M & E HANDBOOKS

M & E Handbooks are recommended reading for examination syllabuses all over the world. Because each Handbook covers its subject clearly and concisely books in the series form a vital part of many college, university, school and home study courses.

Handbooks contain detailed information stripped of unnecessary padding, making each title a comprehensive self-tuition course. They are amplified with numerous self-testing questions in the form of Progress Tests at the end of each chapter, each text-referenced for easy checking. Every Handbook closes with an appendix which advises on examination technique. For all these reasons, Handbooks are ideal for pre-examination revision.

The handy pocket-book size and competitive price make Handbooks the perfect choice for anyone who wants to grasp the essentials of a subject quickly and easily.

THE M. & E. HANDBOOK SERIES

BUSINESS MATHEMATICS

L. W. T. STAFFORD, B.Sc.(Econ.), M.Phil.

Principal Lecturer in Economics at the City of London Polytechnic

SECOND EDITION

MACDONALD AND EVANS

Macdonald & Evans Ltd.
Estover, Plymouth PL6 7PZ

First published 1969
Reprinted 1970
Reprinted 1972
Reprinted 1974
Reprinted 1975
Reprinted 1976
Reprinted in this format 1978
Second edition 1979

ISBN: 0 7121 0282 5

Printed in Great Britain by
Richard Clay (The Chaucer Press) Ltd
Bungay, Suffolk

PREFACE TO THE FIRST EDITION

MATHEMATICS now enters into fields of study which were almost wholly non-mathematical only a few years ago. In business, elementary arithmetic was considered quite adequate for most purposes, although particularly alert and progressive businessmen might pride themselves on the statistical techniques which they or their assistants could deploy. In recent years all this has changed; operational research, the introduction of electronic computers and a generally more numerate and scientific approach to business problems have made mathematics an important and sometimes essential part of the businessman's equipment.

These changes are being reflected in the attitudes of the professional bodies and of the universities, technical colleges and other teaching institutions. Naturally enough, candidates for the qualifications offered by these bodies are increasingly often required to show competence in mathematics. A difficulty is, however, that many people who wish to follow a business career have had a far less thorough grounding in mathematics than, for instance, young people entering a scientific training. Nor, as yet, have many older people established in business a sufficient grasp of the newer techniques to help their junior colleagues. It is hoped that this HANDBOOK may have something to offer to both groups in that it attempts to supply an entry to the world of mathematics, particularly as applied to business, that is free of the obscurity and mystery which so often and so unnecessarily prevents otherwise capable people from attaining mathematical understanding.

PREFACE TO THE SECOND EDITION

THE ABILITY to make effective decisions is one of the most important factors in successful business behaviour. Business mathematics is concerned with improving the quality of decision-making in industry and commerce and it is not surprising that a high degree of mathematical ability has come to be accepted as a necessary part of a manager's equipment at every level of responsibility. This is not to deny that entrepreneurial flair and the ability to take risks, and to distinguish acceptable risks from unacceptable ones, are also important in running a successful business, but even here mathematics has a part to play. It is with these considerations in mind that the new edition of *Business Mathematics* has been prepared. While many familiar things remain, the emphasis has been placed on the mathematics of business decision, including decisions made under conditions of risk and uncertainty.

Important as they are, business decisions can be no better than the information on which they are based and much everyday mathematical work in business is concerned with the prior analysis and presentation of this information. Often, at this level, the methods employed are statistical in nature and over the last ten or fifteen years the sophistication of the techniques available and in common use has grown enormously. In part this has been due to the increase in computing power now able to be brought to bear at comparatively low cost, but it is also due to the fact that new entrants to industry and commerce are now much better trained in quantitative methods. These people, entering as junior management, are moving up the tree so that the general mathematical competence applied at middle management level is likely to increase. Consequently, the standard *required*, without question, from tomorrow's entrants will be higher.

The higher standards of mathematics applied in business have been reflected in the requirements of the professional bodies and in the curricula of the universities, polytechnics and other institutions concerned with education and training for business. Regrettably, though, the basic mathematical foundations for the quite demanding courses offered by all these bodies have not always been securely laid. All too often fundamental concepts in mathematics have never been fully understood or have been forgotten by the time that a career choice is made. Difficulties of this sort are compounded when people established in the earlier stages of a business career find, at some point, that further progress and promotion are blocked because it is not possible to obtain a necessary qualification without mathematical competence. It may be the case, too, that some senior managers, trained in a different environment, find that in dealing with statisticians or operational research specialists their mathematical background is not adequate. It is hoped that this HANDBOOK may have much to offer to each of these groups. It attempts to open the world of mathematics, particularly as applied to business, without any of the mystery and obscurity which so often and so unnecessarily prevent otherwise capable people from understanding and using mathematical techniques.

The scheme of the book. Part I of the book deals with the basic concepts on which the mathematical ideas developed later are based. Because these concepts are so basic, they are accessible to everyone and yet they are so near to the heart of the subject that progress on these foundations can be very rapid. Bearing in mind the higher standards now expected, it is felt that these fundamental ideas ought to be extended to include the differential calculus as an elementary notion rather than as a more advanced method. The presentation, however, is still in fundamental terms.

Part II extends the basic ideas of Part I and in doing so illustrates the slightly more advanced concepts, as they are developed, by examples from business life. Integration, vectors, matrices and the elementary mathematics of probability and statistics are introduced. The statistical ideas, in line with the previously expressed belief that quite sophisticated methods are coming into general use, now include some of the special methods previously regarded as being of a more advanced type. Every opportunity has been taken, in introducing advanced work, to develop the student's competence in mathematics and to increase familiarity with the use of symbols. In Part III the mathematics acquired is used in the specialised field of Finance, with special attention being given to discounting techniques and to the appraisal of investment projects.

Part IV specifically relates mathematical analysis to business decision-making. The essence of business decision is that it is concerned with unknown future conditions. Initially, and perhaps this is appropriate in the less secure business climate with which we are now faced, decisions are considered under uncertainty. Subsequently, ideas introduced in Part II are used in the assessment of the worth of business information and are then applied to probabilistic decision-making. The standard techniques of operational research are then outlined and are developed using both models involving probabilistic approaches and those concerning decisions made under the assumption of certainty. There is a steady development in the standard of mathematical skill required and in the use of symbols, so that the reader should have little difficulty in passing to more advanced work.

In Part V, both the statistical and the mathematical backgrounds are applied to a central business problem: that of forecasting future conditions. All businesses must attempt forecasts, whether by intuitive or by formal methods. This is currently a lively area of work and it is hoped that the final chapters will give some indication of this.

There are Progress Tests at the end of each chapter and worked answers to most of the questions are given in Appendix IV. Where there are no worked answers, the questions are marked with an asterisk and the relevant sections of the text are indicated.

Acknowledgments. My thanks are due to the following examining bodies for permission to quote from past examination papers:

The University of London (B.Sc. (Economics))
The City of London Polytechnic (B.A. (Business Studies) Degree (C.N.A.A.), H.N.D. and C.A. Examinations)
The Institute of Chartered Accountants (C.M.I.)
The Institute of Cost and Management Accountants
The Cambridgeshire College of Arts and Technology (H.N.D.)
The London Chamber of Commerce and Industry (Examinations in Business Statistics and Mathematics)

I must also thank the many colleagues who have commented

on various aspects of the first edition. While I have not always taken their advice, I have invariably found that discussion, whether in person or by correspondence, has deepened my understanding of the problems involved.

July 1979 L.W.T.S.

CONTENTS

LIST OF FIGURES

LIST OF SYMBOLS

Symbol (and name where appropriate)	*Meaning or use*
α (alpha)	often used to indicate a constant
β (beta)	used as a constant or coefficient; indicates a particular type of distribution in statistics
Δ (capital delta)	incremental sign
λ (lambda)	a scalar or constant; the arrival rate in queueing theory
μ (mu)	used as the population mean in statistics and the service rate in queueing theory
ρ (rho)	the traffic intensity
σ (small sigma)	population standard deviation
Σ (large sigma)	the summation sign
θ (theta)	usually indicates an angle
χ (chi)	χ^2 is used to indicate a statistical distribution
$\int$	the integral sign
!	the factorial sign as in $n!$ ("n factorial")
$\{\}$	used to indicate a set
$\|$	the set-builder sign—"such that"
$<$	less than
$\leqslant$	less than or equal to
$>$	more than
$\geqslant$	more than or equal to
$\cup$	union (of sets)
$\cap$	intersection (of sets)
$\wedge$	"and"
$\vee$	"or"
$Pr\ (a\|b)$	conditional probability; "the probability of a given b"
$\longrightarrow$	a mapping
$\longleftrightarrow$	a one-to-one mapping
$f(x)$	function
dy/dx, $f'(x)$, $d/dx\, f(x)$	derivative signs
∂	partial derivative sign, as in $\partial z/\partial x$
A'	transpose of a matrix
π (pi)	Archimedes' constant (= 3·14159 . . .)
e	the exponential constant (= 2·71828 . . .)

PART ONE

BASIC CONCEPTS AND METHODS

CHAPTER I

INTRODUCTION: MATHEMATICS IN BUSINESS

THE GROWING IMPORTANCE OF MATHEMATICS

1. Why use mathematics? In all fields of activity the scientific approach has been gaining ground in this century. Many activities that were previously handled by verbal analysis and description have proved to be more easily dealt with by mathematical techniques. Biology, botany and meteorology are examples of sciences that have yielded to mathematical analysis. The use of mathematics in physics, chemistry and the other natural sciences is of such long standing as to be commonplace.

Business problems, too, can be handled more efficiently:

(*a*) by using the scientific method; and
(*b*) by applying appropriate mathematical techniques where they have been developed.

To a large extent, these two things go together. Mathematical formulation of problems can give certainty in handling complex problems and can enforce a precision in stating the facts of a situation where these would otherwise be lost in emotion and argument. We should use mathematical methods where they can give clear solutions to business problems, because by doing so we can use the limited resources of a business more efficiently. This saves money.

2. The scientific method. If we try to describe the scientific method which has proved so effective in revealing the secrets of the physical world, we should have to list the several stages like this.

(*a*) *Observations* are made and these stimulate ideas about the process being observed.

(*b*) These ideas are expressed as clearly and formally as possible as a *hypothesis*.

(*c*) An experiment is devised to *test* the hypothesis.

(*d*) On the basis of the experiment, which provides new observations, *the hypothesis is either accepted or rejected*.

(*e*) *If it is rejected*, a new hypothesis may be formed, to be tested in turn.

In business, this process is not wholly possible. Experiments merely to test hypotheses are not often possible; moreover, we are usually more concerned to solve a specific problem rather than to find out the exact "truth" of a situation. There are many situations which *can* be dealt with scientifically, even if not in quite the same way.

3. The scientific method in business. If the managers of a business are completely satisfied, then, provided that they are competent, we may take it that there is no problem and the business can be run in the same old way. There are not many business situations that permit that degree of complacency. If the managers are not satisfied, we must track down what is wrong, that is to say we must *define the problem*. This is the most difficult step in the scientific handling of business problems.

The next thing to do is to make a detailed description of the situation or process concerned, together with all the interrelationships between its parts. We may refer to this as *making a model* of the situation. To do this we need to collect information.

When we have collected as much information as we need, and have checked that it is as accurate as we can make it (or can afford to make it: *see* Chapter XXIV), we can *manipulate our model* to see what action will lead to the best result. We *optimise* our model.

Having found the *theoretically* best thing to do, we next need to *formulate a plan* for action in the real world of factory, office or store. The plan must then be applied with sufficient built-in checks to let us know if it is working satisfactorily. If necessary, we must *modify the original plan* in the light of the information gained.

4. Mathematics and the scientific method. It is necessary to go into the place of the scientific method in business because this is the *context* in which management mathematics is applied. Mathematics in business is not just a few short cuts or quick methods of making minor savings. Mathematical analysis provides powerful tools for the solution of major problems. It can weed out fanciful solutions and can provide management with clear-cut alternatives on which decisions can be made.

Often it can provide clear estimates of the additional profits or cost savings that will result from following a particular course of action. However, all this potentially powerful analysis is useless without the will to analyse problems realistically and logically, hence the need for the scientific approach.

5. Mathematical and other models.

(*a*) *Non-mathematical models.* In 3 above, "making a model" was said to be an important part of the scientific approach. The models concerned might be real models in the familiar sense of the word. The siting of office machinery could be assisted by making a miniature representation of the machine room and then moving the small replicas of the machines, desks and so on until the best arrangement was found. Another kind of model, not mathematical but purely conceptual, might concern industrial relations in a factory. If a particular shop was much afflicted by strikes and "go-slow," it would help to write down all the factors affecting the shop, possibly representing them by blocks like this:

Overcrowding in Workshop

and connecting the blocks by arrows to show the inter-relationship between various factors. After isolating the important influences, suggested changes could be discussed and their implications followed.

(*b*) *Mathematical models.* A mathematical model describes a situation in terms of symbols which can be manipulated in accordance with the ordinary rules of mathematics. It is a *symbolic* model.

A SIMPLE EXAMPLE OF A SYMBOLIC (MATHEMATICAL) MODEL

6. Situation. Stone is blasted in a quarry, mechanically loaded into a railed, diesel-powered truck of one-tonne capacity and hauled by the truck to a hopper, into which it is discharged, the stone being taken by a conveyer to a crushing plant. The truck returns empty to the loading point.

7. Making the model. The times shown in Fig. 1 are the shortest practicable times that can be achieved with the existing equipment. Improved equipment could give shorter times. It may be assumed that the hopper-conveyer system can move anything that the truck can dump.

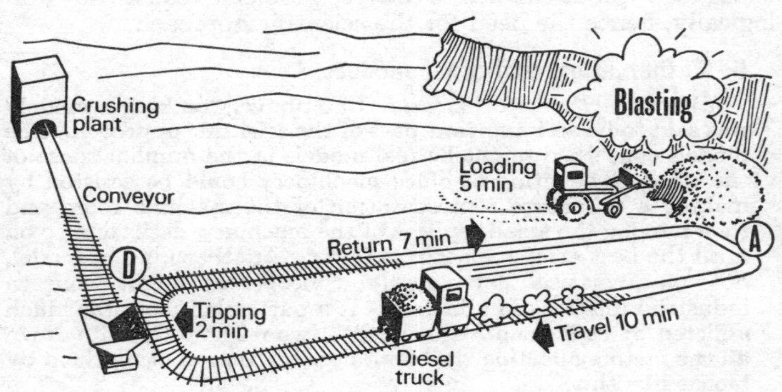

FIG. 1.—*The quarry problem*

8. Problem. We want to construct a model which will give the relationship between the tonnage blasted and the tonnage shifted by the truck.

Allot symbols for each of the times concerned:

Loading time:	m_1 minutes
Travelling time:	m_2 minutes
Tipping time:	m_3 minutes
Return time:	m_4 minutes

Since the truck has a capacity of one tonne, the tonnage per minute handled could be represented as follows:

$$\frac{1}{m_1 + m_2 + m_3 + m_4}.$$

The tonnes per hour handled would be 60 times that amount, that is:

$$\textit{Tonnes per hour} = \frac{60}{m_1 + m_2 + m_3 + m_4}.$$

If the tonnage blasted is to be moved without any "backlog" accumulating, the blasting rate (w) must equal the handling rate. This could be expressed by a simple equation:

$$w = \frac{60}{m_1 + m_2 + m_3 + m_4}.$$

This little equation emphasises that shorter loading or movement times would increase the maximum permissible blasting rate.

9. Manipulating the model. With the times as shown, the maximum blasting rate would be $2\frac{1}{2}$ tonnes an hour. Suppose we wanted to increase this rate to 4 tonnes an hour. We could discuss the possible variations in the times (the m's) that would achieve this result. We might eliminate m_1 altogether by using a drop-sided truck, or we might straighten out curves on the railed track and run the truck at increased speed. Another solution would be to use *two* trucks, running one back empty as the other one carried the stone to the hopper. We show this by writing:

$$w = \frac{2 \times 60}{m_1 + m_2 + m_3 + m_4}.$$

10. Unresolved questions. Could we use a larger number of trucks? If n represents the number of trucks could we write:

$$w = \frac{60n}{m_1 + m_2 + m_3 + m_4}?$$

Would queues develop at the loading point? How can we represent the costs involved?

It would be possible to develop models to handle these questions, but obviously now is not the time. First of all, we must develop the mathematics to handle simple models, then we can introduce complications.

11. Risk and uncertainty in business decisions. In the discussion above it has been assumed that definite and exact times could be allocated to each of the activities. No doubt average values, calculated by observing several days' work, would be used in practice, but the fact is that the actual times for loading the truck, for instance, would vary considerably. On occasions when everything went very slowly, the normal blasting rate could not be maintained. There would also be times when other problems might arise. Trucks would break down; there might be accidents with explosives. Decisions which allowed no margin for the unpredictable occurrence might be unwise and yet excessive allowance for such uncertainties would endanger profitability.

Sometimes business decisions can be made with specific allowance for risk. Possibly running the trucks faster would entail some risk of derailment, with consequent delays at every stage. If this risk could be calculated, a decision about the maximum allowable running rate could be made. Setting this rate too low would reduce profitability, but so would setting it too high. Effective mathematical models ought to take account of these problems, but once again we need special mathematical techniques to deal with them.

THE MAIN FIELDS OF BUSINESS MATHEMATICS

12. Business applications. Naturally, some business activities are more easily treated by mathematical analysis than others. *Finance* is readily dealt with by mathematical techniques since so much of the information is in numerical form, although the figures available are not necessarily reliable. Statistical techniques are very valuable in *market research* as well as in *forecasting* and *quality control.* A whole range of mathematical techniques have been devised to deal with problems of *stocks* or inventories, and methods, in particular linear programming, have been developed to simplify decisions concerning the *allocation of resources* and the choice between alternative products which a firm can make. In many diverse activities *queueing* situations occur and there are specialised techniques to deal with these problems.

Although business men often prefer methods which use

exact figures and which yield precise answers to their problems, there has been a growing realisation in recent years that business decisions concern the future operations of the firm and are often best handled by probabilistic methods. Sometimes, however, it is not possible to estimate the probabilities of future situations although their occurrence is clearly possible. In such cases the theory of games or related methods may be applied.

13. Kind of mathematics required. The mathematics required is a mixture of the old and traditional and the very new. None of it is beyond the reach of the ordinary intelligent man or woman, given patience and a certain amount of determination. The important thing is to set out, as simply as possible, the basic foundations of mathematical reasoning and to start at the beginning, taking nothing for granted. That is why the first two sections of the book are concerned almost entirely with basic techniques and only when these have been mastered are the more glamorous topics introduced.

14. Computers and business mathematics. Many of the methods developed and discussed later in this book can be applied most easily and effectively with the aid of computers. This is so with linear programming, which is not really feasible without computing facilities, and with inventory decisions, investment appraisal methods and forecasting techniques. Computer packages are available for many of these methods, but the standard routines can only be used efficiently and appropriately if the basic ideas are fully understood. Without this understanding, computerised decision methods can be misapplied and inappropriate courses of action recommended. The good analyst or decision-maker needs to understand both the mathematics of the methods and, at least in outline, the way in which they are applied in the standard packages. For the most part, this book is concerned with developing the underlying mathematics, since this is a major task in itself, but references are made to the ways in which computing techniques are applied where these affect the choice of mathematical technique or the way in which the mathematical analysis is to be used.

PROGRESS TEST 1

1.* What do you understand by "the scientific method" and how might it be employed in business? (2)

2. In the example given in **6–8**, how many tonnes of stone could two trucks shift when the loading time was reduced to 3 minutes?

3. Starting one truck at the loading point (A in the diagram) and the other at the hopper (point D), draw up a schedule to show where each of the trucks would be at each minute from the starting time to 24 minutes afterwards. Will the trucks get out of step?

4. What blasting rates would you recommend if the loading time in the example was found to vary between three minutes and six minutes and the travelling time to vary between eight minutes and ten minutes, with all the other times as previously shown? Would your answer be influenced at all if the blasting rate could be controlled only to within half-a-tonne an hour and this variation were acceptable in terms of the general running of the quarry?

* Worked answer *not* given in Appendix IV for questions marked with an asterisk.

CHAPTER II

THE FUNDAMENTALS OF MATHEMATICS: SETS AND NUMBERS

THE IDEA OF A SET

It is probably a good thing to assume that students have little previous knowledge of mathematics and to begin with the most fundamental concept that we can find. Most people, if they were asked to name the most basic idea in mathematics, would say that it was counting or "number," but, before you can count, you must identify the things that you are counting. The most basic idea is *categorisation* and the rock-bottom basic concept is *the set*.

1. Sets. There is a whole world of mathematics to be developed from the idea of the set and yet it is so simple as to be almost trivial. All that we mean by a "set" is a collection of objects that can be distinguished from all other objects.

2. Definition. Any collection of well-defined objects is a set. The word "objects" can be extended to include non-material concepts such as names or numbers. Whatever objects we are dealing with must be "well defined," that is to say they must be distinguishable by some test, so that it is possible to say that a given object is either a member of the set or not. The test of whether an object is in the set or not may be whether it possesses some characteristic or whether it is on some list of members. In the latter case we could say that the members of the set were defined by enumeration.

3. Example of definition by characteristic.

(*a*) *Required set.* The set of all housewives in Extown possessing a refrigerator.

(*b*) *Characteristics.*

(*i*) Residence in Extown.

(*ii*) Possession of a refrigerator.

4. Members of the required set. Only those housewives who pass *both* tests are members of the required set. All others are excluded.

5. Example of definition by enumeration. The following is a list of some employees of the YZ Co. Ltd.:

A. B. Brown; C. D. Smith; E. F. Robinson.

We could divide the employees into two sets, those on the list and those not. Membership of the first set would depend merely on the fact of being listed.

6. The universal set of reference. In the first example we have a small unresolved problem. Should we start by requiring an initial characteristic, "being a housewife"? Perhaps we ought to require an even more basic characteristic, "being a female human." This most basic set, however chosen, is called the *universal set of reference* or just the *universal set.*

In our example the universal set is the set of housewives. This universal set was divided into two *sub-sets*, the set of those living in Extown and those not living there. Finally, the set of those living in Extown was divided into those possessing refrigerators and those who did not.

7. Venn diagrams. The process of division into sub-sets is easily illustrated diagrammatically.

Represent the universal set by a rectangle. This represents the set of housewives in our example. Represent each sub-set

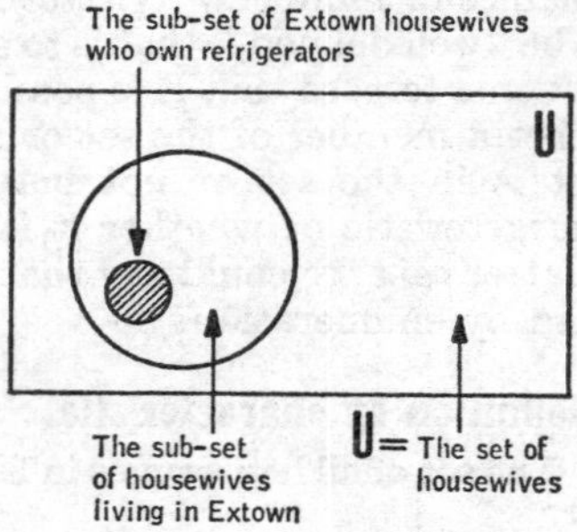

FIG. 2(*a*).—*Venn diagram for Extown example.*

The shaded portion represents the sub-set of Extown housewives owning refrigerators.

by a circle inside the rectangle. Any subsequent sub-set must be within its parent set. (*See* Fig. 2(*a*).)

8. Set notation. In Fig. 2(*b*) the letter U is shown in the top right-hand corner of the rectangle. This is the general symbol for the universal set. In the example, U = the set of all housewives. Other symbols could be allocated as follows:

A = the sub-set of housewives living in Extown.
B = the sub-set of Extown housewives possessing refrigerators.

The Venn diagram would then appear as in Fig. 2(*b*):

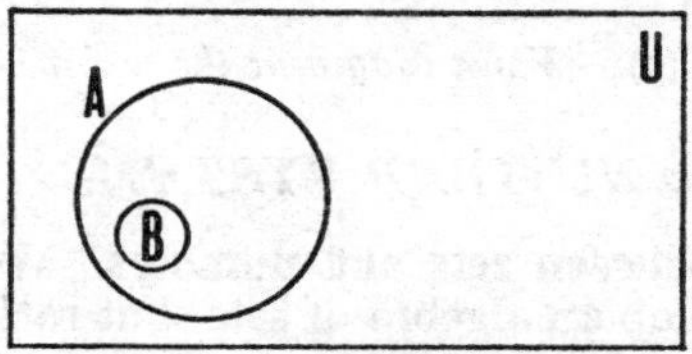

FIG. 2(*b*).—*Revised Venn diagram for Extown example*

If set B had been "the set of *all* housewives possessing refrigerators," the required set of Extown housewives possessing refrigerators would include some members of both the A set (housewives living in Extown) and the B set (housewives possessing refrigerators). This situation, too, can easily be represented by a Venn diagram (Fig. 3(*a*)). The shaded portion represents the required set of Extown housewives possessing refrigerators. This area is the *intersection* of sets A and B and includes all the members who are in set A *and also* in set B.

Another set which concerned both housewives possessing refrigerators and those who lived in Extown would be the set of

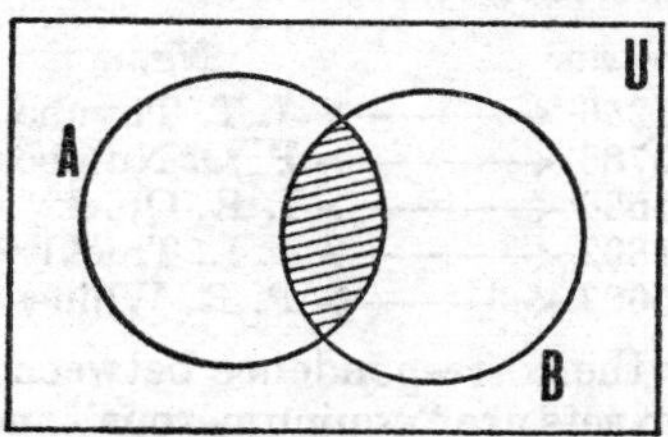

FIG. 3(*a*).—*Venn diagram: the intersection of sets*

all housewives who lived in Extown or those who possessed a refrigerator. Figure 3(*b*) shows this new set, which is known as the *union* of sets A and B.

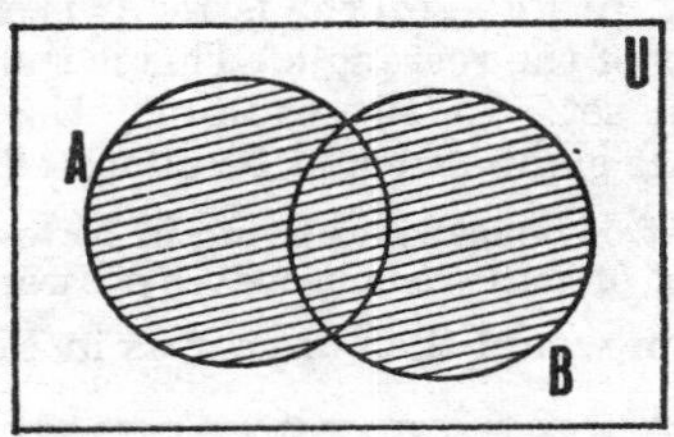

FIG. 3(*b*).—*Venn diagram: the union of sets*

NUMBER SYSTEMS

9. The link between sets and numbers. We are now in a position to develop an algebra of sets, but rather than do this we shall stick to practical matters.

10. Cardinal numbers. Once we have the idea of categorisation, or of putting items into "sets," we can use the idea of the number of items in a set. The most fundamental idea concerning number is that of the *cardinal number*. If we compare two sets and we note that for every member of one set there is a corresponding member of the other set, we can say that these two sets have the same cardinal number. Technically we can say that we can make a one-to-one correspondence between the members (or elements) of the two sets. Suppose that we have a list of reference numbers relating to jobs that have been carried out and that each job must be married up to the name of the customer for whom it was carried out. We should expect to end up with two lists:

Job no.		*Name*
1256	⟷	J. T. Thynne
3789	⟷	P. Q. Numbe
4584	⟷	I. R. Quick
1892	⟷	J. L. Thickly
5687	⟷	P. R. Whine

The arrows show the correspondence between members of the two sets. The two sets are "equinumerous" and have the same cardinal number.

11. Ordinal quality of whole numbers. The cardinal numbers relate to the quantity of items in a set. After acquiring this simple idea, it is an obvious and simple step to put the whole numbers in order of magnitude. We should then have a list of cardinal numbers, each item being bigger than the one before it:

$$1, 2, 3, 4, 5 \ldots$$

The dots signify that the set is infinite.

However many numbers we have in the list, we could always add a larger number. We could add, subtract, multiply and divide these numbers. A set of numbers like this we call a *number system*. The rules for operating the number system are *not* immediately obvious; we could not divide 7 by 4 in this system, for the answer would be $1\frac{3}{4}$ and there is no such number in this simple system of positive whole numbers. Nor could we subtract 7 from 4, since this would give an answer of -3, again a number which is not in this simple system.

12. The system of positive and negative integers. Represent the system of positive whole numbers by a straight line, starting at zero and with some length representing one unit.

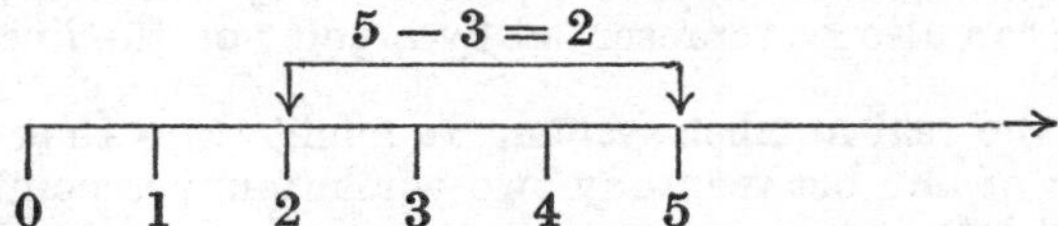

The marked points indicate the whole numbers and the arrow indicates that movement to the right leads to bigger whole numbers. If we subtract 3 from 5, we shall move three places to the left. Movement in a direction opposite to that shown by the arrow indicates subtraction.

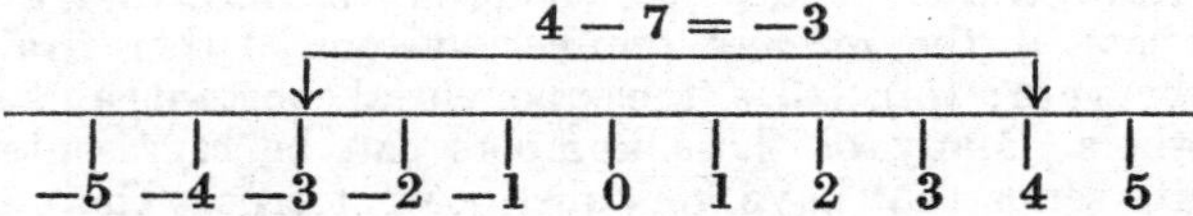

If we subtract 7 from 4, the result will be equal to -3. Sums like these are possible if we extend our number system to include negative whole numbers (negative integers). Mathematicians often use a line to represent a number system. They tend to call such a line a "*directed line segment*," "directed"

because movement along the line leads to greater numbers in one direction and to lesser ones in the other direction. Note that -5 is less than -3 and that both are less than zero.

13. The system of rational numbers. We saw that 7 divided by 4, giving an answer of $1\frac{3}{4}$, was a sum not possible in the system of whole numbers. To accommodate such sums, we need a system which includes *fractions*. This system is called the *rational number system*. If we take the *directed line segment*, we can divide the line between any two integers (whole numbers) into a number of parts.

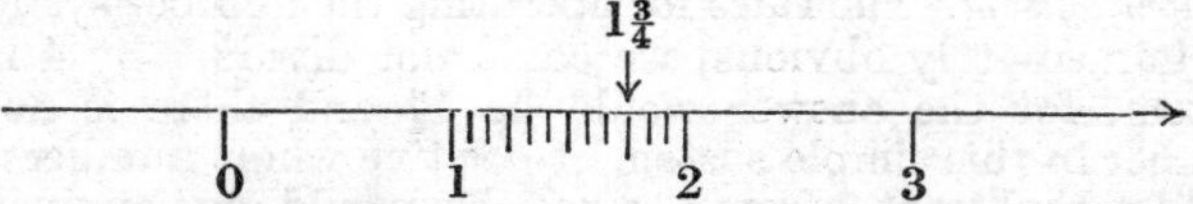

If we want the number $1\frac{3}{4}$ we must take three-fourths of the divisions between 1 and 2. If there are 100 divisions between 1 and 2, we must take 75 of them to find a point on the line representing $1\frac{3}{4}$; if there are only 12 divisions we must take 9 of them; if 4, we take 3. All of these fractions will be equal. Any number which can be represented by a fraction, such as $29\frac{103}{247}$, can also be represented by a point on the line.

14. The real number system. It might seem that since the section of line between any two whole number points can be divided into as many sections as required, *any* number can be represented by a fraction. This, however, is not so. There are many points which cannot be represented by any fraction however elaborately we divide up the line. $\sqrt{2}$ is such a number; there is no fraction which can be multiplied by itself to give the number 2. Numbers which cannot be represented by any fraction are called *irrational* numbers, since they are not members of the *rational* number system. Other irrational numbers are π (pi), $\sqrt{3}$, e (the exponential constant) and a host of others. Many of these numbers can be represented by infinite series that have very distinct patterns. The number usually represented by e is obtained by adding up all the terms of the series:

$$1 + 1 + \frac{1}{2 \times 1} + \frac{1}{3 \times 2 \times 1} + \frac{1}{4 \times 3 \times 2 \times 1} + \cdots$$

and so on. Being an infinite series it can never give an *exact* value, but by taking more and more terms we can get as near to the real value as we like.

If we take all the *rational* numbers and all the *irrational* numbers and put them into a new number system, this new system is called the *real number system*. It includes all the numbers which can be represented as fractions, including the whole numbers as well as those numbers which cannot be so represented.

RULES FOR OPERATING NUMBER SYSTEMS

15. Basic operations. Any number system has two main operations. In our number systems these are addition and multiplication. Subtraction and division are subsidiary operations.

16. Laws governing operations. All number systems obey the following five laws:

(*a*) It does not matter in what order two numbers are added together.

Symbolic representation: $a + b = b + a$.

(*b*) It does not matter how you group several numbers when they are added together.

Symbolic representation: $(a + b) + c = a + (b + c)$.

(*c*) It does not matter in what order two numbers are multiplied together.

Symbolic representation: $a \times b = b \times a$.

(*d*) It does not matter how you group several numbers when they are multiplied together.

Symbolic representation: $a \times (b \times c) = (a \times b) \times c$.

(*e*) If the sum of two numbers is to be multiplied by a third number, this is the same as multiplying each of the two numbers by the third number separately and then adding the two results together.

Symbolic representation: $a \times (b + c) = (a \times b) + (a \times c)$.

NATURE OF SUBTRACTION AND DIVISION

The above laws do not hold for subtraction or division or for mixed calculations that include subtraction and division as well as addition and multiplication.

17. Subtraction. Subtraction *could* be regarded as the addition of a *negative* number:

$$3 - 2 = 3 + (-2).$$

The laws for addition will then hold:

$$3 + (-2) = (-2) + 3.$$

Or again:

$$[3 + (-4)] + 5 = 3 + [(-4) + 5].$$

If this is borne in mind, it will always be possible to think out what is happening when negative numbers are being used.

18. Division. Division can be regarded as multiplication by a reciprocal, that is by one divided by the number being used. For instance:

$$4 \div 3 = 4 \times \tfrac{1}{3}.$$

The rules for *multiplication* will then hold, $4 \times \frac{1}{3} = \frac{1}{3} \times 4$, whereas they obviously would not have done so if the statement had been made in terms of division. The subsidiary nature of division and subtraction is something to be kept at the back of the mind rather than to be worried over, but it can provide a rational explanation for some of those puzzling rules in elementary algebra.

ZERO AND UNITY

19. Zero. If zero is added to a number, that number is unchanged. It retains its identity. We call zero the *identity element for addition*. Since mathematics uses symbols we could familiarise ourselves with them by writing:

$$a + 0 = a.$$

20. Unity. Unity (or one) does a similar job for multiplication. Any number multiplied by unity remains unchanged:

$$a \times 1 = a.$$

CONCLUSION

All the rest of the book is based on the simple, possibly self-evident, ideas in this chapter. If you really understand them, you can reason your way through the rest of the book. They may seem childishly simple, but mathematics is based, and firmly based, on the essential ideas of *the set* and *the number system*. The extensions of these ideas go a very long way and lead to results so powerful that they have changed our whole way of life.

The difficulties that people experience with mathematics are due partly to a false sense of mystery that surrounds the subject and partly to uncertainty about the way in which various manipulations are carried out. In a longer book each algebraic manipulation might be traced back to the essential ideas stated in this chapter, but since this is not possible Chapter III will outline some of the more essential rules of algebra though not always justifying them in detail.

PROGRESS TEST 2

1. In the course of a survey into the characteristics of workers employed by a certain large firm, the following three categories are used.

A: Shift workers.
B: Employees who are members of a trade union.
C: Skilled (*i.e.* fully trained) workers.

(*a*) With the knowledge that these are overlapping categories, display the situation by means of a Venn diagram.
(*b*) Shade (or otherwise indicate) the section of the diagram representing unskilled shift workers who are not members of a trade union.
(*c*) If the number of skilled trade-union members on shift work is 55, the number of skilled shift workers is 60 and the number of unskilled trade-union members in shift work is 38, how many of the 200 shift workers fall in the category mentioned in (*b*) above?

2. Indicate which of the following are rational numbers:

(*a*) $\frac{7}{25}$ (*b*) 8 (*c*) 3 (*d*) *e* (*e*) $0{\cdot}3\dot{3}$ (where this means "point three recurring," the 3s go on and on)
(*f*) 0·5.

3.* "A number system must have two basic operations and its elements must obey five essential rules." Explain and give examples. (15, 16)

CHAPTER III

A REVISION OF ELEMENTARY ALGEBRA

THE NATURE OF ALGEBRA

1. Generalisation of results. Algebra is concerned with the *generalisation* of results. If we add two numbers together we get an answer, another number which is the sum of the previous two. If we want to indicate that this is so for any two numbers we can use symbols instead of the numbers.

The addition sum:

$$3 + 2 = 5$$

is the statement of a *particular* case.

The algebraic sum:

$$a + b = c$$

is a corresponding *general* statement. This is an idea which we have already used in the previous chapter in stating the five laws for number systems. If we want to work out the *general* relationships involved in a certain situation we can use algebraic methods first and afterwards we can slot in particular figures as they become available.

2. An example. Examination of figures for costs shows that every additional unit produced costs a firm £5, but that fixed costs of £500 must be met every month regardless of output.

Total cost for any month can be calculated as: Fixed cost plus five times monthly output. Representing total cost per month as TC, we could write:

$$TC = 500 + 5x,$$

where $x =$ monthly output.

It would now be possible to replace x by any output figure. Suppose fixed cost were to change, however, would it not be prudent to replace the £500 by a symbol which could always be used to represent fixed cost? Let fixed cost per month be shown by the symbol a. Why not replace £5, the marginal cost, by a symbol, say b? Our formula now reads:

$$TC = a + bx,$$

and can always be used, however the detailed figures change. What is *not* changed is the type of relationship between the costs.

In our work we shall almost always be using algebraic symbols to represent numbers, but this need not necessarily be the case. Algebra can be used to state many kinds of general relationships and there is no reason why these need be confined to numerical ones. In Chapter XI we shall refer to algebra of logical statements, although the rules will be a little different.

3. The basic operations of ordinary algebra. In this chapter we shall be concerned with the conventional algebra which is suitable for use where symbols represent numbers and the relationships between them.

The operations which we shall be concerned with and the symbols which we shall use are as follows:

(*a*) *Addition.* Symbol: $+$.
(*b*) *Subtraction.* Symbol: $-$.
(*c*) *Multiplication.* Symbols: $\times$ or . (*e.g.* $a \times b = a \,.\, b$).
(*d*) *Division.* Symbols: $\div$ (*e.g.* $a \div b$) or a/b.

NOTE: Division by zero is not allowed and has no meaning.

(*e*) *Roots.* Symbol: $\surd$ or $\sqrt{\quad}$.

This is the "radical" sign.

(*i*) The sign by itself is used to denote the *square* root of a number and means that the result of the operation is a number which multiplied by itself gives the original number.

EXAMPLE

$$\sqrt{4} = +2 \text{ or } -2.$$

Both these multiplied by themselves give $+4$.

(*ii*) A *cube* root of a number is one of three equal entities which, when multiplied together, produce the original number.

EXAMPLE

$$\sqrt[3]{27} = +3$$
$$(+3) \times (+3) \times (+3) = 27.$$

Note that the same is *not* true of -3. Similarly an nth root would be written $\sqrt[n]{}$ and would signify a quantity which is one of n equal entities which, when multiplied together, produce the original number.

(*f*) *Powers.* Working the other way, a number multiplied by itself a number of times is said to be taken to the nth power.

EXAMPLE: What is the fifth power of 2?

$$2^5 = 2 \times 2 \times 2 \times 2 \times 2 = 32.$$

Symbol: The power to which a number (the base) is taken is shown by a small number just above and to the right of the original number. This is called the "index."

RULES FOR NEGATIVE SYMBOLS

Careful thought about the laws given in the previous chapter and their systematic application would lead to the following working rules.

4. Multiplication: unlike signs. If two numbers are to be multiplied together and their signs are unlike, multiply their absolute values and prefix a minus sign. (The absolute values are the values regardless of sign. This value is sometimes written as $|a|$, where a is the given number.)

EXAMPLE

$$-7 \times 4 = -28.$$
$$|4| \times |7| = |28|$$

The signs are different and the answer is therefore -28.

5. Division: unlike signs. If a number is to be divided into another number and their signs are different, the result is the division of the absolute values prefixed by a minus sign.

EXAMPLE

$$63 \div -9$$
$$|63| \div |9| = |7|.$$

Signs are different, therefore the answer is -7.
This sum could be written as $63/-9 = -7$.

Results of this kind can be confusing when fractions are used.

6. Multiplication and division: like signs. For multiplication or division of numbers with like signs, multiply the absolute values and give the answer a plus sign.

EXAMPLE

$$-a \times -b = ab$$

Note that we must apply the rules to symbols, too. Often we shall be working with a mixture of symbols and ordinary numbers.

7. Addition. If signs are alike there is little problem. $(-3) + (-4) = -7$. We are going in a negative direction along the directed line segment (*see* II, 12).

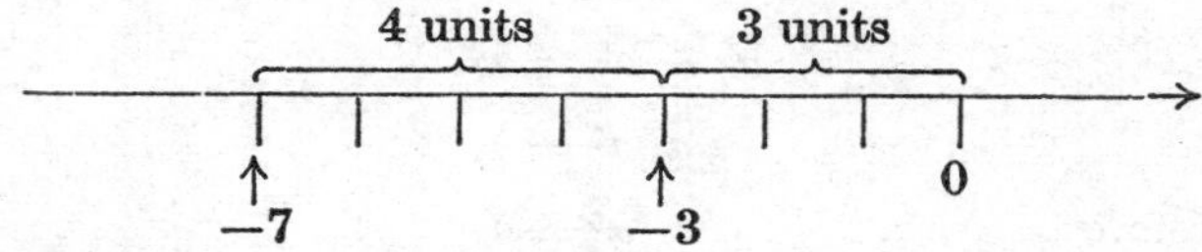

If the signs are *unlike*, find the *difference* between the absolute values and prefix the sign of the greater number.

EXAMPLE

$$-17 + 4 = -13.$$

8. Subtraction. If one number is to be subtracted from another, change the sign and add.

EXAMPLE

$$52 - (-67) = 52 + (+67)$$
$$= \underline{119.}$$

$$(-a) - (-b) = -a + (b)$$
$$= \underline{b - a.}$$

RULES FOR USING INDICES

9. Multiplication. If $a^2 = a \times a$ and $a^5 = a \times a \times a \times a \times a$, then $(a^2 \,.\, a^5)$ (recall that the dot indicates multiplication) must equal $(a \times a) \times (a \times a \times a \times a \times a) = a^7$. The rule is therefore that if two numbers which are powers of the *same base* (*see* **3** above) are multiplied together the indices must be *added*.

10. Division. By similar reasoning, if one number, a power of some base, is to be *divided* into another, this being another power of the same base, the indices must be *subtracted*.

EXAMPLE

$$a^5 \div a^3 = \frac{a \times a \times a \times a \times a}{a \times a \times a}$$
$$= \underline{a^2}.$$

Note the *base* is *a*, the *indices* are 5 and 3. Subtracting these gives the new index of 2.

11. Meaning of a zero index. If the division rule requires the subtraction of the indices:

$$a^2 \div a^2 = a^0.$$

But $$a^2/a^2 = 1.$$

Therefore $$a^0 = 1.$$

Any base taken to the power of zero is equal to **1**.

12. Indices taken to a power. If three elements, a^2, are multiplied together, we have:

$$a^2 \times a^2 \times a^2 = (a \times a) \times (a \times a) \times (a \times a)$$
$$= \underline{a^6}.$$

That is to say:

$$(a^2)^3 = a^6.$$

The rule is that, if we have to take a base taken to some power *to* some power, we must multiply the indices together.

13. Meaning of a fractional index. The index 1 merely shows that the number is to be left as it is, thus $a^1 = a$. The law for the multiplication of two numbers that are powers of the same base (*see* **10** above) requires that the indices be added.

It seems necessary, therefore, that:

$$a^{\frac{1}{2}} \times a^{\frac{1}{2}} = a^1$$
$$= \underline{a}.$$

It follows that $a^{\frac{1}{2}}$ must be a number which multiplied by itself gives *a*, that is, it must be $\sqrt{a}$. From the rule for "powers of powers" we have $(a^{\frac{1}{2}})^2 = a^{\frac{1}{2}\times 2} = a$, which confirms this result.

A fractional index such as $a^{\frac{1}{3}}$ indicates a *cube* root, since

$$a^{\frac{1}{3}} \times a^{\frac{1}{3}} \times a^{\frac{1}{3}} = a^{(\frac{1}{3}+\frac{1}{3}+\frac{1}{3})} = a^1$$
$$= \underline{a}.$$

By the multiplication rule for powers (*see* **12** above), $(a^{1/5})^3 = a^{3/5}$, which thus equals $(\sqrt[5]{a})^3$. The *denominator* (*see* below) gives the *root* of the base of a fractional index, while the *numerator* gives the *power* to which that root is to be taken.

EXAMPLE

$$a^{5/8} = (\sqrt[8]{a})^5.$$

Fractional index is 5/8.

5 is the numerator, 8 is the denominator, regarding 5/8 as a rational number (*see* II, **13**), the denominator tells us how many divisions a unit is broken up into and the numerator indicates how many of these divisions are to be taken.

We are required to find the *eighth root* of the base a, and to take the result to the fifth power.

Put $a = 256$. $\sqrt[8]{256} = 2$, $2^5 = 32$,

$$256^{5/8} = 32.$$

14. Meaning of negative indices. In **11** we said that $a^0 = 1$, whatever value was given to a. Using the addition rule of indices (*see* **9** above):

$$a^2 \times a^{-2} = a^{(2-2)} = a^0$$
$$= \underline{1}.$$

The only meaning that could be given to a^{-2} that would be consistent with this result would be $a^{-2} = 1/(a^2)$. This is the correct meaning. A negative index indicates a *reciprocal*, that is to say it shows "one over" whatever power is taken.

EXAMPLES

$$a^{-5} = \frac{1}{a^5}.$$

$$2^{-3} = \frac{1}{2^3} = \frac{1}{8}.$$

$$10^{-\frac{1}{2}} = \frac{1}{10^{\frac{1}{2}}} = \frac{1}{\sqrt{10}}.$$

15. A warning about the rules for using indices. These rules are *very important*. You will need them for subsequent work. Make sure that you work every example in the test at the end of the chapter.

16. Some useful expressions. It is not possible in a single chapter to review the whole of elementary algebra, but at least some common difficulties can be explored and some useful rules listed. If you cannot remember very elementary techniques such as how to multiply or divide algebraic expressions, consult Appendix III. In the meantime a number of expressions which are met with frequently are shown below. As practice, you should check them by multiplication.

(*a*) $(a + b)^2 = a^2 + 2ab + b^2$.
(*b*) $(a - b)^2 = a^2 - 2ab + b^2$.
(*c*) $(a + b)(a - b) = a^2 - b^2$.
(*d*) $(a + b)^3 = a^3 + 3a^2b + 3ab^2 + b^3$.
(*e*) $(a - b)(a^2 + ab + b^2) = a^3 - b^3$.
(*f*) $(a + b)(c + d) = ac + ad + bc + bd$.

QUADRATIC EQUATIONS

17. Solving quadratic equations. A task which occurs frequently in elementary mathematics is the solution of equations, not as a classroom exercise but as a necessary step in some piece of work. There are three common ways of solving quadratics:

(*a*) By factorising.
(*b*) By completing the square.
(*c*) By using the quadratic formula.

An example of each is given in **18–20** below.

18. Solution by factorising.

$$x^2 + 5x + 6 = 0.$$

If we are to factorise $x^2 + 5x + 6$, we need two numbers of which the sum is 5 and the product 6. The numbers are 3 and 2 and the factors are $(x + 3)$ and $(x + 2)$. Therefore:

$$(x + 3)(x + 2) = 0.$$

If two expressions have a product of zero, one of them must be equal to zero. Therefore *either* $x + 3 = 0$ *or* $x + 2 = 0$. The first will give $x = -3$, the second will give $x = -2$. These values are the roots of the equation.

19. Solution by completing the square. Let us take the equation:

$$2x^2 + 3x + 1 = 0.$$

We have to make the left-hand side into a perfect square.

Step 1. Divide by 2:

$$x^2 + (3/2)x + \tfrac{1}{2} = 0.$$

Step 2. Take $\tfrac{1}{2}$ from both sides:

$$x^2 + (3/2)x = -\tfrac{1}{2}.$$

Step 3. Add half the coefficient of x, squared, to both sides.
Half the coefficient of x is $\tfrac{3}{4}$.
The square of $\tfrac{3}{4}$ is $\tfrac{9}{16}$.

Step 4. Express left-hand side as square:

$$(x + \tfrac{3}{4})^2 = \tfrac{1}{16}.$$

Step 5. Take square root of both sides:

$$x + \tfrac{3}{4} = \pm\tfrac{1}{4}$$

$$x = -1$$

or

$$x = \underline{-\tfrac{1}{2}}.$$

20. Solution by formula. It is fairly easily shown that the roots of a quadratic equation (there are always two of them although they may be equal) are given by:

$$x = \frac{-b \pm \sqrt{b^2 - 4ac}}{2a},$$

when the equation itself is given by:

$$ax^2 + bx + c = 0.$$

EXAMPLE

$$2x^2 + 9x + 1 = 0$$

$$a = 2,\ b = 9,\ c = 1$$

$$x = \frac{-9 + \sqrt{81 - (4 \times 2 \times 1)}}{4}$$

$$= \frac{-9 + \sqrt{81 - 8}}{4}$$

$$= \frac{-9 + \sqrt{73}}{4}$$

$$= \underline{-0{\cdot}115.}$$

The other root is:

$$x = \frac{-9 - \sqrt{73}}{4}$$

$$= \underline{-4{\cdot}385.}$$

PROGRESS TEST 3

1.* What is algebra and why is it an important tool for the businessman? (1, 2)

2. A firm's fixed costs are £5000 per quarter; the variable costs amount to £4 per unit produced.

(*a*) Plot the total cost curve for outputs from zero to 1500 units per quarter.
(*b*) Representing total cost by C and output produced by p, the number of units, represent total cost by an algebraic expression.
(*c*) Calculate total cost when 750 units per quarter are produced.

3. Carry out the following multiplications:

(*a*) $5^3 \times 5^2$ (*b*) $5^2 \times 3^4$ (*c*) $5^{-3} \times 125$ (*d*) $a^3 \times a^{\frac{1}{2}}$ (*e*) $\sqrt[4]{81} \times 7$.

4. Express the following as powers of the base 10 in the simplest way possible:

(*a*) $\frac{1}{10}$ (*b*) 100 (*c*) 1 (*d*) 0·01 (*e*) $10^3 \times 10^2$.

5. Evaluate:

(*a*) $343^{\frac{2}{3}}$ (*b*) $289^{\frac{1}{2}}$ (*c*) $49^{-\frac{1}{2}}$ (*d*) 3617^0 (*e*) $(\frac{1}{2})^0$.

6. Find the factors of:

(*a*) $x^3 - y^3$ (*b*) $a^2 - b^2$ (*c*) $ax + az + bx + bz$.

7. Solve the following quadratic equations:

(*a*) $3x^2 + 14x + 8 = 0$.

(*b*) $x^2 - 7x + 2 = 0$.

CHAPTER IV

MAPPINGS AND FUNCTIONS

MAPPINGS

1. Definition. When it is possible to make a correspondence (*see* **9** below) between members of one set and members of another, the one set can be said to be "mapped" into the other. The members of the real number system could be mapped into the directed line segment. One point on the line then represents each number in the real number system.

Single numbers can be mapped into a line, pairs of numbers can be mapped into a *space*, with each *pair* being represented by a point in the space. This is an idea that most people have already met in drawing graphs or in reading map co-ordinates.

2. Solution sets. In order to see exactly what is going on, it is now necessary to use another new idea, that of the "solution set." A solution set is the collection of entities, not necessarily numbers, for which a certain statement is true. If we were to list several town names:

Malaga
Oslo
Cambridge
Reykjavik
Canterbury
Paris

and then to make the statement: ". . . and . . . are towns in South-East England," with the understanding that the gaps were to be filled by a selection from the six listed towns, Cambridge and Canterbury would be the only ones for which the statement would be true.

3. Set notation. It is usual to denote a particular set by a single capital letter. This is a device which we have already used in II, **8**. If the members of a set are to be listed, the convention is to show the members, or a description of them, inside a pair of "curly brackets." The set of all the even numbers greater than zero could be shown thus:

$$N = \{2, 4, 6, 8, \ldots\}.$$

A *solution set* is usually shown by the capital letter S, so that using the previous example it would be possible to write:

$$S = \{\text{Cambridge, Canterbury}\}.$$

A further refinement is to use a double line to separate a description of the members from some characteristic that they must possess. Thus $S = \{(x, y) \,||\, x + y = 35\}$ would be read, "the set of numbers x and y such that $x + y = 35$." The x and y numbers might be chosen from the real number system, or we might be restricted to whole numbers, or to whole numbers greater than zero. The solution set would be all the members that satisfied the requirement $x + y = 35$.

4. Mapping solution sets into the line and the plane. Suppose we write a set:

$$S = \{(x, y) \,||\, x + y = 10, x \geqslant 0, y \geqslant 0\},$$

this now reads, "the set S, composed of numbers x and y, such that $x + y = 10$, x being greater than or equal to zero, y being greater than or equal to zero." The sign $>$ stands for "greater than"; the sign $<$ for "less than"; while $\geqslant$ means "greater than or equal to."

If our set were:

$$S = \{x \,||\, x \leqslant 5, x \geqslant 0\},$$

we could map the elements of this solution set as follows:

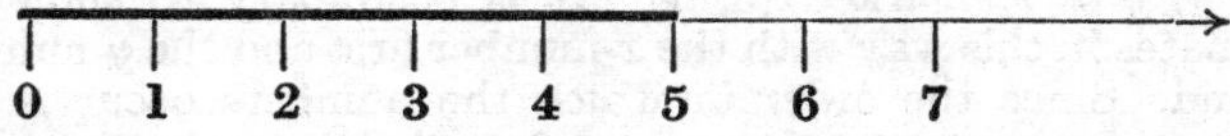

The thickened portion of the line represents the required numbers, with 5 and zero being included. However, if we were required to represent the solution set for $x + y = 10$, we should have two sets of numbers to handle. An easy way of dealing with this would be to have *two* "directed line segments" at right angles to each other, one for the x's and the other for the y's.

In Fig. 4, the solution set:

$$S = \{(x, y) \mid \mid x + y = 10, x \geqslant 0, y \geqslant 0, x, y \text{ integers}\}$$

is mapped into the plane.

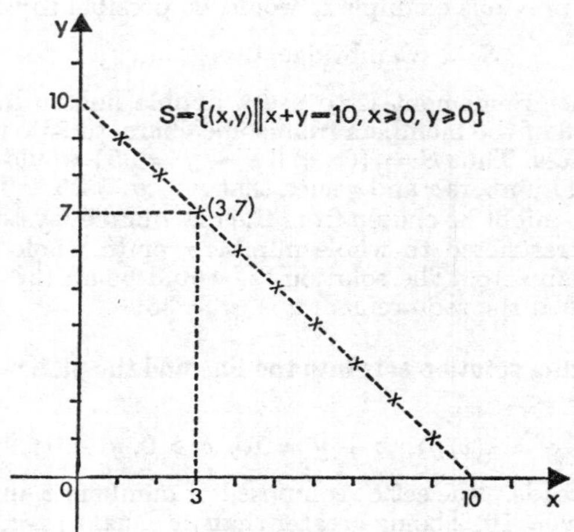

FIG. 4.—*Graphing a solution set*

The point $x = 3$, $y = 7$ would be marked as shown and the other points on the diagram also satisfy the relationship indicated.

5. Ordered number pairs. Figure 4 shows the point where $x = 3$, $y = 7$, marked (3, 7). It is customary to show co-ordinates in this way with the x-number first and the y-number second. Since the order in which the numbers occur is important, such a pair of numbers is called an *ordered number pair*.

6. Other conventions for graphical representation. When a set is mapped into the plane, the horizontal axis is always used for the x-numbers and the vertical axis for the y-numbers. The point where the two axes intersect represents zero values for both x and y and is called the *origin of the co-ordinate system.*

The whole system of co-ordinates can be divided into four quadrants as shown in Fig. 5.

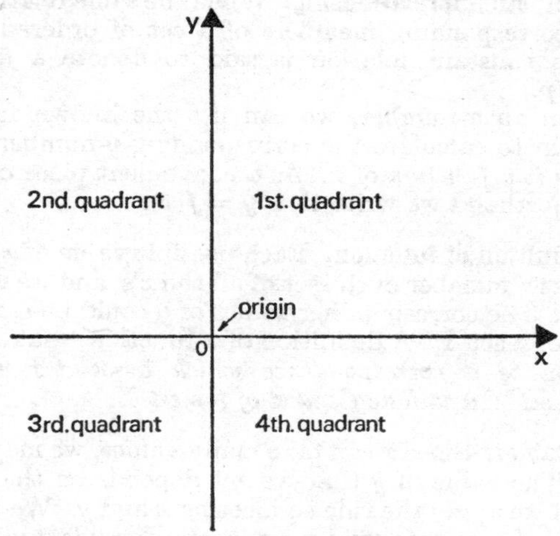

FIG. 5.—*A co-ordinate system*

7. Relation between members of an ordered number pair. In any ordered number pair *some* relation exists between the first and second number. For the ordered number pair (7, 4), the first number is one-and-three-quarter times the second. If we were presented with a set of ordered number pairs it would be possible to work out the relation between the members of each pair. In many cases there would be a different relation for each pair:

Pair	(3, 9)	(5, 17)	(8, 64)	(9, 54)	(7, 14)	(6, 24)
Relation (2nd to 1st)	$\times 3$	$\times 3\frac{2}{5}$	$\times 8$	$\times 6$	$\times 2$	$\times 4$

Sometimes each number pair in the set would exhibit the same relation between second and first members.

(1, 5) (2, 10) (3, 15) (4, 20) (5, 25) . . ., etc.

Regarding the first number as a member of the x-set and the second as a member of the y-set we could write the common relation as $y = 5x$.

FUNCTIONS

8. The functional relationship. When the same relation exists between corresponding members of a set of ordered number pairs, this constant relation is said to denote a *functional relationship*.

If, given an x-number, we can use the known functional relationship to calculate the corresponding y-number, we can say that *y is a function of x*. As a convenient piece of mathematical shorthand we write thus $y = f(x)$.

9. A definition of function. Each possible value of x could be regarded as a member of the set of all the x's, and we could call this set X. The corresponding values of y could be regarded as members of a set Y. A definition of a function would then be: *A function is a correspondence which associates with each element of set X a unique element of the set Y.*

10. Variables. Since x can take many values, we may call it a *variable*. The value of y that we get depends on the value of x to which we apply the rule connecting x and y. We therefore call x the *independent* variable and y the *dependent* variable.

11. The domain of x. The set from which we can choose all the possible values of x is called the *domain* of x. If we have a simple function such as $y = 3 + 4x$, and the domain of x is the system of positive and negative integers, then a mapping of all possible values of x and y would be represented by a set of separate, discrete points, as shown by the crosses in Fig. 6.

If, however, the domain of x was the real number system, there would be a value of x for every point on the directed line segment which forms the x-axis. The line representing all the possible number pairs that satisfied the functional relationship would be a continuous line. The function could be described as a continuous function. Note that the plotted points could be regarded as the members of the solution set

$$S = \{(x, y) \,||\, y = 3 + 4x)\}.$$

The actual members of this set, of course, depend on the set of numbers chosen as the domain of x.

12. The range of y. The possible values of y that correspond to a given domain of x constitute the *range* of y.

SOME USEFUL TYPES OF FUNCTION

13. Linear functions. A function like $y = 3 + 4x$ will always give a straight line when the relationship is shown graphically. Functions of this sort have no powers of the variables higher

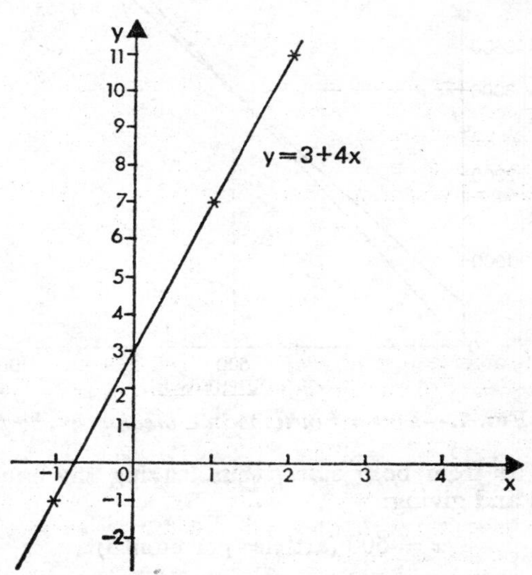

FIG. 6.—*A linear function*

than one (*see* III, 3). The equations describing the relationship are called *first-degree equations* or *linear* equations.

Functions of this type can usefully represent situations that occur when one variable increases or decreases proportionately with another. Break-even charts used by cost accountants exhibit this sort of relationship.

In Fig. 7 the total cost curve is a linear function, in fact the same function as that used in III, 2. Suppose now that each item sold will fetch £6, the difference between the two functions:

$$y = 500 + 5x$$

and $$y = 6x$$

will represent the profit or loss at each output. The firm will break even at the point where the two functions are equal:

$$6x = 500 + 5x.$$

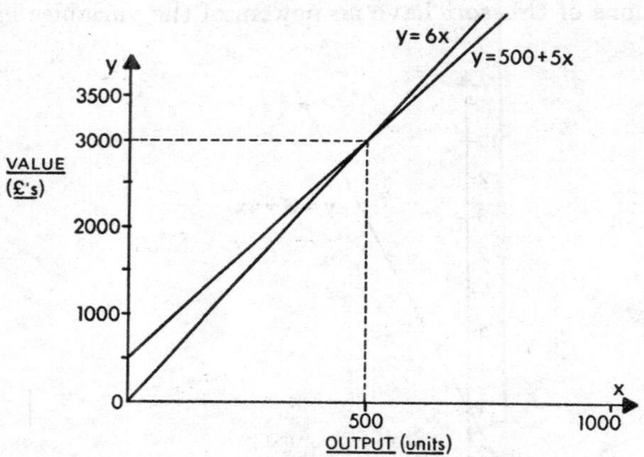

FIG. 7.—*Linear functions in a break-even chart*

Subtract $5x$ from both sides, thus leaving the equality undisturbed and giving:

$$x = 500 \text{ (articles per month).}$$

The correctness of this break-even point can be confirmed from the diagram.

14. Quadratic functions. Quadratic functions can be described by second-degree equations, that is by equations having not only terms involving x, but also terms involving x^2. There will be no powers of x *higher* than the second, however. The following are examples of quadratic functions:

$$y = 3x^2 + 4x + 3$$
$$y = 24x^2 - 6x + 4$$
$$y = 84 - 2x^2 + 4x$$
$$y = x^2.$$

Quadratic functions occur quite frequently in elementary

economics, where marginal and average cost curves may have this form.

15. Functions of the third degree. Second-degree equations give rise to curves with *one* bend; third-degree equations, when plotted as functional relationships, give curves with two bends. Such curves are used to describe total cost curves, among other things, in elementary economics. Third-degree equations contain no powers of x higher than the third.

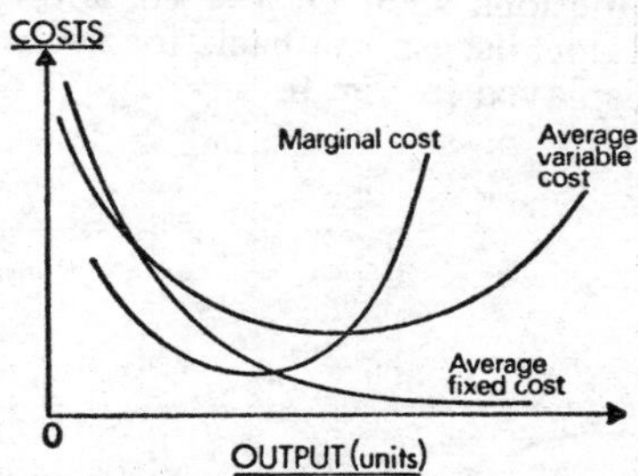

FIG. 8(*a*).—*Quadratic functions in elementary economics*

16. Exponential functions. In all the functions so far discussed the independent variable, x, has been taken to some power. Another type of function uses the variable as a *power* to which some given base is taken. The independent variable is thus acting as an index or exponent and this type of function is therefore known as an exponential function. Thus in the function $y = 2^x$, y would have the value 1 when $x = 0$, 2 when $x = 1$, 4 when $x = 2$ and so on. This type of function is shown in Fig. 8(*b*).

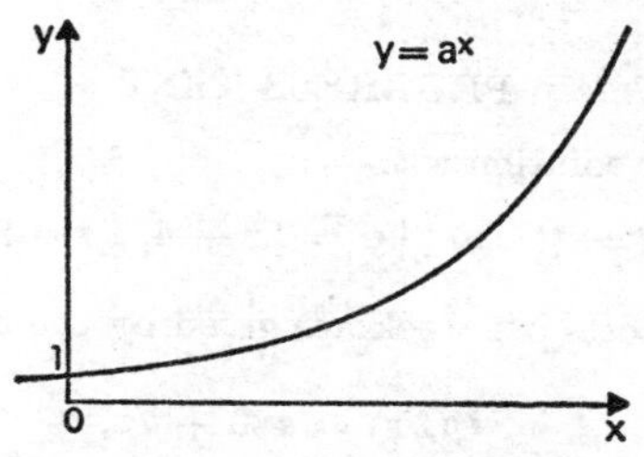

FIG. 8(*b*).—*An exponential function*

Exponential functions describe situations where growth is taking place. An important special type of exponential function is that which uses the base e (*see* **II, 14**).

17. Trigonometric functions. Sometimes, in business situations, we observe systematic fluctuations in the figures with which we are dealing. This may be the case with sales, stocks or many other series which vary over time. One way in which we can incorporate such oscillatory effects is by the use of trigonometric functions such as $y = \cos x$ or $y = \sin x$. Although we shall not discuss the basis for such functions here, an example is displayed in Fig. 9.

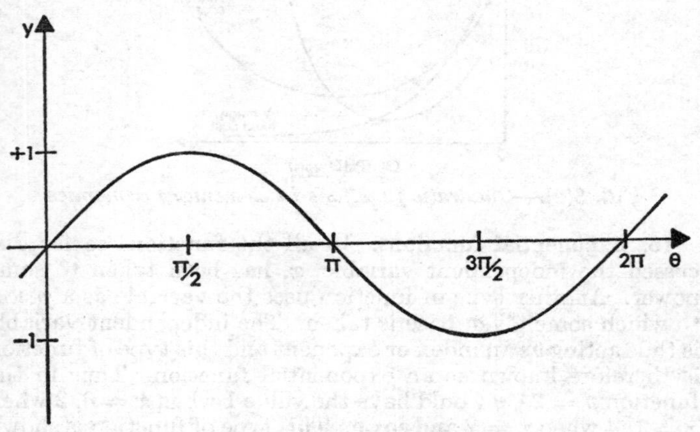

FIG. 9.—*A trigonometric function: $y = \sin \theta$*

PROGRESS TEST 4

1. Graph the solution set:

$$S = \{(x, y) \mid y = \tfrac{1}{2}x + 4, x \text{ real}\}. \quad (4)$$

2. A firm's costs per week are given by the expression:

$$C(\text{£'s}) = 480 + 7x,$$

where x is the number of tonnes of product made.

If the possible outputs from the plant are from a lowest value of 60 tonnes to a maximum of 200 tonnes, state the domain of x and the range of C.

3.* **What is a "mapping"? Discuss the idea of a function as a mapping. (1, 2, 8, 9)**

4. **Plot graphs of the four quadratic functions given in 14.**

CHAPTER V

SEQUENCES, SERIES AND PROGRESSIONS

GENERAL DEFINITIONS

1. Relationships between values at an interval. Sometimes we find either that values have been recorded at regular intervals or that they can be observed at regular intervals. Some such changes take place with the passage of time alone. Thus, we could consider the value of an invested sum of money at yearly intervals or the size of a firm's labour force month by month. This is not to say that it would not be possible to identify the underlying causes of the observed changes, but merely that for the moment we are interested in the size and pattern of the changes from period to period.

2. Sequences. A set of values in order may have no rule by which we can calculate each term from its predecessors, but, if there *is* some regular pattern of growth or decline going on, we should be able to calculate the value of an item from a knowledge of its position in the set. If we *can* do this, we shall call the set of values a *sequence.*

These are examples of sequences:

$$2, 6, 18, 54, 162 \ldots$$

$$\tfrac{1}{3}, \tfrac{1}{5}, \tfrac{1}{7}, \tfrac{1}{9}, \tfrac{1}{11} \ldots$$

3. Series. A sequence of which the terms are connected by plus or minus signs, so that we can calculate a sum for a given number of terms, is called a *series.*

The following are examples of series:

$$1 + \tfrac{1}{2} + \tfrac{1}{6} + \tfrac{1}{24} + \tfrac{1}{120} + \ldots$$

$$1 + 3 + 5 + 7 + 9 + 11 \ldots$$

$$1 - \tfrac{1}{2} + \tfrac{1}{3} - \tfrac{1}{4} + \tfrac{1}{5} - \tfrac{1}{6} + \tfrac{1}{7} \ldots$$

A common problem is to find a rule which will give the sum of a series to any number of terms.

4. Progressions. A series with a constant ratio or difference between successive terms is called a *progression.* If the first term of a series were 3, the second 6, the third 12 and so on, the series would be in geometrical progression with a common ratio of 2. A series with terms 3, 5, 7, 9 and so on would have a common *difference* of 2 and the terms would be in *arithmetic* progression.

ARITHMETIC PROGRESSIONS

5. Definition. Just to avoid any misunderstanding here is a formal definition of an arithmetic progression: *A series is said to be in arithmetic progression if each of its terms increases or decreases by a common difference.*

6. Algebraic description of an arithmetic progression. If we use the symbol a for the first term and d for the common difference, an arithmetic progression can be written as:

$$a + (a + d) + (a + 2d) + (a + 3d) + \ldots + (a + (n - 1)\,d).$$

It will be noted that the second term is $(a + d)$, the third term is the first term plus twice the difference and so on. The "n^{th}" term has had the common difference added on $(n - 1)$ times.

EXAMPLE: Put $a = 5$, $d = 6$.

The series will then be:

$$\begin{array}{cccc} a + & (a + d) + & (a + 2d) + & \ldots \\ 5 + & 11 \quad + & 17 \quad + & \ldots \end{array}$$

The general description will still work if d (the difference) is negative.

EXAMPLE: Put $a = 28$, $d = -4$.

The series is:

$$28 + 24 + 20 + 16 + 12 + \ldots$$

If this series went on for 7 terms, the last term would be:

$$\begin{aligned} a + (n - 1)d &= 28 + (6 \times -4) \\ &= \underline{4}. \end{aligned}$$

7. Sum of an arithmetic progression. The sum of the progression with $a = 28$, $d = -4$ to seven terms would be:

$$\begin{aligned} S &= 28 + 24 + 20 + 16 + 12 + 8 + 4 \\ &= \underline{\underline{112.}} \end{aligned}$$

It would be convenient if there were some general formula for finding the sum of an arithmetic progression to any number of terms. There is such a formula. It is:

$$S_n = \frac{n}{2}[2a + (n - 1)d],$$

where S_n = the sum to n terms. The sum to seven terms of the series above would be:

$$\begin{aligned} S_7 &= \frac{7}{2}(2 \times 28) + (6 \times -4) \\ &= \frac{7}{2}(56 - 24) \\ &= \frac{7 \times 32}{2} \\ &= \underline{\underline{112.}} \end{aligned}$$

GEOMETRIC PROGRESSIONS

More important to the businessman than the arithmetic progression is the geometric progression.

8. Definition. A series of which the terms increase or decrease by some constant ratio is called a geometric progression.

9. Algebraic representation of a geometric progression. Taking the first term as a, as with the arithmetic progression, and the common ratio as r, a geometric progression can be described as follows:

$$a + ar + ar^2 + ar^3 + \ . \ . \ . \ + ar^n.$$

Putting $a = 5$ and $r = 3$, the series would be:

$$5 + 15 + 45 + 135 + \ . \ . \ .$$

10. The sum of a geometric progression. The sum of the series given above to six terms would be:

$$5 + 15 + 45 + 135 + 405 + 1215 = 1820.$$

A formula to give the sum of a geometric progression to any given number of terms is:

$$S_n = \frac{a(1 - r^n)}{1 - r}.$$

If we apply this formula to the example already used the sum to six terms would be:

$$S_6 = \frac{5(1 - 3^6)}{1 - 3}$$
$$= \frac{5(1 - 729)}{-2}$$
$$= \underline{1820.}$$

11. Geometric progression with a common ratio less than one. Perhaps even more common than geometric progressions like the one just considered are progressions where the common ratio is less than unity. If the common ratio in the previous example were $\frac{1}{2}$, with the first term 5 as before, the series would be:

$$5 + (5 \times \tfrac{1}{2}) + (5 \times \tfrac{1}{2} \times \tfrac{1}{2}) + \ldots,$$

giving:

$$5 + 2\tfrac{1}{2} + 1\tfrac{1}{4} + \tfrac{5}{8} + \tfrac{5}{16} + \ldots$$

The expression $\frac{a(1 - r^n)}{1 - r}$ would still give the sum to n terms.

Taking $n = 6$, as before, the sum is:

$$S_6 = \frac{5(1 - (\frac{1}{2})^6)}{1 - \frac{1}{2}}$$
$$= \frac{5(1 - \frac{1}{64})}{\frac{1}{2}}$$
$$= \frac{5(\frac{63}{64})}{\frac{1}{2}}$$
$$= 2 \times 5 \times \tfrac{63}{64}$$
$$= \frac{630}{64}$$
$$= \underline{9\tfrac{27}{32}}.$$

CHECK: The series in geometric progression with $a = 5$, $r = \frac{1}{2}$, to six terms is:

$$5 + 2\tfrac{1}{2} + 1\tfrac{1}{4} + \tfrac{5}{8} + \tfrac{5}{16} + \tfrac{5}{32} = \underline{9\tfrac{27}{32}}.$$

12. Convergence and divergence of series in G.P. If a series in G.P. (the abbreviation G.P. is often used for geometric progression as A.P. is for arithmetic progression) has a common ratio greater than one, each term is bigger than the last. The sum of the series therefore increases *without any limit*. That is to say, if we take any number, however large, we can always make the sum of the G.P. exceed it by taking enough terms. The terms of a G.P. with a common ratio greater than one increases very quickly and consequently the sum of the terms grows even more swiftly.

If the common ratio is less than one, however, each term is *less* than the last and although the series will have a greater sum as more terms are taken there will be some total which will never be exceeded however many terms are taken.

EXAMPLE: Write ten terms of the series in G.P. with $a = 1$, $r = \frac{1}{2}$. Sum these ten terms and estimate the limit of the sum to infinity.

$$1 + \tfrac{1}{2} + \tfrac{1}{4} + \tfrac{1}{8} + \tfrac{1}{16} + \tfrac{1}{32} + \tfrac{1}{64} + \tfrac{1}{128} + \tfrac{1}{256} + \tfrac{1}{512}.$$

The sum to ten terms is $1\frac{511}{512}$. Each term is just half the size needed to bring the series to the sum of 2. We can bring the sum of the series as near as we like to 2, but we can never quite get there.

13. Formula for the sum of a G.P. to infinity. If $r < 1$, the formula $\dfrac{a(1 - r^n)}{1 - r}$ becomes $\dfrac{a}{1 - r}$, since r^n is the nth power of some fraction. Any fraction multiplied by itself becomes smaller as we saw using $r = \frac{1}{2}$. Even if the fraction were very nearly one, say $\frac{99}{100}$, multiplied by itself it would be smaller. Using $\frac{99}{100}$, $(\frac{99}{100})^2 = \frac{9801}{10000}$, which is not much more than $\frac{98}{100}$. If the process were continued for very long, the fraction would become quite small. Continued infinitely, it would become so small that it could be ignored. Re-stating the result, the sum of a G.P. to infinity if the common ratio is less than unity is given by the formula:

$$S_\infty = \frac{a}{1 - r}.$$

EXAMPLE: Find the sum to infinity of the series:

$$8 + 4 + 2 + 1 + \tfrac{1}{2} + \tfrac{1}{4} + \ldots$$

$$S = \frac{8}{1 - \frac{1}{2}}$$

$$= \underline{16.}$$

Note that *dividing* by $\frac{1}{2}$ is the same as multiplying by 2. $8 \div \frac{1}{2} = 8 \times 2$. After all, there are sixteen halves in eight whole units.

USES OF GEOMETRIC PROGRESSIONS IN BUSINESS

Geometric progressions are of special use in business because of their relevance to financial calculations. These special uses will be considered in more detail in Chapter XVI, but some comment on the methods and formulae used is in order here.

14. Geometric progressions and percentages. If the production of a factory was 5000 tonnes of fertiliser in 19–0 and it has increased by 10 per cent per annum each year since then, then the output for successive years (to the nearest tonne) is:

19–0	*19–1*	*19–2*	*19–3*	*19–4*	*19–5*	*19–6*	*19–7*	*19–8*
5,000	5,500	6,050	6,655	7,321	8,052	8,858	9,744	10,718

Inspection of these figures will show that a 10 per cent increase is the same as a multiplication of each tonne by 1·1. The successive yearly outputs are therefore in geometrical progression with a common ratio of 1·1.

Knowing the rate of increase and production in the starting year, it is possible to work out the production in any given year. In 9 above the successive terms of a G.P. were given as $a + ar + ar^2 \ldots$ and so on. With $r = 1{\cdot}1$ and $a = 5000$, production in the 5th year (19–4), for instance, would be $5000\ (1{\cdot}1)^4 = 5000 \times 1{\cdot}4641 = 7320\frac{1}{2}$ tonnes. Similarly, if the same growth rate is to continue, it would be possible to estimate the production for two years after 19–8. Since this would be the tenth year of growth after the initial year, production would be estimated at $5000\ (1{\cdot}1)^{10} = 12{,}969$ tonnes.

15. An alternative notation. The underlying idea of the growth in geometric progression is the same as that of compound interest. In compound interest tables, however, the symbol r is often used to indicate the interest rate in decimal terms. An interest rate of 5 per cent would give an equivalent decimal rate of 0·05. Using $100r$ to represent 5 per cent, $100r$ would be equal to 5 and r would be equal to 0·05. The common ratio between the annually compounded amounts would not be r but $(1 + r)$. Using the symbol A_0 to represent the amount originally invested, the amount accumulated after three years (A_3) would be given by $A_3 = A_0(1 + r)^3$. The amount in any given year (the nth year) would be given by $A_0(1 + r)^n$. Problems of compound interest and related matters are dealt with in Chapter XV.

16. Growth rates. From the previous paragraphs it will be realised that geometric progressions are an excellent description of growth processes. Whenever there is regular percentage growth from year to year it is possible to find the growth rate (the r of the previous paragraph) which corresponds to the observed pattern of increase. If two observations only are made over an interval of time, it is possible to calculate the percentage growth rate per month or year which corresponds to the change. Growth rates between related quantities, say between production and labour force in a firm, can be compared using semi-logarithmic graphs.

THE SIGMA NOTATION

17. Use of the sigma notation. Since a series is the sum of a sequence of values all of which are connected by some rule, it would seem to be reasonable to state the rule and then merely indicate that the terms generated by applying it were to be added together. This is perfectly feasible and can be done very easily by means of the "sigma" notation. The Greek capital letter "sigma" is written like this: Σ, and in mathematics it indicates that all the items of a designated type are to be added together.

18. An example. Using the Σ notation we can write Σr^2. This would mean "add together the squares of all the numbers in the 'r set.'" To make our intention absolutely clear, we ought to add a note of the values that r can take. If r is to take all the values from 1 to n, we should write:

$$\sum_{r=1}^{n} (r^2).$$

A full explanation of this symbol would be:

$$\sum_{r=1}^{n} (r^2) = 1^2 + 2^2 + 3^2 + \ldots + n^2.$$

So long as we can find the rule connecting the terms of the series, we can describe the series or progression in terms of the sigma notation. The general form of an arithmetic progression, for example, could be written as

$$\sum_{r=1}^{n}[a + (r - 1)d],$$

which would give the sum to n terms. With $r = 1$, the expression $a + (r - 1)d$ would be equal to a, with $r = 2$, the second term would be $a + d$ and so on.

19. The sigma notation generally. It is convenient to introduce the sigma notation at this point, but we shall find that it is of very general application. The sigma notation is particularly useful in Statistics. In calculating the arithmetic mean of a set of data it is necessary to add up all the items and then to divide by the number of items. Letting the number of items equal n and representing the mean value by $\bar{x}$ (pronounced "x bar") we could write:

$$\bar{x} = \frac{1}{n}\sum_{i=1}^{n} x_i.$$

This notation is often found in articles and textbooks and allows complicated calculations to be expressed in a very compact form.

PROGRESS TEST 5

1. Write out an expression for the sum of the first n odd numbers.

2. Find the sum of the following progressions to the first seven terms:

(*a*) $1 + 8 + 15 + 22 + \ldots$
(*b*) $-4 - 1 + 2 + 5 + \ldots$
(*c*) $22 + 20 + 18 + 16 + \ldots$
(*d*) $3 + 9 + 27 + 81 + \ldots$

3. (*a*) Prove that the sum of a G.P. to infinity is given by $\dfrac{a}{1-r}$ when $r < 1$.

(*b*) Find the sum to infinity of:

$$\tfrac{1}{4} + \tfrac{1}{12} + \tfrac{1}{36} + \tfrac{1}{108} + \cdots$$

4. A firm's labour force is growing at the rate of 2 per cent per annum. The firm now employs 500 people. How many may it be expected to employ in five years' time?

5. Write the following series in the form $\sum_{r=1}^{n} f(r)$.

(*a*) $1 + 3 + 5 + 7 + \ldots$

(*b*) $2 + 6 + 18 + 54 + \ldots$

6.* Discuss some ways in which sequences, series and progressions may be used in business. Can you think of ways in which these topics might be of use (*a*) to the accountant, (*b*) to the production engineer. (14–16)

CHAPTER VI

THE CALCULUS: DIFFERENTIATION (1)

WHAT THE CALCULUS IS ABOUT

1. The calculus and change. The ideas discussed in this chapter are concerned with the way things change. Profit may change with the quantity produced; demand for one company's product may vary with the price of its competitors' products. We need to know *exactly* how changes are related to each other. The mathematics that deals with changes in functionally related quantities is known as *the calculus* and the technique of differentiation is one part, and an important part, of this area of mathematics. Because it is concerned with change, the calculus can furnish us with an easy way of finding when some changing quantity has reached a maximum or minimum. It is a simple "optimisation" method. This aspect of the calculus is dealt with in Chapter VII.

2. An example from everyday life. Readers of this book will want to apply differentiation to business problems, but its nature is more easily illustrated by an example from another aspect of everyday life.

In Chapter IV, the idea of a *function* was introduced and the particular function $y = x^2$ was mentioned as an example (IV, **14**). Suppose now that y, the *dependent* variable, represents the distance travelled by a car starting from rest and that x, the *independent* variable, gives the time which has elapsed since the vehicle began to move.

Table 1 shows elapsed time (in seconds) and distance gone (in metres). This table could be shown graphically as in Fig. 10 below.

The problem which we want to solve is: "How fast is the car going at any given instant?" This is the speed that would be shown on the speedometer.

USING THE CALCULUS TO FIND SPEED

TABLE 1

x *Elapsed time (seconds)*	y *Distance gone (metres)*
0	0
1	1
2	4
3	9
4	16
5	25
10	100
15	225
20	400

y (distance gone) $= x^2$, when x = time in seconds since start.

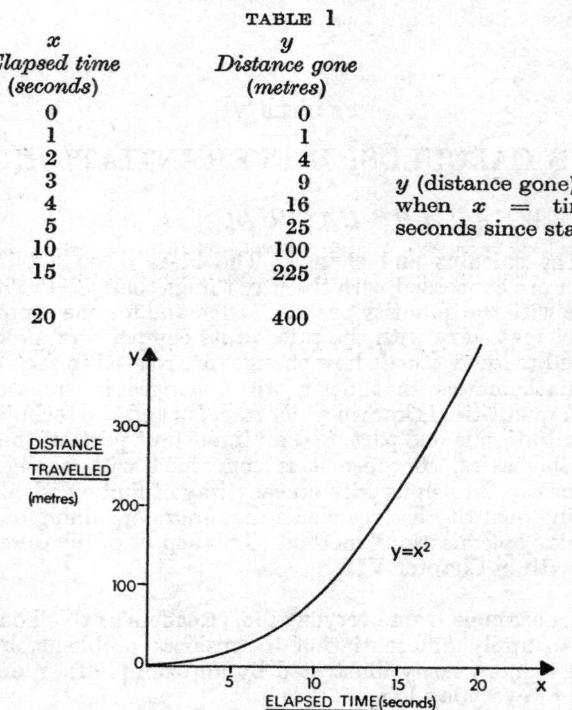

FIG. 10.—*Distance gone as a function of time*

3. Speed, time and distance. Speed can be calculated as *distance gone* divided by *time taken*, but this gives *average speed*, not the speed shown "on the clock." For instance, if a man leaves Cambridge at 11 a.m. one morning and has driven 20 kilometres in the direction of London by 11.20 a.m., his average speed is 20 km $\div \frac{1}{3}$ h = 60 km per hour. The speed *indicated* at 11.20, however, might be 45 km/h or 90 km/h or some other figure. The average takes account of all the times when he was held up at traffic lights as well as the times when his foot was well down on the accelerator.

4. Speed at an instant. A first approach to the problem might be to work out an average speed over a fairly short distance, thus eliminating extreme variations in speed, at least:

A simple calculation will show that if distance in metres equals time in seconds squared, the distance and times given above will hold.

Average speed over 100 *m:* 100/4·142 = 24 metres per second.

Obviously, since the car is accelerating, it will be going faster as it passes the 200-m than it was when it passed the 100-m post. By taking speed over a smaller range of distance it would be possible to make an estimate of the exact speed of the car as it passed the 200-m post:

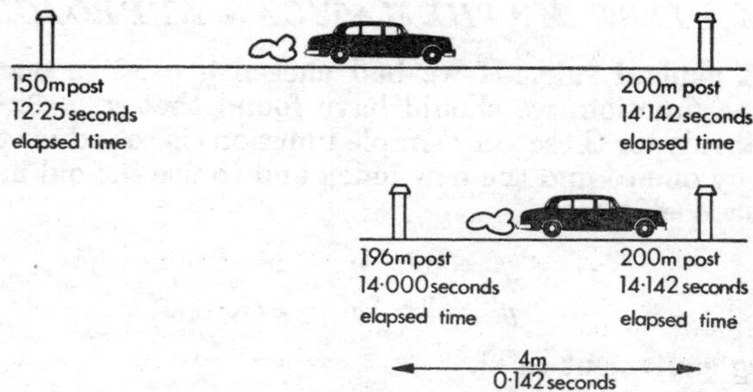

An average speed worked out over the quite small distance would be 4 m/0·142 seconds = 28·2 m.p.s.

Taken over an even smaller distance, say 1 m, average speed would work out to 28·27 m.p.s., and if we could time the last 0·5 m we should get even nearer to the real speed as the car passed the 200-m post. This would be 28·28 m.p.s. (101·8 k.p.h.).

INTERPRETATION IN PHYSICAL TERMS

5. Interpretation. What we have done is to take averages over smaller and smaller distances (and smaller and smaller time intervals) to get closer approximations to the speed at a given instant. This eliminated earlier, lower speeds that were irrelevant to the speed at an instant. All these averages were approximations which got closer and closer to the accurate speed of 28·28 m.p.s.

6. Speed as a function. The original distance/time function (which is not very realistic in terms of the performance of any real car or driver) was $y = x^2$.

$$\text{At } x = 14{\cdot}14,\ y = 200 \text{ m.}$$

If we denote the speed, as calculated, by y':

$$y' = 28{\cdot}28,$$

which is twice 14·14. We should find, and could make calculations to check, that $y' = 2x$ over the whole range of speeds, so that after 12 seconds the car was going at 24 m.p.s. and so on.

A FIRST MATHEMATICAL APPROACH

7. A general rule. If we had chosen $y = x^3$ as our time/distance function, we should have found that $y' = 3x^2$. The general rule for these very simple functions is to reduce the old index by one to find the new index and to use the old index as the new coefficient:

$$\begin{array}{ll} y = x^2 & y = x^3 \\ y' = 2x & y' = 3x^2, \end{array}$$

x being equivalent to x^1.

The *basic differentiation rule* is:

$$\begin{aligned} y &= x^n \\ y' &= nx^{(n-1)} \end{aligned}$$

8. A geometrical interpretation. Let $y = f(x)$ be any suitable function. If we increase x by a certain amount, let this be denoted by Δx (call it "delta x"). Because y depends on x, y will change too. Call the change in y, Δy (delta y).

The average increase in y is $\Delta y/\Delta x$, as shown in Fig. 11 below.

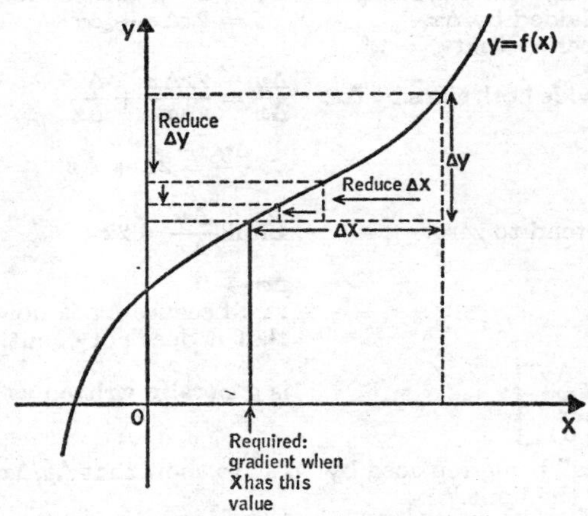

FIG. 11.—*Finding the gradient at a point*

Taking averages over smaller distances can be represented by letting Δx, and therefore Δy, become smaller (shown by the dotted lines and arrows). Now let Δx get very small indeed, in fact let it get as close to nothing as possible; Δy will get very small too and the final, "instantaneous" change will be given by the "limit" of $\begin{pmatrix} \Delta y/\Delta x \\ \Delta x \to 0 \end{pmatrix}$,

reading "$\Delta x \to 0$" as "delta x tends to zero." Note that the derivative, showing how y changes, indicates the *slope* of the curve.

9. Generalising the result algebraically. If we want a "formula" and a method that will work always, we have to resort to algebra. We shall try it first with the easy function $y = x^2$.

Original function.	$y = x^2$
Let x and y increase by a little bit.	$(y + \Delta y) = (x + \Delta x)^2$

Expand $(x + \Delta x)^2$ (recall Chapter III).

$y + \Delta y = x^2 + 2x\Delta x + \Delta x^2$ (remembering that (Δx) and (Δy) are treated as single symbols)

Get the Δy by itself ready to be divided by Δx, remembering that $y = x^2$.

$$\Delta y = x^2 + 2x\Delta x + \Delta x^2 - x^2$$
$$= 2x\Delta x + \Delta x^2$$

Now divide both sides by Δx.

$$\frac{\Delta y}{\Delta x} = \frac{2x\Delta x}{\Delta x} + \frac{\Delta x^2}{\Delta x}$$

$$\therefore \frac{\Delta y}{\Delta x} = 2x + \Delta x$$

Let Δx tend to zero.

$$\underset{\Delta x \to 0}{\text{Limit}} \frac{\Delta y}{\Delta x} = 2x$$

. . . because Δx is now so small that it does not count.

$$\left[\underset{\Delta x \to 0}{\textit{Limit}} \frac{\Delta y}{\Delta x}\right]$$

is generally written as dy/dx, the "deltas" being replaced by "*d*'s" to show that $\Delta y/\Delta x$ has been taken "to the limit."

10. The derivative of a function. The technique of differentiation enables us to find another function which is *derived* from the original function, and so is called the *derivative* of that function. The derivative function makes it possible to calculate the *rate* of change of the original at any point.

EXAMPLE

Original function: $y = x^5$.

Derivative: $\frac{dy}{dx} = 5x^4$.

At the point where $x = 7$, $y = 7^5$ (which is 16,807). At this point y is changing at the rate of $5(7)^4 = 12{,}005$ units for each very small unit change in x.

11. Derivatives as rates of change over a small finite range. This aspect of derivatives will be made clear by a study of the following example:

EXAMPLE: In a certain factory, total cost varies with output in accordance with the function $y = x^3 + 10$, where y = cost in hundreds of pounds and x = output in hundreds of tonnes. x, naturally, must be more than or equal to zero ($x \geqslant 0$).

Original function: $y = x^3 + 10.$

Derivative: $dy/dx = 3x^2.$

(NOTE that 10, a constant, does not affect the derivative)

when $x = 1$ (100 tonnes)

$$dy/dx = 3.$$

An increase of 0·05 "x" units would represent an increase of production of 5 tonnes. $dy/dx = 3$; therefore, for an increase of 5 tonnes, y will increase by $3 \times 0{\cdot}05 = 0{\cdot}15$ "y" units, that is by £15.

CHECK: $x = 1$ (100 tonnes), $y = 11$ (£1100)

$$x = 1{\cdot}05,\ y = (1{\cdot}05)^3 + 10 = 11{\cdot}158$$

Increase: 0·158 (£15·8)

The derivative gives approximate result over a small finite range; it gives the *exact* rate of change at a point.

12. Summary of rules for finding derivatives. Now that the *idea* of a derivative has been established it would be possible to prove, mathematically, that various rules could be used for more complicated functions. We shall save time by stating them and by giving examples.

(*a*) *Basic method:*

$$y = x^n$$
$$dy/dx = nx^{n-1}$$

EXAMPLE

$$y = x^6$$
$$dy/dx = 6x^5$$

(*b*) *Function with a constant:*

$$y = x^n + k$$
$$dy/dx = nx^{n-1}$$

EXAMPLE

$$y = x^4 + 6$$
$$dy/dx = 4x^3$$

(c) *Function with a coefficient:*

$$y = ax^n$$
$$dy/dx = nax^{n-1}$$

EXAMPLE

$$y = 16x^3$$
$$dy/dx = 48x^2$$

(d) *Derivatives of a sum.* Let $u = g(x)$ and $v = h(x)$ so that $f(x) = u + v$, then:

$$\frac{d}{dx}(u + v) = \frac{du}{dx} + \frac{dv}{dx}.$$

EXAMPLE

$$y = 5x^3 + 6x^2$$
$$dy/dx = 15x^2 + 12x.$$

(e) *Derivative of a product.* Suppose that u and v are functions of x, so that $u = g(x)$, $v = h(x)$, and $y = uv$. Then:

$$\frac{d}{dx}(uv) = u\frac{dv}{dx} + v\frac{du}{dx}.$$

EXAMPLE

$$y = (3x + 2)(7x^2 + 9)$$
$$dy/dx = \underbrace{(3x + 2)}_{u} . \underbrace{14x}_{dv/dx} + \underbrace{(7x^2 + 9)}_{v} . \underbrace{3}_{du/dx}$$

(Using the dot symbol for multiplication again.)

(f) *Derivative of a quotient:*

$$y = \frac{u}{v}; \quad \frac{dy}{dx} = \frac{v\dfrac{du}{dx} - u\dfrac{dv}{dx}}{v^2}$$

EXAMPLE

$$y = \frac{6x^2 + 9}{4x^3}$$
$$\frac{dy}{dx} = \frac{4x^3 . 12x - (6x^2 + 9)12x^2}{(4x^3)^2}$$
$$= \frac{4x^3 . 12x - (6x^2 + 9)12x^2}{16x^6}$$
$$= \frac{48x^4 - 72x^4 - 108x^2}{16x^6}$$
$$= -\left(\frac{108x^2 + 24x^4}{16x^6}\right)$$
$$= -\left(\frac{27 + 6x^2}{4x^4}\right)$$

(*g*) *Derivative of a compound function.* In functions like $y = (3x^2 + 2)^3$, we could consider the expression within the bracket as a little "sub-function." Writing this little function as $u = 3x^2 + 2$, the whole major function could be written as $y = u^3$. We could say that y was a "function of a function." The rule here is:

$$dy/dx = dy/du \times du/dx.$$

EXAMPLE

$$y = (3x^2 + 2)^3.$$

Put $\quad u = 3x^2 + 2,$

then $\quad y = u^3$

$$dy/du = 3u^2;\ du/dx = 6x$$

Applying the rule given above:

$$dy/dx = 3u^2 \times 6x$$
$$= 3(3x^2 + 2)^2 \,.\, 6x$$
$$\therefore dy/dx = \underline{18x(3x^2 + 2)^2}.$$

PROGRESS TEST 6

1.* Explain what is meant by a limit and show how it is related to the concept of the slope of a curve at a point. (4, 8, 9)

2. Differentiate the following with respect to x:

(*a*) $x^3 + 4$ (*b*) $2x + 3$ (*c*) $\sqrt{x}$ (*d*) $1/x^2$ (*e*) $(ax - b)(x + a)$.

3. Find the derivatives of the following functions:

(*a*) $y = 3x^2 + 2$ (*b*) $y = 5x^2 + 2x + 3$.

(*c*) $y = 3x^3 - 2x - 1$ (*d*) $\sqrt{x}(x^2 + 4)^2$ (*e*) $\dfrac{x\sqrt{x}}{x + 2}$.

4. At a certain factory, it has been calculated that, if the excess of production over 5000 articles per week is represented by x (in hundreds of articles), average weekly earnings per man varies approximately in accordance with the formula:

$$\textit{Average weekly earnings} = 15 + \frac{x^2}{x + 7}.$$

(*a*) Make a rapid calculation to show by how much you would expect weekly earnings to change if production were stepped up from 6000 to 6350 articles per week.

(*b*) Sketch the curve and check your answer.

5. A firm makes a bulk product and sells it at £80 per tonne. It finds that its variable costs follow a non-linear pattern with respect to sales, the cost function being $C = 0{\cdot}5x^2$, where C represents total variable costs in thousands of £s and x represents monthly output in hundreds of tonnes. The firm calculates fixed costs per month as £1000.

(a) At what output will revenue be changing at the same rate as costs?

(b) Write a function for profit if this is defined as revenue minus costs. At what output will profit cease to increase?

6. Differentiate the function $y = x^3$ from first principles.

CHAPTER VII

THE CALCULUS: DIFFERENTIATION (2)

POSITIVE AND NEGATIVE GRADIENTS

1. Method of finding gradients. The process of differentiation gives a new (derived) function which enables us to find the slope or gradient of a curve at any point. It will be recalled that we do this by finding the derivative function and putting into it the value of x at which we wish to find the slope. Thus, if we are dealing with the function $y = x^3 - 3x + 2$, the methods described in the previous chapter will give the derivative as $dy/dx = 3x^2 - 3$. If we wish to know the slope of the curve when $x = 2$, we put x equal to 2 in this function.

2. Distinction between positive and negative gradients. The gradient when $x = 2$ is $3(2)^2 - 3$, which is equal to $+9$. At this point on the curve every small increase in x gives an increase of nine times as much in y. It should be noted that the sign of the gradient is positive at this point and that, as x increases, y also increases. This is an example of a *positive* gradient and, reading from left to right across the graph of the function, the curve is going *uphill*. A *negative* gradient would represent a "downhill" section of the curve and the value of the gradient, when actually calculated, would have a *negative* sign. Figure 12 shows positive and negative slopes on the curve discussed above.

STATIONARY POINTS

3. The changing slope of a curve. An inspection of the curve in Fig. 12 will show not only that its gradient is different at various values of x, but that it is *constantly* changing. This is usually the case with non-linear functions. The slope of the curve $y = x^3 - 3x + 2$ is very steep at, say, $x = -2$, but it gets less steep as it approaches the point where x is equal to -1. In fact, by the time that it has reached that point it has levelled out entirely and we are "at the top of the hill." After that point the slope of the curve becomes negative, gets more so, then it begins to level out again until we are "at the bottom of a valley." The lowest point of this valley is at the point where $x = +1$, but after this point the curve gets steeper and steeper.

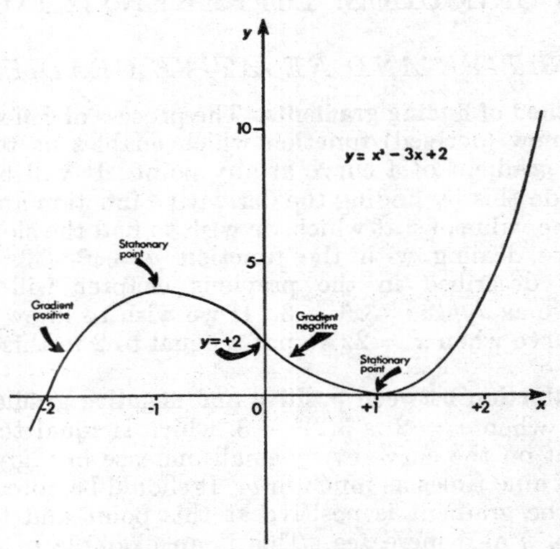

FIG. 12.—*Gradients of a curve*

If uphill sections are indicated by positive gradients and downhill sections by negative gradients, it seems reasonable to assume that level sections will be represented by zero gradients and this is correct. This gives us a method of locating points where there is a zero gradient. For the function $y = x^3 - 3x + 2$, the derivative was $dy/dx = 3x^2 - 3$. To find the points, given by the value of x, where the gradient is zero, put $3x^2 - 3 = 0$. Solving this little quadratic equation (*see* III, 17–20) gives $x = +1$ or $x = -1$, and these are, of course, the two points of zero gradient. These points are known as *stationary points*.

4. Summary of methods for calculating gradients.

(*a*) Calculating gradient at a given point:

	EXAMPLE
Step 1. Differentiate the function to find the derivative.	*Function* $y = 3x^2 - 2x + 4.$ *Derivative* $dy/dx = 6x - 2.$
Step 2. Insert value of x at required points in the derivative function.	Find gradient at point where $x = 2$. $f'(x) = 6x - 2$ $f'(2) = 6(2) - 2 = 12 - 2 = 10.$

(*b*) Finding stationary points:

	EXAMPLE
Step 1. Find derivative as before.	$dy/dx = 6x - 2.$
Step 2. Put derivative equal to zero.	$6x - 2 = 0.$
Step 3. Solve the resulting equation. Stationary point found at value of x which satisfies the equation.	$6x = 2$ $\therefore x = \underline{\tfrac{1}{3}}.$

MAXIMA AND MINIMA

5. Local maximum and minimum points. From the curve shown in Fig. 12 it can be seen that the points at the "top of the hill" and "bottom of the valley" are only "local" highest and lowest points. The summit at $x = -1$ is by no means the highest point on the whole graph, nor is the valley at $x = +1$ the lowest point. These points are local maximum and minimum points and it is local maxima and minima such as these that are found at stationary points.

6. Distinguishing between a maximum and a minimum. The gradient at both maximum and minimum points is zero and we therefore need a means of distinguishing between the two cases. If we approach the maximum point from the left, that is from lower values of x, we can see that the gradient is steeply positive at first but becomes less so. After reaching the local maximum at $x = -1$ the gradient becomes negative. In the region of the maximum, therefore, the gradient is constantly becoming either *less positive* (to the left) or *more negative* (to the right). The *change* in the gradient is therefore constantly moving away from more positive values and towards more negative values.

In the region of the local minimum, the situation is reversed. Approaching the "bottom of the valley" from the left, the gradient of the curve becomes *less negative*, has a zero value at the minimum point and then becomes *more and more positive.* The change in the slope of the curve around the local minimum is away from more negative values and towards more positive values.

7. Second derivatives. The mathematical measure of the way that the gradient of a curve is changing is called the second derivative and is found by differentiating the first derivative function.

EXAMPLE

Function: $y = x^3 - 3x + 2$

First derivative: $dy/dx = 3x^2 - 3$

Second derivative: $d^2y/dx^2 = 6x$

Note the symbol d^2y/dx^2 which is used for the second derivative. This symbol, for which the verbal equivalent is "d-two-y-by-d-x-square," is obviously derived from the idea of taking the derivative of a derivative, thus:

$$\frac{d}{dx}\left(\frac{dy}{dx}\right) = \frac{d^2y}{(dx)^2}.$$

8. Testing stationary points with second derivatives. Since a local maximum or minimum must be at a stationary point, all that is required to define a maximum or minimum is to find the stationary points on a curve and then to test these points in order to distinguish between maximum and minimum and, indeed, between points where the curve flattens out, giving a stationary point, but then goes on in its original direction. Stationary points of this third kind are known as "stationary and inflexional points." As we saw in a previous paragraph the way to distinguish between the different kinds of stationary points is to find out how the gradient, or slope, of the curve is changing. A *negative second derivative* will indicate that the slope is becoming less positive (more negative) at the particular point tested.

EXAMPLE

Function:	$y = x^3 - 3x + 2$
First derivative:	$dy/dx = 3x^2 - 3$
Stationary points:	$x = +1;\ x = -1$
Second derivative:	$d^2y/dx^2 = 6x$
Value of second derivative at stationary points:	When $x = -1$, $d^2y/dx^2 = -6$
	When $x = +1$, $d^2y/dx^2 = +6$.

The value of the second derivative when $x = -1$ is found by putting -1 instead of x in the second derivative function. Since the result (-6) of doing this is negative, the slope of the curve is in process of becoming more negative. The stationary point is therefore at the top of the hill and is a maximum. By similar reasoning, the stationary point at $x = +1$ is a minimum since the second derivative is positive at the given value of x.

9. Inflexional points. When there is an inflexional point, a mere bend on the curve, the second derivative has a zero value. If the inflexional point is stationary and inflexional, the first and second derivatives are both zero, giving a section of the curve which flattens out completely at the bend. Should the point be inflexional and non-stationary, the first derivative will *not* give a zero value, but the second derivative will.

10. Summary of working rules.

	First derivative	*Second derivative*
Local maximum	zero	negative
Local minimum	zero	positive
Stationary and inflexional point	zero	zero
Non-stationary and inflexional point	non-zero (sign depends on direction of bend)	zero

These are working rules; there are some exceptions to them.

11. A minimisation example. If a ship is kept waiting to enter port, costs are incurred during the whole of the time.

The more quickly the ship is turned round, the less these costs of idle time will be. Turning ships round more quickly also costs money, however, since it involves better berthing facilities, mechanical handling equipment and so on. In a particular situation a combination of observation and mathematical analysis gives the relationships discussed in **12–16** below.

12. Cost of idle time. This can be shown as:

$$\frac{C_1}{s-n},$$

where C_1 is the daily cost of keeping a ship idle, n is the average number of ships arriving each day and s is the capacity of the berth in terms of the number of ships that can averagely be turned round each day.

13. Cost of facilities. In the circumstances considered here, the cost of facilities per day is regarded as being a linear function of the number of ships which can be dealt with. The total cost of facilities per day is therefore sC_2, when C_2 is the calculated cost figure for facilities adequate for one ship per day. The cost *per ship* per day is therefore $\frac{sC_2}{n}$.

14. Total cost per ship. The total cost per ship is made up of the cost of idle time *plus* the cost of facilities. The cost of idle time $\left(\frac{C_1}{s-n}\right)$ declines as s, the number of ships that can be handled, increases, whereas the cost of facilities provided get larger as s increases. The total cost (C_T) is given by:

$$C_T = \frac{C_1}{s-n} + \frac{sC_2}{n}.$$

The number of ships averagely arriving per day is an actual figure depending on a calculation made from past records of arrivals. The symbol s is a variable and our problem is to know what level of services to provide in order to minimise total cost per ship. It should be noted that n is regarded as less than s throughout the analysis.

15. Minimising C_T. In order to minimise C_T, we must first find an expression for the gradient of the total cost curve. The curve itself will be of the form shown in Fig. 13.

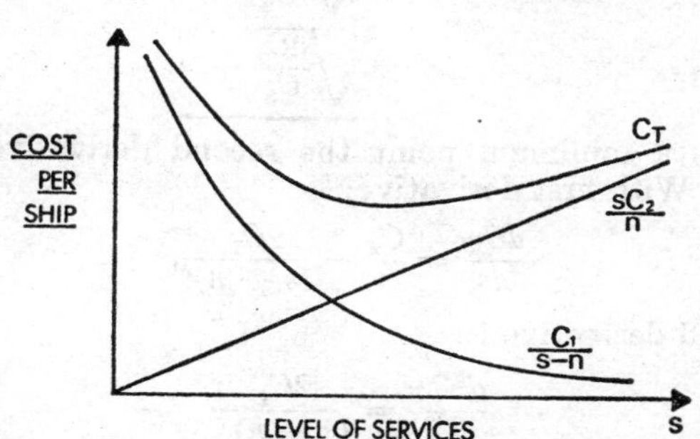

FIG. 13.—*Cost curves for levels of dockside facilities*

Differentiating

$$C_T = \frac{C_1}{s-n} + \frac{sC_2}{n}$$

with respect to s gives:

$$\frac{dC_T}{ds} = -\frac{C_1}{(s-n)^2} + \frac{C_2}{n}.$$

To find the minimum we first need to find a stationary point and to do this we must put:

$$\frac{dC_T}{ds} = 0.$$

Put:

$$\frac{C_2}{n} - \frac{C_1}{(s-n)^2} = 0$$

$$\therefore \frac{C_2}{n} = \frac{C_1}{(s-n)^2}.$$

Multiplying both sides by $(s-n)^2$ and dividing by $\frac{C_2}{n}$ gives:

$$(s-n)^2 = \frac{nC_1}{C_2}.$$

Taking square roots of both sides:

$$s - n = \sqrt{\frac{nC_1}{C_2}},$$

$$s = \sqrt{\frac{nC_1}{C_2}} + n.$$

If this is a minimum point the second derivative will be positive. With first derivative:

$$\frac{dC_T}{ds} = \frac{C_2}{n} - \frac{C_1}{(s-n)^2},$$

the second derivative is:

$$\frac{d^2C_T}{ds^2} = \frac{2C_1}{(s-n)^3}.$$

Since C_1, s and n are all positive and s is bigger than n, this second derivative is positive and the value of s found *is* a minimum.

16. Applying the formula. Suppose that *two* ships on average arrive each day, that the cost of idle time is £200 per ship per day and that the daily cost of facilities adequate to turn round one ship is £100. With these figures, $n = 2$, $C_1 = 200$ and $C_2 = 100$. The level of services required is therefore:

$$s = \sqrt{\frac{nC_1}{C_2}} + n$$

$$= \sqrt{\frac{2 \times 200}{100}} + 2$$

$$= \underline{4}.$$

That is, the level of services which will give minimum overall cost per ship handled is that sufficient to handle four ships per day.

17. A warning. In order to avoid misunderstanding or misuse of the formula it must be emphasised that it was derived to suit a particular set of circumstances. The basis of such models is queueing theory, which is discussed in Chapter XXI.

PROGRESS TEST 7

1. Find first and second derivatives of the following functions:

(*a*) $y = 3x^2 + 5x + 6$. (*b*) $y = \sqrt[3]{x} + 2$.
(*c*) $y = x^3 + 1/\sqrt{x}$.

2. Find the stationary points of the curve $y = x^4 - 3x^2 + 6$, and determine the nature of each of them. Sketch the curve.

3.* Distinguish between stationary points and maximum and minimum points. How is it that a minimum or maximum point may not be the highest or lowest points on the curve? (3–9)

4. In a certain office, examination and analysis of past records shows that there is a relationship between the number of clerks employed and the average cost of processing an order for new business. If q is the number of clerks employed, average cost is given by:

$$C = \frac{3}{2(q - 4)} + 24q.$$

What value of q will minimise this expression and how would you interpret this result?

PART TWO

DEVELOPMENTS AND APPLICATIONS

CHAPTER VIII

INTEGRATION

RESUMÉ

In Part I some very simple but fundamental ideas were considered. The basic concept of a set led on to the idea of a number system and several number systems were examined. To handle numbers in the abstract, when we are not thinking about particular examples but about general relationships, it was necessary to develop, or at least to revise, some ideas about algebra. Although in a fairly short book it was not practicable to develop the rules of algebra from set theory, this could have been done and there would then have been a consistently logical growth from the simplest ideas. The idea that was developed in some detail from set theory was that of the function. When changes in quantities can be related by some clear rule so that given one quantity we can calculate another, we have a functional relationship. To handle quite complex inter-relationships between changing quantitities we need calculus. In discussing rates of change we use the technique of differentiation and we have developed this so that it can detect maximum and minimum points.

AN APPROACH TO INTEGRATION

1. The approach to adopt. It is arguable that, as the techniques used by businessmen become more powerful and sophisticated, their behaviour grows more like that of the ideal entrepreneur, all-knowing and completely rational, who figures in models used by economists. It is also arguable that the economists' models have become more realistic as they have recognised more fully the real forces which influence the decisions of businessmen. We may therefore steal an idea from the economists in order to introduce integration.

2. The revenue of a firm. Most firms have some degree of monopoly power, that is to say if they put up their prices they would still keep some of their customers because of loyalty to their brand of goods or service or because their products do possess some real advantages which competitors' products lack. Conversely, they have the power to increase total sales volume if they put their prices down. Whether increasing the volume of sales increases total revenue received from them depends on how much sales increase and how big a price reduction has to be made. All in all, most firms' total revenue curves over the range of all possible sales might well look like that in Fig. 14.

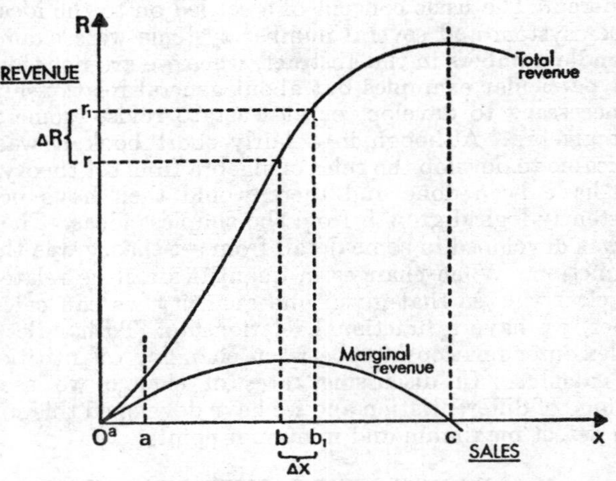

FIG. 14.—*Cost and revenue curves*

From zero to the level of sales marked *a*, revenue climbs slowly; price reductions are not bringing in many customers. From points *a* to *b* lower prices increase sales volume so much that revenue received rises more steeply than sales, but from *b* to *c* revenue rises less quickly and after *c* revenue actually falls, because although sales are rising prices have to be reduced so much that the increased volume is outweighed by the low prices. There is therefore a functional relationship between volume of sales and total revenue received. It should be noted that this graph, like the cost-accountant's break-even chart, shows the position at various *alternative* sales levels.

3. Marginal revenue. If the owner of a business wants to know how many items to sell, he will have to compare the extra *cost* incurred in increasing his sales by, say, fifty items with the extra *revenue* that he will receive from their sale. So long as the extra revenue is more than the extra cost it is worth while increasing sales a little bit more. The *extra* revenue received from an increase in sales is called the marginal revenue.

4. Total revenue as a function of sales. Since the total money received from sales (total revenue) depends on how many items are sold, we could say that total revenue is a *function* of sales. Sales are the independent variable and revenue is the dependent variable. Representing the level of sales by x and revenue by R, we can write: $R = f(x)$.

The marginal revenue derived from increasing sales from level b to level b_1 in Fig. 14 is the difference between r and r_1 on the vertical (revenue) axis. The marginal revenue per unit sold is *increase in revenue* divided by *increase in sales* or, in the notation used in Chapter VI, $\Delta R/\Delta x$. Marginal revenue is, therefore, indicated by the gradient of the total revenue curve and if the increase in sales considered was a very, very small one the expression for marginal revenue would become dR/dx.

5. A comparison of total and marginal revenue. Consider a simple case where output of fertiliser produced by a small plant in the course of a single week can vary from zero to 30 tonnes. If the price is £15 per tonne, customers will take only 5 tonnes, giving a total revenue of £75. However, if price is reduced to £10 per tonne, 10 tonnes can be sold and the revenue received is £100. The marginal revenue for the extra 5 tonnes sold is £25. The whole situation from zero to 30 tonnes is shown in Table 2.

Figure 15 shows the situation graphically. The shaded blocks represent the marginal revenue per 5-tonne lot and the upper, heavy, line represents total revenue. If we wanted to find the total revenue at any sales level, we could calculate it by adding the marginal revenues for that and all previous levels of sales. Thus the total revenue for 15 tonnes is £75 (MR, 0–5 tonnes) + £25 (MR, 5–10 tonnes) + £12½ (MR, 10–15 tonnes) = £112½.

6. Total revenue as area. If the shaded area represents the marginal revenue and the sum of the marginal revenues gives the total revenue at any point, the total shaded area for any sales figure can be found by looking at the height of the total sales bar for that figure. Suppose now that instead of having to increase sales by 5-tonne jumps, we could increase them by

TABLE 2

Sales (tonnes)	*Price per tonne*	*Total revenue*	*Marginal revenue per 5-tonne increase in sales*
0	—	—	
5	£15	£75	£75
10	10	100	25
15	7·50	112½	12·50
20	6·10	122	9·50
25	5	125	3
30	4	120	−5

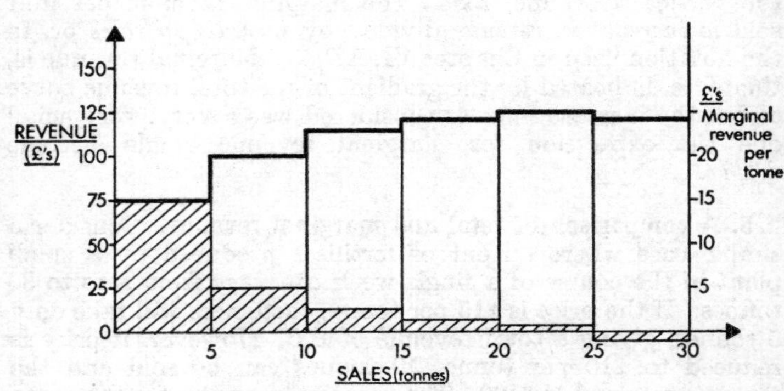

FIG. 15.—*Revenue and sales*

very small amounts. The total revenue could now be shown by a smooth curve. Using figures corresponding to those in the previous example the curves would look something like those in Fig. 16.

Representing the total revenue curve by the function $R = f(x)$, it will be remembered that the marginal revenue is given by the slope of the curve and therefore by the derivative dR/dx. From the discontinuous (5-tonne jump) example we found that the area under the marginal revenue curve (the sum of individual marginal revenues) could be read off from the total revenue curve. It looks as if the area under the marginal revenue (R_m) curve, shaded in Fig. 16, could similarly be read off from the total revenue curve. This must, indeed, be so since we could regard the smooth R_m curve as being composed of a number of very slim marginal revenue blocks which could be stacked up in just the same way as the 5-tonne blocks were in the numerical example.

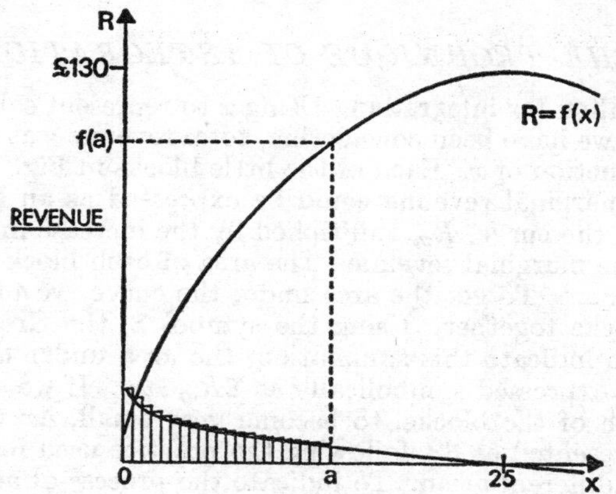

FIG. 16.—*Total revenue as an integral*

7. A generalisation of the marginal revenue result. Suppose that we know the function for marginal revenue and wanted to find the total revenue that would be received at some given sales level such as the point (a) in Fig. 16. We know that the total revenue at sales level a is given by the area under the marginal revenue curve between zero and a. We also know that *if* we knew the total revenue curve we could find the required figure. We know, too, that the marginal revenue function is the derivative of the total revenue function. Finding the total revenue function, therefore, involves finding the function which has the marginal revenue function as its derivative. If we want the area under the marginal revenue curve between zero and a, we must find the function which has the marginal revenue function as its derivative and put x equal to a in that function.

This gives a general rule for finding the area under the curve representing a given function: To find the area under the curve of a function between zero and a given value, find a function which has the given function as its derivative and evaluate this new function at the required value. This new function is known as the *integral* of the old function.

NOTE: This is a working rule only, but it will serve for most functions likely to be met with in a business context.

THE TECHNIQUE OF INTEGRATION

8. Notation for integration. Using x to represent sales in the example we have been considering, total revenue was given by $f(x)$, a function of x. Each of the little blocks in Fig. 16 representing marginal revenue could be expressed as an area, the height of the curve, R_m, multiplied by the increase in x giving rise to the marginal revenue. The area of each block is therefore $R_m \,.\, \Delta x$. To get the area under the curve, we add all the little blocks together. Using the symbol Σ, the Greek letter sigma, to indicate this summation, the area under the curve could be expressed symbolically as $\Sigma R_m \,.\, \Delta x$. If we allow Δx, the width of the blocks, to become very small, Δx would be well represented as dx, following the practice used in Chapter VI with differentiation. To indicate the process of adding up all these infinitely thin areas we replace Σ by the old English long S, $\int$. The whole notation for the area under the marginal revenue curve then becomes $\int R_m \, dx$. The verbal equivalent is "the integral of R_m with respect to x." For any function $f(x)$, the integral of $f(x)$ with respect to x is written: $\int f(x) \, dx$. The integral required, of course, is the function which has $f(x)$ as its derivative.

9. The elementary technique of integration. If we differentiate a simple function such as $y = x^2$, the derivative is given by the rule:

$$\frac{d}{dx}(x^n) = nx^{n-1}.$$

In the case of $y = x^2$, $dy/dx = 2x$. Suppose that we were asked to find $\int 2x\,dx$.

From the previous section, we know that we are required to find the function which has $2x$ as its derivative. Having just carried out the differentiation which gave $2x$ as the result, it is not difficult to write:

$$\int 2x\,dx = x^2.$$

This result is not quite complete, however, as $x^2 + C$, where C is any constant, would also have the derivative $2x$ (*see* VI, 7 if you are in doubt). The full result is, therefore:

$$\int 2x\,dx = x^2 + C.$$

This result is called the *indefinite* integral of $2x$ with respect to x, because of the indefinite nature of the integral which could have *any* constant added to it.

10. General rule for indefinite integrals of simple functions. Differentiation requires the index of the variable x to be reduced by one and for the old index to become the new coefficient of x. Working back the other way to find the integral of a function requires us to increase the power of x by one and then to divide through by a number equivalent to the new index.

EXAMPLE

$$\left.\begin{aligned} y &= 4x^3 \\ dy/dx &= 12x^2 \end{aligned}\right\} \text{Differentiation.}$$

$$\left.\begin{aligned} y &= 12x^2 \\ \int y\,dx &= \frac{12x^3}{3} \\ &= \underline{4x^3 + C} \end{aligned}\right\} \text{Integration.}$$

The general rule is:

$$y = ax^n$$

$$\int y\,dx = \frac{ax^{n+1}}{n+1} + C.$$

NOTE: Integration is a vast subject, a whole mathematical territory on which many books could be, and have been, written. Here we are dealing with ordinary power functions of a single variable and, although we shall occasionally wish that we had more elaborate and advanced techniques of integration available for our use, some simple methods will take us quite a long way.

The basic rule is stated above and the two that follow in **11** and **12** below are extensions of it.

11. Additional rule 1. If a function is multiplied by a constant the integral of that function is also multiplied by the same constant.

Function	*Integral*
$y = \alpha f(x)$	$\int \alpha f(x)\, dx$
(α a constant)	$= \alpha \int f(x)\, dx$

EXAMPLE

$$y = 5x^2 \qquad \int 5x^2\, dx$$

$$= 5\int x^2\, dx$$

$$= 5\frac{(x^3)}{3} + C = \frac{5x^3}{3} + C.$$

12. Additional rule 2. The integral of a function formed by the addition of several other functions is the sum of the integrals of the separate functions.

EXAMPLE

$$y = 5x^2 + 3x + 4$$

$$\int y dx = \frac{5}{3}x^3 + \frac{3}{2}x^2 + 4x + C.$$

It is necessary to add only a single constant at the end of the integral since the constant added to each of the terms would be quite indefinite and the sum of all of the constants would be equally undetermined. It is therefore sufficient to add a single undetermined constant which can assume any value as required in particular cases.

13. Determining the constant of integration. The constant of integration depends entirely on the particular circumstances in which the function is used. This can be shown using a marginal revenue function of the type already discussed. Suppose that the marginal revenue function for a particular firm is given by:

$$R_m = \frac{x^2}{8} - 7x + 100,$$

where x represents weekly sales in hundreds of articles. If we integrate this function we have:

$$\int \left(\frac{x^2}{8} - 7x + 100 \right) dx = \frac{x^3}{24} - \frac{7}{2}x^2 + 100x + C.$$

The total revenue function is therefore given by the integral:

$$R \text{ (total revenue)} = \frac{x^3}{24} - \frac{7}{2}x^2 + 100x.$$

The constant of integration must be zero, since, when sales are zero, $x = 0$ and, at zero sales, *revenue* must be zero. When $R = 0$:

$$\frac{x^3}{24} - \frac{7}{2}x^2 + 100x + C = 0.$$

$C = 0$ is the only value which will satisfy this equation when $x = 0$.

14. The definite integral. When we are merely trying to find the integral of a function we achieve an indefinite result. When we want to find the area between a curve and the x-axis we need a *definite* result, a numerical result giving the actual area in whatever units are being used.

15. Notation for definite integration. Let us take a very simple function, $y = 5x + 4$. If we want to find the area under the curve between $x = 1$ and $x = 4$, we need to integrate the function. In order to show that we require the area under the curve between given limits, we write the integral:

$$\int_1^4 (5x + 4)\, dx.$$

The task of finding the area between the limits falls into two parts, firstly to find the integral function and secondly to use this function to calculate the required area. In following this procedure, we integrate the function and then show the integral in square brackets ready for the second step.

Step 1.

$$y = 5x + 4,$$

$$\int (5x + 4)\,dx = \left[\frac{5}{2}x^2 + 4x\right]_1^4.$$

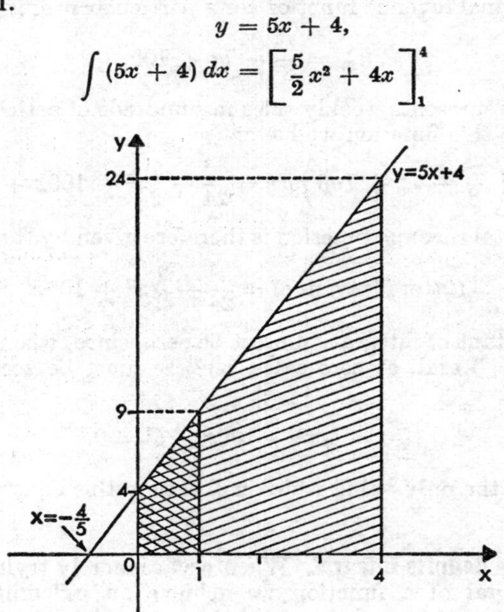

FIG. 17.—*The integral as an area*

Step 2. As a little consideration of the marginal revenue example will show, the area under the curve from zero to a given value of x, say $x = a$, can be found by substituting the given value in the integral function. The area under the curve $y = 5x + 4$ from zero to $x = 4$ is found by putting $x = 4$ in the function $\left(\frac{5}{2}x^2 + 4x\right)$. This area is shown by the shaded area in Fig. 17.

To get the area between $x = 1$ and $x = 4$, we need to subtract the area between zero and $x = 1$, shown by the cross-hatching in the figure. The area to be subtracted is found by putting

$x = 1$ in the function $\frac{5}{2}x^2 + 4x$. The second step of the procedure may be represented by:

$$\int_1^4 (5x + 4)dx = \left[\frac{5}{2}x^2 + 4x\right]_1^4$$
$$= \left[\frac{5}{2}(4)^2 + (4 \times 4)\right] - \left[\frac{5 \times 1^2}{2} + (4 \times 1)\right]$$
$$= \left[\frac{5 \times 16}{2} + 16\right] - \left[\frac{5}{2} + 4\right]$$
$$= 56 - 6\tfrac{1}{2}$$
$$= \underline{49\tfrac{1}{2}} \text{ area units.}$$

NOTE: Square brackets are used to show the definite integral before it is evaluated and during the calculation process.

16. Positive and negative areas. If the area to be calculated in Fig. 17 were that from $x = -2$ to $+4$, the result of the process used in the foregoing paragraphs would give the *net* area. The area between the curve and the axis, to the left of $x = -\frac{4}{5}$, is a negative area. Enclosed areas beneath the x-axis will always give negative results and this must be watched when evaluating definite integrals.

INTEGRALS OF EXPONENTIAL AND LOGARITHMIC FUNCTIONS

17. Integrals of exponential functions. The function $y = e^x$ has the very special characteristic that it is its own derivative. That is to say:

$$\frac{d}{dx}(e^x) = e^x.$$

From this it follows that it must also be its own integral. Putting this symbolically, we have: $\int e^x dx = e^x + C$.

A good way of checking that an integral has been found correctly is to differentiate the integral and to see if this gives the original function. Using this check it can be verified that:

$$\int e^{kx}\, dx = \frac{1}{k}e^{kx} + C,$$

where k is a constant. The differentiation rule to use here is the "function of a function" rule (*see* VI, **12**(g)).

18. Integral of $y = \log_e x$. The function $y = \log_e x$ is closely connected with $y = e^x$ which we have just considered. The derivative of $\log_e x$ is $1/x$ and consequently:

$$\int \frac{1}{x}\, dx = \log_e x + C.$$

Since C is *any* constant we could consider that its value, whatever it is, as the logarithm of some *other* constant which, for the sake of giving it a name, could be called A. Adding logarithms together gives the logarithm of the product of the quantities of which the logarithms were added. Thus:

$$\log_e x + \log_e A = \log_e Ax$$

and:

$$\int \frac{1}{x}\, dx = \log_e Ax.$$

19. Integration and statistics. Integration of probability functions is of great importance in statistics. The method of its use will be discussed in Chapter XII. Some of the integrals used are very complex and difficult to handle, but it is important to understand the *idea* of integration in statistical work. Much of the "pay-off" from this chapter will come from the added understanding of statistical reasoning and of articles on statistical topics.

PROGRESS TEST 8

1. Integrate the following expressions with respect to x:

(a) x^3 (b) $1/x$ (c) $x^2 + 1/x^2$ (d) $9x^3 + 4x$

(e) e^x (f) e^{3x}.

2. Evaluate the following definite integrals:

(a) $\int_0^5 (x^2 + 5)dx$ (b) $\int_0^7 (x - 4)dx$ (c) $\int_3^5 (7x^2 + 2x + 4)dx$

(d) $\int_0^5 3(x^2 + 1)dx$ (e) $\int_0^1 e^x\, dx$.

3.* Distinguish between definite and indefinite integration and relate to the idea of "the area under the curve." **(7, 8, 13–16)**

CHAPTER IX

WORKING IN MORE THAN TWO DIMENSIONS

REPRESENTATION OF SPACES IN SEVERAL DIMENSIONS

1. One-, two- and three-dimensional spaces. The idea of dimension seems, at first glance, to be self-evident and very simple. A line represents a one-dimensional space, a plane surface is a space in two dimensions and a space in three dimensions is a space of the kind in which we exist and move. In actual fact this rather naïve approach soon becomes inadequate and dimensionality can prove troublesome to define mathematically. However, for our modest purposes, the ordinary idea of dimension will prove sufficient, although as mathematicians we must be prepared to progress beyond three dimensions. Only one number is needed to define a point in one-dimensional space. We have already learned to use an ordered number pair to define a point in two-dimensional space. If we write the point as P(2, 3), the number 2 represents the x-co-ordinate and the number 3 represents the y-co-ordinate. Extending this idea, the point P(3, 4, 4) represents a point in three-dimensional space with the co-ordinates $x = 3$, $y = 4$, $z = 4$. This point is shown in Fig. 18.

To reach the point P, we must go 3 units along the x-axis, then turn left and go 4 units in the y direction and, having reached the point (3, 4) in the (x, y) plane, we go upwards 4 units in the z direction.

2. Inequalities in several dimensions. In business we are often more interested in inequalities than in equalities or equations. If £10,000 is available to spend in a month, then what is important is that none of the alternative ways of outlaying the money should exceed this cost ceiling. Inequalities in two, three and four dimensions are considered in 3 to 5 below.

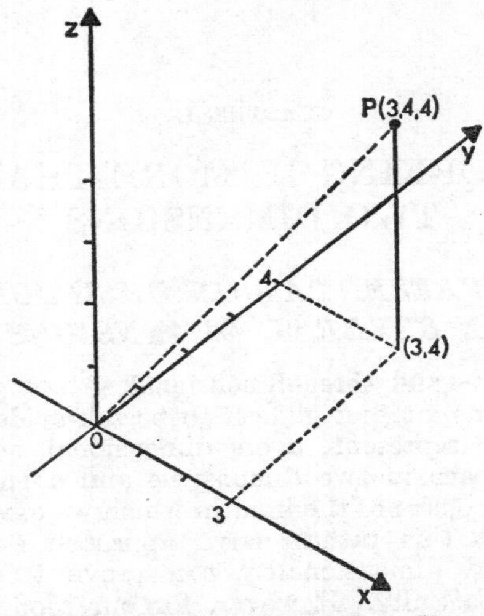

FIG. 18.—*Co-ordinates of a point in three-dimensional space*

3. Inequality in two dimensions. If our productive process involves the purchase of two raw materials one of which costs £10 per tonne and the other £50 per tonne, and if x represents the monthly usage of the first material (in tonnes) and y the monthly usage of the second material, then the relation of usages to the £10,000 can be represented by the inequality

$$10x + 50y \leqslant 10{,}000.$$

This is an inequality in two dimensions and can be represented on an ordinary graph (Fig. 19). Perhaps a further constraint might be that total storage space for the two commodities together was limited to 500 tonnes. If the combined tonnage must not exceed 500, this could be shown by $x + y \leqslant 500$. The two constraints for cost and storage are shown in Fig. 19. If we are now told to order as much as possible within the limits of cost and storage, we must buy 375 tonnes of Material A and 125 tonnes of Material B as shown by the intersection of the upper boundaries of the area of possible tonnages.

4. Inequality in three dimensions. Suppose that our process required *three* materials for our process instead of two. Let the prices per tonne be £10, £50 and £15 and the cost ceiling for the sum that can be spent in the month £20,000. The new inequality will be $10x + 50y + 15z \leqslant 20,000$. In order to represent this inequality, three axes are needed and three dimensions are therefore necessary. The boundary of the space

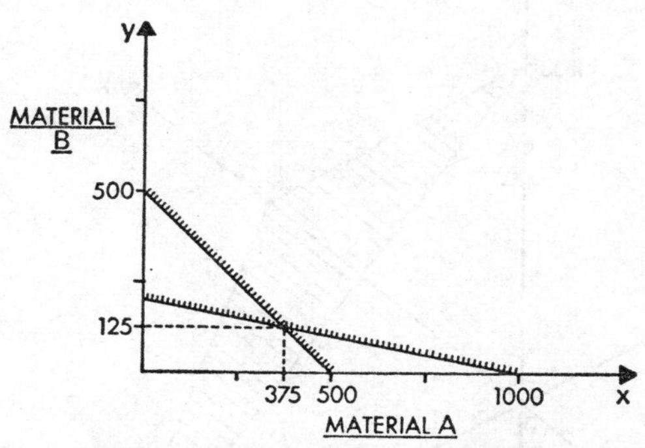

Fig. 19.—*Graphing inequalities*

within which all possible mixes of the three materials are contained is a plane, not a line as in the two-dimensional case. Figure 20 shows how the system might look in a three-dimensional diagram, although a model would be required to show the situation accurately.

5. Inequality in four dimensions. If four different materials were required, four dimensions would be required. There is no possible way of showing this diagrammatically or by means of models, but the equations could be written and would be just as meaningful.

FUNCTIONS IN TWO OR MORE DIMENSIONS

6. Inequalities and functions. The boundary lines between the "more than" and "less than" sides of the two-dimensional inequality shown in Fig. 19 could be represented by functions. The "cash ceiling" inequality is $10x + 50y \leqslant 10,000$, and the boundary is given by the *equality* $10x + 50y = 10,000$ or

$y = 200 - x/5$. The other boundary is given by $y = 500 - x$. These linear functions give straight-line boundaries and the corresponding function in three dimensions, $10x + 50y + 15z = 20{,}000$, gives a plane, a flat surface. Functions with powers of x, y and z higher than the first would give curved surfaces of one kind or another.

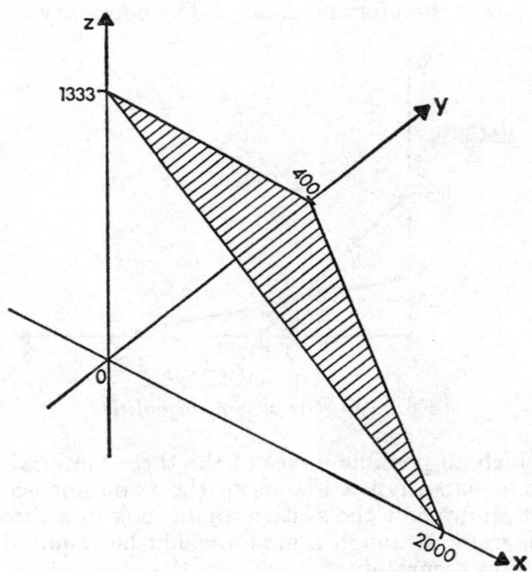

FIG. 20.—*An inequality in three dimensions*

7. Surfaces. A quite usual way to use functions of three or more variables is to designate x and y as independent variables and to let z become the dependent variable, fulfilling the same purpose as y did in the two-variable cases discussed in **IV, 10.** In certain inventory (stock) models cost per unit varies with both the batch size ordered and the quantity in stock at the beginning of the period. Measuring unit cost along the vertical (z) axis, and taking quantity in stock and batch size as the independent variables measured along the x- and y-axis respectively, we have a *cost surface*, rather like that shown in Fig. 21(a). Other situations would give other types of surface and one of these alternatives is also shown in the diagram.

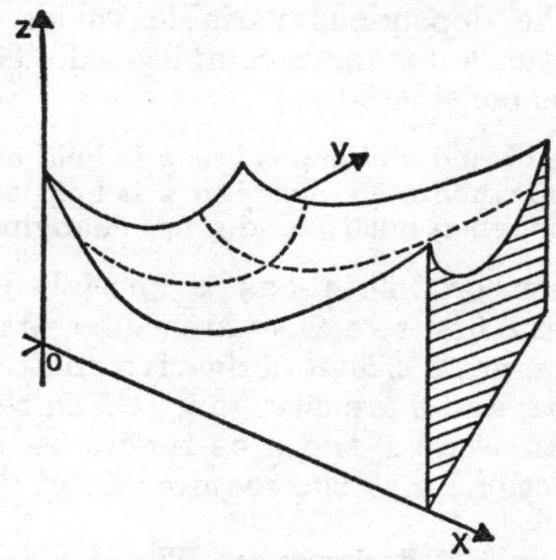

FIG. 21(*a*).—*A cost surface*

If we are using two or more independent variables, the functional notation for a single independent variable, $y = f(x)$, can easily be extended. The notation for "z is a function of x and y" is $z = f(x, y)$.

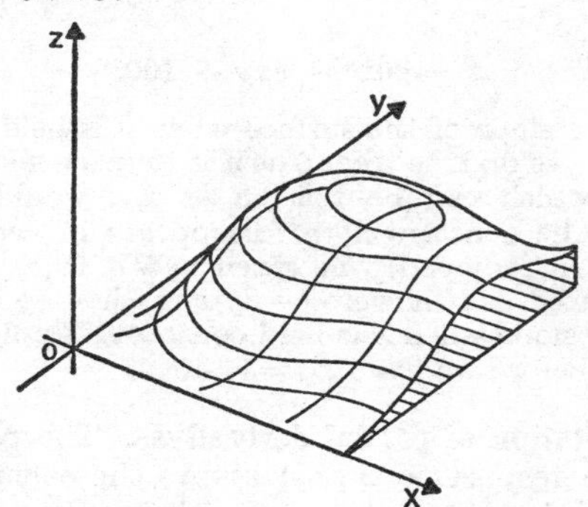

FIG. 21(*b*).—*A function in three dimensions*

DERIVATIVES OF FUNCTIONS OF MORE THAN ONE INDEPENDENT VARIABLE

8. Three cases. The derivative of an ordinary function with y as the dependent variable and x as the independent variable gives a method of finding the slope of the curve for any value of x. When the dependent variable varies with *two* other variables the situation is more complicated. The gradient of a surface could be considered as:

(*a*) the slope when x changes but y is held constant;
(*b*) the slope when y changes but x is held constant; or
(*c*) the slope when both x and y are changing.

Each of these gradients has a special derivative. The derivatives for the first two cases are called *partial* derivatives. The third case requires a *total* derivative and to handle this we must know *how* x and y are changing. Often they change with time and we can write x and y as functions of time and can build these functions into the required total derivative.

9. Rules for partial derivatives. The derivative giving the gradient when x changes but y remains constant is written as $\partial z/\partial x$ and is called the partial derivative of z with respect to x. Naturally the actual slope depends on which of the possible values of y we take as the constant one. The derivative therefore involves both x and y.

EXAMPLE

$$z = 20x^2 - 8xy + 100.$$

To find the slope of the surface when y is held constant, the sensible thing to do is to treat y as if it were a constant. If we do this $\partial z/\partial x$, which can be written as Z_x, would be equal to $40x - 8y$. The constant term disappears in accordance with the familiar (it is hoped) rule given in VI, **12**(*b*), and the term $-8xy$ is treated as if it were $(-8y)x$, with $-8y$ as a constant. Z_y gives the slope when x is held constant. Applying the same principle as before we have $Z_y = -8x$.

10. Interpretation of partial derivatives. The partial derivative of z with respect to x (Z_x) allows the calculation of the gradient at points along paths across the surface parallel to the x-axis. Which of all the possible paths is concerned depends on the value inserted for y. If we could write a profit function for various quantities of a product sold in two different markets, in home and overseas markets for instance, profit could be represented by z and the quantities sold in the two markets by x and y. The partial derivative, Z_x, would then represent the rate of change in profit as sales in market X were varied, sales in market Y being held constant. Similarly Z_y would represent the rate of change in profit as sales (y) in market Y were varied, sales in market X being held constant. Examples of the curves of which the gradients are measured by partial derivatives are shown by dotted lines in Fig. 21(a).

11. Maximum, minimum and saddle points. Imagine that you are a miniature man striding over a cost surface. The higher you climb, the higher are the costs represented by the position on the surface where you are standing.

(a) *Minimum point.* If you were at a position of minimum cost you would be standing at the lowest point of a basin. Looking "due north," parallel with the y-axis, you would be standing on level ground, that is to say Z_x would be equal to zero. Similarly Z_y would have to be equal to zero if you were really standing on level ground at the lowest cost point. The condition for a minimum point must be $Z_x = Z_y = 0$.

(b) *Maximum point.* At a maximum point, or local summit, you would also be standing on level ground whichever way you looked and again Z_x and Z_y would both equal zero.

(c) *Saddle point.* A third type of point at which both partial derivatives are equal to zero is a saddle point. This corresponds to a "minimax" position and is important in the *theory of games* (*see* XVIII, 15–26).

12. Distinguishing between maximum, minimum and saddle points. The task of distinguishing between the three types of "level ground" requires the calculation of *second-order partial derivatives*, in exactly the same way that second derivatives were used to check the nature of stationary points in functions of one independent variable. Second-order partial derivatives are a little cumbersome to calculate and since we shall mostly use first-order partial derivatives in the course of building models with known characteristics, so that we know what type of extreme point to expect, we can safely avoid discussion of them for the present. Should any reader have cause to construct and use a function of several variables of which the optimisation affects his own career or pocket, he would be well advised to test out the maximum or minimum point with full thoroughness, however.

THE USE OF VECTORS

13. Vectors in geometry. In addition to making possible an extension of the simple idea of function, spaces of several dimensions provide a means of categorising and ordering sets of data. In geometry and in elementary mechanics, a vector represents a quantity which has direction as well as magnitude. Thus in a two-dimensional space, the line OP joining the origin to the point P as in Fig. 18 can be regarded as a vector provided that its direction is specified. An arrow conventionally serves to indicate direction.

14. An alternative view. Since the vector from the origin to the point P could be represented adequately by the ordered number pair giving the co-ordinates of its end point, we may regard any ordered number pair as a vector in two dimensions. We must make it quite clear that we are doing this by using small bold italic letters to represent the particular vectors in our calculations. Thus we can write $\boldsymbol{v} = (3, 4)$ and $\boldsymbol{v}$ will always represent the two numbers 3 and 4 in that order throughout our calculations. A vector can therefore be regarded as *an ordering of real numbers*. In effect, a vector is a *list* of numbers, the order of the number in the sequence indicating the variable to which it refers. If each of the variables is assigned a particular meaning, such as the quantity of a commodity purchased in a given period, then a vector will represent one particular point and therefore one particular "mix" of commodities purchased. If there are three commodities concerned, the vector will have three elements and can be considered either as a point in a three-dimensional space or as a line going out from the origin to the point designated by the elements of the vector. In the latter case the length and direction of the line will represent one *particular* mix of the three commodities. If n commodities are concerned, the vector will indicate a point in n-dimensional space in just the same way.

EXAMPLE: A certain engineering product requires the following materials:

54 m	10 mm copper pipe
5	Type "B" couplers
1	4NT pump unit
2	non-return valves
1	flow indicator, Type "N"

Using a five-element vector to represent this list of parts and giving the vector the symbol $\boldsymbol{u}$, we could write $\boldsymbol{u} = (54, 5, 1, 2, 1)$. The position in the row indicates the part referred to and the unit of measurement.

15. Vector addition. The rule for adding vectors together is that corresponding elements should be added together. Naturally, there must be the same number of elements in each of the vectors added, which is the same thing as saying that they are in the same number of dimensions. If a vector $\boldsymbol{w}$ represents an engineering assembly requiring 5 m of copper pipe, one type "B" coupler and one flow indicator, it could be shown as:

$$\boldsymbol{w} = [5, 1, 0, 0, 1].$$

Giving the vector $\boldsymbol{u}$ the same meaning as before:

$$\boldsymbol{u} + \boldsymbol{w} = [59, 6, 1, 2, 2],$$

which would be a new vector specifying the total quantities required for both components.

This concept of vector addition corresponds exactly to the rule which may be familiar to some readers in connection with the "parallelogram of forces" used in elementary mechanics.

16. Scalar multiplication. As previously mentioned, a small bold italic letter is used to indicate a vector. Should it be necessary to indicate the use of a single figure, as distinct from a list of figures, a small Greek letter is used. When single figures are used in combination with vectors, they are referred to as *scalars*. The effect of multiplying a vector by a scalar is to multiply each element of the vector by that scalar. In symbols, we could write:

$$\boldsymbol{u} = [u_1, u_2, u_3 \;.\;.\;.\; u_n],$$
$$\alpha\boldsymbol{u} = [\alpha u_1, \alpha u_2, \alpha u_3 \;.\;.\;.\; \alpha u_n].$$

If $\boldsymbol{u}$ had the meaning assigned in the last paragraph and α was equal to 2:

$$2\boldsymbol{u} = [2 \times 54, 2 \times 5, 2 \times 1, 2 \times 2, 2 \times 1]$$
$$= [108, 10, 2, 4, 2].$$

In this case, scalar multiplication has the effect of giving the quantities required to make two assemblies.

17. Row and column vectors. The vectors so far discussed have been row vectors, with the elements displayed horizontally. It is sometimes necessary to set out the elements vertically and in this case the vector is called a *column* vector. The vector of parts for the engineering assembly would be:

$$u = \begin{bmatrix} 54 \\ 5 \\ 1 \\ 2 \\ 1 \end{bmatrix}$$

18. Vector multiplication. In order to multiply two vectors together, one must be a row vector and the other a column vector and they must both have the same number of elements. The first element of the row vector is then multiplied into the first element of the column vector, the second element into the second element and so on. Symbolically, this could be shown as:

$$uv = [u_1, u_2, u_3 \; . \; . \; . \; u_n] \begin{bmatrix} v_1 \\ v_2 \\ v_3 \\ \\ v_n \end{bmatrix}$$

$$= [u_1 v_1 + u_2 v_2 + u_3 v_3 + \; . \; . \; . + u_n v_n].$$

19. An example of vector multiplication. Take u as a column vector of engineering components as before and let p be a row vector of prices. These prices could be:

Copper pipe	50p per metre
Type "B" couplers	150p each
Pump unit, 4NT	300p ,,
Non-return valves	75p ,,
Flow indicator	120p ,,

The price vector would then be:

$$p = [50, 150, 300, 75, 120]$$

and the product:

$$pu = [50, 150, 300, 75, 120] \begin{bmatrix} 54 \\ 5 \\ 1 \\ 2 \\ 1 \end{bmatrix}$$

$$= [50 \times 54 + 150 \times 5 + 300 \times 1 + 75 \times 2 + 120 \times 1]$$
$$= [2700 + 750 + 300 + 150 + 120]$$
$$= \underline{4020} \text{ (£40·20)}$$

NOTE: The result of multiplying a vector by a vector is a scalar, a single figure. In the case we have just considered, it was necessary, of course, that all the price figures should be expressed in the same units, that is in pence.

PROGRESS TEST 9

1. Discuss the nature of the system of constraints:

$$\begin{aligned} 3x_1 + 5x_2 + 7x_3 &\leqslant 210 \\ x_1 &\geqslant 0 \\ x_2 &\geqslant 0 \\ x_3 &\geqslant 0 \end{aligned}$$

2. (*a*) Find the partial derivatives $\partial z/\partial x$ and $\partial z/\partial y$ of the following functions:

(*i*) $z = 3x^2 + 4y^3$

(*ii*) $z = 2x^2 + xy - y^2$

(*iii*) $z = e^{x+y}$

(*iv*) $z = \sqrt[3]{x} + 1/y + 6$

(*b*)* State the condition for a stationary point on a 3-dimensional surface. What three types of stationary point might exist? (11–12)

3. If $\boldsymbol{u} = [3, 9, 4, 6]$, $\boldsymbol{v} = \begin{bmatrix}1\\3\\5\\9\end{bmatrix}$ and $\boldsymbol{v}' = [1, 3, 5, 9]$ (this is called the "transpose" of $\boldsymbol{v}$), find: (*a*) $\boldsymbol{u} + \boldsymbol{v}$ (*b*) $\boldsymbol{u} - \boldsymbol{v}$ (*c*) $2\boldsymbol{u}$ (*d*) $\boldsymbol{uv}$.

4. Given that $\boldsymbol{q}$ is a vector of quantities and $\boldsymbol{p}$ is a vector of prices, both in appropriate units, find the total expenditure when $\boldsymbol{q} = [17, 4, 36, 18]$ and $\boldsymbol{p}' = [5, 200, 4, 50]$.

CHAPTER X

MATRICES

FUNDAMENTAL IDEAS

1. The matrix. In the previous chapter we saw that a single symbol could be made to stand for a "list" of numbers, each of which represented a point in a multi-dimensional system. This idea can be extended to take in sets of related vectors made up into a rectangular array of numbers. Such rectangular arrays are called matrices.

2. Symbols used for matrices. If we wish to denote a matrix, we use a large Roman letter, as distinct from the small italic letters used to indicate vectors. An example would be:

$$\mathbf{A} = \begin{bmatrix} 1 & 4 & 3 & 2 \\ 3 & 1 & 5 & 6 \\ 9 & 2 & 7 & 4 \end{bmatrix}.$$

Note that instead of the small brackets used to enclose a vector, large brackets are used for the matrix. Other conventions that are sometimes used are double vertical lines

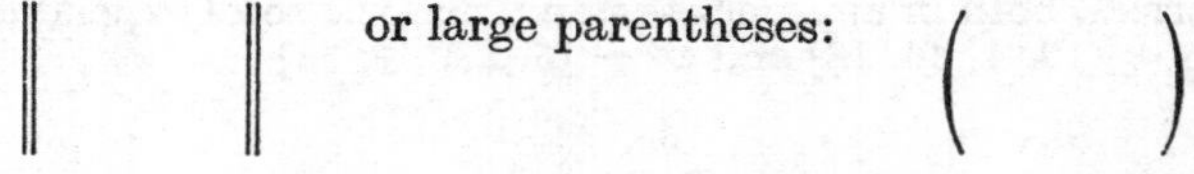

3. The meaning of a matrix. A matrix could be regarded merely as a rectangular array of numbers and then used as a device for handling large sets of numbers in accordance with a set of conventional rules. However, since we have already used the order properties of vectors to indicate values of variables, we should be able to apply similar ideas to matrices. There are two alternative usages open to us: either the elements in a particular position can be used to show the values attaching to a particular variable or the elements of the matrix can represent the coefficients of variables.

MATRICES AS ARRAYS OF QUANTITIES

4. An example from production engineering. Suppose that we are producing three different pump units, each of which has some components in common. The details could be set in tabular form as in Table 3.

TABLE 3

Pump	*Housing*	*Impeller unit*	*Bolts*	*Couplings*	*Inlets*	*Armoured hose*
Type A	1	1	4	3	2	8 m
Type B	1	1	6	2	2	4 m
Type C	1	1	3	4	2	3 m

On the understanding that the parts were always written in this order, the situation could be concisely stated by means of a three-row, six-column (3×6) matrix. Designating this matrix of quantities by **R**, we could write:

$$\mathbf{R} = \begin{bmatrix} 1 & 1 & 4 & 3 & 2 & 8 \\ 1 & 1 & 6 & 2 & 2 & 4 \\ 1 & 1 & 3 & 4 & 2 & 3 \end{bmatrix}.$$

5. A demand vector. On a particular day, our firm might receive an order for four Type "A" pump units, three Type "B" units and one Type "C" unit. Using the conventions adopted in IX, 16, we could write a demand vector $\boldsymbol{d} = [4, 3, 1]$. The quantities of each component required to make up the order could easily be calculated by multiplying each row by the appropriate figure and adding up the quantities obtained. This process could be expressed very simply by regarding each *column* of the matrix as a vector and then applying the "row into column" rule for vector multiplication. The first "column vector" in the matrix is that for housings and is:

$$\begin{bmatrix} 1 \\ 1 \\ 1 \end{bmatrix}.$$

Multiplying the $\boldsymbol{d}$ vector into this gives:

$$[4, 3, 1] \begin{bmatrix} 1 \\ 1 \\ 1 \end{bmatrix} = [4 + 3 + 1].$$

$$= 8 \text{ housing units.}$$

It will be recalled that multiplying a vector by a vector gives a scalar, a single number or quantity. Repeating the process for each *column vector* in the matrix will give six scalars which together will make up a new *row vector*, with the same number of elements as there are columns in the **R** matrix.

The whole process will look like this:

$$\boldsymbol{d}\mathbf{R} = [4, 3, 1] \begin{bmatrix} 1 & 1 & 4 & 3 & 2 & 8 \\ 1 & 1 & 6 & 2 & 2 & 4 \\ 1 & 1 & 3 & 4 & 2 & 3 \end{bmatrix}$$
$$= [8, 8, 37, 22, 16, 47].$$

The elements of this vector represent the quantities required to make up the order, that is 8 housings, 8 impeller units, 37 bolts, 22 couplings, 16 inlets and 47 m of armoured hose.

OPERATIONAL RULES FOR MATRICES AND VECTORS

6. Comparison with vector rules. The rules for operations with vectors and matrices follow very closely the rules for vectors alone.

7. Addition and subtraction of matrices. In order to be able to add matrices together, each of the two matrices concerned must have the same number of rows and columns. The process of addition consists of adding the corresponding elements of the two matrices.

EXAMPLE

$$\mathbf{A} = \begin{bmatrix} 3 & 1 & 2 \\ 4 & 3 & 9 \\ 5 & 6 & 8 \end{bmatrix} \qquad \mathbf{B} = \begin{bmatrix} 0 & 1 & 8 \\ 3 & 7 & 6 \\ 2 & 6 & 4 \end{bmatrix}$$

$$\mathbf{A} + \mathbf{B} = \begin{bmatrix} 3 & 2 & 10 \\ 7 & 10 & 15 \\ 7 & 12 & 12 \end{bmatrix}$$

To subtract one matrix from another, the rule is to subtract corresponding elements.

8. Commutative rule for addition. Just as there is a commutative law for the addition of ordinary numbers, there is a commutative law for the addition of matrices. Provided that the two matrices are of the same pattern so that addition can take place, $\mathbf{A} + \mathbf{B} = \mathbf{B} + \mathbf{A}$.

9. Scalar multiplication of matrices. The rule for scalar multiplication was given in IX, **16**, and it will no doubt be recalled that the effect was to multiply each element of the vector by the scalar. Scalar multiplication for matrices follows exactly the same pattern; each element is multiplied by the scalar.

EXAMPLE

Matrix *Scalar*

$$\mathbf{A} = \begin{bmatrix} 4 & 7 & 9 \\ 3 & 8 & 2 \\ 4 & 1 & 9 \end{bmatrix} \qquad \alpha = 5$$

$$\alpha\mathbf{A} = 5\begin{bmatrix} 4 & 7 & 9 \\ 3 & 8 & 2 \\ 4 & 1 & 9 \end{bmatrix} = \begin{bmatrix} 20 & 35 & 45 \\ 15 & 40 & 10 \\ 20 & 5 & 45 \end{bmatrix}.$$

10. Multiplication of matrices by vectors. A practical example of this has been given in **5** above, and this purely common-sense idea of what is involved in vector multiplication of a matrix is quite sound. The matrix can be treated as a set of column vectors and the "row-into-column" rule applied to produce a new row vector.

11. An additional example.

$$[8 \quad 7 \quad 4 \quad 3]\begin{bmatrix} 4 & 7 & 1 & 2 \\ 3 & 5 & 4 & 2 \\ 2 & 3 & 2 & 1 \\ 1 & 2 & 1 & 1 \end{bmatrix} = [64, 109, 47, 37].$$

Note that the matrix must have the same number of rows as the vector has elements. The vector and matrix must be "conformable" for multiplication to be possible. So long as the matrix and vector do conform, it is possible to multiply a matrix into a column vector. In that case, the matrix must have the same number of columns as the column vector has elements for the row-into-column rule to be applied. The result, as can be seen after a little thought, is a column vector.

12. Multiplication of a matrix by a matrix. The rules for the multiplication of a matrix by a vector can easily be extended to cover the multiplication of a matrix by a matrix. If the first matrix is regarded as a set of row vectors, each row-into-column multiplication carried through the second matrix will produce a row vector. Repeated for each row in the first matrix, a new set of row vectors, that is a new matrix, will be built up as the product of the matrix multiplication.

13. Conditions for matrix multiplication. In order that matrix multiplication may be possible, the matrices concerned must be conformable; that is to say, there must be the right number of rows and columns.

Also, the reader may confirm by experiment that multiplying **A** by **B** does not give the same result as multiplying **B** by **A**. There is, therefore, no commutative law for matrix multiplication.

EXAMPLE

$$\mathbf{A} = \begin{bmatrix} 3 & 4 & 2 \\ 1 & 5 & 1 \\ 2 & 1 & 2 \end{bmatrix} \qquad \mathbf{B} = \begin{bmatrix} 3 & 5 & 2 \\ 4 & 1 & 3 \\ 5 & 3 & 1 \end{bmatrix}$$

$$\mathbf{AB} = \begin{bmatrix} 3 & 4 & 2 \\ 1 & 5 & 1 \\ 2 & 1 & 2 \end{bmatrix} \begin{bmatrix} 3 & 5 & 2 \\ 4 & 1 & 3 \\ 5 & 3 & 1 \end{bmatrix}.$$

The first vector of the new, product matrix is built up by multiplying the row vector [3, 4, 2] into each of the columns of the **B** matrix, giving [35, 25, 20]. The second set of row-into-column multiplications uses the vector [1, 5, 1] and gives the row vector [28, 13, 18]. The final multiplication, using the row vector [2, 1, 2] completes the multiplication, giving the product matrix:

$$\mathbf{AB} = \begin{bmatrix} 35 & 25 & 20 \\ 28 & 13 & 18 \\ 20 & 17 & 9 \end{bmatrix}.$$

14. Types of matrix. A matrix which has the same number of rows as columns is called a square matrix. **A** and **B** above are *square matrices*.

A matrix of which the elements are all zeros will act like zero in ordinary arithmetic and $\mathbf{O} \times \mathbf{A}$ will give $\mathbf{O}$. We could call such a matrix the zero matrix. A square matrix with every element zero except the main diagonal, and this consisting entirely of ones, is called a *unit matrix*. The unit matrix is represented by the symbol **I**. The unit matrix acts exactly like the unity in ordinary arithmetic, multiplication by **I** leaving a matrix unchanged.

EXAMPLE

$$\mathbf{IA} = \begin{bmatrix} 1 & 0 & 0 \\ 0 & 1 & 0 \\ 0 & 0 & 1 \end{bmatrix} \begin{bmatrix} 3 & 4 & 2 \\ 1 & 5 & 1 \\ 2 & 1 & 2 \end{bmatrix} = \begin{bmatrix} 3 & 4 & 2 \\ 1 & 5 & 1 \\ 2 & 1 & 2 \end{bmatrix}.$$

Any other matrix with all elements zero except the main diagonal, and those elements consisting of numbers other than one, is known as a *diagonal matrix*.

EXAMPLE

$$\mathbf{C} = \begin{bmatrix} 3 & 0 & 0 \\ 0 & 4 & 0 \\ 0 & 0 & 5 \end{bmatrix}.$$

15. The inverse of a square matrix. In III, **9–16**, we considered some of the rules governing the use of indices. The symbol a^{-1} represented $1/a$, so that $a \,.\, a^{-1} = 1$. Having acquired a symbol in matrix algebra equivalent to unity, it seems reasonable to suppose that some equivalent to the expression above might exist. Such an expression would be $\mathbf{A}\,\mathbf{A}^{-1} = \mathbf{I}$. The matrix $\mathbf{A}^{-1}$ is, in fact, another matrix such that when multiplied by **A** the result is **I**. Using the symbol **A** to represent the same matrix as in the previous example, we have:

$$\mathbf{A}^{-1}\,\mathbf{A} = \begin{bmatrix} 1 & -\frac{2}{3} & -\frac{2}{3} \\ 0 & \frac{2}{9} & -\frac{1}{9} \\ -1 & \frac{5}{9} & \frac{11}{9} \end{bmatrix} \begin{bmatrix} 3 & 4 & 2 \\ 1 & 5 & 1 \\ 2 & 1 & 2 \end{bmatrix} = \begin{bmatrix} 1 & 0 & 0 \\ 0 & 1 & 0 \\ 0 & 0 & 1 \end{bmatrix}.$$

A method of finding the inverse of a square matrix will be given in **21–23** below.

16. The equality of vectors and matrices. For a vector or matrix to be equal to another matrix or vector, they must have the same number of elements, in the same pattern, and corresponding elements must be equal.

THE SOLUTION OF SIMULTANEOUS EQUATIONS

17. Practical uses. Many situations in business and economics give rise either to systems of simultaneous equations or to simultaneous inequalities. Whenever there are limitations which cannot be exceeded, such as upper limits on the availability of plant or skilled labour, the constraints can be expressed as inequalities. One such situation, although a very simple one, was discussed in IX, **3–5**. That problem was dealt with by considering the two inequalities concerned at their extreme values so that they could be solved as simultaneous equations. Simultaneous equations occur when certain restrictions must be met exactly. Matrix methods offer a straightforward means of solving simultaneous equations, moreover they are methods which can easily be adapted for use with calculating machines or can be programmed for computers.

18. Solution by row transformations. Consider the simultaneous equations:

$$7x_1 + 4x_2 = 80$$
$$5x_1 + 3x_2 = 58.$$

If we concerned ourselves only with the coefficients, we could write the left-hand sides of the equations as a matrix, on the understanding that the first column of the matrix represented coefficients of the variable x_1 and the second column the coefficients of the variable x_2. The matrix would be:

$$\begin{bmatrix} 7 & 4 \\ 5 & 3 \end{bmatrix}.$$

Such a matrix could be extended by putting in a division to represent the equals signs and then using a third column to show the right-hand-side constants. The matrix would then be a *partitioned* matrix and would appear as:

$$\left[\begin{array}{cc|c} 7 & 4 & 80 \\ 5 & 3 & 58 \end{array}\right].$$

19. Manipulating the partitioned matrix. Since the two sides of an equation are equal, this equality will be maintained if the whole equation is multiplied or divided by some figure or if equal quantities are added to both sides.

Our aim must be to get the left-hand side of the partitioned matrix to look like this:

$$\left[\begin{array}{cc|} 1 & 0 \\ 0 & 1 \end{array}\right],$$

which would read: $x_1 = \ldots, x_2 = \ldots$ If we can obtain this result without disturbing the equalities, that is by dividing rows right through by some figure or by adding or subtracting multiples of rows to other rows, we shall have solved the simultaneous equations.

EXAMPLE

Partitioned matrix: $\left[\begin{array}{cc|c} 7 & 4 & 80 \\ 5 & 3 & 58 \end{array}\right]$

representing: $\left[\begin{array}{c} 7x_1 + 4x_2 = 80 \\ 5x_1 + 3x_2 = 58 \end{array}\right]$

A sensible strategy is to work through the columns one by one, getting the chosen element equal to unity and the others equal to zero.

Step 1. Divide row 1 by 7:

$$\left[\begin{array}{cc|c} 1 & \frac{4}{7} & \frac{80}{7} \\ 5 & 3 & 58 \end{array}\right]$$

Step 2. Subtract 5 times row 1 from row 2:

$$\left[\begin{array}{cc|c} 1 & \frac{4}{7} & \frac{80}{7} \\ 0 & \frac{1}{7} & \frac{6}{7} \end{array}\right]$$

Step 3. Multiply new row 2 by 7:

$$\left[\begin{array}{cc|c} 1 & \frac{4}{7} & \frac{80}{7} \\ 0 & 1 & 6 \end{array}\right]$$

Step 4. Subtract 4/7ths of (multiplied) row 2 from row 1:

$$\left[\begin{array}{cc|c} 1 & 0 & 8 \\ 0 & 1 & 6 \end{array}\right]$$

Solution. Taking the first column to represent x_1 and the second to represent x_2, as before, the final matrix is read as:

$$x_1 = 8$$
$$x_2 = 6.$$

20. Larger systems of equations. The same procedure, exactly, can be used to find solutions to larger systems of equations. For a system of equations to be solvable, there must be as many equations as variables. The sub-matrix to the left of the partition must therefore be square. Readers may try their hands at a 3×3 matrix system in Question 5 in the Progress Test which follows this chapter. The full working is shown in the answer in Appendix IV.

FINDING THE INVERSE OF A SQUARE MATRIX

21. Method. A fairly easy method of finding the inverse of a square matrix uses methods very similar to those demonstrated in 19 above.

22. Setting up the partitioned matrix. Finding the inverse of a square matrix involves finding the solution to several sets of equations. Taking our matrix as:

$$\mathbf{A} = \begin{bmatrix} 4 & 3 & 1 \\ 2 & 1 & 4 \\ 3 & 0 & 1 \end{bmatrix},$$

the inverse can be found by setting up the initial tableau as:

$$\left[\begin{array}{ccc|ccc} 4 & 3 & 1 & 1 & 0 & 0 \\ 2 & 1 & 4 & 0 & 1 & 0 \\ 3 & 0 & 1 & 0 & 0 & 1 \end{array}\right].$$

Our objective is to show the unit matrix on the left-hand side of the partition and the inverse matrix on the right-hand side. The process involves "row transformations" as before, but they are carried out across all six columns of the partitioned matrix.

23. Solution to problem of finding inverse of A.

Tableau 1.

$$\left[\begin{array}{ccc|ccc} 4 & 3 & 1 & 1 & 0 & 0 \\ 2 & 1 & 4 & 0 & 1 & 0 \\ 3 & 0 & 1 & 0 & 0 & 1 \end{array}\right]$$

Divide row 1 by 4.

Tableau 2.

$$\left[\begin{array}{ccc|ccc} 1 & \frac{3}{4} & \frac{1}{4} & \frac{1}{4} & 0 & 0 \\ 2 & 1 & 4 & 0 & 1 & 0 \\ 3 & 0 & 1 & 0 & 0 & 1 \end{array}\right]$$

Eliminate non-zero elements from column 1 by subtracting twice row 1 and three times row 1 from rows 2 and 3 respectively.

Tableau 3.

$$\left[\begin{array}{ccc|ccc} 1 & \frac{3}{4} & \frac{1}{4} & \frac{1}{4} & 0 & 0 \\ 0 & -\frac{1}{2} & 3\frac{1}{2} & -\frac{1}{2} & 1 & 0 \\ 0 & -2\frac{1}{4} & \frac{1}{4} & -\frac{3}{4} & 0 & 1 \end{array}\right]$$

Bring second element in row 2 to unity by multiplying by -2.

Tableau 4.

$$\left[\begin{array}{ccc|ccc} 1 & \frac{3}{4} & \frac{1}{4} & \frac{1}{4} & 0 & 0 \\ 0 & 1 & -7 & 1 & -2 & 0 \\ 0 & -2\frac{1}{4} & \frac{1}{4} & -\frac{3}{4} & 0 & 1 \end{array}\right]$$

Eliminate non-zero elements from column 2 by subtracting $\frac{3}{4}$ of row 2 from row 1 and adding 9/4ths of row 2 to row 3.

Tableau 5.

$$\left[\begin{array}{ccc|ccc} 1 & 0 & \frac{11}{2} & -\frac{1}{2} & \frac{3}{2} & 0 \\ 0 & 1 & -7 & 1 & -2 & 0 \\ 0 & 0 & -\frac{31}{2} & \frac{3}{2} & -\frac{9}{2} & 1 \end{array}\right]$$

Bring third element in row 3 to unity by multiplying by $-2/31$.

Tableau 6.

$$\left[\begin{array}{ccc|ccc} 1 & 0 & \frac{11}{2} & -\frac{1}{2} & \frac{3}{2} & 0 \\ 0 & 1 & -7 & 1 & -2 & 0 \\ 0 & 0 & 1 & -\frac{3}{31} & \frac{9}{31} & -\frac{2}{31} \end{array}\right]$$

Remove non-zero elements from column 3 by adding 7 times row 3 to row 2 and subtracting 11/2 times row 3 from row 1.

Tableau 7.

$$\left[\begin{array}{ccc|ccc} 1 & 0 & 0 & \frac{1}{31} & -\frac{3}{31} & \frac{11}{31} \\ 0 & 1 & 0 & \frac{10}{31} & \frac{1}{31} & -\frac{14}{31} \\ 0 & 0 & 1 & -\frac{3}{31} & \frac{9}{31} & -\frac{2}{31} \end{array}\right]$$

The required inverse is:

$$\mathbf{A}^{-1} = \begin{bmatrix} \frac{1}{31} & -\frac{3}{31} & \frac{11}{31} \\ \frac{10}{31} & \frac{1}{31} & -\frac{14}{31} \\ -\frac{3}{31} & \frac{9}{31} & -\frac{2}{31} \end{bmatrix}$$

as shown by the right-hand side of Tableau 7.

24. Using the inverse to solve simultaneous equations. Suppose that the **A** matrix of the example had been derived from the set of equations:

$$\begin{aligned} 4x_1 + 3x_2 + x_3 &= 8 \\ 2x_1 + x_2 + 4x_3 &= -4 \\ 3x_1 + x_3 &= 1 \end{aligned}$$

Putting **A** as the matrix of coefficients:

$$\begin{bmatrix} 4 & 3 & 1 \\ 2 & 1 & 4 \\ 3 & 0 & 1 \end{bmatrix},$$

remembering that a zero entry is required for the missing variable, x_2, in the third equation, we could let the variables be represented by a vector:

$$\boldsymbol{x} = \begin{bmatrix} x_1 \\ x_2 \\ x_3 \end{bmatrix}.$$

Taking another vector:

$$\boldsymbol{c} = \begin{bmatrix} 8 \\ -4 \\ 1 \end{bmatrix},$$

for the right-hand-side constants, the whole system could be written as $\mathbf{A}\boldsymbol{x} = \boldsymbol{c}$. In case the reader is uncertain that this is so, the system is written out in matrix and vector form below:

$$\begin{array}{ccc} \mathbf{A}\boldsymbol{x} & = & \boldsymbol{c} \end{array}$$

$$\begin{bmatrix} 4 & 3 & 1 \\ 2 & 1 & 4 \\ 3 & 0 & 1 \end{bmatrix} \begin{bmatrix} x_1 \\ x_2 \\ x_3 \end{bmatrix} = \begin{bmatrix} 8 \\ -4 \\ 1 \end{bmatrix}.$$

Row-into-column multiplication gives the first element of the product vector for $\mathbf{A}x$ as $4x_1 + 3x_2 + x_3$. This can be regarded as a special kind of scalar, since the three terms added together with the correct values of x_1, x_2, x_3 would give a single figure. For two vectors to be equal, each element in one must be equal to the corresponding element in the other. The result of the first multiplication must equal 8, giving the required equation. The remaining multiplications complete the system. Writing the system compactly as $\mathbf{A}x = \mathbf{c}$ we can proceed to solve the equation by multiplying both sides by $\mathbf{A}^{-1}$, giving:

$$\mathbf{A}^{-1}\mathbf{A}x = \mathbf{A}^{-1}\mathbf{c}.$$

However, $\mathbf{A}^{-1}\mathbf{A} = \mathbf{I}$, which is equivalent to 1.
The equation can now be written:

$$x = \mathbf{A}^{-1}\mathbf{c}.$$

Actual multiplication, using the inverse already found, gives the required values as the elements of a column vector.

$$\mathbf{A}^{-1} = \begin{bmatrix} \frac{1}{31} & -\frac{3}{31} & \frac{11}{31} \\ \frac{10}{31} & \frac{1}{31} & -\frac{14}{31} \\ -\frac{3}{31} & \frac{9}{31} & -\frac{2}{31} \end{bmatrix} \quad \mathbf{c} = \begin{bmatrix} 8 \\ -4 \\ 1 \end{bmatrix}$$

$$\begin{bmatrix} \frac{1}{31} & -\frac{3}{31} & \frac{11}{31} \\ \frac{10}{31} & \frac{1}{31} & -\frac{14}{31} \\ -\frac{3}{31} & \frac{9}{31} & -\frac{2}{31} \end{bmatrix} \begin{bmatrix} 8 \\ -4 \\ 1 \end{bmatrix} = \begin{bmatrix} 1 \\ 2 \\ -2 \end{bmatrix}$$

The solution is $x_1 = 1$, $x_2 = 2$, $x_3 = -2$.

THE ADVANTAGES OF MATRIX NOTATION

25. Compactness. Matrix notation enables us to represent whole arrays of figures by a single symbol, to manipulate the symbols freely and then to "untie the parcel" and carry out the final operations when the solution has been found in terms of matrix algebra. The methods, although tedious to carry out by hand, are systematic and ideal for mechanical or electronic calculation.

26. Matrices in business. Some of the more obvious applications are detailed below.

(*a*) *Linear programming*. This important class of problems is solved by a technique known as the "Simplex" method, which is dependent on matrix operations and can be understood properly only in terms of matrices.

(*b*) *Technical applications.* Matrices can be used to show requirements of parts and their relationship to completed assemblies as in 4 above. These ideas can be extended to methods involving inverses and other aspects of matrix algebra. A simple example is given in Question 6 in the Progress Test at the end of the chapter.

(*c*) *Accounting.* An accounting system can be represented almost entirely in terms of matrices and vectors and many operations can be carried out by means of matrix operations. This has implications for electronic data processing although the full implications have not yet been followed out.

(*d*) The *operations of a firm* or of the whole economy can be described on terms of matrix algebra, although somewhat inexactly in the latter case.

PROGRESS TEST 10

1.* Say exactly what is meant by a matrix and give some examples of the possible uses of matrices in business situations. (**3–5, 25**)

2.* To what extent is it justifiable to talk of "an algebra of matrices"? (**6–17** and discussion in light of previous knowledge of algebra as in Chapter III.)

3. Taking $\mathbf{A} = \begin{bmatrix} 1 & 4 & 3 \\ 2 & 1 & 8 \\ 1 & 1 & 2 \end{bmatrix}$, $\mathbf{B} = \begin{bmatrix} 2 & 1 & 2 \\ 0 & 4 & 8 \\ 6 & 1 & 4 \end{bmatrix}$,

calculate (*a*) $\mathbf{A} + \mathbf{B}$ (*b*) $\mathbf{A} - \mathbf{B}$ (*c*) $\mathbf{AB}$.

4. (*a*) If $\boldsymbol{a} = [3, 1, 4]$ calculate $\boldsymbol{a}\mathbf{B}$ with $\mathbf{B}$ as in Question 1.

(*b*) Using the requirements matrix ($\mathbf{R}$) of **4**, and a demand vector $\boldsymbol{d} = [6, 1, 4]$ calculate $\boldsymbol{d}\mathbf{R}$ and say what your calculation and answer mean.

5. Find $\mathbf{A}^{-1}$ when $\mathbf{A} = \begin{bmatrix} 1 & 3 & 4 \\ 0 & 1 & 2 \\ 6 & 3 & 1 \end{bmatrix}$.

6. If $\mathbf{Q}$ is a triangular matrix showing the relationship between various parts, sub-assemblies and a completed engineering piece, it can be shown that the number of parts, sub-assemblies, etc., to be made is given by the equation $\boldsymbol{r} = \boldsymbol{r}\mathbf{Q} + \boldsymbol{d}$, where $\boldsymbol{d}$ is a vector of both parts and completed assemblies required by customers and

$\boldsymbol{r}$ is a requirement vector showing quantities of all parts to be produced, both for direct sale and for making up other assemblies.

(*a*) Show that $\boldsymbol{r} = \boldsymbol{d}[\mathbf{I} - \mathbf{Q}]^{-1}$.

(*b*) Calculate $\boldsymbol{r}$ if $\mathbf{Q} = \begin{bmatrix} 0 & & & & \\ 8 & 0 & & & \\ 1 & 2 & 0 & & \\ 3 & 0 & 1 & 0 & \\ 0 & 3 & 4 & 1 & 0 \end{bmatrix}$ and $\boldsymbol{d} = [0, 0, 2, 4, 9]$.

CHAPTER XI

PROBABILITY

THE MEANING OF MATHEMATICAL PROBABILITY

1. Probability and business. Business policy is concerned with future markets, costs and price movements and is therefore subject to uncertainty. In the ordinary way every businessman has to make some forecast of future events; mathematical probability builds into our attempts to foresee the future, the uncertainty which must necessarily be present. The basis of mathematical probability may be either a subjective estimate of future events, a statistical examination of comparable past events or a theoretical model of a situation. The relationship between these approaches and the conflict between them is a subject for learned discussion but need not concern us greatly here.

2. A definition of probability. A fairly simple definition can serve as a beginning for our examination of probability in relation to business problems. Suppose that some event (E), which is of advantage to us, can happen in m ways, but that there are n other possibilities that exclude the occurrence of the desired event. The total number of possible courses which events (favourable or unfavourable) can take is $(m + n)$. The probability of E can be defined as: $Pr(E) = m/(m + n)$.

EXAMPLE: If a six-sided unbiased die is thrown once, there are six possible results of the throw.

Possible results: 1 2 3 4 5 6.

Event: Let the event (E) be the throwing of a six.

Number of ways the event can happen = 1
Number of ways it can fail to happen = 5
$Pr\,(E) = 1/(1 + 5) = \frac{1}{6}$.

The result accords with common sense and this is something that we require of our system of mathematical probability.

3. Probability and Venn diagrams. If the event of the example in the previous section is defined by a statement, that statement would be "a six will be thrown." Let us represent the statement by a symbol, p. In a Venn diagram (see II, 7–8) let the universal set be the set of all the possible outcomes of the dice throw and let a circle represent P, the set of all the cases for which the statement p would be true. This Venn diagram is shown in Fig. 22.

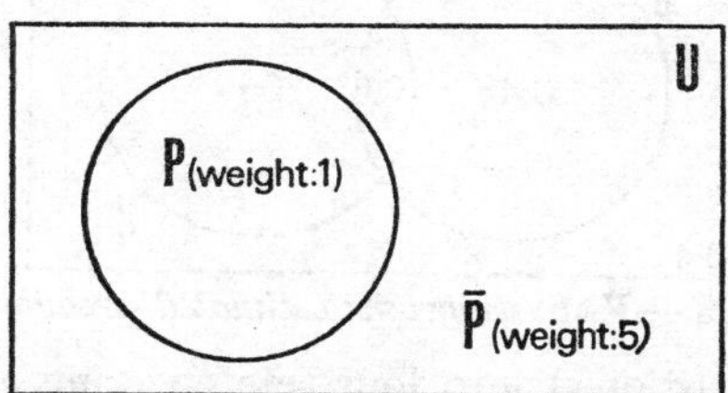

FIG. 22.— *Venn diagram for probabilities*

Since all the events are equally likely, the single event satisfying p could be represented as the weighting for the set P. We could call this weighting 1 unit. The weighting of $\bar{P}$, the "not-p" set, would be 5 units and the universal set, comprising all the events under consideration, would be 6 units. The probability of the universal set must be represented as 1, since unity must indicate an event or combination of events which is bound to happen, at least within the framework of the model under discussion. The probability of p is then represented as:

$$Pr(p) = \frac{\text{Weighting of P}}{\text{Weighting of U}} = \tfrac{1}{6}.$$

4. Probabilities based on estimations. Suppose that a firm of contractors submits tenders for two civil engineering contracts, one for a sewerage scheme and the other for a highways development. The managing director, wishing to calculate what resources will be available for use elsewhere, makes a subjective estimate of the probability of getting the sewerage scheme and assesses this probability as 0·5, that is a "fifty-fifty" chance. He reckons that there is a 20 per cent chance of getting the highways contract and only a 10 per cent chance of getting both contracts. Letting the set S represent the sewerage scheme, and H the highways scheme, our Venn diagram would appear as shown in Fig. 23.

The weighting for the probability of getting both contracts applies to the intersection of the sets S and H (*see* II, **8**, if you have forgotten the meaning of "intersection") and the weighting of the remainder of the S set is therefore 0·4. The universal

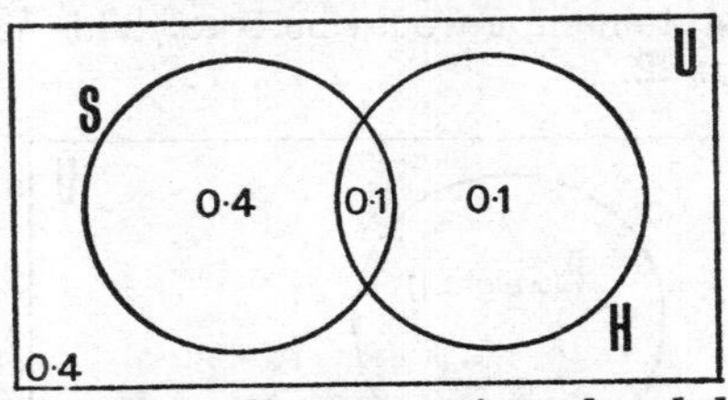

FIG. 23.—*Venn diagram: estimated probabilities*

set can be partitioned into four sets covering all the logical possibilities, which are as follows:

Event	*Probability*
Sewerage contract only awarded	0·4
Highways contract only awarded	0·1
Both contracts awarded	0·1
Neither contract awarded	0·4
Total	1·0

The total of the separate probabilities is necessarily 1 since it covers all cases possible. It is quite legitimate to use probabilities in this way, and, although the subjective element in calculations renders them uncertain, the quantification of the estimated probabilities is likely to promote more informed discussion than mere statements that "we shall be unlikely to get both contracts" or "we should be unlucky if we landed neither scheme."

ADDITION AND MULTIPLICATION RULES FOR PROBABILITY

5. The event space. The set of all the logical possibilities is called the *event space*. This is equivalent to the denominator in the expression $Pr(E) = m/(m + n)$, that is, the number of elements in the event space is $(m + n)$. In the case of the single die throw, the number of elements in the event space was six, the six possible scores.

6. The addition law. Let us consider the probability of throwing a three *or* a four with a single die throw. The event space consists of the same six possibilities as before, but this time the desired event is satisfied by *two* of the cases. The probability of throwing either a three or a four is therefore $\frac{2}{6}$, that is $\frac{1}{3}$. It can be seen that this result is obtained by adding together the probabilities of the two events, each of which precludes the other. There are similarly *mutually exclusive* events in the contracts problem. The probability of getting the highways contract only or the sewerage contract only is $0{\cdot}4 + 0{\cdot}1 = 0{\cdot}5$.

The rule is that to calculate the probability of several mutually exclusive events occurring, the probabilities of the separate events must be added.

7. The multiplication law. While some events exclude each other so that they *cannot* occur together, there are many cases where events can be expected to occur together and the probability of the separate occurrence of each event is known. If the occurrence of one such event does not affect the probability of the occurrence of the other, the events are said to be *mutually independent*. An example would be the result of a second coin toss following after a first toss. There is no mystic bond by which the first result affects the second. The rule for the joint occurrence of mutually independent events is that the probabilities should be multiplied.

8. A sample space for a double dice throw. If two dice are thrown together, there are thirty-six possible results. People have been known to doubt this and the array of possible scores is therefore displayed in Table 4.

TABLE 4

1st 2nd die/die	*1st 2nd die/die*	*1st 2nd die/die*	*1st 2nd die/die*	*1st 2nd die/die*	*1st 2nd die/die*
1 : 1	1 : 2	1 : 3	1 : 4	1 : 5	1 : 6
2 : 1	2 : 2	2 : 3	2 : 4	2 : 5	2 : 6
3 : 1	3 : 2	3 : 3	3 : 4	3 : 5	3 : 6
4 : 1	4 : 2	4 : 3	4 : 4	4 : 5	4 : 6
5 : 1	5 : 2	5 : 3	5 : 4	5 : 5	5 : 6
6 : 1	6 : 2	6 : 3	6 : 4	6 : 5	6 : 6

There is therefore an event space with thirty-six elements.

Let the chosen event be defined by the statement $p =$ "a double six will be thrown." Of the thirty-six possible results only one fills the bill: a six with each of the dice. We can write $Pr(p) = \frac{1}{36}$. As we know very well, the probability of either one of the dice showing a six was $\frac{1}{6}$ and since these two events are mutually independent the two probabilities must be multiplied together giving $\frac{1}{6} \times \frac{1}{6} = \frac{1}{36}$, thus confirming the multiplication law.

9. Coin tosses as independent events. It has already been remarked that there is no magical tie between successive tosses of a coin. Let us consider the case of two fair coins thrown together. The chance of either coin coming up heads is equal to its chance of coming up tails. There are thus four equally likely outcomes, each of which excludes the other three, but each of which is itself made up of two independent events. The array of possibilities is as follows:

Coin 1	*Coin* 2
Head	Head
Head	Tail
Tail	Head
Tail	Tail

Each of these four outcomes has a probability of $\frac{1}{4}$ or 0·25.

For three tosses, there would be eight possible outcomes which could be represented as a tree diagram. Each branching shows the alternative outcome, head being denoted by H and tail by T.

The succession of independent events is found by following any of the possible paths through the network or tree. Since the events *are* independent, their joint occurrence calls for a multiplication of probabilities, thus the path H H H (three heads) has the probability $\frac{1}{2} \times \frac{1}{2} \times \frac{1}{2} = \frac{1}{8}$, which is confirmed by the fact that there are eight equally likely paths through the tree and only one of them is the H H H path. Each of these eight outcomes excludes the others, however, and to find the probability of throwing two heads and a tail, for instance, we must add all the mutually exclusive ways of reaching that result. There are three such paths, marked with an asterisk in Fig. 24, and the required probability is therefore $\frac{3}{8}$.

CONDITIONAL PROBABILITIES

10. Explanation. When we laid out the event space for the double dice throw we saw that there were 36 possibilities. If we threw the two dice in succession we could pause after having thrown, say, a six with the first die and ask, "Having thrown a six, what is the probability of gaining a score of ten or more?" Such probabilities are called "conditional probabilities." If the two statements "a six is thrown with the first

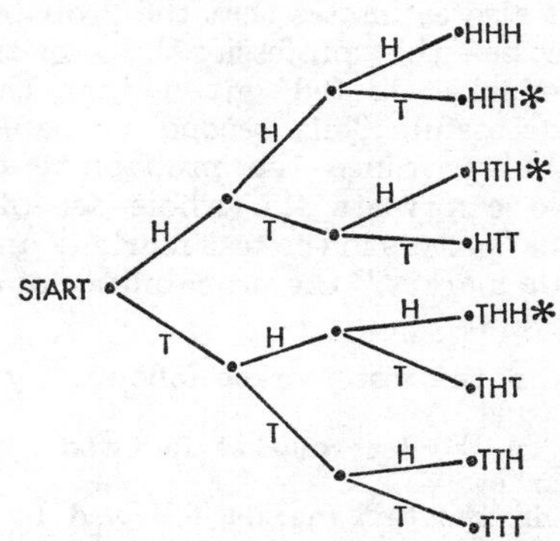

FIG. 24.—*Coin tosses: a tree diagram*

die" and "the total score is ten or more" are given the labels a and b respectively, the conditional probability required is called the "probability of b, given a" and is written $Pr(b \mid a)$.

11. Redefining the event space. Once a thing has happened it is outside the field of conjecture and no probabilities are required to be calculated. It is therefore necessary to reconsider the set of possibilities and to see which of the remaining possible events refer to the required event. Once a six has been thrown only six further events are now possible, the six scores that can be made with the second die. Of these six scores, the four, five or six would bring the total score with the two dice to the required sum of ten or more. The *conditional probability of scoring ten or more with two dice, given that one six has been thrown* is $\frac{3}{6}$ or 0·5. The method of calculating conditional probabilities is, therefore, to eliminate the event that has happened from the universal set or event space and to use the remaining possible outcomes as the new universal set on which further calculations will be based.

12. An example from business life. Very often a firm will carry out a sales campaign in a small test market, chosen to be representative of the large-scale market, before launching a new product. Let us suppose that a firm intends to carry out such a test and that it estimates beforehand that the probability of the test-market sales reaching a certain target sales figure is 0·7. It also estimates that the probability of success in the large-scale—the professionals sometimes say the "broadscale"—market is 0·8, given that the test-market operation is successful. This second probability is a conditional probability. Since the probability of "not p" is $[1 - Pr(p)]$, we can write the whole set of probabilities. Designating p as "success in the test market" and q as "success in the broadscale market," the probabilities of all the possible events are as follows:

(*a*) Success in the test market followed by success in the broadscale market.

(*b*) Success in the test market followed by failure in the broadscale market.

(*c*) Failure in the test market followed by success in the broadscale market.

(*d*) Failure in the test market followed by failure in the broadscale market.

Using the symbol $\bar{p}$ to mean "not p" and the symbol $\wedge$ to mean "and," this being the conventional notation for describing statements of this kind, the situation can be shown on a tree diagram, treating the events as independent as we did with the coin tosses (*see* Fig. 25).

Needless to say, the probabilities add up to 1. If we were required to state the probability of success in the large-scale market on the basis of these probabilities we should add the probability of $(p \wedge q)$ to the probability of $(\bar{p} \wedge q)$, q representing success in the large-scale market. This probability is 0·80 or 80 per cent.

NOTE: This example is rather unreasonably simplified, since the probabilities would be unlikely to be independent, that is success in the large-scale market would be likely to be *less* probable following a *failure* in the test market.

BAYESIAN PROBABILITY

13. The essential idea. Bayesian probabilities are based on ideas originally put forward by the Rev. Thomas Bayes, an eighteenth-century English mathematician. The essence of the Bayesian probability is that it affords a means of re-assessing probabilities in the light of additional information.

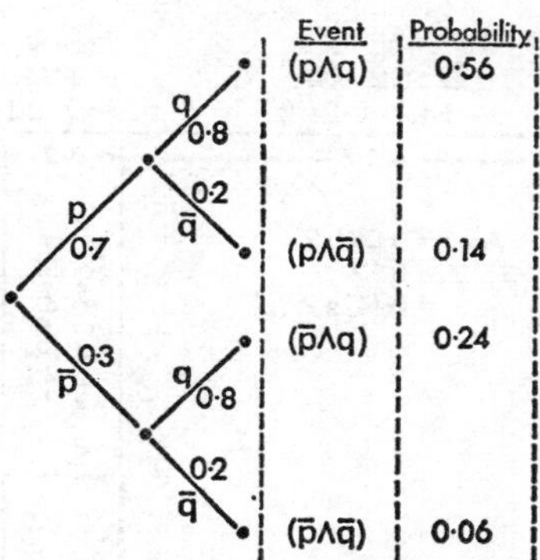

FIG. 25.—*A tree diagram with conditional probabilities*

14. Prior and posterior probabilities. The probability of an event before the new information is available is called the prior probability; the probability afterwards is called the posterior probability. When new information is received, it means that an event or events which had previously existed only as possibilities have now become actualities and the event space must be redefined.

15. A Bayesian example. Suppose that operatives in a certain workshop consist of those trained in the firm's own training school and those who have undergone conventional apprenticeships. Only 20 per cent are products of the firm's school. A scrutiny of the operatives' output records shows that they can be divided into "high performers" and "low performers." Of those coming from the firm's training school, 40 per cent rank as high performers; only 10 per cent of the conventionally trained operatives are high performers.

Suppose an employee is selected at random, possibly by using random number tables to select a time-clock number, *given that the selected employee is a high performer, what is the probability that he is a product of the firm's training school?*

16. A useful diagrammatic approach. Let the sides of a square be of unit length, so that the square has unit (1 × 1) area. If one side is now divided in the ratio 80 : 20, this will

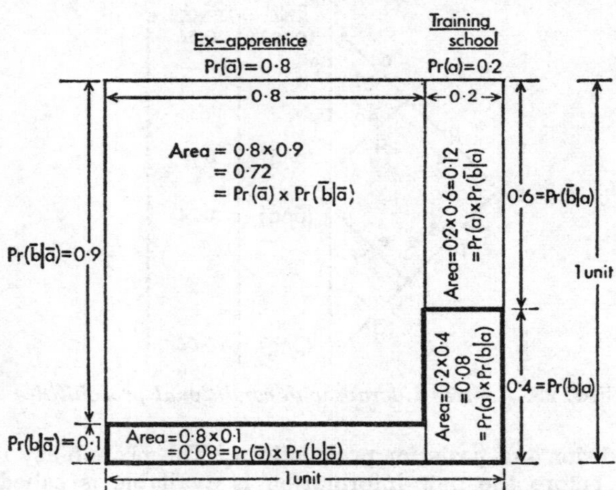

Fig. 26.—*Bayesian probabilities*

represent the division of the operatives into ex-apprentices and training-school men. This division is shown by the central vertical line in Fig. 26. Selecting an employee at random is now equivalent to selecting a point at random within the square, since the area is divided in the same ratio as the side. Each of the two areas within the square may now be divided in accordance with the conditional probabilities. The unit side of the smaller (training-school) area is divided in the ratio 60 : 40 and the unit side of the larger area in the ratio 90 : 10. Representing "training-school product" by (a) and "high performer" by (b), the division of the whole area may be expressed in terms of probabilities and conditional probabilities as is shown in Fig. 26.

We are required to state the probability that a high-performance operative selected at random would have been trained at the firm's own school. The additional information that the employee is a high-performance executive restricts the universal set of reference to the area enclosed by the heavy lines. The required probability is given by the probability of being both a training-school man *and* a high-performance operative related to the probability of being a high performance operative at all. These probabilities are the known *prior* probabilities. In mathematical symbols we have:

$$Pr(a \mid b) = \frac{Pr(a \wedge b)}{Pr(b)} = \frac{0{\cdot}08}{0{\cdot}08 + 0{\cdot}08} = 0{\cdot}5.$$

This is a posterior probability, that is a probability calculated in the light of the information that the selected employee is a high-performance operative.

17. Bayesian formulae. If these prior and posterior probabilities are carefully related to the diagram, the following formulae for turning prior probabilities into a posterior probability may be derived quite easily.

The probability of "*a and b*" ($a \wedge b$) is represented by the area in the bottom right-hand corner of the unit square. That is:

Formula 1.

$$Pr(a \wedge b) = Pr(a) \,.\, Pr(b \mid a)$$

(Just in case the reader has forgotten, we are using the dot notation for multiplication here.) This probability must be related to (divided by) the probability of being a high-performance operative = $Pr(b)$. $Pr(b)$ is given by the sum of the two lower areas:

Formula 2.

$$Pr(b) = Pr(\bar{a}) \,.\, Pr(b \mid \bar{a}) + Pr(a) \,.\, Pr(b \mid a)$$

The required probability is $Pr(a \mid b)$ and is given by:

Formula 3.

$$Pr(a \mid b) = \frac{Pr(a \wedge b)}{Pr(b)} = \frac{Pr(a) \,.\, Pr(b \mid a)}{Pr(\bar{a}) \,.\, Pr(b \mid \bar{a}) + Pr(a) \,.\, Pr(b \mid a)}$$

BINOMIAL PROBABILITIES

18. A simple case. An important application of probability in business is in the field of the statistical sampling of attributes. The required theoretical basis can be developed from the simple ideas considered in **8** and **9** above in connection with coin tosses and dice throws. The simplest possible case is that of a single coin tossed once only. There are only two, equally likely, results, a head or a tail. Two coins gave four possible results and three coins would give eight results. The possible results for tosses of up to four coins are shown in Table 5.

TABLE 5

1 coin		*2 coins*		*3 coins*		*4 coins*	
						$4H$	1
				$3H$	1		
		$2H$	1			$3H/1T$	4
				$2H/1T$	3		
H	1						
						$2H/2T$	6
		H/T	2				
T	1			$2T/1H$	3		
		$2T$	1			$3T/1H$	4
				$3T$	1		
						$4T$	1

The interested reader who has not met this pattern of numbers before may try to estimate the frequencies for five coin tosses. Once the pattern has been grasped, it may be continued indefinitely.

19. Binomial coefficients. The pattern generated by listing the frequencies with which combinations of heads and tails may be expected is also the pattern of coefficients generated by writing down the expansion of $(p + q)^n$ when n assumes various values from 1 to n. A few of the simpler expansions have been given in Chapter III, but the pattern can be appreciated more clearly if a number of examples are seen together.

$$(p + q)^1 = p + q$$
$$(p + q)^2 = p^2 + 2pq + q^2$$
$$(p + q)^3 = p^3 + 3p^2q + 3pq^2 + q^3$$
$$(p + q)^4 = p^4 + 4p^3q + 6p^2q^2 + 4pq^3 + q^4$$
$$(p + q)^5 = p^5 + 5p^4q + 10p^3q^2 + 10p^2q^3 + 5pq^4 + q^5.$$

Remembering that the coefficient of p^2, for instance, is 1, the pattern can be represented by "Pascal's triangle" in which each figure except the "ones" is the sum of two figures immediately above it.

$$
\begin{array}{ccccccccccccc}
 & & & & & 1 & & 1 & & & & & \\
 & & & & 1 & & 2 & & 1 & & & & \\
 & & & 1 & & 3 & & 3 & & 1 & & & \\
 & & 1 & & 4 & & 6 & & 4 & & 1 & & \\
 & 1 & & 5 & & 10 & & 10 & & 5 & & 1 & \\
1 & & 6 & & 15 & & 20 & & 15 & & 6 & & 1 \\
\swarrow & & & & & & & & & & & & \searrow
\end{array}
$$

It should be noted that the sum of the powers of p and q always add up to the power of the expansion and that, as the powers of p decline, those of q grow larger. The expansion of $(p + q)^6$ would therefore be:

$$p^6 + 6p^5q + 15p^4q^2 + 20p^3q^3 + 15p^2q^4 + 6pq^5 + q^6.$$

20. Probability and the binomial expansion. Let p represent the constant probability of the occurrence of an event at a single trial such as the toss of a coin or the throw of a die, and let q represent the constant probability of the event not happening at a single trial. The probability q will then equal $1 - p$, since the event must either happen or not happen and $(p + q)$ must therefore sum to 1. If n trials are made, the successive terms of the expansion of $(p + q)^n$ will give the probability of the event occurring a given number of times, the number of times being indicated by the power of p.

EXAMPLE: Let p be the probability of a six being shown on the face of a die at a single throw. The probability of some other score appearing is $q = 1 - p$. In this case $p = \frac{1}{6}$ and $q = \frac{5}{6}$. What is the probability of two or more sixes being scored in four dice throws? The expansion required is $(p + q)^4$, n, the number of trials, being equal to four.

$$(p + q)^4 = p^4 + 4p^3q + 6p^2q^2 + 4pq^3 + q^4.$$

Put $p = \frac{1}{6}$ and $q = \frac{5}{6}$ and the expansion reads:

$$(\tfrac{1}{6})^4 + 4(\tfrac{1}{6})^3(\tfrac{5}{6}) + 6(\tfrac{1}{6})^2(\tfrac{5}{6})^2 + 4(\tfrac{1}{6})(\tfrac{5}{6})^3 + (\tfrac{5}{6})^4,$$

which equals:

$$\frac{1}{1296} + \frac{20}{1296} + \frac{150}{1296} + \frac{500}{1296} + \frac{625}{1296}.$$

These terms represent the probability of 4, 3, 2, 1, 0 sixes being shown in four throws. We are required to find the probability of throwing two or more sixes. The expansion of $(p + q)^4$ shows the five possible outcomes and we require the sum of the first three terms, since each excludes the other two, that is, we can score four sixes *or* three sixes *or* two sixes, but since there is only one *actual* result we cannot score all three.

The required probability is, therefore, $\frac{1}{1296} + \frac{20}{1296} + \frac{150}{1296} = \frac{171}{1296}$ or 0·132. An alternative method would have been to subtract the sum of the last two terms from unity, since these represent the probabilities of getting one six or none.

21. Relation to sampling. A particular number of dice throws can be considered as a random sample from all the possible dice throws. Mathematically this situation is no different from taking a random sample of individuals from some population which is so large in comparison with the sample that the subtraction of a few hundred individuals does not affect the probability of any one individual having some chosen characteristic. This is precisely the situation when a sample of, say, two thousand is taken from a population of some fifty million. The mind boggles at the thought of calculating the expansion of $(p + q)^{1000}$, but fortunately this is not necessary as some further developments of the theory give more streamlined methods of comparing a particular sample with the theoretical probability of its occurrence. These points are expanded in Chapter XII.

22. Calculating the binomial coefficients. The coefficients of the binomial expansions can be taken direct from Pascal's triangle, but we really ought to be able to calculate them as this calculation yields a formula which is useful in other contexts.

Consider the case of three sixes scored out of four dice throws. This probability is given by the term $4p^3q$, with $p = \frac{1}{6}$, $q = \frac{5}{6}$ as before. The p^3q part of this term gives the probability of any of the ways of throwing three sixes out of four, and the coefficient, 4, gives the number of ways in which this could occur. With four dice—call them dice A, B, C and D—the three sixes could have been scored by:

(*a*) Dice A, B and C.
(*b*) Dice A, B and D.
(*c*) Dice A, C and D.
(*d*) Dice B, C and D.

The coefficient of p^3q represents, in fact, the number of ways in which three dice can be selected from four. We could say that the coefficient is given by the number of *combinations* that can be made from four items taken three at a time.

23. Formula for combinations. The symbol for the number of combinations of n items taken r at a time is ${}^nC_r$ or sometimes $\binom{n}{r}$. The formula for calculating this number of combinations is given by:

$$ {}^nC_r = \frac{n!}{(n-r)!\,r!}, $$

where $n!$ stands for all the whole numbers from n down to 1 multiplied together. This is called "factorial n." Using this notation, $4! = 4 . 3 . 2 . 1 = 24$. For ${}^4C_3$, the formula gives:

$$ {}^4C_3 = \frac{4!}{(4-3)!\,3!} = \frac{24}{1 \times (3 \times 2 \times 1)} $$
$$ = 24/6 = \underline{4}. $$

An alternative form is found by cancelling $(n - r)!$ into $n!$, giving:

$$ {}^nC_r = \frac{n(n-1)(n-2)\ .\ .\ .\ (n-r+1)}{r!}. $$

This involves multiplying together all the whole numbers from n down until $(n - r + 1)$ is reached. For ${}^4C_3$, $(n - r + 1)$ equals $(4 - 3 + 1)$, giving the number 2 as the last number in the product, and producing the same result as before.

HYPERGEOMETRIC PROBABILITIES

24. A problem. A small batch of parts consists of ten items of which three are known to be defective. Two parts are taken from stores at random. What is the probability that one, and only one, of the parts is defective?

25. A simple solution. The probability that the first part taken off the shelf will be defective must be $\frac{3}{10}$, since each of the ten parts are equally likely to be chosen. The probability that the second part is not defective, given that the first one is, is $\frac{7}{9}$, since seven of the nine remaining parts must be sound. This is one of the two ways of getting one, and only one, defective in a sample of two. The other way is to have taken first a sound part (probability $\frac{7}{10}$) and then a defective part (probability $\frac{3}{9}$).

The required probability is then:

First way (one defective, then one sound): $\frac{3}{10} \times \frac{7}{9} = \frac{21}{90}$
(Multiplication law applies)
Second way (one sound, then one defective): $\frac{7}{10} \times \frac{3}{9} = \frac{21}{90}$
Total probability (the two ways are mutually exclusive):
$\frac{42}{90} = \underline{0{\cdot}47}$

26. An alternative view. Another way of dealing with this problem would be to ask how many ways one defective item could be chosen from three, thus making up the defective part of the sample. Each of these ways could be combined with any of the ${}^{7}C_1$ ways of making up the "good" half of the sample of two. The probability of getting this mixed sample would be the number of ways of making it up divided by the total number of ways of making up any sample of two from ten items. This last number would be ${}^{10}C_2$. The required probability would be given by:

$$\frac{{}^{3}C_1 \times {}^{7}C_1}{{}^{10}C_2} = \frac{3 \times 7}{45}$$
$$= \underline{0{\cdot}47}, \text{ as before.}$$

The general expression for the hypergeometric distribution can be found as follows:

Let N = the number of items in the batch,
R = the number of defectives in the batch,
n = the number of items in the sample,
and r = the number of defectives in the sample.

Then the probability of drawing a sample of size n containing r defectives is given by:

$$\frac{{}^{R}C_r \, . \, {}^{N-R}C_{n-r}}{{}^{N}C_n}.$$

PROGRESS TEST 11

1. An office machinery salesman has a 20 per cent chance of selling an adding machine to a certain firm, a 40 per cent chance of selling a typewriter and a 10 per cent chance of selling both. Represent this situation by means of a Venn diagram and estimate the probability of his not making a sale at all.

2. (*a*) An unbiased six-sided die is rolled three times in succession. What is the probability of a six being thrown on each of the three occasions? **(8, 9)**

(*b*) An unbiased six-sided die is to be thrown twice. Given that the first throw is a six, what is the probability of the total score being less than nine? **(10, 11)**

3. 60 per cent of a particular type of unbranded shoes sold in a large store are made by a single major manufacturer, the remainder coming from a variety of smaller manufacturers. 1 per cent of the major manufacturer's shoes are likely to have a defect, whereas the proportion defective in other manufacturers' shoes is 5 per cent. If a pair of shoes purchased from the store is defective, what is the probability that it was made by the major manufacturer?

4. Evaluate:

(*a*) $^{5}C_{2}$ (*b*) $^{10}C_{4}$ (*c*) $^{100}C_{2}$.

5. A batch of eight articles is known to contain three defectives. In how many ways can a sample of three containing two good pieces and one defective be drawn from the batch? What is the probability of getting such a sample if three articles are taken from the batch at random? **(24–26)**

6. It is estimated that 3 per cent of a company's employees have been reported for a breach of safety regulations in the past year. The chairman is in the habit of requiring twelve employees of good repute to be presented to him for an "informal" morale-boosting chat on the firm's sports day, but is known to check up afterwards in order to see that the selected employees deserved the honour. As personnel manager you have fifteen minutes to select the twelve employees and you resolve to do so at random using some adequate technique. The chairman is keen on safety; what is the probability that less than two of the selected employees have a blot on their safety records in the past year?

CHAPTER XII

SOME STATISTICAL CONCEPTS

THE NATURE OF THE USE OF STATISTICS

1. A warning. First of all, it is necessary to give a warning about the place of statistics in this book. Statistics is one of the most useful and most used areas of applied mathematics. It is not merely a collection of methods for juggling with figures but is based on well-reasoned and highly sophisticated mathematical concepts. In this chapter, we shall investigate these ideas, but we shall *not* develop the computational techniques needed to handle statistical methods with full confidence, since this would require a separate book in itself. An excellent introduction to statistical method is *Statistics* by W. M. Harper (an M. & E. HANDBOOK).

2. The nature of statistics. In ordinary language, the word statistics is used in several ways. We speak, for instance, of "the statistics of foreign trade," meaning the actual collected figures relating to foreign trade. This is not the sense in which the word is used in this book. Here we are concerned with the *science* of statistics. Our introduction to statistics, in this latter sense, consists of two parts, firstly an examination of concise, mathematical methods of describing data and, secondly, a consideration of some techniques of making inferences from data that have been collected or acquired.

3. Using statistics in business and industry. Business is now too big and plays too important a part in the life of a modern society for major decisions to be made on intuition alone. If decisions are to be good ones, they must be based on the best possible information. Top management cannot concern itself with masses of figures, however, and when information is presented to management it must be in as clear and compact a form as possible. We must therefore develop means of describing quite complicated situations by means of a few key indicators and of making comparisons between one period and another or between one plant or market and another.

Often the information about a situation is so complex that it is hardly possible to describe it completely. It is therefore necessary to use sampling techniques in order to assess what is happening. These techniques are familiar in the contexts of market research surveys and public opinion polls, but similar or related methods may be applied to sample the utilisation of machines in workshops, the quality of output from a production process or the incidence of mistakes in a clerical process.

A further aspect of statistical work is concerned with the way in which observed changes in one variable are related to changes in another. The association between advertising and sales in a particular market might be a case in point. Techniques of correlation and regression analysis are used in dealing with this sort of problem.

Part IV of the book deals with some of the techniques of operational research. These have statistical aspects and in some respects depend heavily on statistical reasoning.

4. The scope of the present chapter. A more detailed review of statistical techniques and their use is undertaken in XIII, XIV and Part V, but in this chapter some of the essential groundwork is covered since later development depends on this. The topics handled are:

(*a*) a basic descriptive tool: the frequency distribution and the measures associated with it; and

(*b*) the concept of a sampling distribution and the nature of the three main theoretical distributions.

THE FREQUENCY DISTRIBUTION

5. The basic situation. An operation forming part of a simple clerical task is timed over twenty cycles of the whole task and the times shown in Table 6 are recorded.

If we were asked to describe the results by quoting two measures calculated from these figures we should need a *representative* figure to indicate the time that the operation might be expected to take and another measure to indicate the *variability* of the time taken. These would be practical measures on which allowed work times could be based. A good representative figure is the ordinary average or *arithmetic mean*; a simple measure of the way that the times vary could be calculated by subtracting the lowest recorded value from the highest, to give the *range* of times.

TABLE 6.—MANUAL POSTING, DEBTORS' LEDGER, DEPT Y

Cycle no.	*Time taken (seconds)*	*Cycle no.*	*Time taken (seconds)*
1	9	11	12
2	17	12	11
3	11	13	10
4	14	14	13
5	13	15	12
6	15	16	13
7	13	17	12
8	11	18	13
9	13	19	14
10	14	20	12

6. Formula for the arithmetic mean. If we designate the times recorded by the general symbol x, any particular time could be indicated by the symbol x_i, the subscript i showing the cycle number in Table 6. Using the "sigma" notation described in V, **17–19**, the sum of all the recorded values would be given by $\sum_{i=1}^{n} x_i$. The arithmetic mean is found by adding up all the values and then dividing this total by the number of items concerned. Denoting the number of items concerned by the symbol n and the arithmetic mean by the symbol $\bar{x}$ (pronounced "x bar"), the process of calculating the arithmetic mean is described completely by:

$$\bar{x} = \frac{1}{n} \sum_{i=1}^{n} x_i.$$

If we miss out the subscripts we could give a more compact but less precise formulation, as:

$$\bar{x} = \frac{\Sigma x}{n}.$$

7. Calculations for the example. In the example quoted $\Sigma x = 252$ seconds, $n = 20$, and the arithmetic mean is therefore 12·6 seconds. The range is 17 seconds minus 9 seconds that is 8 seconds.

8. The example as a frequency distribution. An alternative vay of setting out the job times given in Table 6 would be to abulate the values that occur and then to set against each value the number of times that it was observed. The number of times that a value occurs could be called the *frequency*; the listribution of frequencies over all the observed values is a requency distribution (Table 7).

ABLE 7.—FREQUENCY DISTRIBUTION OF LEDGER-POSTING TIMES

Time taken (seconds):	9	10	11	12	13	14	15	16	17
Frequency observed:	1	1	3	4	6	3	1	0	1

9. The means of a frequency distribution. If the times are aken as the x values and the frequencies are given the symbol , the mean of the frequency distribution may be given by the ormula:

$$\bar{x} = \frac{\Sigma fx}{n}.$$

This is obviously the appropriate formula, since the sum of ll the values is found by taking each value and multiplying it y the number of times it occurs and then adding all these roducts together.

10. A grouped frequency distribution. Suppose that, instead f having a simple distribution of twenty values, we were equired to deal with a much larger distribution of, say, wo hundred items which ranged from values of 30 seconds or o up to values of 1200 seconds (20 minutes). Such a distribution might be observed if all the telephone calls going hrough a PBX switchboard were timed and recorded for a ertain period. A method of dealing with this problem would e to record not individual values but classes of values. We hould then note the number of calls lasting from 2 minutes to minutes, 4 minutes to 6 minutes and so on. A possible listribution might be that given in Table 8.

11. Graphical representation of a grouped frequency distribution. A suitable graphical representation, which clearly hows the form of the distribution of Table 8, is given in Fig. 27 n p. 132. This form of diagram is called a *histogram*. The line oining the middle points of the blocks, and incidentally enclosing the same area as the blocks, is called a *frequency polygon.*

TABLE 8.—DISTRIBUTION OF TELEPHONE CALLS

Date——————

Length of call (seconds)	*No. of calls*
0– 120	30
120– 240	60
240– 360	50
360– 480	24
480– 600	16
600– 720	10
720– 840	4
840– 960	2
960–1080	3
1080–1200	1
Total	200

12. The mean of a grouped frequency distribution. The mean of a grouped frequency distribution is found by letting the mid-point of each class stand as a representative value for all the items in the class. Thus, the first class is "0 to 120 seconds" and its middle point is 60 seconds. Letting x now represent the mid-point values, the arithmetic mean is given by $\bar{x} = \Sigma fx/n$, or, since n is equal to the number of frequencies (observations), $\bar{x} = \Sigma fx/\Sigma f$. The mean of the distribution in Table 8 is found by calculating Σfx, which works out at 62,040 seconds, and dividing by n, which is equal to 200. The mean is therefore 62,040/200 seconds = 310·2 seconds. This may be checked by the reader.

13. Frequency density. A slightly more general way of setting out the situation described by the frequency distribution of telephone calls would be to show the percentage of calls falling into each class or, almost the same thing, to show the proportion in each class as a decimal of the whole. This proportion would be the *frequency density* for each class. Table 9 gives the results of calculating these frequency densities.

14. Probability densities. Suppose that we felt justified in regarding this distribution of frequency densities as being a good guide to the length of telephone calls that could be expected at this switchboard. Asked for the probability that any telephone call would last for ten minutes or more we should no doubt add up the frequency densities for all the classes of calls of 600 seconds or more. These total to 0·1 and we should say that there was a 10 per cent probability of an incoming call lasting for ten minutes or more. We should be using the distribution of calls as a typical or ideal distribution on the basis of which probabilities of future durations of calls might be calculated. We should be using the frequency densities as probability densities.

TABLE 9.—DISTRIBUTION OF TELEPHONE CALLS: FREQUENCY DENSITIES

Length of call (seconds)	*Frequency density*
0– 120	0·150
120– 240	0·300
240– 360	0·250
360– 480	0·120
480– 600	0·080
600– 720	0·050
720– 840	0·020
840– 960	0·010
960–1080	0·015
1080–1200	0·005
Total	1·000

THE STANDARD DEVIATION

15. Devising a measure of dispersion. In describing frequency distributions so far we have used the arithmetic mean, with just a passing reference to the range. The range is not an entirely satisfactory measure of how the distribution is spread out among all the observed values. A possible measure would be the average deviation from the arithmetic mean, but it is a quality of the arithmetic mean that positive and negative deviations from it just balance out each other. One way of getting round this difficulty is to ignore the signs of the deviations and if we did this we should have calculated the *mean deviation*. A better way of avoiding the cancelling out of the plus and minus signs would be to *square* the deviations.

16. Calculating the standard deviation. In order to appreciate the nature of the standard deviation let us work with a single set of ten values. The times for the first ten cycles in Table 6 make a suitable set. They are:

9, 17, 11, 14, 13, 15, 13, 11, 13, 14.

The mean of these values is 13 seconds. Our measure of dispersion requires that we square the deviation of each of these values from the mean time of 13 seconds. To get a *general* measure of dispersion it would be appropriate to take the mean of these squared deviations. This average of the squared deviations needs to be reduced to the same dimension as the other values and a fairly obvious final step is to take the square root. If we indicate our measure of dispersion by the symbol s, its calculation is given by the formula:

$$s = \sqrt{\frac{\Sigma(x - \bar{x})^2}{n}}.$$

For the ten values we are using the calculations are as follows:

Times in seconds	9	17	11	14	13	15	13	11	13	14
Deviations from mean	−4	+4	−2	+1	0	+2	0	−2	0	+1
Squared deviations	16	16	4	1	0	4	0	4	0	+1

Sum of squared deviations 46 (seconds).
Mean of squared deviations 4·6 seconds.
Standard deviation (square root of squared deviations):
2·14 seconds (approximately).

17. Calculation of *s* for a frequency distribution. If we now calculate the standard deviation of a frequency distribution, each deviation from the mean will have to be multiplied by the frequency with which it occurs. The revised formula will be:

$$s = \sqrt{\frac{\Sigma f(x - \bar{x})^2}{n}}.$$

A simple modification which lends itself to easy calculation with a desk machine can be derived as follows:

$$s = \sqrt{\frac{\Sigma f(x - \bar{x})^2}{n}}.$$

Expanding $(x - \bar{x})^2$ gives $(x^2 - 2x\bar{x} + \bar{x}^2)$ and the formula becomes:

$$s = \sqrt{\frac{\Sigma f(x^2 - 2\bar{x}x + \bar{x}^2)}{n}}.$$

Since, for any given value of x, the frequency, f, can be multiplied into the term inside the bracket, this gives:

$$s = \sqrt{\frac{\Sigma(fx^2 - 2\bar{x}fx + f\bar{x}^2)}{n}}.$$

The Σ operator acts on each term in turn; it is a *linear operator*. Each term is changed as follows:

fx^2 becomes Σfx^2

$2\bar{x}fx$ becomes $2\bar{x}\Sigma fx$.

> $(2\bar{x})$ is a definite figure, a constant, and multiplying every value of (fx) by it gives $2\bar{x}$ times Σfx.

$f\bar{x}^2$ becomes $\bar{x}^2\Sigma f$

or $(n\bar{x}^2)$ since $\Sigma f = n$.

The full formula is now:

$$s = \sqrt{\frac{\Sigma fx^2 - 2\bar{x}\Sigma fx + n\bar{x}^2}{n}}.$$

Dividing each term under the radical sign by n, the common denominator of them all, gives:

$$s = \sqrt{\frac{\Sigma fx^2}{n} - 2\bar{x} \cdot \frac{\Sigma fx}{n} + \bar{x}^2}$$

Since $\dfrac{\Sigma fx}{n} = \bar{x}$, this can be written as:

$$s = \sqrt{\frac{\Sigma fx^2}{n} - \bar{x}^2}.$$

A method of calculation would be to square up each value, multiply the squared values by the frequencies and to divide the sum of the products by the total number of values. The mean, squared, is then subtracted before the square root is found.

FREQUENCY CURVES

18. Curve and polygon. The histogram, Fig. 27, shows a distribution with a fairly small number of classes and relatively few observations. Imagine a distribution comprising a great many observations grouped into a great number of rather narrow class intervals. The shape of the distribution would tend to be smoothed out because of the great number of narrow intervals. The frequency polygon (*see* diagram) would become a curve. When discussing frequency distributions, it is often convenient to consider them as if they were continuous curves.

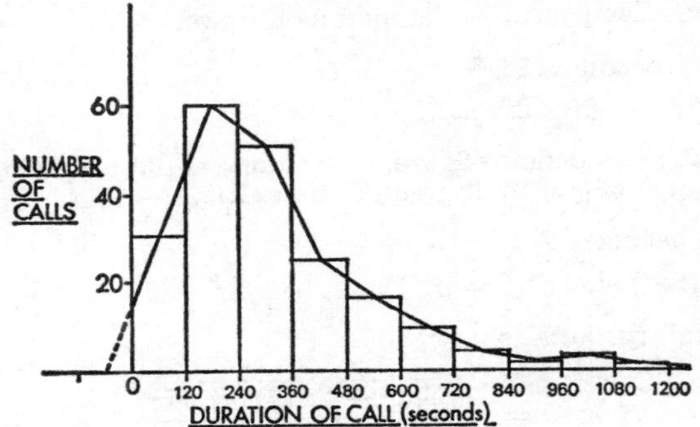

FIG. 27.—*Distribution of telephone calls: histogram and frequency polygon*

19. Frequency curves and functions. If the frequency, or alternatively the frequency density, is measured on the vertical, y, axis and the values of the variable on the x-axis, the frequency curve that closely represents a distribution can be regarded as a frequency function. As we shall see very shortly, we often need to use theoretical distributions which represent various "ideal" or typical situations. When these theoretical distributions are continuous distributions, so that a frequency density can be calculated for every value of x (the variable being measured) over a given range, an actual function in the familiar, $y = f(x)$, form exists (f, here, being the conventional short-hand for "function of," *not* the symbol for frequency).

20. Applying the mean and standard deviation. The mean is a representative value and gives some idea where the central part of a distribution lies on the x-axis. It is analogous to the "centre of gravity" of the distribution. It is one of several possible *measures of central tendency* and it locates the distribution on the x-axis.

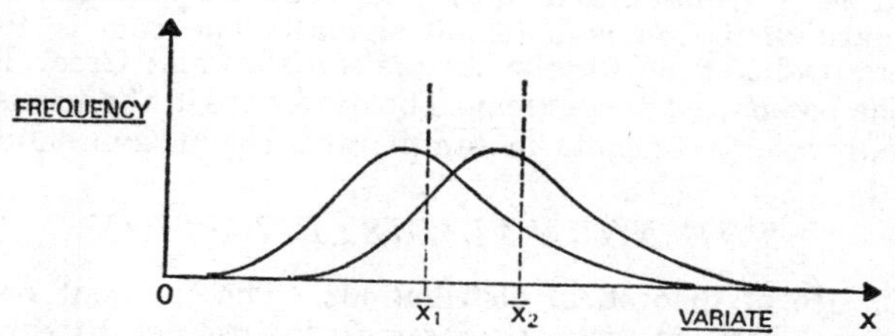

FIG. 28(*a*).—*Frequency distributions with differing means*

The standard deviation, being a measure of spread, or dispersion, does nothing to locate the distribution, but tells us how spread out it is once we have located it.

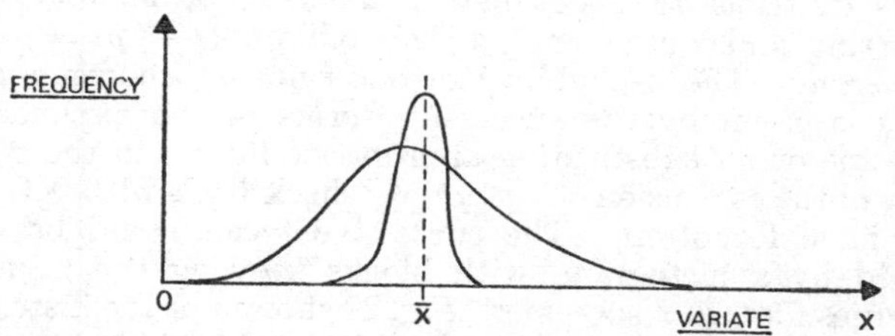

FIG. 28(*b*).—*Dissimilar distributions with identical means*

An additional service performed by the standard deviation is that, provided that the distribution is reasonably symmetrical about the mean, we can make some assumptions about the proportion of all the observations that are within a given number of standard deviations of the mean.

21. Sample and population. In discussing the calculation of the mean and standard deviation it was assumed that the data came from a sampling operation. This is a very usual situation and the symbols s and $\bar{x}$ are used for the standard deviation and mean respectively in these circumstances. The sample is taken from a background *population*. The word "population" is used here in a technical sense, to indicate the set of all the values from which the sample could be taken. An equivalent term is, in fact, a *universe*, a term similar to the *universal set* discussed in earlier chapters. The symbol for the population mean is μ (pronounced mu) and that for the population standard deviation is σ (small sigma). The rule is Roman letters (italic style) for the *sample statistics* and Greek letters for the *population parameters*. The difference in the terms used for equivalent concepts in sample and population should be noted.

THE NORMAL DISTRIBUTION

22. Use of theoretical distributions. The frequent need to compare observed distributions with theoretical distributions has already been mentioned. Perhaps the most important of these theoretical distributions is the normal distribution.

23. Binomial and normal distributions. In Chapter XI on probability we considered the situation where in each of a series of trials an event had a constant probability, p, of occurring, and consequently a probability of $(1 - p) = q$ of not happening. The probability of observing r occurrences in n trials is given by the successive terms of the expansion of $(p + q)^n$ or by substituting appropriate figures in the general term of the expansion ${}^nC_r\, p^r\, q^{n-r}$ (check back with XI, **23**, if you have forgotten). The successive terms could be represented by a histogram, with blocks showing the frequency densities for 0 to n successes. Fig. 29 shows not the histograms but the frequency polygons for binomial distributions with $p = 0{\cdot}1$ and $n = 5$, $n = 10$ and $n = 50$. It will be seen that as n grows larger the polygon becomes more symmetrical. As n approaches infinity, the curve becomes perfectly smooth and *perfectly* symmetrical. This symmetrical curve is known as the normal curve of distribution.

24. Interpreting the normal curve. The normal curve is bell-shaped and symmetrical and has the equation:

$$y = \frac{1}{\sigma\sqrt{2\pi}}\, e^{\frac{-(x-\mu)^2}{2\sigma^2}}.$$

Formidable though it is we can disentangle this equation. First of all, y gives the height of the curve above the x-axis in the usual way and in this case y gives the frequency density. Secondly, we can see, with a bit of thought, that since π and e are constants (both are irrational numbers: recall II, **14** above) the only things that can be altered in the equation are μ and σ. The location and spread of the curve are determined by the mean

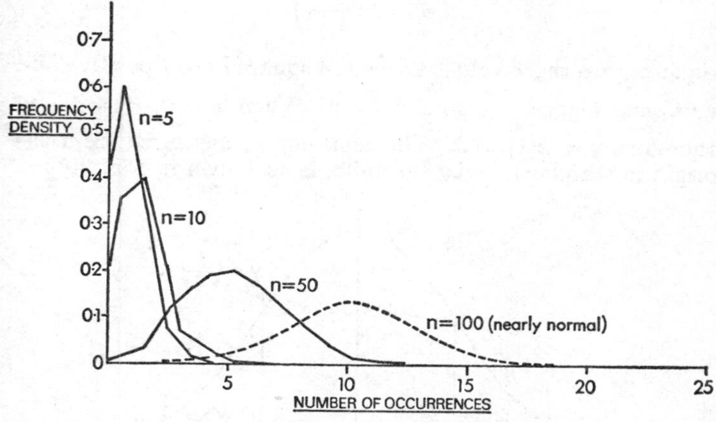

FIG. 29.—*Binomial distributions compared*

and standard deviation. A further simplification can be made by measuring all the values from the mean, that is by putting the mean at the origin. The value of the mean will then be zero with values below the mean registering negatively and those above the mean positively. The equation with μ equal to zero, as described, looks like this:

$$y = \frac{1}{\sigma\sqrt{2\pi}} e^{\frac{-x^2}{2\sigma^2}}.$$

In order to simplify the whole thing a little more, we could measure in standard deviation units. In the example of a grouped frequency distribution given in **11** above, the standard deviation is 214 seconds. A value of 535 seconds would represent 2·5 standard deviations, that is $2\frac{1}{2} \times 214$ (seconds). Putting $\sigma = 1$ in the normal curve function gives:

$$y = \frac{1}{\sqrt{2\pi}} e^{-\frac{x^2}{2}}.$$

The expression $1/\sqrt{2\pi}$ is a constant, so we can now write:

$$y = ke^{-\frac{x^2}{2}}$$

or even:

$$y = k\left(\frac{1}{e^{\frac{1}{2}x^2}}\right).$$

Squaring up the x-values keeps the squared term positive and as x gets bigger $\frac{1}{e^{\frac{1}{2}x^2}}$ gets smaller. When $x = 0$, $e^0 = 1$ and therefore $y = k(1) = k$. The final curve, measured from the origin in standard deviation units, is as shown in Fig. 30.

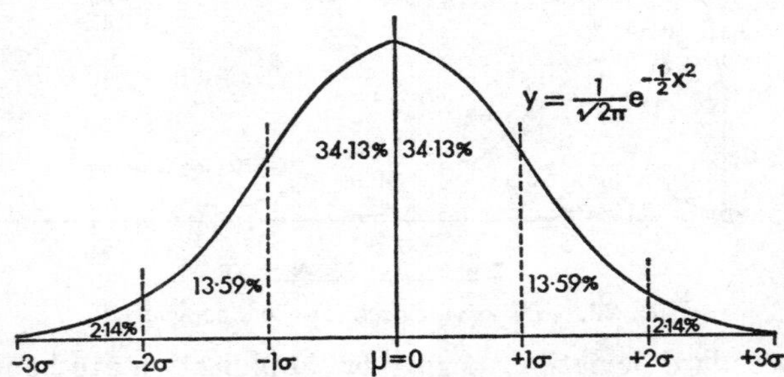

FIG. 30.—*Areas under the normal curve*

25. The occurrence of the normal curve. When the normal curve was being discussed by the great mathematicians at the beginning of the nineteenth century, it was thought of principally as a mathematical curve which could be used to describe variations that appear in nature. It is certainly the case that natural measurements such as the heights of men or women, measurements of plants and so on do conform closely to the normal distribution. Of at least as great importance to statisticians is the fact that statistics of samples drawn from a background population are normally distributed regardless of the form of the population distribution. If a large number of samples of incomes earned in a particular area or country were taken and the mean income calculated for *each* of the samples, a frequency distribution of the values of the sample means would be a normal distribution. It would be most unlikely that the incomes in the background population were normally distributed. Because this normal distribution of sample statistics is known, the probability of an actual sample drawn being an odd and unrepresentative one can be calculated.

26. Areas under the normal curve. Since the spread of the normal curve is controlled by the standard deviation and its shape is otherwise unaltered, the area under the curve between the mean, taken as zero and any given value can be calculated. The whole area under the curve from minus infinity to plus infinity is equal to unity, that is:

$$\frac{1}{\sqrt{2\pi}}\int_{-\infty}^{+\infty} e^{-\frac{x^2}{2}}\,dx = 1.$$

Areas under the curve between the mean and plus or minus one, two and three standard deviations are shown in Fig. 30 and are tabulated in more detail in Appendix II.

27. Example of normal distribution in use. A section of tunnelling is lit by 2000 electric bulbs which are kept burning night and day. The manufacturers say that the lives of the bulbs are normally distributed about a mean life of 820 hours with a well-established standard deviation of 90 hours. How many electric bulbs will be expected to fail before 1000 hours?

METHOD: First calculate the difference between the mean and 1000 hours. Designate the value 1000 hours as x.

$$\begin{aligned} x - \mu &= 1000 \text{ hours} - 820 \text{ hours} \\ &= \underline{180 \text{ hours.}} \end{aligned}$$

Calculate this in standard deviation units.

$$\begin{aligned} \frac{x-\mu}{\sigma} &= \frac{180 \text{ hours}}{90 \text{ hours}} \\ &= \underline{2 \text{ standard deviations.}} \end{aligned}$$

Reference to the curve in Fig. 30 or to tables shows that approximately 47½ per cent of the curve lies between the mean and +2 standard deviations. Since 50 per cent of the curve is represented by values less than the mean of 820 hours, 97½ per cent of the curve is therefore below the value of 1000 hours and may be expected to fail before that time.

$$\text{Number expected to fail} = 97\tfrac{1}{2} \text{ per cent of } 2000$$
$$= \underline{1950 \text{ lamps.}}$$

THE POISSON AND NEGATIVE EXPONENTIAL DISTRIBUTIONS

28. Random events. Another theoretical distribution which is particularly important in queueing theory is the Poisson distribution. This distribution, too, can be derived from the binomial distribution and is equivalent to $(p + q)^n$ with large n and a small value of p. It, therefore, approximates to a large number of trials with the event in question occurring only occasionally. This is the situation which corresponds to the observation of lightning strikes, air disasters and other relatively uncommon events of random occurrence.

29. The form of the Poisson distribution. The Poisson distribution is a *discrete* distribution since it is concerned with the *number* of observations which can be observed. The probability of 0, 1, 2, 3, etc., occurrences is given by writing out the series represented by $(e^m \,.\, e^{-m})$, where e is the exponential constant mentioned in II, **14** above and used in the normal curve formula. Using the factorial notation:

$$e^m = 1 + m + \frac{m^2}{2!} + \frac{m^3}{3!} + \frac{m^4}{4!} + \ldots + \frac{m^r}{r!} + \ldots$$

This is an infinite series with each term smaller than the previous one. It is therefore "convergent" and has a limiting value which is found by taking e as 2·71828 . . . and then taking this to the given power. Multiplying this series by e^{-m}, term by term we obtain:

$$e^m \,.\, e^{-m} = e^{-m} + me^{-m} + \frac{m^2e^{-m}}{2!} + \ldots$$
$$+ \frac{m^re^{-m}}{r!} + \ldots$$

The terms of this series give the required probabilities where m is the average number of occurrences previously observed in

the given unit of time. If we believed that cars passed an automatic level crossing on a quiet country road in an absolutely random manner, without any regular pattern, and had observed that on average *four* cars passed every ten minutes, then m would equal 4. The terms of the expansion would give the probability of 0, 1, 2, 3 and so on, cars passing in any given ten-minute period. The probability that no cars would arrive would be $e^{-m} = e^{-4}$. Writing e^{-4} as $1/e^4$ we could calculate this probability as 0·0183 or less than 2 per cent. The probability of any given number, r, cars passing is given by evaluating the general term $Pr(r) = m^r e^{-m}/r!$ for the appropriate values of m and r. It will be realised that since $e^m . e^{-m}$ is a probability distribution, and since the series generated is an infinite one, covering all possible values of r, the sum of all the terms must add up to unity. This must be so since $e^m . e^{-m} = e^0$ and any number taken to the power zero equals one.

30. The negative exponential distribution. If the Poisson distribution represents the probability of the occurrence of random events, the negative exponential distribution represents the distribution of the times between these random events. It is often referred to as merely the "exponential distribution." Consider the line segment (Fig. 31) as repre-

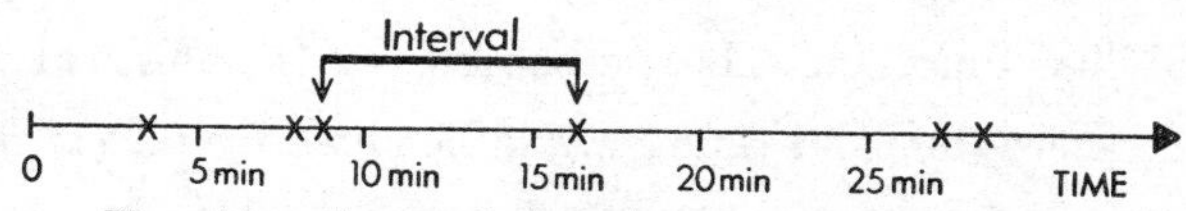

FIG. 31.—*Intervals between random occurrences*

senting a period of time measured from a starting point at $t = 0$. It is divided up into 5-minute intervals, using 5 minutes as a standard time unit. The crosses on the line represent the occurrence of random events; some intervals have one cross in them, some have two, one has none. A similar pattern would no doubt be repeated if the line were continued to the right for an indefinite distance. The distance from cross to cross represents the time interval between two events. The exponential distribution gives the distribution of these "inter-event times."

31. Function for the negative exponential distribution. From the Poisson distribution, the probability of no events occurring can be calculated from the first term, e^{-m}. This must be the probability that the interval between two events is greater than one time unit, for otherwise an event would occur in the given interval. This may need a little reflection, but is correct, as a consideration of the marked interval in the diagram will show. Designating the length of the time interval as t, the probability of no events occurring in time t becomes the probability of the interval between events being greater than time t. This could be developed as follows:

Probability of time between events being greater than $t = e^{-mt}$, where m is the average occurrence per time unit and t is the number of time units that have gone by. Thus, if $m = 2$ and the time unit is a 5-minute interval, the probability of no events occurring in 15 minutes is $e^{-(2 \times 3)}$ or 0·0025. The probability of the time between events being less than the unit interval t must be $(1 - e^{-mt})$ since the two probabilities together cover all the cases, the probability of the interval being *exactly* t being minutely small, since it is merely the boundary between the other two cases. Following our reasoning with the normal curve, it seems likely that there is some probability function that would give the probability density for any value of t. The probability of the interval between events being greater than t would then be given by $\int P(x)\,dx$, where $P(x)$ is the required probability function. The probability of the interval being between zero time and time t would be given by $\int P(x)\,dt$, but we know that this probability is also equal to $(1 - e^{-mt})$. We therefore know that:

$$\int P(x)\,dt = 1 - e^{-mt}.$$

The function that gives this definite integral is $y = me^{-mt}$ and this is the function for the negative exponential distribution.

32. Using the negative exponential distribution. The negative exponential distribution is the probability distribution for the time intervals between randomly occurring (Poisson) events. It is therefore possible to find the probability of a machine failing in a given time interval if the failures occur at random intervals but there is some recorded history of previous failures, so that m can be calculated.

EXAMPLE: A compressor is becoming rather old and tends to fail after about 100 hours' running time. This time between failures is based on an average of the previous recorded failures but the records do not show any particular pattern in the occurrence of breakdowns. The compressor is required to operate for 120 hours in order that an important job may be completed. What is the probability of a breakdown within this time?

The symbol m represents the average number of events in unit time and the average time between occurrences is therefore $1/m$. (If this is not intuitively obvious consider a case where the time unit was 1 hour and $m = 3$. The time between events would be averagely 20 minutes if three events occur every hour and this is confirmed since $1/m = \frac{1}{3}$ hour.) In the example $1/m = 100$ and $m = \frac{1}{100}$. The probability of an event occurring between $t = 0$ and $t = 120$ is given by:

$$\int_0^t me^{-mt}\,dt = \Big[-e^{-mt}\Big]_0^t$$
$$= -e^{-mt} + e^0$$
$$= \underline{1 - e^{-mt}}.$$

Putting $t = 120$ and $m = \frac{1}{100}$ gives:

$$\int_0^t \frac{1}{100}e^{-\frac{t}{100}}\,dt = 1 - e^{-\frac{120}{100}}$$
$$= 1 - \frac{1}{e^{1\cdot 2}}$$
$$= 1 - 0{\cdot}3012$$
$$= \underline{0{\cdot}6988}$$

The probability of a breakdown during the 120 hours' running time is just under 70 per cent.

33. The exponential distribution and queueing theory. In queueing theory, it is often convenient to assume that customers, or whatever other units are forming the queue arrive randomly in accordance with a Poisson law and that the time taken to deal with them at the service point varies in accordance with the negative exponential distribution.

PROGRESS TEST 12

1.* What is a frequency distribution and why is it important in statistics? **(5, 8–11, 19)**

2. Calculate the mean and standard deviation for the following twenty times, which represent the delays between placing orders and receiving consignments of turbine blades.

Lead times in days:

25	34	20	18	32	24	16	28	27	30
22	31	25	17	29	27	23	19	22	26

3. Find the derivative of $y = e^{-t^2}$ and sketch the curve. Discuss the relationship of this curve to that of the normal distribution.

4. Delays in sailing, incidents in passage and so on prevent the manager of an oil terminal from ever being quite sure when a tanker will arrive and so require a berth and unloading facilities, or how many ships will arrive on a given day, but previous experience indicates that the average number of arrivals is 2 ships per day. What is the probability that more than three ships will arrive on any given day? **(29)**

5. Show that (*a*) $\int_0^\infty me^{-mt}\,dt = 1$

(*b*) $\frac{d}{dt}(-e^{-mt}) = me^{-mt}$.

6. If a certain part in a complicated piece of automatic machinery breaks it will cost a company £5000 owing to delays and other penalties. The part averagely runs for 240 hours before breakdown. What would be the expected loss, due to a breakdown, of attempting a production run which required the part to function for 300 hours? (*Expected loss = Loss due to event × probability of event occurring.*) **(30–32)**

CHAPTER XIII

SAMPLING AND SIGNIFICANCE

TAKING SAMPLES

1. Sampling distribution. When we take samples we need to know whether they are really representative and whether they can safely be taken as guides to action. The method of assessing the reliability of a sample is to compare it with a suitable theoretical model that shows the distribution of the particular sample statistic which we are testing. Thus, if we are concerned with the mean of a sample, we wish to know whether it is a good estimator of the population mean. We therefore turn to the theoretical distribution of all the means of samples that could have been drawn from the population. This distribution, we have already discovered, follows the normal form, and we can therefore calculate the probability that the *population* mean is within stated limits. The theoretical distribution of sample means is a *sampling distribution.*

2. Some important theoretical distributions. There is a continuing development of ever more elaborate theoretical distributions that form the basis of very sophisticated tests. We shall confine our attention to a few of the better-known ones. We have already discussed the form of the binomial, normal and Poisson distributions (*see* XII, 22–29). To these, we shall add some tests based on "Student's" *t*-distribution and on the χ^2 (chi-squared) distribution.

3. The sampling requirements. In using the tests which follow it is important that the sample should have been drawn randomly from the parent population. The idea of randomness has occurred several times in this book in various contexts and here it means that every item in the background population must have an equal chance of being selected when a sample is drawn, or, a more exact statement, that every possible sample should have an equal chance of being the chosen sample.

Practical considerations often rule out the truly random selection of a sample, but, even if "quasi-random" or other special sampling methods are used, the ideal which should never be forgotten is that selection of the sampling units should be completely and strictly random.

Most of the tests which are used are appropriate only when the sample is a reasonably large one. In other cases, special small sample tests must be used. A convenient dividing line between large and small samples is that, for large sample tests to be used, n (the sample size) must be greater than 30. Unless it is otherwise stated it will be assumed that the population from which the samples are drawn is very large in comparison with the sample size.

SAMPLE STATISTICS AS ESTIMATORS

4. Estimation. We require our sample to reflect, as exactly as possible, the characteristics of the background population from which it is drawn. These characteristics would be summarised, if we knew them, by the population parameters such as the mean (μ) and the standard deviation (σ). When we do not know them, or when we do not feel it necessary to take the sample, we use the corresponding sample statistics as estimators of the population parameters.

5. Point estimates. The simplest use of a sample statistic as an estimator is to assume that the corresponding population parameter is exactly reflected in the sample statistic. Often it is true that this is the best estimate of the population parameter that we can make.

EXAMPLE: An aircraft manufacturer wishes to make an estimate of the time taken to install and connect fuel tanks into the airframe of a certain type of aeroplane. From the records of several hundred jobs that have been carried out a random sample of 50 is taken. The mean time to install the tanks is calculated as 40 hours.

Estimate: Since $\bar{x} = 40$ hours, μ is estimated to be 40 hours.

6. Confidence limits. The question immediately arises of how sure we can be that the estimate in the above example is correct. The right approach to the problem is to ask what is the probability that the population mean, in this case the mean of all jobs of this type, is *not* 40 hours. This probability would be very high indeed, but it can be lowered if we set limits to our estimate of the population mean. We could, for instance, say that our estimate of the population mean was between 35 and 45 hours, that is 40 hours $\pm$ 5 hours, but it would still be legitimate to ask with what probability we could make this statement.

What is really required is an estimate, with upper and lower limits stated, together with an assessment of the probability that the parameter does lie within the stated limits.

7. Setting up a confidence interval. If we approach the problem from the other end and begin by stating that we want an estimate of the population mean about which we can be 95 per cent confident that it is correct, we may be on surer ground. We already know that, if we could make a frequency distribution of the means of samples that are drawn from a background population, this distribution would be normal in form. We may state this result more formally as the *central limit theorem*, which states: *Provided that n is large, the theoretical sampling distribution of $\bar{x}$ is approximately normal.*

If we could find out the standard deviation of this theoretical distribution we could refer to a table of areas under the normal curve (*see* Appendix II) and could estimate the probability that the population mean lay within given limits. The standard deviation of the distribution of the sample mean is called *the standard error of the mean.* If we wanted to be 95 per cent confident that the population mean was within the limits that we stated, we should have to set them 1·96 standard errors (refer to diagram of normal curve areas in XII, 23–27) above and below the estimate of the mean.

EXAMPLE: The standard error of the mean time to install the tanks in the previous example has been calculated as 30 minutes. Our estimate of the population mean can be restated:

At the 95 per cent confidence level, the estimate is 40 hours $\pm$ (1·96 $\times$ $\frac{1}{2}$ hour) or approximately 40 hours $\pm$ 1 hour.

The *confidence limits* are then 39 hours to 41 hours.

8. Calculating the standard error of the mean. Where σ is the population standard deviation and n is the sample size, the standard error of the sample mean is given by the formula:

$$\text{Standard error of the sample mean} = \frac{\sigma}{\sqrt{n}}.$$

Since we do not know the population standard deviation we use the sample standard deviation (s) as an estimator and re-write the formula:

$$\textit{Standard error of the sample mean} = \frac{s}{\sqrt{n}}.$$

EXAMPLE: The standard deviation of the sample of 50 jobs was found to be 3 hours 32 minutes,

$$\therefore \textit{Standard error of the sample mean} = \frac{3{\cdot}53}{\sqrt{50}}$$

$$= \underline{0{\cdot}5 \text{ hours.}}$$

9. Attribute sampling. When we are concerned with estimating the proportion of people, or other units, in a population that possess some particular characteristics, we are sampling for the *attribute* possessed.

EXAMPLE: In a study concerned with package design a manufacturer wishes to know what proportion of a type of men's toiletries are purchased by women. Out of a random sample of 900 purchases, 280 are made by women. Construct a 95 per cent confidence interval for the actual proportion of the article bought by women.

We proceed exactly as we did for the sample of a variable in the previous example, but the required standard error is the standard error of the sample proportion. This is given by the formula:

$$\textit{Standard error of the sample proportion} = \sqrt{\frac{pq}{n}},$$

where p is the proportion in the sample possessing the attribute and $q = (1 - p)$.

As we discovered earlier, when n is large, the binomial distribution approaches the normal distribution in form. We may, therefore, use the areas under the normal curve as approximations for the areas under the frequency polygon of the discontinuous binomial distribution. Having calculated the standard error of the sample proportion, we may take the confidence interval as being:

$$p + 1{\cdot}96\sqrt{pq/n}$$

and

$$p - 1{\cdot}96\sqrt{pq/n}.$$

In the example, $p = 0{\cdot}31$ and $q = 0{\cdot}69$, giving a standard error of

$$(1{\cdot}96 \times \sqrt{(0{\cdot}31 \times 0{\cdot}69)/900}),$$

which is equal to $1{\cdot}96 \times 0{\cdot}015$ or $0{\cdot}029$. The confidence interval is 31 per cent $\pm$ 2·9 per cent. In practical terms we should say that we were 95 per cent confident that the population proportion was not less than 28 per cent or more than 34 per cent. It is often the practice to take two standard errors rather than 1·96 at the 95 per cent level in order to simplify calculation.

10. The confidence interval and accuracy. At the 95 per cent confidence level, the end points of the confidence interval are 1·96 standard errors above and below the mean. If we wanted to increase our confidence in the estimate, we should have to widen the confidence interval. At the 99 per cent confidence level we must take 2·58 standard errors above and below the estimate. Our estimate of the population proportion in the example would be $0{\cdot}31 \pm (2{\cdot}58 \times 0{\cdot}015)$ or 31 per cent $\pm$ 4 per cent. We should now expect there to be only a one-in-a-hundred chance of being wrong, but there would be less to be sure about, since the proportion might be as low as 27 per cent or as high as 35 per cent.

11. Confidence level and sample size. In planning a survey, we should be sure of how accurate we wished the result to be before the sample was taken. In the men's toiletries example, we should probably have had some rough idea of the proportion in the population. If we decided that we wanted the result to be within plus or minus 2 per cent with only a one-in-twenty chance of being wrong, we should then have defined the confidence level at 95 per cent and the standard error of the sample proportion as 1 per cent, that is, 2 standard errors would be equal to 2 per cent. The sample size would be determined as follows:

$$\textit{Standard error} = 1 \text{ per cent} = \sqrt{\frac{pq}{n}}.$$

Suppose that the original guess at the population proportion was 25 per cent, a figure which turned out to be on the low side according to the example. Then:

$$\textit{standard error} = 0{\cdot}01 = \sqrt{\frac{0{\cdot}25 \times 0{\cdot}75}{n}}$$

$$\therefore\ 0{\cdot}01 = \sqrt{\frac{0{\cdot}1875}{n}}$$

$$\text{and } 0{\cdot}0001 = \frac{0{\cdot}1875}{n}$$

$$\text{Therefore } n = \underline{1875.}$$

NOTE: We should have had to *double* the sample size (in the example $n = 900$) in order to reduce the standard error from $1\frac{1}{2}$ per cent to 1 per cent. Increased accuracy tends to be expensive, but under some circumstances it might be worth the expense of increasing the sample size even to get $\frac{1}{2}$ per cent off the ends of the confidence interval.

TESTING HYPOTHESES

12. Basic procedure. When we wished to know whether a correlation coefficient was significant we set up a hypothesis that it was *not* significant and then set about disproving it. This is a typical procedure which we must now develop in more detail.

13. Setting up the hypothesis. A plastic (nylon) sleeve forms part of a bulkhead seal in an aircraft. This sleeve has a nominal mean internal diameter of 30 millimetres. An automatic machine produces these sleeves, which are a standard part, in large quantities and periodic samples are taken to ascertain that the parts are being produced to the correct measurements. Previous, and accurate, information is that the standard deviation of the machine's output is 2 mm. Samples of size 25 are taken in order to check that the machine is still producing parts to the correct diameter. The hypothesis is set up that the population mean is 30 mm if the sample mean is between 29·2 mm and 30·8 mm. A usual notation for this is:

$$H\colon \mu = 30 \text{ mm if } 29{\cdot}2 \text{ mm} \leqslant \bar{x} \leqslant 30{\cdot}8 \text{ mm.}$$

14. Type I errors. The distribution of sample means if the hypothesis were correct would be as shown in Fig. 32(*a*). We only accept the hypothesis that the population (output) mean *is* 30 mm if the sample mean falls somewhere between the two "*Z*-marks." There is thus a definite chance that a sample may occur having a mean outside the limits even though the population mean is at the correct value of 30 mm. This is the chance of *falsely rejecting a true hypothesis.*

15. Calculating the probability of making a Type I error. In the diagram the shaded areas (α) show the parts of the sampling distribution that represent the probability of making a Type I error. Calculating this probability, therefore, involves finding the area under the curve at the tails of the normal distribution. To do this, we need to calculate the distance of the "*Z*-marks" from the mean in standard deviation (standard error) units. To do this we proceed as follows:

$$Z_1 = \frac{30{\cdot}8 - \mu}{\textit{Standard error mean}}$$

$$\textit{Standard error mean} = \frac{\sigma}{\sqrt{n}}$$

$$= \frac{2}{5} = 0{\cdot}4 \text{ mm.}$$

$$\therefore Z_1 = \frac{30{\cdot}8 - 30{\cdot}0}{0{\cdot}4}$$

$$= 2 \textit{ standard errors from the mean.}$$

Similarly:

$$Z_2 = \frac{29{\cdot}2 - 30{\cdot}0}{0{\cdot}4}$$

$$= -2 \text{ standard errors.}$$

By reference to the normal curve areas (*see* Appendix II) or recalling previous work, we know that there is just over $2\frac{1}{2}$ per cent of the area in each of the tails with these values of *Z*.

16. Type II errors. If *H* is not correct, there is nevertheless a probability that it may still be accepted. This probability is shown by the shaded area marked β in Fig. 32(*b*). We could calculate the actual probability if we knew the value of μ, but, since μ is different from 30 mm only because the machine has wandered from its correct setting, we are not likely to be in this position.

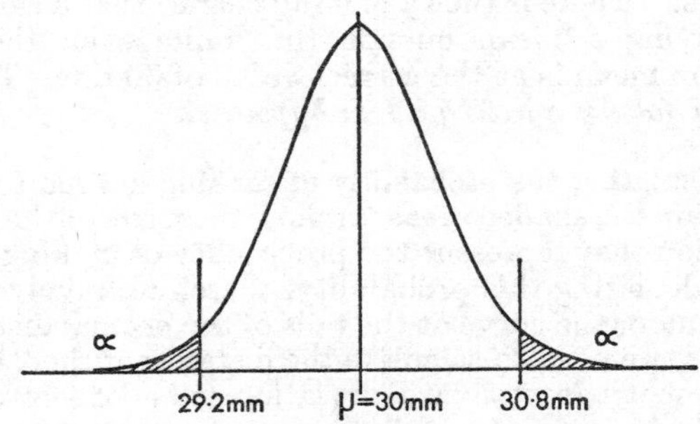

FIG. 32(*a*).—*Distribution of sample means showing probability of Type I error*

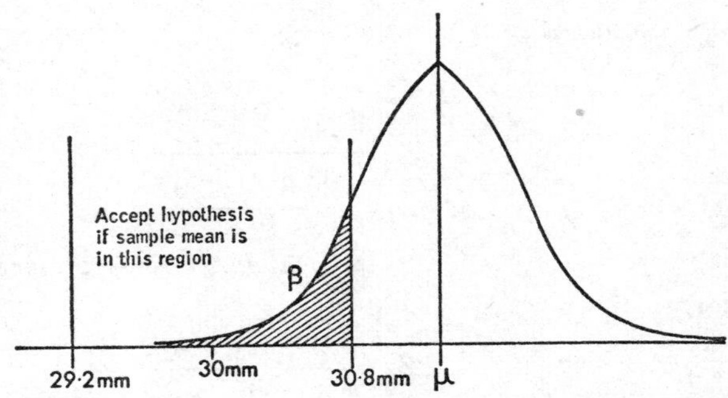

FIG. 32(*b*).—*Distribution of sample means showing probability of Type II error*

17. The operating characteristics curve. What we can calculate, however, is the probability of making a Type II error while using a given hypothesis if μ were to assume various values different from the correct one. Figure 33 shows the operating characteristics curve for the hypothesis just discussed.

18. Type I and Type II errors summarised. Students sometimes find a little difficulty in remembering which type of error is which. A diagram is therefore appended.

	Accept	*Reject*
H True	√	Type I
H False	Type II	√

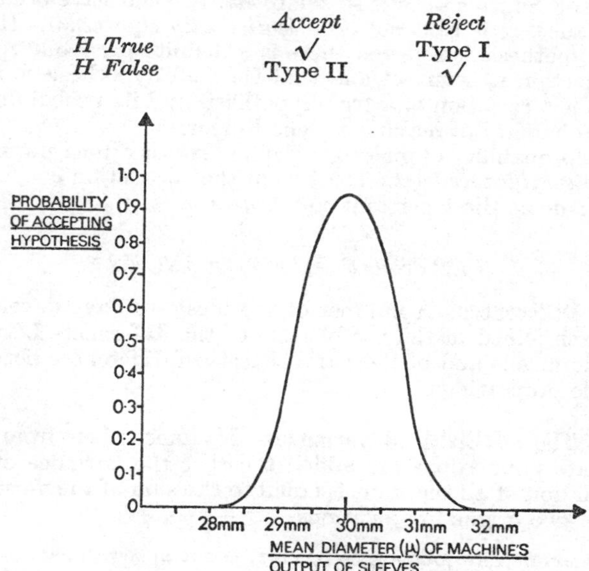

FIG. 33.—*Operating characteristics curve for hypothesis that μ = 30 mm if sample mean is greater than 29·2 mm but less than 30·8 mm*

19. The null hypothesis. The null hypothesis is one which states that there is *no* difference between two situations that are being compared. A null hypothesis can be disproved by an adverse observation and this is often the best way of setting up a hypothesis that is capable of being tested.

EXAMPLE: Salesman Smith averages 20 sales per week; salesman Jones is to be promoted to sales manager if he can be shown to be a better salesman than Smith.

H: There is no difference between the performance of Smith and Jones.

Criterion. Reject the null hypothesis if Jones's average weekly sale during the next quarter is more than 24.

20. Significance. A difficulty in making tests such as the one just discussed is to know where to set the level at which the hypothesis is to be rejected. If the difference between Jones's sales and Smith's sales is so small that it could have occurred by chance, it is said *not to be statistically significant*. If the null hypothesis is rejected there is a definite probability that its rejection is incorrect and that the null hypothesis is true. There is a rejection of a true hypothesis and its probability is the probability of making a Type I error.

The probability of making a Type I error is often referred to as the *significance level*. The test of the correlation coefficient was made at the 1 per cent *significance level*.

TESTS OF DIFFERENCES

21. Differences. A number of the ideas we have developed are exemplified in the use of tests of the differences between sample means and of the parallel tests of differences between sample proportions.

22. The additivity of variances. If items taken from two separate populations are added together the variance of the population of all the sums is equal to the sum of the variances of the two original populations.

EXAMPLE: Two jobs are to be carried out in sequence:

(*a*) Inspecting and repairing pump:

$$\bar{x}_1 = 2{\cdot}2 \text{ hours}$$
$$\sigma_1^2 = 1{\cdot}0 \text{ hour.}$$

(*b*) Refitting pump:

$$\bar{x}_2 = 1{\cdot}0 \text{ hour}$$
$$\sigma_2^2 = 0{\cdot}4 \text{ hour.}$$

The mean time and the variances of job times have been obtained from past records in both cases. We are required to estimate the mean and standard deviation for the two jobs carried out together.

Expected time to inspect, repair and refit pump

$$= \bar{x}_1 + \bar{x}_2$$
$$= \underline{\underline{3{\cdot}2 \text{ hours.}}}$$

Variance of time to inspect, repair and refit pump

$$= \sigma_1^2 + \sigma_2^2$$
$$= 1{\cdot}0 \text{ hour} + 0{\cdot}4 \text{ hour}$$
$$= \underline{1{\cdot}4 \text{ hours.}}$$

$$\textit{Standard deviation} = \sqrt{\sigma_1^2 + \sigma_2^2} = \sqrt{1{\cdot}4} \text{ hours}$$
$$= \underline{1{\cdot}18 \text{ hours.}}$$

With a little thought it can be seen that the variance of a population of differences will also be equal to the sum of the variances of the component populations, since the differences may include cases where very small values have been taken from very large ones and vice-versa for negative differences.

23. The standard error of the differences between sample means. It frequently happens that we must compare the means of two samples in order to decide whether the two samples have come from the same parent population. If sample 1 is of size n_1 and standard deviation s_1 the standard error calculated for the corresponding theoretical sampling distribution would be $s_1/\sqrt{n_1}$. The standard error calculated from a second sample of size n_2 and with standard deviation s_2 would be $s_2/\sqrt{n_2}$. If we imagine a distribution of differences between sample means drawn from the two populations of means with the standard errors given above, this distribution of differences would have a variance of:

$$\frac{s_1^2}{n_1} + \frac{s_2^2}{n_2}.$$

The square root of this variance would be the *standard error* of the difference between the sample means. Stating the formula, we have:

$$\textit{Standard error of difference between means} = \sqrt{\frac{s_1^2}{n_1} + \frac{s_2^2}{n_2}}.$$

EXAMPLE: A sample of 100 electronic components proves to have a mean life of 1080 hours and a standard deviation of 80 hours. A second sample of 150 components has a mean of 1100 hours and a standard deviation of 90 hours. Have these two samples been drawn from the same population? We shall set up the null hypothesis that there is no significant difference between the sample means.

24. The test. The hypothesis will be tested by comparing the difference between the means with the standard error of the difference between the sample means. Before we make the test we must set the significance level that our experience and knowledge of the situation leads us to believe to be appropriate. Let us set this at the 5 per cent level.

In symbolic terms, the test is given by the formula:

$$Z = \frac{\bar{x}_1 - \bar{x}_2}{\sqrt{\frac{s_1^2}{n_1} + \frac{s_2^2}{n_2}}}.$$

We shall reject the null hypothesis if $Z > 1{\cdot}96$.

25. Calculation. The data are:

$$\bar{x}_1 = 1080 \text{ hours}, \ \bar{x}_2 = 1100 \text{ hours}.$$
$$n_1 = 100, \ n_1 = 150.$$
$$s_1 = \quad 80 \text{ hours}, \ s_2 = \quad 90 \text{ hours}.$$

$$Z = \frac{1080 - 1100}{\sqrt{\frac{6400}{100} + \frac{8100}{150}}}$$

$$= \frac{-20}{\sqrt{64 + 54}}$$

$$\therefore Z = \underline{-1{\cdot}84.}$$

Since Z, disregarding the sign, is less than 1·96, the null hypothesis cannot be rejected.

26. The difference between sample proportions. Reasoning in exactly the same way, the standard error of the difference between the sample proportions is found to be:

$$\textit{Standard error of difference between proportions} = \sqrt{\frac{p_1q_1}{n_1} + \frac{p_2q_2}{n_2}},$$

where p_1 and p_2 are the observed proportions in samples 1 and 2 and n_1 and n_2 are the sample sizes.

This formula must be somewhat revised if our hypothesis contains the assumption that the samples have come from the same population. In that case, we must make an estimate of the population proportion from the data supplied by the two samples. If the observations have all come from the same population, then we have $(n_1 + n_2)$ items of which $(p_1n_1 + p_2n_2)$ have the given attribute, since p_1 and p_2 are the proportions of the samples of size n_1 and n_2 having the attribute. The estimate of the population proportion will be:

$$\hat{p} = \frac{p_1n_1 + p_2n_2}{n_1 + n_2}.$$

The standard error of the differences between the populations will now be:

$$\textit{Standard error difference (proportions)} = \sqrt{\frac{\hat{p}(1-\hat{p})}{n_1} + \frac{\hat{p}(1-\hat{p})}{n_2}}$$

$$= \sqrt{\hat{p}(1-\hat{p})\left(\frac{1}{n_1} + \frac{1}{n_2}\right)}.$$

The test value, Z, will be:

$$Z = \frac{p_1 - p_2}{\sqrt{\hat{p}(1-\hat{p})\left(\frac{1}{n_1} + \frac{1}{n_2}\right)}}.$$

EXAMPLE: A sample of 1000 housewives in Uptown shows that 520 of them use our product, whereas a sample of 800 housewives in Downtown shows 480 of them using it. Test the hypothesis that the proportion in the two districts is the same.

H: There is no significant difference between the two sample proportions.

Criterion: Selecting the 5 per cent significance level, reject H if $|Z| > 1{\cdot}96$.

Data: $p_1 = 0{\cdot}52$; $p_2 = 0{\cdot}60$; $n_1 = 1000$; $n_2 = 800$.

Calculation:

$$p = \frac{p_1n_1 + p_2n_2}{n_1 + n_2}$$

$$= \frac{520 + 480}{1800}$$

$$= \underline{0{\cdot}56}$$

$$Z = \frac{0{\cdot}52 - 0{\cdot}60}{\sqrt{(0{\cdot}56 \times 0{\cdot}44)\left(\frac{1}{1000} + \frac{1}{800}\right)}}$$

$$= \frac{-0{\cdot}080}{\sqrt{0{\cdot}246 \times 0{\cdot}002}}$$

$$= \frac{-0{\cdot}080}{0{\cdot}022}$$

$$= \underline{-3{\cdot}6}.$$

Since $|Z|$ is greater than 1·96, the null hypothesis must be rejected; the difference is significant.

PROGRESS TEST 13

1.* Discuss the idea of a sampling distribution and show clearly its relevance to the testing of hypotheses. **(1, 2, 12–20)**

2. A sample of 64 pieces of thread gives a mean breaking load of 31 N with a standard deviation of 1 N. Construct a 95 per cent confidence interval for the breaking load of this thread. Could this sample have come from the output of a machine producing thread with a mean breaking load of 30 N?

3. One hundred of the large number of female employees of an electronics firm are given a test of manual dexterity in order to find out whether they can be trained to handle a new process. In the event, 40 per cent of the employees tested fail to achieve the required standard. Dismayed by this high proportion failing the test, your general manager directs you to take a further sample and to design it so that you can be 99 per cent sure that your result is correct to within $2\frac{1}{2}$ per cent of the indicated result. Report to your manager: (*a*) on the sample size; (*b*) on the reasonableness of his request.

4. (*a*)* Distinguish between Type I and Type II errors. **(14–18)**

(*b*) A maker of a special type of window knows his market to be related to the possession of central heating apparatus. A random sample of households in a certain area in post-1945 housing shows that 26 per cent have central heating whereas a sample of households living in pre-1939 housing indicates 21 per cent only as having central heating. The sample size in the first case was 400 and in the second 260. Do the samples show a significant difference between the proportions in the two types of houses having central heating? State your hypothesis carefully and test so that the probability of a Type I error is 5 per cent only.

CHAPTER XIV

SMALL SAMPLE AND OTHER SPECIAL TESTS

SMALL SAMPLE TESTS

1. Standard deviation for small samples. When our samples are small, say of size less than 30, our standard tests become unreliable. The sample standard deviation is no longer a very good estimator of the population standard deviation and must be calculated by means of a more exact formula.

2. Degrees of freedom. Once the mean of a set of n values has been calculated, only $(n - 1)$ independent values remain. This must be so since the mean is given by $\bar{x} = \Sigma x/n$ and so $n\bar{x}$ is the total of the values. With the total given, once $(n - 1)$ values have been identified, there is only one possible remaining value: the last value has been determined by the others. The true formula for the standard deviation relates the sum of the squared deviations from the mean to the number of independent values and so should be:

$$s = \sqrt{\frac{\Sigma(x - \bar{x})^2}{n - 1}}.$$

The number of independently ascertainable values is called the number of degrees of freedom.

3. The "*t*" statistic. If we wanted to test whether a sample came from a given population, we should compare the sample mean with the population mean by seeing how many standard errors it was away from the population mean. Using the familiar notation, we should test:

$$Z = \frac{\bar{x} - \mu}{s/\sqrt{n}}$$

$$= \frac{\bar{x} - \mu}{s}\sqrt{n}$$

against the normal distribution. If the sample is small, however, the sample mean is no longer normally distributed. The actual form of the theoretical distribution which should be used for small-sample tests depends on the number of independent observations concerned, that is on the *number of degrees of freedom*. The revised formula to take account of this is:

$$t = \frac{\bar{x} - \mu}{s}\sqrt{\nu + 1},$$

where ν is the number of degrees of freedom.

4. The "*t*" distribution. The distribution of this "*t*" statistic is called "Student's" *t*-distribution, after its discoverer, W. S. Gosset, who wrote under the pen-name of "Student." Since the shape of the distribution is different for each number of degrees of freedom, the usual way of tabulating t is to show the values of t which would be exceeded with a given probability at the various degrees of freedom. As the number of degrees of freedom increases, the *t*-distribution approaches the normal distribution.

5. Using "*t*" to set up a confidence interval. The formula:

$$t = \frac{\bar{x} - \mu}{s}\sqrt{\nu + 1}$$

gives a value for t. To establish a 95 per cent confidence interval we must keep the value of t to one which will only be exceeded by chance 5 per cent of the time. This value is written $t_{0\cdot025}$ since there will be a $2\frac{1}{2}$ per cent chance of $+t$ being exceeded and the same chance for $-t$. Using mathematical notation, which is more compact and economical than verbal description, we can make the whole statement in the form of a simple inequality:

$$-t_{0\cdot025} < \frac{\bar{x} - \mu}{s}\sqrt{\nu + 1} < t_{0\cdot025}$$

Multiplying by $s/\sqrt{\nu + 1}$ we have:

$$-t_{0\cdot025}\left(\frac{s}{\sqrt{\nu + 1}}\right) < \bar{x} - \mu < t_{0\cdot025}\left(\frac{s}{\sqrt{\nu + 1}}\right),$$

which can be shown to be equivalent to:

$$\bar{x} - t_{0\cdot025}\left(\frac{s}{\sqrt{\nu+1}}\right) < \mu < \bar{x} + t_{0\cdot025}\left(\frac{s}{\sqrt{\nu+1}}\right).$$

This, interpreted, means that at the 95 per cent confidence level the population mean will lie between:

$$\bar{x} + t_{0\cdot025}\left(\frac{s}{\sqrt{\nu+1}}\right) \text{ and } \bar{x} - t_{0\cdot025}\left(\frac{s}{\sqrt{\nu+1}}\right).$$

EXAMPLE: A sample of five metal pieces taken from the output of a machine has an average length of 1·025 cm. Calculate a 95 per cent confidence interval for the mean length of the pieces produced.

From tables, $t_{0\cdot025}$ with 4 degrees of freedom is 2·78. (Note that $n = 5$; therefore $= n - 1 = 4$.) The standard deviation is given as 0·042 cm, therefore:

$$\frac{s}{\sqrt{\nu+1}} = \frac{0\cdot042}{\sqrt{5}} = \frac{0\cdot042}{2\cdot236}$$
$$= \underline{0\cdot018 \text{ cm}}$$

$$\textit{Confidence interval} = \bar{x} \pm (2\cdot78 \times 0\cdot018) \text{ cm}$$
$$= \underline{1\cdot025 \pm 0\cdot050 \text{ cm}}$$

Note that the use of the normal distribution would give an interval of 1·025 "± 0·035," which is considerably narrower. Because our sample is so small we can be less sure of our result and the t-distribution shows this by giving the wider interval.

THE χ^2 DISTRIBUTION

6. A more complex approach. While the ideas behind the statistical distributions used so far have been fairly straightforward and not difficult to understand, there are occasions on which we have to use methods which are derived from quite abstract mathematics. Such ideas may nevertheless be very useful and surprisingly easy to apply. An illustration is provided by the χ^2 distribution.

7. Establishing the distribution. Consider a circle with radius χ. The formula for a circle with radius r is $x^2 + y^2 = r^2$. In our case, we should have $x^2 + y^2 = \chi^2$ and the question is:

what might x and y represent in such a situation? We shall say that x represents the difference between some arbitrary value x_1 and its expected value $\bar{x}_1$. Letting y, similarly, be the difference between another such arbitrary value, x_2, and its expected value $\bar{x}_2$ and expressing both deviations in standardised units by dividing through by the appropriate standard deviation (*see* XII, **24**), the expression for χ^2 with *two* comparisons would be:

$$\left(\frac{x_1 - \bar{x}_1}{\sigma_1}\right)^2 + \left(\frac{x_2 - \bar{x}_2}{\sigma_2}\right)^2 = \chi^2$$

With three squared standardised deviations from their expected values, the χ^2 formula would correspond not to a circle but to a sphere, since the general expression for a sphere is $(x^2 + y^2 + z^2) = r^2$, where the x-, y- and z- values are measured along the three axes as explained in IX, **2**. With k deviations, the full χ^2 formula is found:

$$\chi^2 = \left(\frac{x_1 - \bar{x}_1}{\sigma_1}\right)^2 + \left(\frac{x_2 - \bar{x}_2}{\sigma_2}\right)^2 + \ldots + \left(\frac{x_k - \bar{x}_k}{\sigma_k}\right)^2$$

For any *given* value of χ^2, only $(k - 1)$ terms are independent, since the value of the last term can always be found when $(k - 1)$ terms are known.

8. A random value of χ. An expression in k dimensions would represent not a circle (two dimensions) or a sphere (three dimensions) but a hypersphere. It is not difficult to think of the idea of a random or chance value of χ, and therefore of χ^2, as being the value given to the radius of the hypersphere (think of it as a 3D sphere to simplify matters) by joining a random point within the sphere to the centre.

9. The practical use of the χ^2 hypersphere. There are many cases in business statistics in which we have to compare an expected value with an observed value. We have to decide whether the difference from the expected value is due to chance or whether it is statistically significant. The question is exactly the same, in formal analysis, as the question of whether a particular value of χ, the radius of the hypersphere, differs from the radius produced by a randomly selected point.

The number of comparisons made, of course, would correspond to the number of dimensions of the hypersphere.

10. A probability integral. To complete the discussion, it is necessary to show that the formal analysis does produce a useful probability distribution. Although, strictly speaking, the mathematics is a little advanced, most of the work can be followed easily by students who have worked this far through the book. It would be possible to work out the probability of a random point occurring in some given locality within the sphere. Consider a shell formed by expanding the radius of the sphere a little. Now ask the question, how has the probability of getting a given value of χ changed with the increase of χ itself? The change in probability is the only difficult part of the mathematical work and follows from the assumption that the observations are drawn from normal distributions. The expression required for the change in probability (*dP*) with a small extension of χ is:

$$dP = Ae^{-\frac{1}{2}\chi^2}\,\chi^{k-2}\,d\chi,$$

where A is a constant and e is the familiar exponential constant. This could be written:

$$\frac{dP}{d\chi} = Ae^{-\frac{1}{2}\chi^2}\,\chi^{k-2}$$

and integrating both sides gives:

$$P = A\int e^{-\frac{1}{2}\chi^2}\,\chi^{k-2}\,d\chi.$$

Recalling the geometrical equivalent, χ must lie somewhere between zero and infinity. This gives a probability of 1 for the definite integral evaluated from zero to infinity that is:

$$A\int_0^\infty e^{-\frac{1}{2}\chi^2}\,\chi^{k-2}\,d\chi = 1.$$

If we require the probability that a particular value of χ will be exceeded by chance, we must evaluate the integral from the given value to infinity. There are special tables which aid this integration and, better still, tables of the value of χ^2 which will be exceeded with given key probabilities such as 0·01, 0·05 and so on.

APPLICATIONS OF χ^2

11. Differences from an expected value. The quantity $\sum\frac{(O-E)^2}{E}$, where O represents an observed value and E the corresponding expected value, is distributed in the same way as χ^2 and, in fact, is usually referred to as χ^2. The χ^2 distribution acts as the theoretical distribution against which $\sum\frac{(O-E)^2}{E}$ can be tested in much the same way as other statistics have been tested against theoretical distributions. When we have to test whether the observed facts accord with some hypothesis, we can use χ^2.

12. An example. Following a change in Government policy, an organisation conducts a survey of the views of firms in four industries in order to ascertain whether they consider their prospects to be "better," "unchanged" or "worse." The results are shown in Table 10.

The investigating organisation wishes to know whether there is any significant difference between the attitudes of firms in the different industries. The appropriate significance level has been decided to be 5 per cent.

13. The null hypothesis again. In order to test whether there is any significant difference between the four industries' attitudes we must set up the null hypothesis that there is *no* significant difference between their attitudes.

14. The expected frequencies. If the null hypothesis were correct, the proportion of each industry's returns that fell into

TABLE 10

Prospects	*Number of firms reporting*				*Total*
	Industry 1	*Industry* 2	*Industry* 3	*Industry* 4	
Better	28	12	25	11	76
Unchanged	30	32	23	25	110
Worse	27	11	12	14	64
Totals	85	55	60	50	250

the "Better," "Unchanged" and "Worse" rows would not be significantly different from the proportions in each category for the four industries taken together. These proportions are $\frac{76}{250}$, $\frac{110}{250}$ and $\frac{64}{250}$. The expected frequency for the Industry 1/"Better" cell would be $\frac{76}{250} \times 85 = 25{\cdot}8$; in the Industry 1/"Unchanged" cell it would be $\frac{110}{250} \times 85 = 37{\cdot}4$; and for the Industry 1/"Worse" cell, $\frac{64}{250} \times 85 = 21{\cdot}8$. These figures, and the corresponding ones for the other three industries are entered in Table 11(*a*) below, a rounding adjustment having been made to preserve the totals.

TABLE 11(*a*)

SURVEY OF FIRMS' ESTIMATED PROSPECTS IN FOUR INDUSTRIES

Prospects	*Expected (theoretical) frequencies*				*Totals*
	Industry 1	*Industry* 2	*Industry* 3	*Industry* 4	
Better	25·9	16·7	18·2	15·2	76
Unchanged	37·4	24·2	26·4	22·0	110
Worse	21·7	14·1	15·4	12·8	64
Totals	85	55	60	50	250

These figures are now transferred to the "Expected" column of Table 11(*b*) and the calculation of:

$$\chi^2 = \sum \frac{(O - E)^2}{E}$$

is completed by following through the remaining columns and totalling the results entered in column 7.

15. Degrees of freedom for χ^2. Taking it that there are r rows and k columns in the table of expected values, it can be seen that, when we have fitted in the first $r - 1$ rows and $k - 1$ columns, the remaining values are determined by the row and column border tables. There are thus $(r - 1)(k - 1)$ degrees of freedom. In the example, there are $(3 - 1)(4 - 1) = 6$ degrees of freedom.

16. Checking χ^2. The sum of $(O - E)^2/E$ is equal to 13·76 in the example, the significance level has been set at 5 per cent

TABLE 11(*b*)

CALCULATION OF χ^2

(1) *Industry*	(2) *Prospects*	(3) (*O*) *Observed*	(4) (*E*) *Expected*	(5) $O - E$	(6) $(O - E)^2$	(7) $\frac{(O - E)^2}{E}$
1	Better	28	25·9	2·1	4·41	0·17
	Unchanged	30	37·4	–7·4	54·76	1·46
	Worse	27	21·7	5·3	28·09	1·29
2	Better	12	16·7	–4·7	22·09	1·32
	Unchanged	32	24·2	7·8	60·84	2·51
	Worse	11	14·1	–3·1	9·61	0·68
3	Better	25	18·2	6·8	46·24	2·54
	Unchanged	23	26·4	–3·4	11·56	0·44
	Worse	12	15·4	–3·4	11·56	0·75
4	Better	11	15·2	–4·2	17·64	1·16
	Unchanged	25	22·0	+3·0	9·00	0·41
	Worse	14	12·8	+1·2	1·44	1·03
	Totals	250	250	$\sum \frac{(O - E)^2}{E} = 13·76$		

(the probability of making a Type I error) and the number of degrees of freedom is 6. Consulting the tables of χ^2 (*see* Appendix II for a miniature version) we find that at $P = 5$, $\nu = 6$, the tabulated value is 12.59. The calculated value of 13·76 is too large to have occurred by chance with a probability of 5 per cent. We must therefore reject the null hypothesis.

Had the 1 per cent significance level been chosen, we could not have rejected the null hypothesis. Note that determining the significance level to be used is *not* a statistical decision. All the factors concerned in the decision must be weighed and the harm that could come from a Type I error assessed before setting an appropriate level.

17. χ^2 and "goodness of fit." Since χ^2 serves as a good test of the agreement between observation and hypothesis, it is an excellent test of whether a series of values is adequately described by a particular type of frequency distribution or a particular function. The method of making the test is to calculate the theoretical values, using the given distribution or function, and then to test against the observed values as before.

STATISTICAL QUALITY CONTROL

18. Reducing costs. A complete inspection of the output of a machine or of man and machine systems is very expensive. By applying sampling techniques it is possible to reduce this expense considerably and yet still to ensure that the process remains under control.

19. Quality. The term "quality" used in the context of statistical quality control means some property of the product that can be measured or identified as being present or not present. The distinction is exactly that which was made earlier between the sampling of attributes and the sampling of variables.

20. Variability in processes. No process, however accurate, produces to exact measurements nor are parts produced by the same machine ever exactly alike. There is always some variability in the output which is due to chance variations in the precise conditions under which production takes place. These variations may be minute differences in the quality of the materials used, in cutting speeds and so on. This chance variation is statistically similar to that observed in random processes.

21. Statistical control. If the variation present in a process can effectively be limited to that which is due to chance, the process is said to be *under statistical control.*

22. Control charts for variables. The method of ensuring that the process remains under statistical control is to set up a control chart. The form of these charts is shown in Fig. 34(*a*).

A central line is used to indicate the calculated process mean, the calculated average measurement to which the process is working. On either side of the central line are upper and lower control limits. The process is assumed to be under control as long as the means of samples taken from the output are within the control limits.

23. Setting the control limits. Taking repeated samples from the output and entering them on the control chart is really the same as repeatedly testing the hypothesis that there is no significant difference between the sample mean and the population (process) mean. The usual way of setting the control limits is to place them three standard errors above and below the desired process mean, thus limiting the probability of *wrongly* deciding that the process was out of control (a Type I error) to about 0·3 per cent. The "3-sigma" limits are fairly generally accepted as being a reasonable compromise between making a Type I error, and thus stopping production unnecessarily while the process is checked and machines re-set, and making a Type II error and so allowing defective parts to reach customers.

24. Simplification of control limits. Quality control has normally to be operated by non-statisticians and it is therefore desirable that they should be able to work with the simplest measures possible. The concepts of standard deviation, standard error and so on are not entirely uncomplicated and quality control schemes are set up in terms of the two simple measures, the *sample mean* and the *sample range*. The actual limits must be set in terms of standard errors about the process mean and this difficulty is dealt with by using tables which relate the sample range to the standard error of the sample mean and to the desired control limit. The actual setting of the control limits is done by calculating the mean range of a number of samples and then multiplying by a constant read-off from tables according to the sample size.

EXAMPLE: Before setting up a control chart, ten samples of five items are taken from the output of an automatic machine.

The machine is set to produce parts 1 cm in length and the range of the ten samples is as follows:

Sample no.	*Longest* (*cm*)	*Shortest* (*cm*)	*Range* (*cm*)
1	1·010	0·972	0·038
2	1·080	1·010	0·070
3	1·080	0·960	0·120
4	1·020	0·940	0·080
5	1·080	0·960	0·120
6	1·080	1·000	0·080
7	1·060	0·940	0·120
8	1·020	0·900	0·120
9	1·090	0·920	0·170
10	1·100	1·000	0·100

Sum of ten ranges: 1·018 cm

$$\text{Mean sample range} = \frac{1{\cdot}018}{10}$$

$$= 0{\cdot}102 \text{ cm}$$

to the nearest thousandth of a centimetre.

From tables, the appropriate constant for converting a mean sample range to a "3-sigma" limit is 0·577. Putting $\bar{w}$ equal to the mean sample range and A_5 as the constant for sample size 5 and $\bar{\bar{x}}$ as the process mean, the limits are:

$$\text{Upper limit: } \bar{\bar{x}} + (A_5 \times \bar{w}) = 1{\cdot}000 + 0{\cdot}059$$

$$\text{Lower limit: } \bar{\bar{x}} - (A_5 \times \bar{w}) = 1{\cdot}000 - 0{\cdot}059$$

or 1·059 cm and 0·941 cm. These are the limits shown on Fig. 34(*a*).

25. The meaning of the tabulated constant. The limits must be three standard errors above and below the process mean. There is a fairly firm relationship between the mean range and population standard deviation for samples of various sizes. Writing this range factor as a_n, $\sigma = a_n\bar{w}$. For samples of size 5, $a_5 = 0{\cdot}430$, giving an estimate of the population standard deviation of $\sigma/\sqrt{n} = (0{\cdot}430 \times \bar{w})/\sqrt{5}$, recalling that the population is one of sample means. Our control limits must be 3 standard errors above and below the central line, that is they must be at plus or minus $3(\sigma/\sqrt{n}) = (3 \times 0{\cdot}430 \times \bar{w})/\sqrt{5}$. The factor A_5 is equal to $(3 \times 0{\cdot}430)/2{\cdot}236 = 0{\cdot}577$.

26. Using the control charts. So long as the means of samples are within the limits, the null hypothesis that there is no significant difference between the output mean and the desired process mean has not been disproved and we may consider the process under control. However, sometimes a steady drift of successive sample means is observed, as in the last three entries on the chart in Fig. 34(*a*). In such cases we may prefer to play safe and stop the process, since it appears that, although the control limits are not being exceeded, the process is wandering away from the correct process mean.

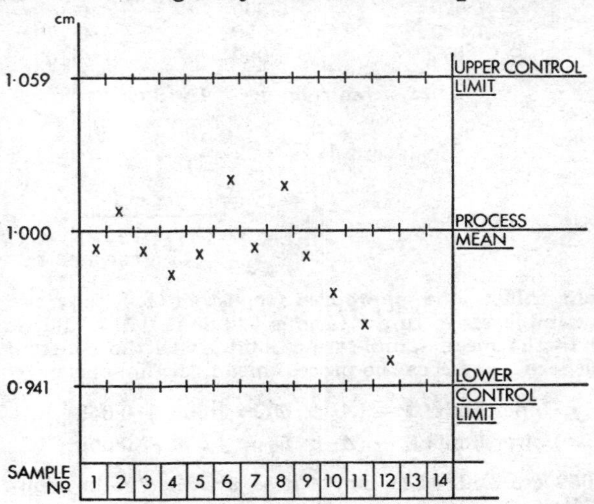

FIG. 34(*a*).—*Control chart for sample means*

27. Range charts. Charts set up in a similar way to control the process by checking the sample range are usually used in conjunction with mean charts. This is necessary because a perfectly acceptable mean for a sample may mask the fact that excessively high and excessively low values are offsetting each other.

28. Control charts for attributes. Some aspects of quality may not be measurable although they are observable. Pieces of material may be flawed, workmanship may be of poor quality, electrical assemblies may not function. In situations like this, the item inspected is either passed or rejected. The control chart therefore shows the number of defectives per sample and the control limit shows the number of defectives permitted before the process is assumed to be out of control. To achieve a fairly normal distribution of defectives, the sample size must be fairly large (recall **1**) and the average number of defectives to be expected is $n\hat{p}$, where $\hat{p}$ is the estimated proportion of defectives to be expected in the output. The control limit is then $n\hat{p} + 3x\sqrt{npq}$. An attribute control chart is shown in Fig. 34(*b*).

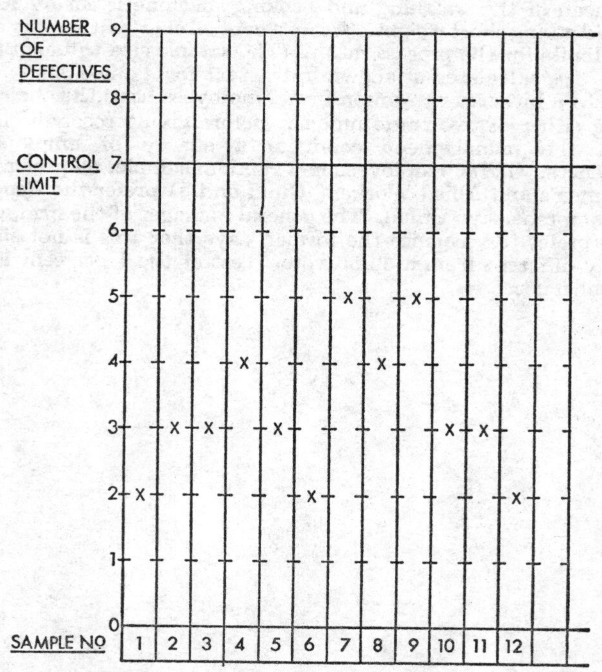

FIG. 34(*b*).—*Control chart for sample proportions*

PROGRESS TEST 14

1. (*a*) Construct a 99 per cent confidence interval for the mean estimated from the following observations:

Diameter in millimetres

42	41	45	43
40	39	44	40
44.			

2. "Quarter-kilo" packets of dried fruit are sampled in batches of 10. Before setting up a control chart, twenty samples of size 10 are taken and the mean sample range is found to be 6 g. The process mean of the weighing and packing machine is set at 260 g to avoid giving short weight. Set up a control chart with upper and lower limits for the process mean. (The sample size will continue as 10. A_{10}, calculated as shown in the text for A_5, is 0·308.)

3. In a hitherto non-union firm, employees have the choice of joining either of two trade unions. Before giving recognition to either, the management conducts a survey of employees' preferences. Of 150 employees in a random sample, 69 prefer the Craftsmen's and Allied Workers' Guild and 81 prefer the General and Comprehensive Union. The general manager of the firm, who would prefer to recognise the former, says that this is not significantly different from a 50:50 vote. Test at the 1 per cent level of significance.

PART THREE

THE MATHEMATICS OF FINANCE

CHAPTER XV

COMPOUND INTEREST

THE MEANING OF FINANCE

1. The gap. Income does not always match up to expenditure. This is a common experience for both firms and individuals and both bridge the gap by borrowing. There is no suggestion that either firms or individuals need to borrow because they are improvident; it is merely that expenditure tends to be "lumpy" and that expensive purchases occur at irregular intervals. The essence of finance is the provision of money at the time when it is needed. Some people have excess funds which they are prepared to lend; others require money for projects and are prepared to pay interest in order to have the use of it.

2. The importance of time. Since finance is concerned with the provision of money at the right time and with levelling out requirements for funds over time, it is obvious that the mathematics of finance must be concerned with time. An essential idea is that money now is more valuable than the same sum at some future time. This is quite regardless of increasing prices. If we had the money now we could make it work for us and we should have more at the future time. Consequently those who lend money, and so give up the chance of using it themselves, expect to be reimbursed. The sum paid as compensation for what they could otherwise have made is called *interest*.

COMPOUND INTEREST

3. A first approach. Let the rate of interest be $100r$ per cent, so that a 5 per cent rate would be represented by $r = 0{\cdot}05$. If £1 is invested at a rate of $100r$ per cent per annum, after a year the investment will be worth £$(1 + r)$. At the end of the year we have the original £1 plus £$(1 \times r)$. Suppose that not £1 but

£100 was invested; at the end of the year we should have the original £100 plus £100r.

EXAMPLE: Put $r = 0{\cdot}06$, giving $100r = 6$ or 6 per cent. £200 is invested at 6 per cent per annum. At the end of the year we have the original £200 plus £200 × 0·06, giving £200 + £12 or £200 (1·06).

4. A first interest formula. Following the example used in the previous paragraph, the original sum invested could be represented as £A and after a year we shall have £$A(1 + r)$.

5. A formula for compound interest. At the time of the original investment we have £A; after a year this has grown to £$A(1 + r)$. If the sum is left invested for another year, we could regard it as a new initial sum so that after another year it will have grown to £$A(1 + r)(1 + r)$, which is equal to £$A(1 + r)^2$. It follows that after £A has remained invested for n years it will have grown to £$A(1 + r)^n$.

EXAMPLE: A man places £300 into a savings account which pays 3 per cent interest each half year. Calculate the balance after four years.

The period here is not a year but a half-year, so that after four years the interest has been paid for eight periods. At a rate of 3 per cent per period, $r = 0{\cdot}03$. The balance after four years is therefore equal to:

$$
\begin{aligned}
\pounds A(1 + r)^n &= \pounds 300\,(1{\cdot}03)^8 \\
&= \pounds 300\,(1{\cdot}2668) \\
&= \underline{\pounds 380{\cdot}04.}
\end{aligned}
$$

6. An alternative notation. There is an obvious chance of confusion if we allow r to represent either the interest rate per annum or the rate for a shorter period. A similar confusion can occur if n can represent either the number of periods or the number of years concerned. In order to avoid confusion, we could keep the symbol r for the annual rate and substitute i as the symbol for the rate per period when the period is not a year. Similarly we could use m for the number of periods per year and keep n for the number of years.

The revised formula can be found by realising that $i = r/m$ and is £$A[1 + r/m)]^{mn}$. In the example, m was equal to 2; since interest was added twice yearly, the full rate per annum was 6 per cent, giving $r/m = 0{\cdot}06/2$ or 0·03 as shown. With the number of years (n) equal to four, mn gives a value of 8, again the figure used in the example.

7. A link with the exponential constant. Suppose that interest is being paid at the rate of 100 per cent per annum. Unlikely though this may be, it yields an interesting and illuminating mathematical result. The value of r would be 1·00 since $100r$ must equal 100. The formula for £1 invested for one year would be $[1 + (1/m)]^m$. It is apparent that, the more often the interest is compounded, the greater will be the interest earned, but that there is some limit to this, since $1/m$, the rate per period, will get smaller as m gets larger. In fact, the sum of £1 invested at 100 per cent per annum, with interest paid and compounded m times per year, could never grow to more than £2·71828 . . . however many times the interest was compounded. Readers will no doubt recall (II, **14** and XII, **24**) that the figure of 2·71828 . . . is the irrational number which is usually represented by the symbol e; in fact we could write:

$$e = \underset{m \to \infty}{Limit} \left(1 + \frac{1}{m}\right)^m$$

or: the exponential constant is the limit of $(1 + \frac{1}{m})^m$ as m tends towards infinity.

8. Continuous compounding. The rate of 100 per cent per annum is an unlikely one in most circumstances. To adapt the formula to more conventional rates, we have merely to substitute r instead of 1. Thus:

$$e^r = \underset{m \to \infty}{Limit} \left(1 + \frac{r}{m}\right)^m.$$

We could regard this as a description of what happens when the yield from an investment is available immediately it is earned and is immediately ploughed back to earn more. It is the formula for *continuous compounding*.

COMPOUND INTEREST WITH GROWING ANNUAL INVESTMENT

9. The problem. Starting again with £A invested at the beginning of the first year, let an additional sum £p be added to the investment in each subsequent year. No withdrawals are to be made and the whole sum invested is to be allowed to accumulate at a compound rate.

10. Time subscripts. The initial investment can be designated A_0, the zero subscript showing that it is the investment in the starting year. Using the notation, A_1 is the investment in the next year, A_2 in the year after and so on. The investment in any given year could be shown by the symbol A_t where the t subscript can take the value for any desired year. To find the investment in any given year, we should have to solve the equation:

$$A_t = A_{t-1}(1 + r) + p \quad . \; . \; . \; \text{(equation 1)}.$$

11. Difference equations. An equation such as that shown above is called a difference equation. The solution of difference equations generally is outside the scope of a fairly simple introduction, but this one is not difficult and so the stages of the solution are indicated in **12–15** below.

12. Stage 1: a first approximation. The original compound interest problem could have been expressed in the form:

$$A_t = A_{t-1}(1 + r),$$

each year's total being $(1 + r)$ times the previous year's total. The solution to the problem, expressed in the form of a difference equation, would be:

$$A_t = A_0(1 + r)^t,$$

which agrees with the solution given earlier in the chapter (**5**) if we take A_0 as the starting value. A corresponding solution here would have to be modified to take account of the constant term p. It would seem reasonable to add on some final term, and perhaps we should not be too sure that the other constant in the solution would be A_0. Making these allowances, a tentative solution would be:

$$A_t = K(1+r)^t + z, \ . \ . \ . \text{ (equation 2)}$$

with K and z to be determined.

13. Stage 2: finding a value for z. The next stage is based on the idea that equation 2 is really the sum of two partial solutions. The first partial solution is valid for the original compound interest problem, ignoring the constant added sum, p, but to this must be added the second part of the answer, z, which must be valid for equation 1 at all times. To find the value of this second part, therefore, we substitute z for both A_t and A_{t-1} in equation 1, giving:

$$z = z(1+r) + p \ . \ . \ . \text{ (equation 3)}$$

or:

$$z = z + zr + p,$$

and therefore:

$$-zr = p$$

or:

$$z = -\frac{p}{r}.$$

14. Stage 3: finding a value for *K*. At this stage of the solution we are in a position to re-write equation 2 with $z = -\frac{p}{r}$, which gives:

$$A_t = K(1+r)^t - \frac{p}{r} \ . \ . \ . \text{ (equation 4)}.$$

If we go back to the start of the investment process, we can write equation 4 with $t = 0$, to give:

$$A_0 = K(1+r)^0 - \frac{p}{r},$$

and since any base to the power zero equals unity this is equivalent to writing:

$$A_0 = K - \frac{p}{r}$$

or:

$$K = A_0 + \frac{p}{r}.$$

15. Stage 4: the solution. Now that we have values for both K and z, it is possible to substitute these values in equation 2 and to test it to see if it really is a solution.

This substitution would give:

$$A_t = \left(A_0 + \frac{p}{r}\right)(1 + r)^t - \frac{p}{r} \quad . \; . \; . \text{ (equation 5).}$$

Putting $t = 0$ does give A_0, the initial sum invested. With $t = 1$:

$$\begin{aligned} A_1 &= \left(A_0 + \frac{p}{r}\right)(1 + r) - \frac{p}{r} \\ &= A_0 + A_0 r + p \\ &= \underline{\underline{A_0(1 + r) + p.}} \end{aligned}$$

This again is correct, since we have the initial investment plus one year's interest on it plus the new investment p. Testing for further values of t confirms that the solution is the correct one.

16. An example. £5000 is invested at the beginning of 19–4. It remains invested and, on 1st January each subsequent year, another £400 is added to it. What sum will be available six years later on 19–0 if interest is compounded each year at the rate of 5 per cent per annum? The formula is given by equation 5:

$$A_t = \left(A_0 + \frac{p}{r}\right)(1 + r)^t - \frac{p}{r}.$$

Here:

$$\begin{aligned} A_0 &= £5000 \\ p &= £400 \\ r &= 0{\cdot}05 \\ t &= 6. \end{aligned}$$

Therefore:

$$\begin{aligned} A_6 &= \left(5000 + \frac{400}{0{\cdot}05}\right)(1 + 0{\cdot}05)^6 - \frac{400}{0{\cdot}05} \\ &= (13{,}000)\,(1{\cdot}05)^6 - 8000 \\ &= 13{,}000 \times 1{\cdot}3401 - 8000 \\ &= 17{,}421{\cdot}3 - 8000 \\ &= \underline{\underline{£9421{\cdot}30}} \end{aligned}$$

SOME APPLICATIONS OF THE BASIC FORMULA

17. A generalisation. In a sense, the formula derived in the previous section is the *basic* compound interest formula, since the earlier formula can be derived from it by putting p equal to zero.

Basic formula.

$$A_t = \left(A_0 + \frac{p}{r}\right)(1 + r)^t - \frac{p}{r}.$$

With $p = 0$: $$A_t = A_0(1 + r)^t.$$

We can thus use the basic formula to find the eventual values of a sum left to grow at compound interest for a certain number of years, or find the value of a sum which is added to year by year. If we put p equal to a negative figure, we can use the same formula for the situation in which withdrawals are made year by year.

18. Example with annual withdrawals. A man invests £10,000 and withdraws £1500 at the end of each year, starting at the end of the first year. How much will he have left after seven years if the money is invested at 4 per cent per annum?

$$A_0 = £10{,}000;\ r = 0{\cdot}04;\ t = 7;\ (1{\cdot}04)^7 = 1{\cdot}3159$$

$$p = -£1500$$

$$\begin{aligned} A_t &= \left(A_0 + \frac{p}{r}\right)(1 + r)^t - \frac{p}{r} \\ &= (10{,}000 - 37{,}500)\,(1{\cdot}04)^7 + 37{,}500 \\ &= -(27{,}500)\,(1{\cdot}3159) + 37{,}500 \\ &= \underline{£1312{\cdot}75} \end{aligned}$$

Drawing at this rate he will only have £1312·75 at the end of seven years.

19. Finding amount to produce a given income. We should like to invest a sum which would yield an annual income of £2000, paid in equal annual instalments each year for ten years. We are counting on being able to invest the sum so that the invested balance yields 5 per cent per annum.

Let the amount to be invested be P. Since we are to make withdrawals of £2000 each year, $p = -2000$. The number of years is 10, the rate per cent is 5, therefore $n = 10$ and $r = 0{\cdot}05$. $(1{\cdot}05)^{10}$ is approximately equal to 1·6289.

The investment is to be just used up after ten years, giving a terminal sum of zero. The calculation is, therefore:

$$\begin{aligned} 0 &= \left(P + \frac{p}{r}\right)(1+r)^t - \frac{p}{r} \\ &= \left(P + \frac{-2000}{0{\cdot}05}\right)(1{\cdot}05)^{10} - \frac{(-2000)}{0{\cdot}05} \\ &= (P - 40{,}000)\,(1{\cdot}05)^{10} + 40{,}000 \\ &= 1{\cdot}6289(P) - 65{,}156 + 40{,}000. \end{aligned}$$

This gives $0 = 1{\cdot}6289(P) - 25{,}156$

or $1{\cdot}6289P = 25{,}156$

$$\therefore\ P = \frac{25{,}156}{1{\cdot}6289} = \underline{£15{,}442{\cdot}912}$$

The amount to be invested is just under £15,443.

PROGRESS TEST 15

1.* (*a*) "The rate of interest is 100*r* per cent." Explain. (3)

(*b*) £450 is invested at 4 per cent per annum at the beginning of 19–6. To what sum will this have amounted by the end of 19–9, interest being paid annually? (4)

2.* (*a*) What is the connection with $y = e^x$? (7, 8)

(*b*) What is the relationship between the ordinary compound interest formula, the formula for compound interest with increasing annual investment and that for the situation with annual withdrawals? (15, 19)

3. £4500 was invested on 1st January 19–4 and £500 was added to it on 1st January 19–5 and on each subsequent 1st January. If the sums remained invested at the rate of 5 per cent per annum, what amount of money was available on 31st December 19–7? (15, 16)

CHAPTER XVI

DISCOUNTING AND PRESENT VALUES

TIME AND THE VALUE OF A MONEY SUM

1. Discounting. As we saw in XV, 2, time is an essential element of finance. £500 right now is obviously worth more than £500 in a year's time, and £500 in a year's time is worth more than the same amount in two years' time. The question which remains is: "How much more?"

Offered the choice of £100 in a year's time or some other sum right now, we should have to adopt some criterion by which to compare the two alternatives. A useful way would be to ask: "What sum, invested now, would yield £100 after a year?" This is the sum now that would be just equal to £100 in a year's time. The method of finding the required sum is simple. Let the rate of interest be $100r$ per cent, in the usual way, and let £x be the sum of money of which we are trying to find the value. The formula which would give £100 after a year is $100 = x(1 + r)$, which, dividing both sides by $(1 + r)$, gives a value of:

$$£x = \frac{100}{(1 + r)}$$

or

$$£x = 100(1 + r)^{-1}.$$

The value £x is the *discounted* value of £100 or £100 *discounted for one year at the rate of* $100r$ *per cent per annum.* The problem of finding the value *now* of £100 actually, and certainly, to be received in two years' time is straightforward. The present value of £100 in a year's time is £100 $(1 + r)^{-1}$ and the present value of £$[100/(1 + r)]$ itself received only after another year would be £$[100/(1 + r)] \times 1/(1 + r)$ or £$100/(1 + r)^2$. Naturally enough, each year that we have to wait for the money involves another year's discounting, so that the formula for £100 to be received in n years' time is:

$$P = \frac{100}{(1 + r)^n},$$

where P is the present value.

2. Present value. Readers meeting this idea for the first time may find it somewhat elusive, but if present value is first thought of in very practical terms there should be no real difficulty. Future money can be exchanged for present money, in actual fact, by borrowing. The rate of interest paid equates present and future values. A borrower sacrifices a larger sum of future money for a smaller sum of present money. The future sum can be brought down to its present value by discounting.

ANNUITIES

3. Definition. A series of annual cash flows of constant amount is known as an annuity. To find the present value of a series of cash flows, each annual amount must be discounted according to the number of years it is away in the future. Thus, if the first sum is to be received next year, it will have to be discounted for one year only and must be divided by $(1 + r)$, whereas the second amount will be divided by $(1 + r)^2$ and so on.

4. The present value of an annuity. Using the symbol P for the present value and applying the methods of the previous paragraph, we have:

$$P = \frac{A}{(1 + r)} + \frac{A}{(1 + r)^2} + \frac{A}{(1 + r)^3} + \cdots + \frac{A}{(1 + r)^n},$$

supposing that the annuity is to continue for n years. Recalling what we have learned about geometric progressions, we can see that each term is the previous term multiplied by $1/(1 + r)$. In the terminology of Chapter V we can say that $1/(1 + r)$ is the common ratio. Giving the common ratio the symbol R to distinguish it from our annual rate (r), the sum of a geometrical progression is found by:

$$(\textit{First term}) \times \left[\frac{(1 - R^n)}{(1 - R)}\right].$$

Our first term is $A/(1 + r)$ and $R = 1/(1 + r)$. The present value of the annuity of £A per annum for n years is therefore:

$$P = \frac{A}{(1 + r)}\left[\frac{1 - \left(\frac{1}{1 + r}\right)^n}{1 - \frac{1}{(1 + r)}}\right].$$

This can be written as:

$$P = \frac{A}{1+r}\left[\frac{1-(1+r)^{-n}}{r/(1+r)}\right]$$

or:

$$P = A\left[\frac{1-(1+r)^{-n}}{r}\right]$$

5. Use of tables. Although values of the expression in the square brackets could be found by ordinary arithmetical methods, it is more convenient to use discount tables. These normally show a range of percentages along the top of the table and the number of years for which the annuity is to run down the side. The conventional symbol used in such tables is:

$$a_{n/r} = \frac{1-(1+r)^{-n}}{r}$$

to indicate that the values (a) are tabulated against n and r. The value tabulated is for one unit and must, of course, be multiplied by the annual sum to be received.

EXAMPLE: An investment will yield £1000 per annum for eight years. If finance can be obtained at 7 per cent per annum and the investment costs £5000, is it worth undertaking?

$A = £1000$ From tables $a_{n/r} = 5{\cdot}9713$

$r = 0{\cdot}07$

$n = 8$

$$P = A\left[\frac{1-(1+r)^{-n}}{r}\right]$$

$$= £1000\left[\frac{1-(1{\cdot}07)^{-8}}{0{\cdot}07}\right]$$

$$= £(1000 \times 5{\cdot}9713)$$

$$= \underline{£5917{\cdot}3}$$

Since the investment's actual cost is £5000 and the present value of the cash flow series is £5917·30, the investment should be made.

6. Risk and tax. In computing the present value in the example, all questions of risk and tax have been ignored. This book is primarily concerned with the mathematical methods used, but readers will be sufficiently alert to realise that the certainty of the cash flow and the tax which may have to be paid must be taken into account when actual decisions are made.

7. Perpetual annuities. The present value formula:

$$P = A\left[\frac{1-(1+r)^{-n}}{r}\right]$$

gives the value of a series of cash flows for n years. If the annuity is to continue for so long that we cannot see its end, we can regard the flow as a perpetual annuity and can let n tend to infinity. The term $(1+r)^{-n}$ is equivalent to $[1/(1+r)]^n$ and, since $1/(1+r)$ is less than unity, this will tend to zero as n tends to infinity. The present value of the series as n tends to infinity is therefore:

$$P = A\left[\frac{1-0}{r}\right].$$

$$= \frac{A}{r}$$

SINKING FUNDS

8. Terminal value. Another problem which can be handled by very similar methods is that of the terminal value of a series of amounts invested year by year. At the end of each year a sum of money is available for investment, this sum being the same every year. Naturally, the first amount put by for investment earns more interest than sums invested later on. If the whole process lasts for n years and the constant annual sum becoming available at the end of each year is £A, then the first investment will have been earning for $(n-1)$ years by the end of the period. The value of this £A will be £$A(1+r)^{n-1}$ when the n years have elapsed, bearing in mind that the investment was not made until the end of the first year. Each successive amount will have one year less than its predecessor in which to earn interest and the last £A will not be invested at all, but will only become available right at the end of the period. The *terminal value* (S) of the series will be:

$$S = A(1 + r)^{n-1} + A(1 + r)^{n-2} + \ldots + A(1 + r) + A.$$

This is a G.P. with a common ratio of $(1 + r)^{-1}$ and an initial term $A(1 + r)^{n-1}$. The sum to n terms gives the total value of the amounts invested plus the interest earned.

This would be:

$$S = A(1 + r)^{n-1}\left[\frac{1 - (1 + r)^{-n}}{1 - (1 + r)^{-1}}\right],$$

which equals:

$$S = A(1 + r)^{n-1}\left[\frac{1 - (1 + r)^{-n}}{r/(1 + r)}\right],$$

which, when tidied up, gives:

$$S = A(1 + r)^{n}\left[\frac{1 - (1 + r)^{-n}}{r}\right]$$

or

$$S = A\left[\frac{(1 + r)^{n} - 1}{r}\right].$$

9. Tables for sinking fund calculations. The expression $\frac{(1 + r)^{n} - 1}{r}$ is tabulated in much the same way as are the annuity present values. Conventionally the symbol used is $S_{n/r}$, S standing for "sinking fund" just as a stood for "annuity" and the tabulated values being based on a unit investment.

10. Using the sinking-fund formula. The sinking-fund problem usually arises when it is necessary to put aside a sum each year in order to provide for the replacement of equipment at some future date. Since the sums put aside can be invested and will earn interest, the total of the sums themselves can be less than the amount required for the replacement. The formula derived above will give the total of sums and investment and can be adapted to solve the complementary problem of what annual sum to invest in order to produce a given total sum in a given number of years.

EXAMPLE 1: A firm intends to invest £150 at the end of each year and to receive interest on the amounts invested at 5 per cent per annum. What sum of money will be available at the end of the fifth year?

$$r = 0{\cdot}05; \quad A = £150; \quad n = 5$$

$$S_{n/r} = 5{\cdot}5256$$

$$\begin{aligned} S &= A\left[\frac{(1+r)^n - 1}{r}\right] \\ &= AS_{n/r} \\ &= £150 \times 5{\cdot}5256 \\ &= \underline{£828{\cdot}84.} \end{aligned}$$

EXAMPLE 2: A firm needs to provide £5000 in six years' time and can invest at 5 per cent per annum. How much should be set aside at the end of each year?

The sum at the end of six years is known and is the S in the formula. We therefore have the following data:

$$S = £5000; \; r = 0{\cdot}05; \; n = 6; \text{ and, from tables, } S_{n/r} = 6{\cdot}8019$$

$$S = A\left[\frac{(1+r)^n - 1}{r}\right]$$

$$\therefore \; S = AS_{n/r}$$

or

$$5000 = A \times 6{\cdot}8019,$$

giving

$$A = \frac{5000}{6{\cdot}8019}.$$

Using conventional arithmetic methods we calculate:

$$A = \underline{£735{\cdot}089,}$$

Just over £735 must be invested at the end of each year to produce the required £5000.

YIELDS ON INVESTMENTS

11. Rate of return. The true rate of return on an investment is the discount rate which will just bring the present value of a series of cash flows down to the actual cost of the investment.

When the investment concerned is the purchase of a security, this rate is often known as the *yield rate.* The general method of calculating such yields is outlined in XVII, 6. The cash flows should be those forecast for future years and, strictly, should be net of tax. If the returns arise from investment in the shares of a company, some allowance should be made for the expected future growth of the dividend per share purchased. While the detail is not pursued here, it could easily be shown that the yield on the shares (r) is:

$$r = \frac{R_0}{V_0} + g$$

where R_0 is the initial net-of-tax return in the first year, V_0 is the purchase price and g is the estimated rate of growth of the dividends. If the investor merely wished to make a short-term comparison between alternative investments, he might choose to consider only the first term (R_0/V_0), the *dividend yield.*

12. Redemption yield. In many cases, the investment considered is a fixed interest security, the nominal value of which is to be refunded at some definite future time. The return then consists of a series of constant cash flows at regular intervals (each year or half-year, usually) plus the final refund of the nominal sum invested. Since the security is likely to have been purchased at less than its face value, the nominal rate of return on the security will not be the true rate. The calculation of the yield to redemption, which must relate the capital gain at the end of the period to an equivalent annual (or period) return, reinvested to give the final redemption value, is not easy—particularly as the reinvestment element represents a gradually increasing amount of capital tied up in the investment. This, in turn, affects the calculation of the redemption yield, since the greater the capital tied up, the lower will be the rate of return.

Without following all the stages of this complex argument, the formula which gives the best approximation to the redemption yield is

$$r = \frac{R}{V_0} + \frac{\frac{1}{2}(V_n - V_0)}{V_0 \times S_{n/r}}$$

where V_0 represents the purchase price (or initial value), V_n is the value at redemption and $S_{n/r}$ is the sinking fund formula developed in **8–10** above. R is the annual (or regular) interest payment and r, on the left-hand side of the formula, is the best estimate of the eventual redemption yield, obtained either without calculation or from a more primitive formula such as

$$r = \frac{nR + (V_n - V_0).}{\frac{n}{2}(V_0 + V_n)}$$

EXAMPLE: A £100 debenture, redeemable at face value in ten years' time, gives interest at 6 per cent per annum. What is the true yield rate if the debenture is purchased for £85?

$$r = \left[\frac{6}{85} + \frac{\frac{1}{2}(100 - 85)}{85 \times S_{n/r}}\right].$$

The best "guestimate" of the yield is taken to be 6½ per cent, giving $S_{10/6\frac{1}{2}} = 13{\cdot}5$ (approximately).

This calculation gives:

$$r = \frac{6 + \frac{15}{27}}{85}$$

$$= \underline{7{\cdot}7 \text{ per cent.}}$$

It may be verified by experiment that the calculation is fairly stable in its results even if the estimate of r in $S_{n/r}$, is not a good one. The second formula could be used as a first-stage calculation if desired.

PROGRESS TEST 16

1.* State the formula for the present value of an annuity and derive it from first principles. (4)

2. Calculate the present values of the following annuities. (5)

	Rate per cent	*Annual flow starting after one year*	*Number of years*
(*a*)	5	£1000	10
(*b*)	4	£800	7
(*c*)	8	£1500	5

3. Replacement of a machine is expected to cost £2500; what sum must be set aside at the end of each year and invested at 5 per cent per annum to provide the necessary sum after 5 years? (8–10)

CHAPTER XVII

THE EVALUATION OF CAPITAL INVESTMENT PROJECTS

METHODS OF APPRAISING INVESTMENT PROJECTS

1. Rule-of-thumb techniques. Decisions to invest in capital equipment are among the most important that the managers of a business ever make. Not only do they tie up large sums of money, they also determine to a large extent the firm's future profitability and probably the productive techniques that the firm will be using for years ahead as well. Yet the methods that many, or even most, businesses use in the evaluation of capital investment projects are primitive and misleading. Two examples of such methods are the "pay-back period" method and the "average rate of return on capital" method. These are examined in **2** and **3** below.

2. Pay-back period. This method of comparing alternative investment projects consists of calculating for each project the period in which the profits earned will just have paid back the original capital outlay. If the competing projects are exactly comparable in other ways, the one with the shortest pay-back period will be chosen. In previous chapters we have discussed the time-value of money, and the pay-back method does take this into account to some extent by giving preference to capital investment projects with shorter pay-back periods. The method is unsatisfactory, however, because it takes no account of returns after the pay-back period has ended.

3. Annual rate-of-return methods. While it seems very sensible to choose between competing projects by comparing the annual rate of return on the capital invested, it is very difficult to express, as a single figure, the varying returns that may be expected over the life of the project. An even more basic fault in this method is that it ignores the time-value of the successive annual returns. Further objections lie in the possible ambiguities inherent in calculating annual profits, since alternative methods of depreciation can give quite different results, in the failure to take account of the length of the productive life of the investment and, in many cases, in the failure to take investment grants, investment allowances and other recoveries from the Government into account.

4. Discounting methods. The method of discounting future sums to give present values was explored in the previous chapter. This gives a relatively simple way of taking the time-value of money into account and of comparing projects over the whole of their productive lives, even though the returns from the projects are not constant from year to year. By comparing the discounted present value of the flow of returns with the outlay, allowing for Government grants or other payments, it is possible to construct a measure which can be used as a basis for comparison and which meets the objections raised against the other methods discussed. It is suggested that the appropriate measure of the returns from a capital project is not the "profit," which is necessarily a somewhat hypothetical concept, but the actual *cash flow*. This cash flow should be the actual cash return expected, less the cash expenses directly attributable to the project and less taxation. Two methods of calculating and using the discounted net cash flow from a project are discussed below.

DISCOUNTED CASH FLOW

5. Effects of taxation. In this section we are really concerned only with the application of discounting techniques in the special set of circumstances involved in constructing some simple measures for the appraisal of capital investment projects. This practical use requires a considerable familiarity with company taxation and current investment incentives. Such matters are beyond the scope of this book and in any case are liable to change from time to time. Readers are therefore referred to specialist works, such as those mentioned in Appendix I of this book, for detailed guidance in this field. The treatment of taxation and investment incentives as outlined below merely indicates the approach to be followed in order to take these factors into account in the calculations.

6. Yield method. The method requires, essentially, the calculation of a discount rate that will just bring the present value of the net cash flow down to the actual net cash outlay. In any one year the discounted net cash flow will be:

$$(\textit{Net cash flow for year}) \times \frac{1}{(1+r)^n},$$

where r is the discount rate and n is the number of years that expected flow lies in the future. Of course, a similar calculation will have to be carried out for each year and a value of r found that would make the cost of the project (C) just equal to the sum of the discounted cash flows. Writing the value of each year's cash flow as a_t, where the subscript denotes the number of years since the original outlay, the situation is given by the equation:

$$C = \frac{a_1}{1+r} + \frac{a_2}{(1+r)^2} + \ldots + \frac{a_n}{(1+r)^n}$$

or

$$C = a_1(1+r)^{-1} + a_2(1+r)^{-2} + \ldots + a_n(1+r)^{-n}.$$

7. Method of calculation. The problem is to find the discount rate, that is the value of r, which would bring about this equality. Fortunately tables of values of $(1+r)^{-n}$ are available giving the "discount factor" for various percentage rates and for a range of years. A miniature version of such a table is given in Appendix II. Our method of finding the appropriate discount rate is to set up a schedule showing the net cash in-flows year by year, this inflow being calculated by:

(*a*) taking the profit due to the investment, *before* depreciation;
(*b*) deducting corporation tax on the previous year's profit at the rate in force;
(*c*) adding back any tax savings due to investment allowances, etc.; and
(*d*) adding back any scrap values recovered in the year.

A similar schedule is set up for cash outflows, giving a year-by-year breakdown of expenditure on the project. These must be *net* outflows with investment grants, etc., deducted.

Both inflows and outflows must be "netted back" to the starting year by discounting at an appropriate rate. This is done by trial and error, using discount factors derived from likely rates and choosing a rate which just brings the discounted inflows into equality with the discounted outflows.

8. An example.

SCHEDULE OF CASH OUTFLOWS

Year	*Net outflow*	*Discount rate: 7%*		*Discount rate: 10%*		*Discount rate: 12%*	
		Factor	*Resultant*	*Factor*	*Resultant*	*Factor*	*Resultant*
0	£1000	—	1000	—	1000	—	1000
1	£250	0·9346	233·6	0·9091	227·3	0·8929	223·2
2	£20	0·8734	17·5	0·8264	16·5	0·7972	16·0
3	£10	0·8163	8·2	0·7513	7·5	0·7118	7·1
4	£10	0·7629	7·6	0·6830	6·8	0·6355	6·4
5	£40	0·7130	28·5	0·6209	24·8	0·5674	22·7
Totals	£1330	/	£1295·4	/	£1282·9	/	£1275·4

SCHEDULE OF CASH INFLOWS

Year	*Net cash inflow*	*Discount rate: 7%*		*Discount rate: 10%*		*Discount rate: 12%*	
		Factor	*Resultant*	*Factor*	*Resultant*	*Factor*	*Resultant*
0	—	—	—	—	—	—	—
1	£120	0·9346	112·3	0·9091	109·1	0·8929	106·8
2	£300	0·8734	262·0	0·8264	247·9	0·7972	239·1
3	£500	0·8163	408·2	0·7513	375·6	0·7118	355·9
4	£500	0·7629	381·5	0·6830	341·5	0·6335	316·8
5	£250	0·7130	178·2	0·6209	155·2	0·5674	141·8
Totals	£1670	/	1342·2	/	1229·3	/	1160·4

Comparison of net cash inflows with net cash outflows shows that a discount rate of 7 per cent is not sufficient to bring the discounted inflow down to the discounted outflow. However, a discount rate of 10 per cent is too great, since it reduces the net cash inflow to £1229·3 as against a discounted net cash outflow of £1282·9.

9. Linear interpolation. Since the 7 per cent rate is too low and the 10 per cent rate is too high, it is necessary to find the rate between the two which will just bring the inflows and outflows to equality. When discounted inflows and outflows are equal, the ratio of inflows to outflows will be unity. At 7 per cent this ratio is 1342/1295 or 1·04 and at 10 per cent the ratio is 1229/1283 or 0·96, both correct to two places of decimals. To give a ratio of 1 we need four of the second places of decimals. The interpolation calculation is, therefore:

7 per cent ratio	1·04	7 per cent ratio	1·04
10 per cent ratio	0·96	Required ratio	1·00
Difference	0·08	*Difference*	0·04

Difference between the discount rates is 3 per cent; therefore the required rate is:

$$7 + \left(\frac{0{\cdot}04}{0{\cdot}08} \times 3\right) = 8\tfrac{1}{2} \text{ per cent.}$$

There is an element of approximation here and the true rate that would bring the flows to equality is just a little higher, but any increased accuracy in calculation would be meaningless since the cash inflows, particularly, are estimates of future yields. In practice, there would also be a degree of approximation in calculating the capital cost of a project.

10. Interpretation of result. We could regard this result as indicating that the returns from the capital investment project would be sufficient to pay back the original outlay and still earn 8½ per cent per annum. If the firm is able to obtain capital at 7 per cent per annum, the project will be worth carrying out.

11. The present value method. If the projects under discussion are mutually exclusive, so that if one is taken up the other is ruled out, the actual magnitude of the excess of net cash inflows over outflows is important as well as the rate of return earned. The correct method of evaluating competing projects of this sort is to agree to some rate that *must* be earned and then to find the *net present value* when the cash flows are discounted at that rate. The chosen rate would be either the cost of obtaining capital or the rate that could be earned on the most profitable outside alternative investment.

12. A basic inequality. If C is used to represent the initial capital cost, a_i represents the cash flow in year i and r is the chosen discount rate, we can write:

$$C < a_1(1 + r)^{-1} + a_2(1 + r)^{-2} + \ldots a_n(1 + r)^{-n}.$$

Letting S be the sum of the discounted cash inflows from year 1 to year n, C must be less than S if the project is worth considering at all. If $C < S$, then we can write $S - C = v$, where v is the net present value of the project. The sum S is the maximum amount that should be paid out for the investment if finance is to cost $100r$ per cent per annum; anything over this represents a gain which can be compared as between alternative projects.

13. An example. A firm may buy either of two machines to make a metal part which is sold to a major motor manufacturer. The cost of the machines and the estimated cash flows (net) are tabulated below. Which machine should be purchased?

Within the limits of accuracy of the expected returns, both machines would cover the cost of finance at 7 per cent per annum, but the NPV of Machine 1 is more than that of Machine 2. Although it costs more it still gives a return in Year 5 and this is worth while. Machine 1 is a better investment. Note that it is assumed in this example that the costs are all incurred at the beginning of the project.

COMPARISONS OF TWO MACHINES, COSTS AND CASH FLOWS

Year	*Cost (£'s)*	*Net cash flow (£'s)*				
	0	1	2	3	4	5
Machine 1	10,000	1000	2000	5000	5000	1000
Machine 2	8000	1500	2000	6000	1000	—

Flows are to be discounted at 7 per cent per annum.

Year	*Machine 1*			*Machine 2*		
	Cash flow	*Discount factor*	*Resultant*	*Cash flow*	*Discount factor*	*Resultant*
1	1000	0·9346	934·6	1500	0·9346	1401·9
2	2000	0·8734	1746·8	2000	0·8734	1746·8
3	5000	0·8163	4081·5	6000	0·8163	4897·8
4	5000	0·7629	3814·5	1000	0·7629	762·9
5	1000	0·7130	713·0	—	0·7130	—
Totals:	14,000	/	11,290·4	£10,500	/	8809·4
		Less cost	10,000·0		*Less* cost	8000·0
Net present value			£1,290·4			£809·4

RISK AND THE EVALUATION OF INVESTMENT PROJECTS

14. Allowing for uncertainty. As has been said before in other sections of this book, forecasting any future event is a chancy and uncertain business, but management is constantly called upon to do just this. In many cases there will be a considerable degree of uncertainty attaching to each of the estimated cash flows and, if the uncertainty is judged to be significant, some attempt should be made to allow for it. The most crude way, but one that is often resorted to, is to require a greater NPV or a greater rate of return than would ordinarily be the case. Sometimes this may be the only practicable way, but there is a danger of ruling out quite viable projects on purely subjective grounds.

15. Using mathematical probability. Mathematical expectation, it will be recalled (*see* Test 12), is the anticipated return multiplied by the probability of achieving it. If the factors which produce the cash flow, that is the sales levels, costs and so on, are considered in detail, a number of possible alternative combinations of events are possible. Each of these alternatives can be weighted by the probability of its occurrence and the single estimate of a cash flow replaced by a weighted average of the possible cash flows. Alternatively, the most probable figure could be used.

In the case of investment projects which are of major importance to the firm's future, an even more careful analysis should be made and the probabilities of the net present value of each competing project falling within the various possible or feasible ranges should be calculated and considered.

16. The role of management. It cannot be too strongly stressed that, when all the calculations have been carried out and every effort has been made to highlight the factors involved, the final choice is still one to be made by the senior managers concerned. Because of the uncertainty of future events and because of the subjective factor in investment decisions, no method can relieve management of the necessity and responsibility for the final choice.

PROGRESS TEST 17

1.* (*a*) What advantages have D.C.F. and similar methods of evaluating capital investment projects over traditional methods? (1–4)

(*b*) Distinguish between yield and present-value methods of evaluating capital investment projects. (6, 11, 12)

2. A machine can be purchased for £5000 and thereafter produces the following cash inflows and requires maintenance which gives rise to the listed series of cash outflows (Year 1 and onwards).

COSTS AND OUTFLOWS

Year	*Costs* (£)	*Cash inflows* (£)
0	5000	—
1	50	1000
2	50	1200
3	75	1500
4	150	800
5	200	800
6	150	600

Assuming that the inflows and outflows occur at the beginning of the listed years and that six years after its original purchase the machine is sold for £500, calculate the D.C.F. rate of return on the investment. (7–10)

3. Two alternative machines are being considered for purchase, one at a cost of £10,000 and the other at a cost of £9000. The cash

flows resulting from their operation over their expected lives have been calculated and are as follows:

NET CASH FLOWS AT YEAR END

Year	*Cash flow* (*Machine* 1)	*Cash flow* (*Machine* 2)
	£	£
1	1000	1200
2	1600	1500
3	2500	3500
4	2500	2000
5	2500	2000
6	1500	1000
7	1000	—

The listed cash flows do not include salvage values at the end of the machines' useful lives of £1500 and £1000 respectively. Which machine would you recommend for purchase? (**13**)

PART FOUR

MATHEMATICS AND DECISION-MAKING

CHAPTER XVIII

UNCERTAINTY AND BUSINESS DECISIONS

APPROACHES TO DECISION-MAKING

1. Decisions and the future. It is too seldom recognised that *all* decisions are concerned with future events and that these events can never be fully anticipated. In the strictest sense, the future does not exist and is necessarily unknown. In making business decisions, whether they concern the affairs of a multinational company or a "corner shop," the decision-maker is confronted with a trading situation which involves uncertainty. Estimates may be made of the future demand for a company's products, but changes in the public taste or the appearance of a rival producer may bring about a totally different situation. Similarly, on the production side, rises in the prices of raw materials or labour troubles or many other quite unforeseeable events may invalidate the most careful estimates of future costs. In more purely commercial activities, too, decisions concern future conditions. A decision to invest in the stock of a particular company, to grant a loan to an individual or to buy or sell commodities would all be cases in point. We now consider the contribution which mathematics can make to effective decision-making under uncertainty.

2. The structure of business decisions. All decisions, including business decisions, involve selection from a set of alternative courses of action. Each course of action, if selected, will actually be carried out in some future "state of the world" and the outcome of the course of action will depend on which of the many "futures" is the one which actually occurs. In most business situations each outcome will give rise to a profit or loss and it is comparison of these expected gains or losses, under the various possible future states of the world, which will determine which course of action is selected. In tabular form, the situation could be shown as follows:

		States of the World		
		W_1	$W_2 \ldots$	W_n
	A_1	C_{11}	$C_{12} \ldots$	C_{1n}
	A_2	C_{21}	$C_{22} \ldots$	C_{2n}
Actions	.	.	.	.
	.	.	.	.
	.	.	.	.
	A_m	C_{m1}	$C_{m2} \ldots$	C_{mn}

This will be recognised from earlier chapters as a *matrix* of outcomes or consequences (C_{ij}). Even if the values associated with each outcome are known, it is still necessary to know the probability of each relevant "state of the world" before an evaluation can be made.

3. Decision trees. The structure of the decision can be shown more clearly by means of a *decision tree*. Suppose that we have a situation in which there are two courses of action, A_1 and A_2, and two relevant states of the world, W_1 and W_2. With a little thought it can be seen that there are four possible outcomes. A matrix such as that used in 2 would have four outcome elements, C_{11}, C_{12}, C_{21}, C_{22}. Substituting a tree-diagram (recall XI, 10 and XI, 12) for the matrix convention, the structure of the decision under uncertainty is shown in Fig. 35(*a*). The convention used here is that the "box" □ shows an alternative course of action and the "circle" ○ indicates an "event fork." At the end of each final branch is the

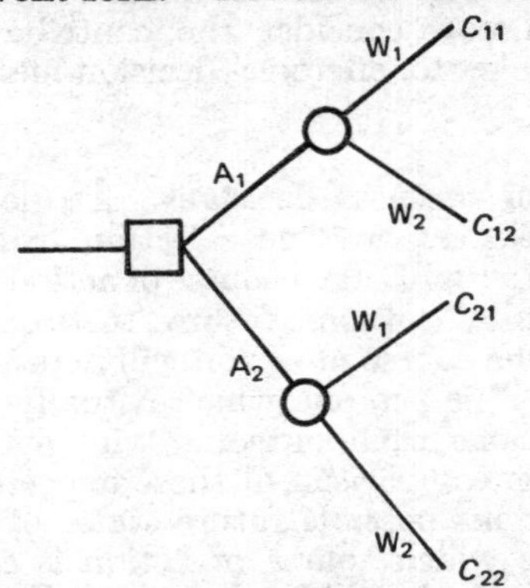

FIG. 35(*a*).—*Decision under uncertainty*

outcome corresponding to a course of action in conjunction with a particular state of the world, that is with a particular future situation. Clearly if we knew the probabilities associated with each state of the world, we could evaluate the alternative courses of action.

4. Decisions under certainty. If decisions are so much concerned with future and unknown states of the world, it might be wondered why business men ever use non-probabilistic methods. One reason is that it is enormously difficult to assign probabilities to future events. Another is that many decision-makers find it much more natural to work with exact quantities even when they know that the outcomes of their decisions are uncertain. Much business information is derived from the accounting system and many forecasts must be embodied in budgets. In neither case is it easy to allow for uncertainty or to conduct discussions in probabilistic terms. A further reason may be that business men are often, necessarily, risk-takers. It is then more natural to hazard a guess at likely future conditions and then to evaluate alternative

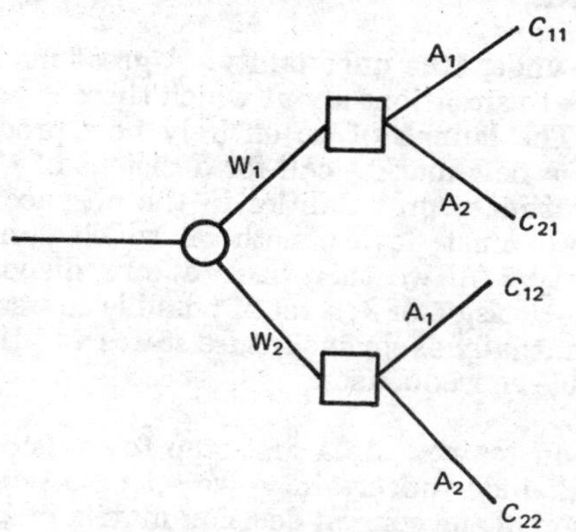

FIG. 35(*b*).—*Decision under certainty*

courses of action *as if* the chosen state of the world, and all the information relating to it, were certain. The decision then has the form shown in Fig. 35(*b*). If W_1 is forecast, W_2 is ignored. (Note here the slightly different use of the event circle.) Linear programming, among other techniques, is often applied as if certainty existed, although variants such as *stochastic programming* do embody probabilistic elements.

DECISIONS UNDER TRUE UNCERTAINTY

5. Risk and uncertainty. In ordinary speech, and in some parts of this book, the terms "risk" and "uncertainty" are used in ways which, although quite proper, lack precision. In the sections which follow, however, the term *risk* is reserved for situations about which there is a statistical history of past occurrence. It would be possible to obtain insurance against such risks. With the term risk reserved for insurable (or potentially so) situations, *uncertainty* becomes the appropriate word to be used when there is a complete lack of information about the likelihood of the occurrence under discussion. In this strict sense, then, we are prevented under such conditions from using probability. Many people find that this scheme, although logical, is too restrictive and so use the term *quasi-risk* to refer to situations for which there are no statistical data and yet in which it would be useful to apply familiar probabilistic methods.

6. Decisions under true uncertainty. A great many business decisions relate to situations about which there is no statistical information. The launch of an entirely new product or the penetration of a new market call for decisions of this sort. If we refuse to estimate probabilities in the absence of definite information, we must devise methods which can deal with true uncertainty. All we then have at our disposal are the elements of the decision of **2**: a set of possible courses of action, a number of mutually exclusive future states and the resulting array of possible consequences.

7. The pay-off matrix. As a first step towards dealing with decisions made under uncertainty, we set up a *pay-off matrix.* This is a version of the general decision matrix of **2** adapted to show the possible outcomes of a particular decision. An example is shown in Table 10, where the situation represented is that of a company facing union negotiators across the bargaining table at the beginning of a pay round. The circumstances envisaged are that prices are rising, that the Government has just initiated an incomes policy but that it is not known whether the policy will be effective (W_1) or only partially effective (W_2). It is possible that, if the negotiations are prolonged, the incomes policy could be abandoned (W_3) before they are completed. These three possibilities form the alternative "negotiating climates" with which the company may be faced and which it is unable to affect. The company must choose whether to adopt a "tough" bargaining strategy (A_1) or a "pliant" one (A_2). The choice of strategy will determine the selection of the company's negotiating team and, once this has been done, it will not be possible to reverse the company's strategy. Each outcome will have a different net effect on the company's profits for the coming year and it is the estimates of these changes, in £ thousands, which have been entered in Table 10.

8. Evaluation of the matrix elements. One advantage of setting up the pay-off matrix is that it is necessary to make a careful evaluation of the consequences of each possible course of action in each future situation that could occur. In the case outlined, the important factors are the increase in the wage bill resulting from the negotiations, the estimated permitted rise in the prices of the company's products over the period, any productivity increases expected and any costs associated with industrial action arising from the strategy followed. It has been assumed that in three cases, readily identifiable from the matrix, price rises in excess of wage costs and productivity increases will secure increases in profit, but that an incomes policy which is only partially effective will lead to reduced profits, particularly if a tough strategy leading to industrial action is followed. Should the government abandon its income policy before the negotiations are completed, it is expected that a tough negotiating stance will lead to a more modest eventual settlement, since there will be no bargaining "norm," and to higher profits. Attempts to be conciliatory in the absence of an incomes policy, however, will lead to increased settlements and to reduced profits.

The validity of these evaluations depends entirely on the correctness of the assumptions underlying them, of course.

9. Decision criteria. Selecting the best course of action depends on the criterion applied by the decision-makers. Even assuming that they wish to maximise profit (or minimise loss), the criterion used will depend on the attitude of the decision-makers and their degree of optimism or pessimism. If, for instance, their attitude were one of great optimism and disregard of risk, they would select strategy A_1, the tough line, since that *might* lead to a gain of £21,000. Such a choice would be based on a *maximax* criterion.

10. Maximax and Maximin. In addition to the elements of the pay-off matrix, Table 10 has marginal columns showing the maximum and minimum "gains" from each strategy. The entry 21 is the largest element in the *Max* column. The strategy A_1 is the one which has the maximum of the maximum outcomes: it is the *maximax* choice. An alternative criterion would be more conservative. Each strategy is examined to find the least advantageous outcome as listed in the *Min* column of the table. The strategy having the greatest of these minimum results would be the one which offered the least disadvantageous outcome even in the most disadvantageous circumstances. By this *maximin* criterion, strategy A_2, the pliant approach, would be chosen with a maximum profit reduction of £6000.

TABLE 10.—THE PAY-OFF MATRIX

£s thousand

Strategy	*Policy situation* *Effective* (W_1)	*Not effective* (W_2)	*Abandoned* (W_3)	*Max*	*Min*	*Average*
Tough (A_1)	20	−20	21	21	−20	7
Pliant (A_2)	19	−4	−6	19	−6	3

11. Regret. If an incorrect choice is made, the decision-maker will experience regret that the most advantageous strategy was not selected. Should the pliant strategy (A_2) be selected and the incomes policy prove to be effective (state W_1), a sacrifice of profit of £1000 would be made. The potential regret associated with A_2 and W_1 is measured by this sacrifice. The regret associated with A_1 and W_1 is zero, since the tough strategy would be the best one in the circumstances. For each cell of the pay-off matrix, a regret entry could be calculated and a new matrix formed. Designating the elements of this *regret matrix* as R_{ij}, it can be seen that R_{11} is equal to zero, R_{21} is equal to 1 (£1000) and so on.

12. Minimax regret. For each policy situation column there will be one zero and one non-zero entry in a two-row regret matrix. The full regret matrix is shown, together with the maximum regret for each strategy, in Table 11. To minimise the maximum regret, we must select strategy A_1, the tough approach, since the maximum regret is limited to 16 (£16,000), whereas A_2 could lead to a regret of £27,000.

TABLE 11.—THE REGRET MATRIX

£s thousand

Strategy	*Policy situation* W_1	W_2	W_3	*Maximum regret*
A_1	0	16	0	16
A_2	1	0	27	27

13. Average outcome values. While a maximax criterion would seem, to many decision-makers, to require an excessively optimistic attitude towards the future, the maximin approach would seem too conservative. A reasonable compromise would be to calculate the average of all the possible outcomes and to select the strategy for which this was greatest. Inspection of Table 10 shows this to be strategy A_1.

An objection to this method, which is often called selection by Bayes' criterion, is that it is equivalent to assuming that each relevant state of the world is equally probable. This conflicts with the idea that under true uncertainty, probabilities are quite unknown.

14. The Hurwicz criterion. An alternative way of evaluating the various courses of action, without taking either an extremely optimistic position or an equally pessimistic one, would be to take a weighted average of the maximum and minimum outcomes. The weighting applied would be chosen by the decision-maker according to the degree of optimism experienced. A decision-maker feeling moderately optimistic about the future course of events might apply a weighting of 0·8 to the greatest outcome and 0·2 to the minimum. The results of the calculation, based on the figures given in Table 10, are

$$A_1: (0{\cdot}8 \times 21) + (0{\cdot}2 \times -20) = 12{\cdot}8$$
$$A_2: (0{\cdot}8 \times 19) + (0{\cdot}2 \times \;\; -6) = 14{\cdot}0.$$

On a moderately optimistic view, the pliant (A_2) strategy should be chosen.

It will be noticed that this criterion, which is due to L. Hurwicz, makes it very clear that selection of a strategy depends both on the calculations of the gains and losses in each situation and on the attitudes of the decision-makers. There is no one absolutely correct way of evaluating decisions under uncertainty.

CONFLICT AND THE THEORY OF GAMES

15. Conflict and competition. Often the uncertainty in a business situation is due not so much to general conditions as to the way in which rivals and opponents may react to our decisions. In circumstances like these the choice of a strategy must be determined not only by the decision-maker's view of his best advantage but by the actions, or anticipated actions, of a competitor or opponent. Situations of this sort are not easy to handle mathematically, but some special problems can be solved by a technique which is allied to linear programming (*see* Chapters XXII and XXIII). The methods appropriate to these competitive situations form the *theory of games.*

16. The essentials of a game. We shall suppose that there are two opponents, or players, and that a number of courses of action are open to each of them. As before, we shall call these alternative *strategies* and associated with each strategy are a series of "pay-offs." These pay-offs are now seen to vary according to the strategy chosen by the player's opponent. The players are assumed to be rather conservative by nature, so that they play safe and never take an excessive risk even though the rewards might be great. Their policy is to *minimise the maximum possible loss.* This is sometimes called a *minimax* strategy.

17. The game matrix. The game matrix for a competitive situation is shown in Table 12, bordered by maximum and minimum values. The quantities gained or lost are looked at from the point of view of one of the players rather than from a neutral point of view. Thus, positive entries in the matrix represent gains to player A and negative entries gains to B. In the games which we shall consider, A's losses are B's gains and vice-versa. A game of this sort with two players is known as a *two-person zero-sum game*, the sum of gains and losses being zero. In the matrix in Table 12 the pay-offs for A's strategies (A_1 and A_2) are shown in the rows and those for B's are shown in the columns.

TABLE 12.—THE GAME MATRIX

Strategies	B_1	B_2	*Row minima*
A_1	−1	3	−1
A_2	−3	2	−3
Col. max.	−1	3	/

18. The solution of the game. Player A will try to minimise his greatest loss. He can only do this by choosing between Strategy A_1 and Strategy A_2. The biggest loss that can befall him if he chooses A_1 is −1, which occurs when B chooses Strategy B_1. If A chooses Strategy A_2, his greatest loss will be −3, again occurring when player B chooses Strategy B_1. In order to minimise his losses, player A will choose Strategy A_1, thus limiting his greatest loss to −1.

Player B's losses are represented by the positive values, since we are looking at the game from A's point of view. If B plays Strategy B_1, his greatest "loss" is a gain of 1; if he plays B_2 his greatest loss is a real loss of 3. He will therefore play B_1. It is noteworthy that in this case there is a single result that satisfies both players. If player A *always* chooses A_1 and player B always chooses B_1, the result will be the best that either of them can achieve. When a solution of this sort is possible, there is said to be a "*saddle point*."

19. The method of solution. To find A's losses, enter the minimum value at the right-hand side of each row. Since B's losses are positive figures, write the maximum of the columns at the bottom of each one. To find the least loss we must select the greatest of the row minima, remembering that -3 is less than -1. To find the least loss for B, we must select the least of the column maxima. The selected values are in bold type. If the least of the column maxima is equal to the greatest of the row minima, a saddle point exists.

20. Pure and mixed strategies. In a game such as that just discussed, there is no problem about which strategy to choose; the same strategy must be used all the time. A situation like this is said to require a *pure strategy*. When first one strategy and then another must be chosen, the overall strategy is said to be a "mixed" one.

21. Dominance. When one pure strategy is at least as favourable as another in all respects and is clearly better for one of the possible choices, the first strategy is said to *dominate* the second. From B's point of view, B_1 dominates B_2 and he would be foolish ever to use his second strategy.

THE THEORY OF GAMES IN BUSINESS SITUATIONS

22. Market shares. The situation is that two firms share the market for a certain consumer good. The maximising firm, Firm A, has calculated the share of the market that it will gain by (*a*) increasing its advertising outlay by a given percentage (A_1), (*b*) reducing its price (A_2) or (*c*) restyling the product (A_3). Similar policies are open to its rival, Firm B. Shares gained by Firm A are lost to Firm B and gains by Firm B are losses to Firm A. The situation is displayed in the matrix in Table 13.

Taking the greatest of the row minima and the least of the column maxima, we find that A's safest course is to follow Strategy A_1 consistently and to increase its advertising. If Firm B is equally prudent, it will follow Strategy B_2 and will lower its prices. If it is not consistent, Firm A can only gain. Once again, there is a saddle point.

23. The value of the game. The expected return to Firm A is called the *value of the game*. This quantity is represented by the symbol g and in our example $g = -1$.

TABLE 13.—PERCENTAGE OF MARKET SHARE GAINED BY FIRM A

		Strategies, Firm B			
		B_1	B_2	B_3	*Row minima*
Strategies, Firm A	A_1	10	−1	4	−1
	A_2	−4	−1	−5	−5
	A_3	6	−2	4	−2
	Column maxima	10	−1	4	

24. Mixed strategies. Suppose that, as time goes by, the relative strength of the two products changes and that Firm B has made so much of its present product that the option of restyling it has been lost for the present. The new situation might be represented by the revised matrix (Table 14).

TABLE 14.—THE REVISED GAME

		Strategies, Firm B		
		B_1	B_2	*Row minima*
Strategies, Firm A	A_1	11	−1	−1
	A_2	−2	3	−2
	A_3	5	2	2
	Column maxima	11	3	

There is no longer a saddle point and it is no longer true that a pure strategy is the best one. The problem is to find out what mixture of strategies is the best one.

THE ALGEBRA OF THE GAME

25. The basic inequalities. Continuing with the same problem, let the value of the game be g, the precise value being as yet unknown. Firm A will pursue a mixed strategy. Let the frequency with which the firm follows Strategy A_1 be x_1, that with which it follows A_2 be x_2 and the frequency for A_3 be x_3. The value of the game is the best that A can get out of the game when the worst happens. Using the concept of expectation and realising that $x_1 + x_2 + x_3 = 1$, since together they account for all Firm A's actions, we can write two inequalities

$$(x_1 \times 11) + (x_2 \times -2) + (x_3 \times 5) \geqslant g$$
$$(x_1 \times -1) + (x_2 \times 3) + (x_3 \times 2) \geqslant g$$

When x_1, x_2 and x_3 are at their optimum values, these inequalities will give the value of the game.

Looking at the position from Firm B's point of view, we can write B's optimum frequencies as y_1 and y_2. B's expectations are given by three "less than" inequalities; after all, Firm B wants to reach the lowest negative figure. The inequalities are

$$(y_1 \times 11) + (y_2 \times -1) \leqslant g$$
$$(y_1 \times -2) + (y_2 \times 3) \leqslant g$$
$$(y_1 \times 5) + (y_2 \times 2) \leqslant g$$

26. A graphical solution. In order to plot the inequalities on a two-dimensional graph, we must recall that $y_1 + y_2 = 1$ and that $y_2 = (1 - y_1)$. It is therefore possible to plot y_1 on the horizontal axis and g on the vertical axis.

The inequalities could be written as:

$$11y_1 - y_2 \leqslant g$$
$$-2y_1 + 3y_2 \leqslant g$$
$$5y_1 + 2y_2 \leqslant g$$

Substituting $(1 - y_1)$ for y_2, we have:

$$11y_1 - (1 - y_1) \leqslant g$$
$$-2y_1 + 3(1 - y_1) \leqslant g$$
$$5y_1 + 2(1 - y_1) \leqslant g,$$

which simplify to:

$$12y_1 - 1 \leqslant g \text{ . . . representing } A_1$$
$$-5y_1 + 3 \leqslant g \text{ . . . representing } A_2$$
$$3y_1 + 2 \leqslant g \text{ . . . representing } A_3$$

From previous work it will be remembered that inequalities can be represented by plotting the lines of equality that separate the "more than" from the "less than" sides of the two-dimensional space. This has been done in Fig. 36.

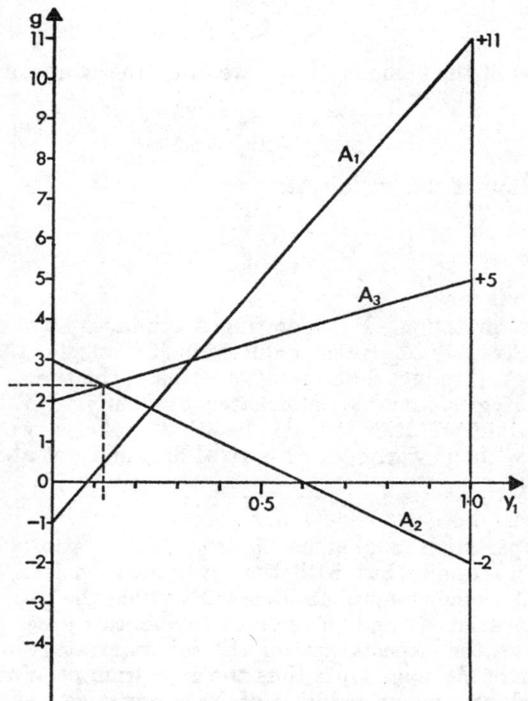

FIG. 36.—*Graphical solution of game*

27. Reading the graph. The value of the game is "underpinned" by the three "less than" constraints. If Firm B does its worst it can reduce the value of g to $2\frac{3}{8}$ ($2\frac{3}{8}$ per cent market share gain). If Firm A follows Strategies A_2 and A_3 it can make sure that the value of the game never falls below this level; but Firm A must play these strategies in the proportions that correspond to Firm B's most damaging strategy.

28. Choosing the frequencies. The constraints for Firm A were given earlier. Putting x_1 equal to zero because we are not going to use strategy A_1, and using them as equalities because the value of g lies *on* the constraint lines, we have:

$$-2x_2 + 5x_3 = g$$
$$3x_2 + 2x_3 = g$$

The value of the game is $2\frac{3}{8}$ and we must therefore solve:

$$-2x_2 + 5x_3 = 2\tfrac{3}{8}$$
$$3x_2 + 2x_3 = 2\tfrac{3}{8}$$

The solution of this little system is:

$$x_2 = \tfrac{3}{8}$$
$$x_3 = \tfrac{5}{8}$$

29. Interpretation. By operating a minimax strategy and playing Strategy A_2 (price reduction) $\frac{3}{8}$ths of the time and Strategy A_3 (product differentiation) $\frac{5}{8}$ths of the time. Ideally these strategies would be alternated randomly. No doubt a realistic interpretation would be that policies would be changed without warning to the rival firm and not at regular intervals.

30. Expectation and game theory. If the strategies are operated randomly but with the given frequencies, the frequencies become the probabilities with which the gain or loss will be experienced and the sum of frequencies times gain or loss will be the expectation for the mixed strategy applied. The *value of the game* (g) is thus the gain from each outcome multiplied by the probability of its occurrence. We have, therefore, another instance of the idea of *mathematical expectation* already encountered in Chapters XII and XVII. Although probability has not been used in setting up the decision situation, it has re-emerged in the solution of the game.

It is also possible that the values entered in the pay-off matrix may not be exact values, since they will be calculated future gains and losses. It will sometimes be appropriate to enter the mathematical expectation associated with the strategies concerned.

31. Summary of methods of solution. The methods used will serve for an $m \times n$ game which has a saddle point or an $m \times 2$ game which requires mixed strategies.

(*a*) *Games with pure strategies.* Proceed as follows:

(*i*) Find cell values by using mathematical expectation if the values are not given.
(*ii*) Enter pay-off matrix from viewpoint of the maximising player.
(*iii*) Enter row minima and column maxima in margins.
(*iv*) Select maximum of "row min's" and minimum of "column max's." If they have the same value and this value is the smallest in the row and the largest in its column, there is a saddle point.

Players then follow the pure strategies indicated.

(*b*) *Games with mixed strategies* ($m \times 2$ games only). Proceed as before and if pure strategies are not possible proceed as follows:

(*i*) Check for dominance and eliminate the dominated strategy.
(*ii*) Set out the constraints for Player A, using $x_1, x_2 \ldots x_m$ as the frequencies to be followed.
(*iii*) Set out the constraints for Player B, using y_1 and y_2.
(*iv*) Substitute $(1 - y_1)$ for y_2 and re-write. The result will be a set of "less than or equal to" inequalities in terms of y_1 and g.
(*v*) Graph these inequalities.
(*vi*) Check the least possible value of g within the constraints. Identify (1) the constraints concerned, (2) the value of y_1 which is best for Firm B and (3) the value of g.
(*vii*) Substitute the value of g into the x-constraints and find values for the frequencies with which the strategies are to be used.
(*viii*) Interpret the solution.

PROGRESS TEST 18

1. Draw a decision tree for a situation in which a business man faces *three* possible courses of action and *two* possible future states of the world using the conventions of sections 2 and 3. Distinguish clearly between decisions under certainty and those under uncertainty. (1–3)

2. The directors of a firm are uncertain about the effects of Government policy on the demand for their product. The Government may take action to stimulate demand, it may take no such action, or it may stimulate demand but also increase corporation tax. There are thus three uncertain future trading states. The company must decide, in advance of the Government action, either to increase its labour force or to keep the labour force at its current level. The six possible effects on profits are shown below:

	Estimated profit £(000*s*)
Increase labour force: no policy action	5·5
Increase labour force: demand stimulated	7·0
Increase labour force: stimulation plus tax	4·0
No increase in labour force: no policy action	6·0
No increase in labour force: demand stimulated	6·5
No increase in labour force: stimulation plus tax	4·5

(*i*) Set up the pay-off matrix.

(*ii*) Indicate what policies you would recommend under the maximax, maximin and Bayes' criteria. (5–14)

3. Set up a regret matrix for the data of Question 2 and use an appropriate criterion to recommend a course of action. (5–14)

4. What is the Hurwicz criterion? Apply the criterion to the situation of Question 2, assuming that the decision maker is of a relatively pessimistic disposition. (14)

5. Leakytub Traders is a company which runs small vessels between various ports in a part of the world which is subject to hurricanes at certain times of the year. If a hurricane occurs when one of the company's vessels is at sea, the ship is 80 per cent certain to founder with a net loss to the company of £5000, and, even if the vessel is not lost, damage to the value of £1000 will be caused, this figure being based on past experience. Should there not be a hurricane, the company will make a profit of £10,000 on each voyage.

These risks can be avoided by chartering vessels from another company operating in the same area. This company's vessels are larger and more modern than those operated by Leakytub Traders and will complete the voyage whether there is a hurricane or not. Because of market conditions, Leakytub will make a profit of £3000 if the chartered vessel delivers a cargo after weathering a hurricane but only £2000 if no hurricane has occurred.

A third course of action would be to take out additional insurance cover on vessels and cargoes. This would ensure that a hurricane during one of Leakytub's own ships' voyages would result in no loss but no profit either. Taking the heavy premium into account would reduce the profit on a voyage during which no hurricane was met with to £4000.

What strategy should Leakytub Traders adopt? (25–31)

CHAPTER XIX

INFORMATION, PROBABILITY AND DECISION

INFORMATION AND EXPECTATION

1. Information and decision. Information flows are important for the effectiveness of business decisions. These flows may be of many kinds. They may be the result of market research, they may be statistical forecasts, or they may be internally generated information flows concerning production conditions or industrial relations. Whatever the nature of the information, it is hardly ever costless. An additional level of decision is that concerning the outlay of money or resources which should be made in order to gain further information on which the major decisions of the business will be based. The decision to acquire information requires some method of evaluating the likely worth of the information, even though it has not yet been obtained and even though it relates to the uncertain future.

2. Mathematical expectation. The concept of mathematical expectation has been mentioned several times. It is defined as the value of an expected event multiplied by the probability of the event occurring. If business men are willing to assign probabilities to possible future events, rational decisions can be made even though the outcomes are uncertain. Alternative strategies may be evaluated by comparing the mathematical expectations associated with them. It follows that the value of information which would influence the probabilities estimated for future outcomes ought also to be capable of evaluation.

3. Objections to the use of probabilities. One objection to the use of probability in business decision-making is that such methods are quite at variance with the way that business men think. For many business men, judgment and experience, not probabilistic calculation, are the proper basis for major decisions. More technically, it is objected that very often no statistical basis exists for probabilistic decision-making. The probabilities must, at best, be subjective estimates. Against this, it might be urged that the use of numerical probabilities, even those intuitively determined, enforces a more careful consideration of the risks involved. It also ensures consistency in the evaluation of possible courses of action.

4. Expectation and decision. In order to show how expectation may be used, we now consider a specific situation.

(*a*) *The Situation.* An importer deals in a commodity of high value density. This substance is used in small quantities in the manufacture of many foodstuffs. The basic product is derived from an agricultural crop and is traded internationally, the market being influenced at some stages by speculation. Each month, the importer must decide whether to increase his stocks or to run them down and this decision depends on his estimate of whether the price will rise or fall.

(*b*) *The Decision.* Three courses of action are open to the importer:

(*i*) A_1: to buy at the beginning of the period
(*ii*) A_2: to sell at the beginning of the period
(*iii*) A_3: to operate a "hedging" sale or purchase and so to remove the risk.

Two possible states of the market are relevant to the decision:

(*i*) W_1: price rises
(*ii*) W_2: price falls.

(For simplicity the "no-change" state is omitted.)

The outcomes from each of the strategies, together with the probabilities which the importer estimates for the future market states, are set out in Table 15.

TABLE 15.—THE IMPORTER'S DECISION

Decision and State of Market	*Probability*	*Gain* (+) *or Loss* (−) (£)	*Expectation* (£)
A_1: *Importer buys*			
Forecast state of market:			
W_1: Price rises	0·75	50,000	37,500
W_2: Price falls	0·25	−10,000	−2,500
	Evaluation of strategy A_1		35,000

TABLE 15.—*continued*

Decision and State of Market	*Probability*	*Gain (+) or Loss (−)* (£)	*Expectation* (£)
A_2: *Importer buys*			
Forecast state of market:			
W_1: Price rises	0·75	−5,000	−3,750
W_2: Price falls	0·25	80,000	20,000
	Evaluation of strategy A_2		16,250
A_3: *Importer hedges*			
W_1: Price rises	0·75	0	0
W_2: Price falls	0·25	0	0

5. The nature of the problem. As was emphasised in Chapter XVIII, the attitude of the decision-maker is an essential element of the decision, even when it is structured mathematically. Here, the decision-maker has three courses of action open to him when he believes that prices may change during the coming month. If he is a risk avoider, he may cover his ordinary commercial contracts with a forward contract, thus avoiding the risk of either gain or loss. We shall now assume that our decision-maker is *not* a risk avoider but likes to make a speculative profit when he can. He therefore has strategies A_1 and A_2 to consider. If he buys more than usual at the beginning of the month and the price rises, he will be able to make a profit when he sells the excess at the end of the period. Conversely, if the price should fall, he will make a loss, or at least a reduction of profit. If he anticipates a price fall, he would do well to run down his stock and to buy in at the lower price. Whatever the strategy selected, the actual course of prices is not a matter of certainty and all that the importer can do is to estimate the probability that the rise or fall will take place. If only the importer's subjective estimates of the probabilities are available, together with the gains or losses associated with them, the mathematical expectations may be calculated.

6. Selecting a strategy. The strategy selected will be the one with the greatest mathematical expectation. The expectations are listed in Table 15, but in order to make the method quite clear, the calculation for strategy A_1 is given below

$$\begin{aligned}\text{Expectation } A_1 &= \text{Gain from } A_1 \text{ given that } W_1 \text{ occurs} \times Pr(W_1)\\ &\quad \text{plus}\\ &\quad \text{Gain from } A_1 \text{ given that } W_2 \text{ occurs} \times Pr(W_2)\\ &= £(50{,}000 \times 0{\cdot}75) + (-10{,}000 \times 0{\cdot}25)\\ &= \underline{£35{,}000.}\end{aligned}$$

The evaluation of A_2 can be followed from the table. It is clear that A_1 should be selected: the importer should buy.

7. Probability and information. The importer will only occasionally be "caught out" by a price fall, but he may still wish to improve his decision-making. One way of doing this will be to obtain an expert forecast of future price changes. Even with the best forecasts, there is a chance of being wrong. The importer will wish to know whether it would be worth his while to pay for a forecast. By enquiry in the trade he finds that the chance of a forecast of a price rise being correct when prices are, in fact, rising is rather better than "evens." He estimates this probability at 60 per cent.

Using the notation of conditional probability (recall XI, **10**) this probability would be shown as

$$Pr(I^* \mid W_1) = 0{\cdot}6$$

Here I^* indicates a "bullish" forecast, that is a forecast of a price rise, and W_1 shows an actual price rise. The symbols should be read as "the probability of a forecast price rise, given that the market is actually rising, is 0·6."

The forecast might be an incorrect one, that is a falling price might be forecast even though the market were rising. Representing the forecast of a price fall as I', we should have

$$Pr(I' \mid W_1) = 0{\cdot}4$$

the two probabilities summing to unity. The remaining probabilities, relating to the cases when the market is actually a falling one (W_2), are estimated as

$$Pr(I^* \mid W_2) = 0{\cdot}2$$
$$Pr(I' \mid W_2) = 0{\cdot}8$$

The reader is left to translate these symbols into words. For the sake of simplification, the "no price change" is again omitted from the analysis.

8. Using Bayes' theorem. In order to find a solution to the importer's problem of whether or not to obtain and to act on a price forecast, we must apply Bayes' theorem. Referring back to the Bayesian formula of XI, **17**, we can now estimate the probability that the market will *actually* experience a price rise given that a "bullish" forecast has been made. This is the probability that a forecast of rising prices will be correct. Using Bayesian Formula 3 of Chapter XI, we have

$$Pr(W_1 \mid I^*) = \frac{Pr(W_1) \,.\, Pr(I^* \mid W_1)}{Pr(W_2) \,.\, Pr(I^* \mid W_2) + Pr(W_1) \,.\, Pr(I^* \mid W_1)}.$$

Using the probabilities given in Table 15 as well as those of **6**, we calculate this probability as

$$Pr(W_1 \mid I^*) = \frac{0{\cdot}75 \times 0{\cdot}6}{(0{\cdot}25 \times 0{\cdot}2) + (0{\cdot}75 \times 0{\cdot}6)}$$

$$= \underline{0{\cdot}90}$$

There is thus a very high probability that the forecast will be correct, but it will be realised that this is due to the already high probability (0·75) that the price of the commodity will, in any case, rise.

9. The probability of a given forecast. The problem of evaluating the worth of a forecast *before* the forecast has been made requires one more figure. This is the probability that a given forecast, either I* (rise) or I′ (fall) will be made. To do this, we apply Bayesian Formula 2 (XI, **17**). Substituting $Pr(I^*)$ for $Pr(b)$ in the formula as given in Chapter XI and $Pr(I^* \mid W_2)$ for $Pr(b \mid \bar{a})$ and so on, we have

$$Pr(I^*) = Pr(W_2) \,.\, Pr(I^* \mid W_2) + Pr(W_1) \,.\, Pr(I^* \mid W_1)$$

$$= 0{\cdot}05 + 0{\cdot}45$$

$$= \underline{0{\cdot}50}.$$

It follows that $Pr(I')$ should also be equal to 0·50. There is an even chance of being given either forecast.

10. The problem. The first question to be answered is whether it is worthwhile obtaining a forecast. A further problem is: how much ought to be paid for the forecast? As is often the case, a good way of clarifying the problem is to draw a decision tree. It is shown in Fig. 37.

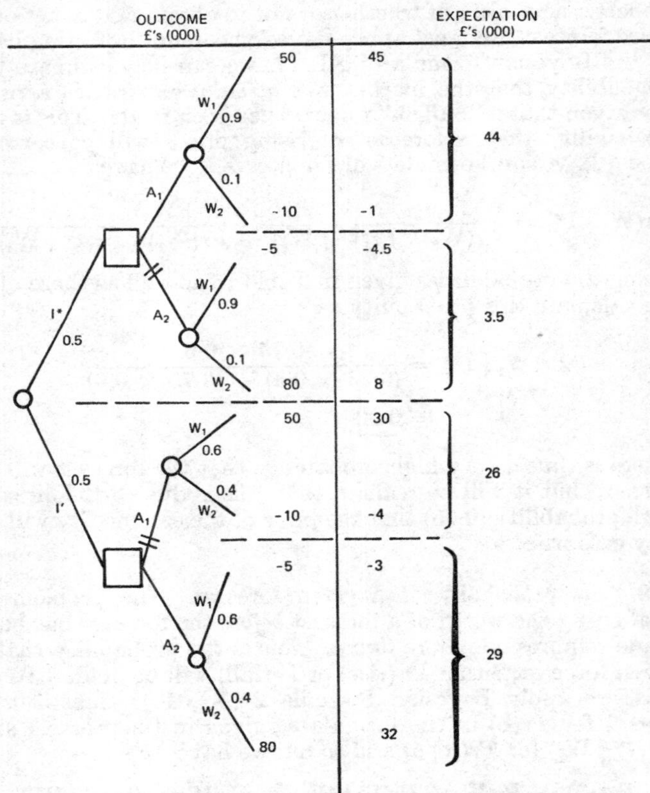

FIG. 37.—*Information and Bayesian probabilities*

11. Interpreting the diagram. The probabilities found in the preceding sections are transferred to the diagram. There is an 0·5 probability of either forecast being given. After each forecast, the alternative courses of action, A_1 and A_2, are still open to the importer and the conditional probabilities such as $Pr(W_1 \mid I^*)$ and $Pr(W_2 \mid I^*)$ are then applicable. At the end of each branch, the return that would be received if the state of the market, W_1 or W_2, followed the selected course of action is shown. The expectation, calculated by multiplying the appropriate return by the conditional probability of the event, is also shown. If forecast I* is given, strategy A_1 will carry the greatest expectation (£44 thousand), so that under those circumstances strategy A_2 would be discarded. This is indicated by the double bar on the lower of the branches from the decision box. Should forecast I′ be received, strategy A_2 will have the higher expected value (£29 thousand) and A_1 is barred.

Since the forecast of a price rise will be followed by an increased purchase of the commodity, the expectation associated with the forecast I* will be the £44,000 from course of action A_1. Similarly, the forecast of a price fall will be followed by a sale, with consequent expectation of £29,000. It will be noted that the receipt of a forecast changes the probabilities assigned to the market states and so the expectations. Since there is now an expected value associated with each forecast and the probability of each forecast being received has been calculated, the expected value of the decision as taken in the light of the forecast can now be found.

12. The value of the forecast. The value of the forecast is calculated as the expected value of the decision with the forecast *less* the expected value of the decision as estimated without the forecast. Using the symbols G_{11} for the monetary gain when action A_1 is followed by market state W_1 and G_{22} for the gain when action A_2 is followed by market state W_2, the expected value of the decision with the forecast is given by

$$\begin{aligned} E &= £[(Pr(I^*) \times 44{,}000) + (Pr(I') \times 29{,}000)] \\ &= £(0{\cdot}5 \times 44{,}000) + (0{\cdot}5 \times 29{,}000) \\ &= \underline{£36{,}500} \end{aligned}$$

The expected value of the decision without the forecast was £35,000 with strategy A_1 selected as shown in **6** and Table 15.

It would be worth paying up to £1500 for a forecast of the future market state.

13. Summary of method. The procedure to be applied is best considered in two parts, which are:

(*a*) evaluating and selecting strategies;
(*b*) re-evaluating strategies in the light of new information (the forecasts).

The case without the new information is summarised first. The stages are as follows

(*a*) List all the strategies together with the alternative outcomes.
(*b*) Estimate the probabilities for each outcome.
(*c*) Calculate the mathematical expectation for each outcome by multiplying the probabilities by the estimated monetary return.
(*d*) Evaluate the expectation for each strategy by adding the separate expectations for the mutually exclusive outcomes.
(*e*) Compare the expectations of the various strategies and select the one with the greatest expected value.

The second case is a little more complex but follows the same basic principles. The stages are as follows.

(*a*) List all the strategies together with all the alternative outcomes.
(*b*) Estimate the probabilities for each outcome before new information is obtained.
(*c*) On the best advice, estimate the (conditional) probabilities of getting accurate information (forecasts) about the alternative states (of the market).
(*d*) Using Bayesian formulae to secure consistency, calculate the probabilities of the various alternative outcomes on the basis that the information has been received (the posterior probabilities).
(*e*) Apply the posterior probabilities in the evaluation of the expected monetary values of the various outcomes and combine them to give expectations for each strategy under both (or all) information conditions.
(*f*) Calculate the probabilities of receiving the alternative types of information and evaluate the decision in the light of the expected information.
(*g*) Compare the decision *with* information with the decision based only on the crude subjective probabilities.

14. A cautionary note. The evaluation of the probable worth of information before the information is received is a complicated business. It involves many stages and employs probabilities which are either quite subjective or are based on slender evidence. Such an elaborate process would be justified only if the savings were considerable and if excellent professional advice were available. Consequently, such procedures would be likely to be employed only on major projects. In the case discussed above, the analysis might be justified because repeated decisions of the same kind would be made and the decision to obtain the forecast would pay for itself over time.

SEQUENTIAL DECISIONS

15. Information and activities. In the situation discussed in the earlier part of this chapter, the course of action selected depended on the forecast of future prices. Such a forecast would be derived from past records of prices (some methods are discussed in Chapter XXV). Information which is helpful in guiding future action can be obtained not only from records but also from activities. This is not an unusual state of affairs; we all learn from experience.

16. Simplifying the evaluation. The rather complicated calculations of **7–9** above could have been avoided if the decision-maker had decided at the beginning to buy if the forecast were "favourable" and to sell if it were "unfavourable." This would have eliminated the barred strategies at the outset and would have simplified the tree diagram. The evaluation of the strategies "with information," that is with the forecast, would have remained unchanged at £36,500. Once a definite decision to obtain information and to act on it has been made, the complicated Bayesian formulae can be avoided.

17. Sequential decisions. Many real-life decisions are much more complex than the examples used so far. The business decision-maker is confronted by a sequence of activities, the outcome of each of which will determine the action to be taken at the next stage. The sequence of *decisions* is reduced to a sequence of *events*. The probabilities to be applied are still conditional ones at each stage after the first, but they can be estimated directly, partly on the basis of past experience and partly subjectively, for each event. Consistency is ensured because the probabilities from each event fork must sum to unity.

18. The multiplication and addition laws. Each sequence of decisions now involves the joint occurrence of mutually independent events and the multiplication law of probability (recall XI, 7) must be used. At the end of a sequence of decisions, a number of alternative final outcomes will be determined. These will be mutually exclusive and the addition rule will apply. If the calculations have been carried out correctly, the probabilities of these final outcomes will automatically add up to unity.

19. Comparison of strategies for sequential decisions. The method is essentially that outlined in earlier sections. The return (or contribution towards expenditure) that would result from each final outcome is multiplied by the probability of that outcome, calculated as discussed above, to find the expectation. The mutually exclusive expected values are added together and the strategy with the greatest total expectation is selected. It might be added that since we are now concerned with a set of sequential decisions, the term strategy is much more appropriate than in the simpler cases.

SEQUENTIAL DECISIONS: AN EXAMPLE

20. The situation. A firm which is about to launch a new consumer product is faced with two alternative strategies. They are detailed in 21 and 22 below.

21. Strategy 1. A market-research survey costing £50,000 will establish whether or not the product has the potential for success. If it has not, the firm will cut its losses by selling all its rights in the product for £20,000. If the survey shows that the product has potential, a test-marketing operation will be carried out in a carefully selected locality at a cost of £100,000. Should evaluation of the test-market results be very favourable, a large-scale launch of the product involving capital expenditure of £1·5 million will be undertaken and, if successful, will yield an estimated £3 million contribution over the life of the product. Should the test-market result be only moderately favourable, a relatively small-scale launch, involving capital expenditure of only £500,000 will be undertaken. This smaller project is expected to yield a contribution of £1 million. An unfavourable test-market result will lead to the firm selling all its rights in the product, although the publicity associated with the test operation will have reduced the amount that they will fetch to £5000. A forward look at the probabilities associated with the three stages of the project estimates that there is a 60 per cent chance of the market research survey showing that the new product has potential and that there is a 70 per cent chance of the test-market result indicating that the product is a real winner, with a 20 per cent chance that it shows only a moderately favourable result and a 10 per cent chance that the test is really unfavourable. If the large-scale launch takes place it is estimated, tentatively, that it will have an 80 per cent chance of success, while the more modest small-scale launch will have a 90 per cent chance.

22. Strategy 2. The alternative strategy is much simpler; it is to make the large-scale launch if the market research survey shows that the product has potential and to sell out if it does not do so. Naturally, the probability of the survey indicating that the product is likely to succeed is the same as before (60 per cent), but without the survey it is not possible to be quite so sure of the large-scale launch being a success, since there has been no local market test to precede it. The probability of the large-scale success is therefore placed at only 60 per cent. The contributions to be expected towards the capital expenditure and profits are the same as before. If the market research survey indicates that the product is not likely to succeed, the rights will be sold for £20,000 as before.

23. Summary of data. In real life, problems emerge as a result of evolving situations and their final form often becomes clear only after long discussions between the managers concerned. In examinations and in textbook examples there is often a rather long explanation of the case from which the essential particulars must be extracted. For this example, the relevant details are summarised in Table 16.

24. Calculating the probabilities. The large-scale launch of the new product will take place only if (*a*) the market-research survey is favourable and (*b*) the test-market result is very favourable. Only if both these things happen will the product go into large-scale production and the probability of this happening is:

Probability of favourable M.R. survey × probability of very favourable test market result $= 0{\cdot}6 \times 0{\cdot}7$
$= \underline{0{\cdot}42}.$

The probability of the large-scale launch being successful is 80 per cent if both these things happen. That is, the probability of a successful large-scale launch

$$= 0{\cdot}8 \times 0{\cdot}42$$
$$= \underline{0{\cdot}336}.$$

These are independent probabilities and so are multiplied together to find the probability of their joint occurrence. The result for each possible combination of events is shown in the tree diagram, Fig. 38.

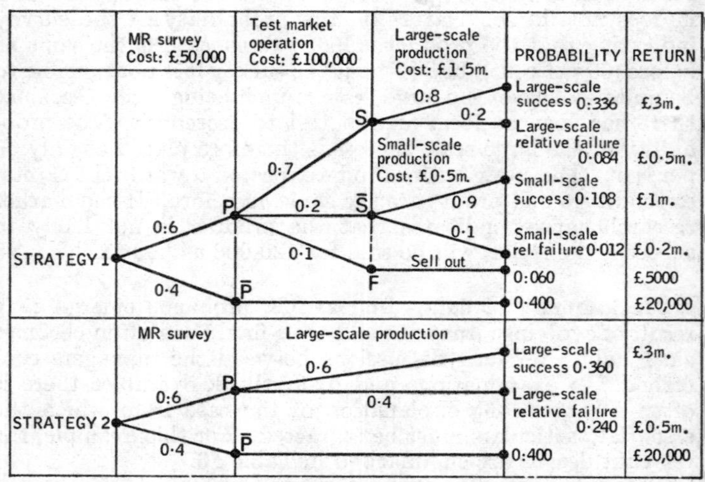

FIG. 38.—*Tree diagram: evaluation of strategies*

KEY: P = Market potential indicated by survey; P̄ = Market potential not indicated by survey; S = Success indicated by test market; S̄ = Success not indicated by test market; F = Failure indicated by test market.

TABLE 16

Operation	*Probability*	*Cost*	*Contribution*
STRATEGY 1.			
M.R. survey:	1	£50,000	—
Market potential indicated	0·6	—	—
Market potential not indicated	0·4	—	—
Test market:			
If M.R. survey good	1	£100,000	—
Chance of indicating good success	0·7	—	—
Chance of indicating moderate success	0·2	—	—
Chance of indicating failure	0·1	—	—
Large-scale launch:			
If test market indicates good success	1	£1·5 m.	—
Chance of success	0·8	—	£3·0 m.
Return if relative failure	0·2	—	£0·5 m.
Small-scale launch:			
If test market indicates modest success	1	£0·5 m.	—
Chance of success	0·9	—	£1·0 m.
Return if relative failure	0·1	—	£0·2 m.
Sell out:			
If M.R. survey indicates no potential	1	—	£20,000
If test market indicates failure	1	—	£5,000
STRATEGY 2.			
M.R. survey (as before)			
Large-scale launch:			
If M.R. survey indicates potential	1	£1·5 m.	—
Chance of success	0·6	—	£3·0 m.
Return if failure	0·4	—	£0·5 m.
Sell out:			
If M.R. survey indicates no potential	1	—	£20,000

25. The cash return for each set of events. In the case of the eventual successful large-scale launch, the probability was 0·336. To find the corresponding mathematical expectation this must be multiplied by the expected return.

The costs incurred were as follows:

	£
M.R. survey	50,000
Local market test	100,000
Capital and advertising costs for large-scale launch	1,500,000
	£1,650,000
Contribution (sales less variable costs over life of product)	£3,000,000
Net return from successful launch of product	£1,350,000

26. Expectation. The expectation for the successful large-scale launch is therefore:

$$\pounds(0{\cdot}336 \times 1{,}350{,}000)$$
$$\text{or} \quad \underline{\pounds 453{,}600.}$$

(*a*) *Expectation from Strategy* 1. Using the probabilities and returns shown in the tree diagram we have:

Gains

	£	
0·336 × £1·35m. =	453,600 (as above)	
0·108 × £0·35m. =	37,800	
Totals		491,400
Less expected losses		
0·084 × £1·15m. =	96,600	
0·012 × £0·45m. =	5,400	
0·060 × £0·145m. =	8,700	
0·400 × £0·030m. =	12,000	122,700
Net expectation		£368,700

(*b*) *Expectation from Strategy* 2. Working in the same way, the expectation from Strategy 2 is:

		£
	0·36 × £1·45m. =	522,000
Less		
	£	
0·24 × £1·05m. =	252,000	
0·40 × £0·03m. =	12,000	
		264,000
		£258,000

Note that we add the expectations for the separate events because they are mutually exclusive.

27. Comparison. On the basis of the two expectations Strategy 1 is preferable, since it may be expected to yield £368,700 against Strategy 2's £258,000.

PROGRESS TEST 19

1. A man has the choice of running either a hot-dog stall or an ice-cream van at a popular sea-side resort during the summer season. If it is a fairly cool summer, he should make £4000 by running the hot-dog stall, but if the summer is hot he can only expect to make £1000. If he operates the ice-cream van, his profit is estimated at £6000 if the summer is hot, but only £750 if it is cool. There is only a 40 per cent chance of the summer being hot. Should he operate the hot-dog stall or the ice-cream van? (1–13)

2. A company owns the mineral rights in a certain area but is considering whether to sell them to a rival concern. The directors consider that there is a 50 per cent chance that valuable minerals will actually be found, but if they *are* found, the royalties from them will be worth £1 million. If the company makes excavations, which would entail outlays of £500,000, but finds no minerals, the rights will be worthless. If the concession is sold before excavations are made, it will realise £100,000. The directors estimate that if minerals are present, the geologists have an 80 per cent chance of making a correct report, with a 20 per cent chance of making an incorrect report. If there are actually no minerals present, the probability of the geologists making a report that this is so is only 50 per cent, the terrain being in some respects difficult and misleading. Should the directors commission a survey? (7–13)

3. An import/export merchant is hoping to get the exclusive U.K. agency for a certain foreign product. If he gets the agency, and there is a 75 per cent chance of this, he will open a Manchester office, appoint new staff and make other arrangements at an outlay of £50,000. Should he not get the agency, he will clear out all existing stocks of the product, which he has already been handling on a small scale, at knockdown prices but will still show a profit of £5000. Should he get the agency, there is an 80 per cent chance of the venture being a success and yielding him a profit of £150,000, although this figure does not take into account the amount outlaid for the Manchester office, etc. There is a 20 per cent chance that the product will not be successful, and in that case the expected profit will be £60,000 only, again before deducting the Manchester expenses. Evaluate the merchant's expectation from this strategy. **(15–19)**

CHAPTER XX

INVENTORY CONTROL

THE CENTRAL PROBLEM OF INVENTORY CONTROL

1. The natures of inventories. Inventories, to use the increasingly popular synonym for stocks, may be accumulations of (*a*) raw materials, (*b*) semi-finished goods or spare parts or (*c*) finished goods. In each case, the function of the stocks is to act as a cushion between uneven flows, so that the processes of production and distribution can continue without interruption.

2. The need for adequate stocks. To be quite certain that no customer ever has to wait for any but the shortest time between placing his order and receiving the goods and that no machine is ever idle because materials are not available, large stocks must be held. Large stocks give security against interruption of the process.

3. The disadvantage of holding large stocks. The larger the stocks that are held, the less the risk of disappointing customers or of experiencing hold-ups in production; but stocks cost money. Goods that are on the shelves rather than already sold represent working capital tied up and not available for re-investment in new supplies of materials or for other uses. Every £'s worth of excess inventory represents a real cost to the business because of the loss of earning power of the tied-up capital.

4. The problem stated. The central problem of inventory control should now be obvious; it is to reconcile the possible loss to a business through interruption of production, or failure to meet orders, with the cost of holding stocks large enough to give security against such loss. The techniques that have been devised over the last forty years or so seek to quantify this reconciliation.

BUILDING INVENTORY MODELS

5. The nature of inventory models. Inventory models are simplifications of the very complicated situations which exist in all factories or stores of any size. Although they are abstractions from reality, they must preserve the central features of the problems which confront the production manager or the purchasing officer. For reasons already discussed (*see* XIX, 3) business decision-makers often prefer to use models designed as if the decision were to be made under certainty. The first models which we consider are devised under the certainty assumption, but later a probabilistic element is introduced.

6. The assumptions underlying the model. The simple model which is outlined in this section is based on the following assumptions:

(*a*) We shall assume that there is a fixed ordering cost that is constant whatever the size of the order placed with suppliers. This is made up of wage costs, clerical costs and so on.

(*b*) Over and above this constant cost we assume that there is an additional cost, representing the price per unit, which varies directly with the size of the batch purchased.

(*c*) We shall assume that by inspection of past records and by inferences from the current position, using available costing data, it is possible to find the cost of holding a unit in stock for a given period of time. This cost is expressed as a percentage of the cost of procuring a unit of the goods stocked.

7. The symbols used. Basing our mathematical model of the situation on these assumptions, we can show the cost of procuring the goods *and* of holding them in stock as a function of the size of batch purchased. In developing the model. these are the symbols that will be used:

Unit cost of procuring and holding goods	C_U
Cost of placing on order (or "set-up" costs)	C_s
Size of batch ordered (or produced)	Q
Optimum batch size	Q^*
Sales (or usage) per period of time (t)	S
Unit cost (price charged to buyer) of good	m
Stock-holding cost for one time period as percentage of cost of procuring goods	$100P$

8. Preparing the model for assembly. The first expression that we must derive is one for the cost of purchasing one unit of whatever goods we are considering. The total cost of purchasing will consist of *ordering costs* plus *total purchase price*, the total purchase price being quantity ordered multiplied by unit price. The expression required will be:

$$\textit{Cost of procuring batch} = C_s + mQ.$$

Cost per unit purchased is found by dividing through by Q, the number of items purchased:

$$\textit{Unit cost of purchasing batch of size } Q = \frac{C_s}{Q} + m.$$

The next expression required is that for the cost of holding an item in stock for one time period, that is for one month or year or whatever period is appropriate. This last item has been given as a percentage of unit cost of purchasing $(C_s/Q) + m$. If this percentage is $100P$, then the equivalent decimal fraction will be P (recall XV, **5**: 5 per cent is equivalent to the decimal 0·05). The cost of holding one stock unit for one time period is therefore:

$$P\left(\frac{C_s}{Q} + m\right).$$

We now need to know the average length of time for which goods remain in stock. If the sales rate per unit of time (say per month) is given by S and the batch purchased is of size Q, then the batch will be entirely sold out in Q/S months. If the sales are quite regular throughout this time, then the average time in stock will be half this period, that is $Q/(2S)$.

9. Assembling the model. All the pieces of the model are ready: they merely require assembly.

(*a*) *Verbally*, we could state the basic relationships as follows:

The total cost of procuring and holding one stock unit is equal to:

(*i*) the cost of procuring one unit; plus
(*ii*) the cost of holding one unit for one unit of time, multiplied by the average time for which one unit is held in stock.

(*b*) *Symbolically*, this becomes:

$$C_T = \left(\frac{C_s}{Q} + m\right) + P\left(\frac{C_s}{Q} + m\right) \times \frac{Q}{2S}$$

Cost per unit = Cost of buying one unit + Cost of holding one unit in stock × Average time in stock

10. Optimising the model. The requirement now is to find the batch size that will minimise the cost per unit, that is that will minimise C_U. It can be seen that C_U is made up of two parts: the buying cost, which declines as Q increases, and the cost of holding stocks, which increases as Q increases. Tidying up the model proceeds as follows:

$$C_U = \left(\frac{C_s}{Q} + m\right) + P\left(\frac{C_s}{Q} + m\right)\frac{Q}{2S}$$

$$= \frac{C_s}{Q} + m + \frac{PC_s}{2S} + \left(\frac{Pm}{2S}\right)Q,$$

which is obtained merely by clearing the brackets. The next step is to segregate the terms according to the powers of Q, which is our independent variable. This gives:

$$C_U = \left(\frac{Pm}{2S}\right)Q + C_sQ^{-1} + \left(\frac{PC_s}{2S} + m\right).$$

To find the minimum cost we must differentiate C_U with respect to Q (recall VI, **12**) and then put the derivative equal to zero to find the stationary point:

$$C_U = \left(\frac{Pm}{2S}\right)Q + C_sQ^{-1} + \left(\frac{PC_s}{2S} + m\right)$$

$$\frac{dC_U}{dQ} = \frac{Pm}{2S} - C_sQ^{-2}.$$

Putting:

$$\frac{dC_U}{dQ} = 0,$$

$$\frac{Pm}{2S} - C_sQ^{-2} = 0$$

$$\frac{C_s}{Q^2} = \frac{Pm}{2S}$$ (remembering that Q^{-2} is the same as $1/Q^2$),

$$\therefore Q^2 = \frac{2SC_s}{Pm}$$

$$\therefore Q^* = \sqrt{\frac{2SC_s.}{Pm}}$$

Finding the second derivative and testing the stationary point will confirm that this value of Q is a minimum.

11. The optimum batch size. The symbol Q^* is used for the optimum (best) batch size and the actual quantity to be ordered is found by substituting the appropriate values of the other quantities.

EXAMPLE: In a particular firm it is estimated that it costs £6 to place an order. A particular part, Frame Assembly Part No. 4PN27, costs £3 and the cost of holding one item in stock for one month is estimated at one half of one per cent of the total (unit) cost of procuring the item. Usage is at the rate of 50 per month.

$$Q^* = \sqrt{\frac{2SC_s}{Pm}}$$

$S = 50$ items; $C_s = £6$; $P = 0{\cdot}005$; $m = £3$.

Substituting in the formula gives:

$$Q^* = \sqrt{\frac{2 \times 50 \times 6}{0{\cdot}005 \times 3}}$$
$$= \sqrt{\frac{600}{0{\cdot}015}}$$
$$= \sqrt{40{,}000}$$
$$= \underline{200 \text{ articles.}}$$

A VARIANT

The previous model was built up in detail in order to illustrate the important mathematical process of model building. Subsequent models will be dealt with more briefly.

12. Assumptions for a different approach. Suppose that our requirements are considered over some fairly long time period, which we shall designate T. Assuming that we start with a full optimum batch in stock and that sales (or usage if the articles are required within the firm) take place at a constant rate, the optimum batch will be used up entirely in some shorter time period, represented by the symbol t. Graphically, this situation is represented in Fig. 39.

13. A sketch of the model. If the total requirements in the longer time period, T, are R, then the number of batches that must be ordered in period T is R/Q. Taking the ordering costs per batch as C_s, as before, the total ordering costs in period T will be $(C_sR)/Q$. The total stockholding costs in time period T will be the *average number in stock* × *stock-holding costs per unit, per unit of time* (C_1) × *time in stock*. The expression for total stock-holding costs can fairly easily be shown to be $(C_1TQ)/2$. Putting these two expressions together we shall have the total costs for time period T. It is convenient to call this the *total expected cost* or TEC. We therefore have:

$$\text{TEC} = \frac{C_sR}{Q} + \frac{C_1TQ}{2},$$

which again has a term which declines as Q, the batch quantity, increases and another which increases with Q. To find the minimum cost, we differentiate, as before, and put the derivative equal to zero. This gives:

$$Q^* = \sqrt{\frac{2C_sR}{TC_1}}.$$

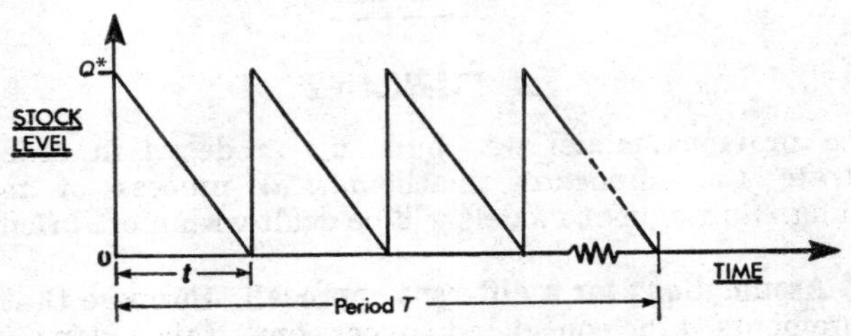

FIG. 39.—*The stock cycle*

INTERPRETATION OF THE MODELS

14. First model. The formula is:

$$Q^* = \sqrt{\frac{2SC_s}{Pm}}.$$

The batch size (Q^*) becomes larger as C_s, the ordering cost, increases. This is sensible, since larger batches mean fewer orders. The optimum batch also increases as sales (S) increase, which again accords with common sense. The batch size declines as m, the price, increases because this increases the amount of capital tied up in stocks. The batch size also declines as P, the stock-holding cost function, increases. The square root prevents the batch size from varying as much as the expression under the radical.

15. Second model. In this model larger set-up costs (C_s) and larger total requirements (R) necessitate larger batches, and larger stock-holding costs reduce the batch size. The T in the denominator relates R to the time period concerned and the square-root sign moderates the effect as before.

USING EOQ MODELS

16. A warning. Models such as those just discussed are often called EOQ (economic ordering quantity) models or merely square-root models. Although these models, and rather more elaborate variants of them, can form the basis of quite effective inventory control systems, they need to be applied with care. They can, in some cases, lead to excessive investment in stocks since they take no account of the yield which might have been earned had money invested in stocks been put to other use. In some circumstances, too, unthinking application of the formula may give answers which are theoretically correct but are, in fact, not practicable. In addition it is not often practicable to calculate EOQ's for each of the many items which a manufacturing company will have in its stores.

17. Developments and variants of the EOQ models. In a short discussion of the mathematics of inventory models there is not space to discuss all the adaptations that might be made, but one simplification would be to split the square root formula into two parts. The basic formula is:

$$Q^* = \sqrt{\frac{2SC_s}{Pm}}.$$

This could be written as:

$$\left(\sqrt{\frac{2C_s}{P}} \cdot \sqrt{\frac{S}{m}}\right).$$

The $\sqrt{2C_s/P}$ part is not likely to change very much from period to period, but may be different from one class of stores to another. P, the storage cost fraction, may be high for goods requiring a great deal of storage space or special storage conditions, and C_S, the ordering or set-up costs, may be high in some circumstances. A ready simplification, therefore, is to write $\sqrt{2C_s/P}$ as k, a constant, and to use this same constant for whole groups of broadly similar stores. A further simplification would be to replace S/m, which varies directly with sales and inversely with unit price, by a single symbol, V, representing the money value of usage in the period. This can be seen by taking the original formula and multiplying both sides by m, the price of the item. We then have

$$\begin{aligned} Q^*m &= \left(k\sqrt{\frac{S}{m}}\right)m \\ &= k\sqrt{\frac{Sm^2}{m}} \\ &= k\sqrt{Sm} \end{aligned}$$

The formula must be applied with care in times of rising price, since with V in money terms, the batch quantity Q would tend to decline.

18. Periodic review models. Where a number of major parts have to be stored and replenished at intervals it may be preferable to review the whole stock position at intervals rather than to replenish each item as minimum stocks are reached. In that case, it is necessary to ask whether there is an optimum length of time for this review period. An inspection of Fig. 39 shows the cyclic nature of the usage and replenishment process. If a mathematical model of the whole stock process can be made and a variable n, for the number of cycles completed within the time period T, included, this model can be optimised for n. Having found the optimum *number* of cycles, the optimum period follows when T is divided by the optimum value for n. Such models are known as periodic, or cyclic, review models.

STATISTICAL ASPECTS OF INVENTORY CONTROL

19. The problem of variable lead time. The time between placing a firm order and receiving the goods, or materials, is called the *lead time*. Unless special arrangements have been made for regular periodic deliveries, this lead time is likely to vary. One result of this is that the stocks used between placing an order with suppliers and actually receiving a replenishment is not constant and that if a re-order level is established it must take account of this varying lead time.

20. The problem of varying rates of demand. Not only is the lead time likely to vary, but the actual rate of demand, the rate at which the goods in stock are required, is likely to vary during the lead time. In dealing with the joint problems of varying lead time and varying rate of demand, we shall use the statistical concepts of the *mean* and the *standard deviation* of the distributions of lead times and demands.

21. A distribution of lead times. Suppose that a company selling certain chemical products operates a depot at which a particular liquid is stored in a 20,000-litre tank. When the contents of the tank are becoming low, deliveries are made direct from a major chemical manufacturer. Although this major supplier endeavours to make deliveries promptly, there is naturally an inevitable delay of a few days before the delivery is effected. Scrutiny of past records reveals the following pattern over recent months:

DISTRIBUTION OF LEAD TIMES

Lead times	*No. of occasions*
Under 2 days	3
2–4 days	10
4–6 days	26
6–8 days	6
Over 8 days	5

A simple calculation, taking due account of the pattern of lead times of over 8 days and under 2 days, shows the mean lead time to be approximately $5\frac{1}{4}$ days and the standard deviation to be just a little under 2 days.

22. Calculating a re-order level. If we disregard the slightly skewed nature of the distribution of past lead times we can proceed as if the population of all possible lead times were normal. Using $5\frac{1}{4}$ days and 2 days as estimates of the mean and standard deviation respectively of the distribution of all possible lead times, we can calculate the probability of experiencing lead times of any given length. There will, for instance, be only a 5 per cent chance of experiencing lead times of more than 1·65 standard deviations above the mean lead time of $5\frac{1}{4}$ days (check with XII, 23–26, and Appendix II). Suppose that there is a regular demand of 800 litres a day. Nineteen times out of twenty (95 per cent of the time) the lead time will not be more than $5\frac{1}{4}$ days + (1·65 × 2 days). This makes us 95 per cent certain that the lead time will not exceed 8·55 days, or in practical work-a-day terms $8\frac{1}{2}$ days. In that time the demand for the chemical would be 6800 litres and this would be our re-order level. (A calculation accurate to 0·05 of a day would give 6840 litres.)

23. Lead time demand variance. The same result could be obtained using the variance of the lead time demand. With demand (D) constant at 800 litres a day and the standard deviation of the lead time (σ_L) at 2 days, the standard deviation of the lead time demand (σ_{LD}) is given by

$$\sigma_{LD} = D\sigma_L$$

the multiplication bringing the units from days to litres. The variance would be

$$\sigma_{LD}{}^2 = D^2\sigma_L{}^2.$$

The re-order level is found by taking the mean lead time demand ($D\bar{L}$) and adding ($1{\cdot}65 \times D\sigma_L$). This will reduce the risk of exhausting the tank to 5 per cent. Checking that this will give the same result as the previous method is left as an exercise.

24. Re-order level with varying demand. If the daily demand varies as well as the lead time, the formula for the variance of the lead time demand must be modified. The constant demand, D, must be replaced by the mean demand, $\bar{D}$, and some allowance made for the variance of the demand. With variance of the daily demand $\sigma_D{}^2$, the new formula for the variance of the lead time demand would be

$$\sigma_{LD}{}^2 = \bar{D}\sigma_L{}^2 + \bar{L}\sigma_D{}^2.$$

The demand variance must be multiplied by $\bar{L}$ even though it is in the correct units (litres) because it is expected to continue for $\bar{L}$ days. The standard deviation of the lead time demand is then

$$\sigma_{LD} = \sqrt{\bar{D}^2\sigma_L{}^2 + \bar{L}\sigma_D{}^2}.$$

Taking the mean daily demand as 800 litres and the standard deviation of the demand as 60 litres, the standard deviation of the lead time demand is

$$\sigma_{LD} = \sqrt{800^2 \times 2^2 + 5{\cdot}25 \times 60^2}$$
$$= 1606 \text{ litres.}$$

To find the re-order level with the same risk of "stock-out" as before, we must take the mean lead time demand, $\bar{L}\bar{D}$, plus 1·65 times the standard deviation of the lead time demand.

This gives:

Re-order level = 4200 litres + (1·65 × 1606 litres)
= 6850 litres (to nearest litre).

It will be seen that in this case the inclusion of the additional term makes no practical difference to the re-order level.

25. Unresolved problems. While we have considered the problem of the lead-time demand being greater than expected, we have given no consideration to the possibility that it will be less than expected. It could happen that an unusually short lead time coincided with an unexpectedly low rate of demand. In such a case the danger would be not that we ran out of stock but that the storage space was insufficient. This problem can be tackled by a similar method.

Another problem would occur if demand were not approximately normally distributed but followed a Poisson distribution (recall XII, 28–29). Readers may care to speculate on ways of dealing with this situation. Other inventory control models could be constructed to take into account the cost of running out of stock, but, since this would be a very difficult cost to estimate, such models have not been included. Stock control problems form a large and well-explored area of business mathematics and operational research and a number of useful texts are mentioned in Appendix I.

PROGRESS TEST 20

1.* Why is inventory control important for every business firm and what are the basic problems of inventory control? **(1–4)**

2. A firm's requirement of an article which costs £15 is 10 per week. The cost of placing each order for a supply of these items is £1·20 and the cost of holding them in stock is 20 per cent per annum of the value of the goods in stock. What size batch should be ordered? (Assume a 50-week year.) **(10)**

3. Differentiate the expression:

$$\text{TEC} = \frac{C_s R}{Q} + \frac{C_1 T Q}{2}$$

with respect to Q and show that the EOQ is given by:

$$\sqrt{\frac{2C_s R}{TC_1}}. \qquad \textbf{(12, 13)}$$

4. For a certain class of stores, a firm applies a general value of 8 for $k = \sqrt{2C_s/P}$ in arriving at its economic ordering quantities. Compare the effect of this on the stocks held for items with annual usages of (*a*) £2500, (*b*) £100, (*c*) £10,000. What classes of stocks would you expect to have smaller values of k? **(17)**

5. At a certain depot a firm has a 40,000-litre storage tank from which collections of a liquid product are made. If the mean daily demand for the product is 1500 litres with a standard deviation of 100 litres and the delay between the depot manager placing an order and having the tank replenished is averagely 4 days, with a standard deviation of 1 day:

(*a*) suggest a re-order level for the manager's guidance, and
(*b*) comment on the size of the tank.

The standard re-order quantity is 25,000 litres. **(24)**

CHAPTER XXI

QUEUEING THEORY

QUEUEING SITUATIONS

1. The general queueing problem. Queueing situations have been part of most people's lives for many years. We queue at supermarket check-out points, we queue for 'buses and we sit in our motor cars queueing at roundabouts and traffic lights. There are many other situations which are mathematically similar to these everyday queues: examples are aircraft waiting to use airport runways, machines waiting for repair or maintenance, workpieces waiting to be machined and so on. If it is possible to devise a general mathematical model that will describe all these situations, it should be possible to manipulate it in order to find ways of minimising queueing time or to determine what level of services, how many check-out points for example, is required.

2. Elements of the queueing situation. As a preliminary to describing queueing situations mathematically, it will help if the basic elements of the situation can be described. Essentially, individuals arrive at the end of the queue, wait in the queue, receive the service they have been waiting for and then leave the system. Schematically, the situation is:

ARRIVALS → QUEUE → SERVICE → EXIT FROM SYSTEM

3. Varieties of queueing situations. The simplest situation consists of a single queue and a single service point. Fig. 40(*a*) shows this simple system.

An alternative system which is often seen in banks and elsewhere is where there are several service points each with its own queue. Arrivals choose which queue to join. This is shown in Fig. 40(*b*).

A further variant would be to have a single queue which the queue members leave to go to any service point which happens to be vacant. Fig. 40(*c*) shows this situation.

Fig. 40(*a*).—*Queueing situation with single queue and sing[le] service point*

Fig. 40(*b*).—*Queueing situation with several queues and sever[al] service points*

Fig. 40(*c*).—*Queueing situation with single queue and sever[al] service points*

Our analysis will be concerned in the main with the simple ituation involving a single queue and a single service point, ut there will be some development of the multiple channel ituation. More difficult situations are probably best dealt ith by *simulation* (*see* **16–22** below).

4. Ways of ordering queues. Even when the number of channels" has been determined, there is room for further ifferentiation between situations. The *queue discipline* may llow priorities or may be strictly on a "first come, first erved" basis. Priorities tend to increase the average time pent in the queue. The *arrival pattern* may vary: people, or hatever queueing units are concerned, may arrive at regular itervals or may arrive randomly. The *service time* may be onstant or may vary in some way. When models of a queueing tuation are built, all these things must be taken into account.

THE SIMPLEST QUEUEING MODEL

5. The model defined. This simple queueing situation is one here there is a single queue and a single service point. The ueue discipline is "first in, first out" (FIFO) and arrivals are ndom. The service times, too, are random or, more exactly, llow a negative exponential distribution (recall XII, **30–32**).

6. Notation. The arrivals are random but, if we can estimate e *average* number of arrivals that may be expected in the osen time unit, we can use the *Poisson* distribution (*see* XII, **3–29**) to calculate the probability that any given number of rivals will occur. The average number of arrivals in one time nit is designated by the symbol λ (lambda). The average umber of services that may be expected to be completed in nit time is given by the symbol μ (mu).

7. Arrival times and service times. If the average number of rivals in the given time is λ, the average time between arrivals ill be $1/\lambda$. Similarly, if the average number of services mpleted in the given time period is μ, the average time taken r each service is $1/\mu$.

EXAMPLE: On the average, 6 cars an hour arrive at a car-wash. The average time between arrivals is $\frac{1}{6}$ hour or 10 minutes.

$$\lambda = 6; \frac{1}{\lambda} = \tfrac{1}{6} \text{ (hours)}.$$

The "inter-arrival time" is 10 minutes.

If one service is completed every 6 minutes, averagely $1/\mu = 6$ minutes $= \frac{1}{10}$ hour, therefore $\mu = 10$ (services pe hour).

8. Formulae derived from the simple queue model. In thes formulae, the expression λ/μ occurs frequently and in accordanc with the usual convention this measure, the "traffic intensity," is represented by the symbol ρ (rho), that is $\rho = \lambda/\mu$.

Using probability theory, we can deduce the followin formulae:

(*a*) The probability that there is no one in the system at given time (no one in the queue and no one being dealt with a the service point) is:

$$P_0 = 1 - \frac{\lambda}{\mu}$$
$$= 1 - \rho.$$

(*b*) The probability that there are *n* people in the system is:

$$P_n = (1 - \rho)\,\rho^n.$$

(*c*) The probability of having to queue on arriving

$$= \frac{\lambda}{\mu} \text{ (or } \rho).$$

(This is equal to [1 − probability that there is no one in th system].)

(*d*) The average (expected) number of people in the queu (including the occasions when no one is queueing)

$$= \frac{\rho^2}{1 - \rho}.$$

(*e*) The expected number of people in the queue when there a queue

$$= \frac{1}{1 - \rho}.$$

(*f*) The expected number of people in the system

$$= \frac{\rho}{1 - \rho}$$
$$= \frac{\lambda}{\mu - \lambda}.$$

(*g*) The average waiting (queueing) time

$$= \frac{\rho}{\mu(1-\rho)}$$

$$= \frac{\lambda}{\mu(\mu-\lambda)}.$$

(*h*) The average time spent in the system

$$= \frac{\lambda}{\mu(\mu-\lambda)} + \frac{1}{\mu}$$

$$= \frac{1}{\mu-\lambda}.$$

(This is waiting time plus service time.)

9. Importance of the traffic intensity. In many queueing situations and in the model that we are discussing, arrivals and departure are random. Sometimes, by chance, a time interval will have few arrivals and the services will be completed easily; at other times there will be a large number of arrivals and the jobs will be difficult as well. It is found that, unless the service rate is well below the arrival rate, the service will not be adequate and there will be times when the queue becomes very long indeed.

The relationship between arrivals and services completed is given by the ratio λ/μ, the *traffic intensity*. The effect of changes in the traffic intensity can be shown by plotting against the time spent in the system, using the formula $1/(\mu-\lambda)$.

EXAMPLE: In a certain large workshop, men are required to go to a stores window to draw materials from time to time. The men are engaged on non-routine work and consequently both the number of workers coming to the stores window and the range of items required vary randomly. Past observations show that the stores clerk takes five minutes (averagely) to fulfil a request for spares. Show how the time spent away from work, queueing or being served, will vary as the number of operatives requiring spares increases.

The service rate (μ) = 12 per hour. Plotting lost time (time in system) for arrival rates from 1 to 12 per hour produces the following table.

ARRIVAL RATES, TRAFFIC INTENSITIES AND WAITING TIMES IN A WORKSHOP

Arrival rates (λ)	*Traffic intensities* (ρ)	*Time in system* (*min*) $\left(\frac{1}{\mu - \lambda}\right)$
1	0·08	5·5
2	0·16	6·0
3	0·25	6·6
4	0·33	7·5
5	0·42	8·6
6	0·50	10·0
7	0·58	12·0
8	0·66	15·0
9	0·75	20·0
10	0·83	30·0
11	0·92	60·0
12	1	becomes very large as ρ approaches 1

This situation is shown graphically in Fig. 41.

It can be seen from the example that as ρ reaches and exceeds 0·8, the time in the system becomes very long. In general λ/μ should not be allowed to exceed 0·8. Many managers do not realise that the mean arrival rate must not approach the mean service rate too closely or very long queues will result. It is the failure to provide sufficient facilities (that is a sufficiently large μ) that results in such long queues in some supermarkets and such large backlogs of work

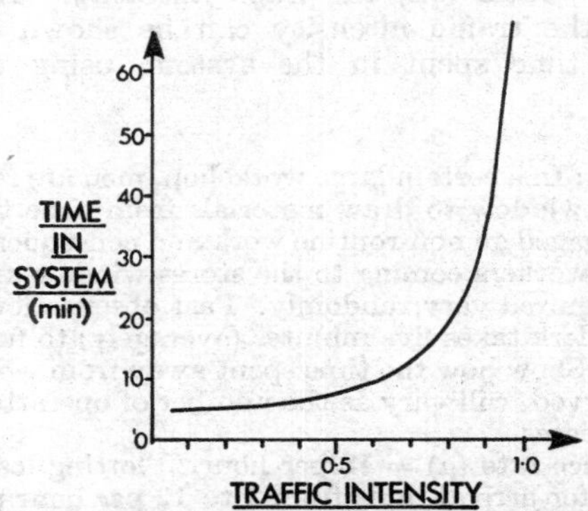

Fig. 41.—*The effect of increasing traffic intensity*

in some offices. The course of action that should be taken depends on whether the queues or the backlogs are considered to be tolerable or not. Inspection of the formulae given above will show that other quantities such as the expected number in the queue will also increase as ρ increases.

10. Using the queueing model. A taxi firm estimates that on the average four of its cars break down every day. Every day that a car is out of commission costs the firm £100 in lost earnings. At present the taxi firm's own repair shop can deal with five cars per day although the actual repair times vary. The cost of operating the repair shop is £300 per day. The alternative is to close the repair shop, thus saving £300 daily cost and to contract out the repairs to a firm whose charges would be equivalent to a daily charge of £400. A representative of the repair firm has produced data which indicate that his firm's facilities could handle up to six cars a day. Should the taxi firm continue to use its own repair shop or should it contract out its repairs?

OWN REPAIR SHOP

Number of cars expected to be out of action

Average number in the repair system $= \dfrac{\lambda}{\mu - \lambda}$

$= \dfrac{4}{5 - 4}$

$= \underline{4 \text{ cars.}}$

Averagely 4 cars would be either under repair or awaiting repair.

Cost of lost time $= 4 \times £100$

$= £400$ per day

Plus daily repair shop costs £300

Total daily cost $= \underline{£700}$

CONTRACTING OUT

Number of cars expected to be out of action $= \dfrac{\lambda}{\mu - \lambda}$

$= \dfrac{4}{6 - 4}$

$= \underline{2 \text{ cars}}$

Cost of lost time	$= 2 \times$	£100
	$=$	£200 per day
Plus contractor's daily cost		£400
		£600 per day

Conclusion. It would be cheaper to contract out the repairs.

MULTI-CHANNEL QUEUES

11. Situation. Suppose that the customers form a single queue as before, but that as they leave it a choice of service points is available. This is the situation shown in Fig. 40(c).

All the results previously obtained have to be modified because the number of channels available affects all the expected times, number in queue and so on.

12. Traffic intensity for a multi-channel system. As before, the system will only have stable results, that is it will only be in a "steady state," if the traffic intensity is less than one. The only modification in calculating the traffic intensity is that the service rate for a single channel must be multiplied by the number of channels available. If the service rate for a single channel is given by μ, the required formula is:

$$\textit{Traffic intensity } (\rho) = \frac{\lambda}{c\mu},$$

where c is the number of channels. As before, ρ also gives the probability of having to queue.

EXAMPLE: Modifications must be carried out urgently to a small but complex radar set. One of the few firms technically capable of carrying out the modification has sufficient skilled staff and equipment to modify five sets at any one time, each modification taking one hour to complete. It is expected that twenty sets will arrive for modification during each eight-hour working day. What is the probability that any set arriving at the works will not receive immediate attention?

Working with a time period of one day, $\lambda = 20$. The number of channels (c) is 5 and, since each channel can handle one job an hour, $\mu = 8$.

The probability of a set having to wait for modification is:

$$\frac{\lambda}{c\mu} = \frac{20}{5 \times 8}$$
$$= \underline{0 \cdot 5}$$

The probability of a set having to "queue" for attention is 0·5; there is a "fifty-fifty" chance that a set will not be able to be repaired immediately.

13. Formulae for multi-channel systems. Although the quivalent formula for the traffic intensity is quite straightorward the remaining expressions are by no means so easy to erive. In deriving the formulae for the one-channel, steadytate system, we began by stating the probability that there ras no one in the system (P_0). This was equal to $(1 - \rho)$ since gave the probability that there *was* someone in the system. Vith several channels this is no longer the case. The expression is now equal to $\lambda/(c\mu)$ and gives the probability that all the hannels will be engaged when a unit arrives at the end of the ueue. The new expression for P_0 is much more complicated nd is:

Probability that there is no unit in the system
$$= \frac{c!(1-\rho)}{(\rho c)^c + c!(1-\rho)\left\{\sum_{r=0}^{c-1} \frac{1}{r!}(\rho c)^r\right\}}$$

Denoting this probability by P_0, examples of other multihannel formulae are as follows:

(*a*) Average number of units in the system

$$= \frac{\rho(\rho c)^c}{c!(1-\rho)^2} P_0 + \rho c.$$

(*b*) Average time in queue

$$= \frac{(\rho c)^c}{c!(1-\rho)^2 c\mu} P_0.$$

(*c*) Average time in system

$$= \frac{(\rho c)^c}{c!(1-\rho)^2 c\mu} P_0 + \frac{1}{\mu}.$$

14. Example of use of formulae. Using the same data as in he previous example, but now supposing that the workshop can only modify three radar sets at a time, calculate how long each radar set will be out of service if it can be brought back into use immediately the modification is completed.

We need to find the "time in the system" if we are to calculate how long a radar set is averagely out of action and to do this we need a value for P_0.

Using the formula previously given:

$$P_0 = \frac{c!(1-\rho)}{(\rho c)^c + c!(1-\rho)\left\{\sum_{r=0}^{c-1} \frac{1}{r!}(\rho c)^r\right\}}.$$

Our basic data are now:

$$c = 3$$
$$\mu = 8$$
$$\lambda = 20$$
$$\rho = \frac{\lambda}{c\mu} = \frac{20}{24}$$
$$= \underline{0{\cdot}8\dot{3}.}$$

This gives:

$$P_0 = \frac{3!(1 - 0{\cdot}8\dot{3})}{(0{\cdot}8\dot{3} \times 3)^3 + 3!(1 - 0{\cdot}8\dot{3})\ 6{\cdot}625}$$
$$= \frac{6 \times 0{\cdot}1\dot{6}}{15{\cdot}625 + 6(0{\cdot}1\dot{6})\ (6{\cdot}625)}$$
$$= \frac{1}{15{\cdot}625 + 6{\cdot}625}$$
$$\therefore P_0 = \underline{0{\cdot}045.}$$

This is the probability that all the channels are completely idle. Substituting this value into the formula for "time in the system" gives:

$$\frac{(\rho c)^c}{c!(1-\rho)^2 c\mu} P_0 + \frac{1}{\mu} = \frac{15{\cdot}625 \times 0{\cdot}045}{6(0{\cdot}027)(24)} + \tfrac{1}{8}$$
$$= \frac{15{\cdot}625}{(0{\cdot}162)(24)}(0{\cdot}045) + \tfrac{1}{8}$$
$$= \frac{15{\cdot}625 \times 0{\cdot}045}{4} + \tfrac{1}{8}$$
$$= \underline{0{\cdot}3\ \text{(days)}}\ \text{approximately.}$$

15. Some points to note. This model is based on the same assumptions as the previous, single-channel model, in that there is a Poisson stream of arrivals (check back with **5** and **6** above if you cannot quite remember what this means) and a negative exponential pattern of service times (*see* XII, **30–32**). Queue discipline is the same as before.

In interpreting these results, it should be remembered that our time-unit of this example was one eight-hour working day. The value of 0·045 could be understood as indicating that all three channels could be expected to be unused for 4½ per cent of the time. Finally, it should be noted that even this model, which is a fairly simple one, necessitates quite nasty calculations. Instead of pursuing our analysis into more difficult situations such as the multi-channel, multi-queue model required for the situation shown in Fig. 40(*b*), we shall investigate an alternative approach.

SIMULATION

16. Simulation models. When problems become too complex for ready solution by analytical methods one way of proceeding is to set up a "simulation" model, a model that will behave like the system under observation. Since many of the systems with which we are concerned involve probabilistic or even random elements, any model which we set up to simulate the real system must also contain random elements. Because of this "gambling" element these are often called "Monte Carlo" models.

Simulation models are an ideal application of computers and very large systems indeed can be handled in this way. Simulation methods can be applied to a wide range of problems from company strategy to aircraft movements and, in a very different field, the silting up of rivers.

17. Randomisation. When several events can happen with equal probability and nothing but chance determines which of the events actually does occur, we can say that these are random events. If our "events" are the appearance of each of the digits from 0 to 9, and each of the ten possible digits is equally likely to appear, then we can refer to the digit which actually "shows up" as a *random digit*. It would be possible to have a succession of random digits and these could be arranged as a *random number table.*

18. A random number table. The short table of numbers which follows has been constructed so that each of the ten possible digits stood an equal chance of appearing in each place.

72945	27812	21252	03493
27899	99703	95315	09191
27491	43405	99176	91184
20650	52331	21797	26765

19. Using the random number table. We can use the random number table to introduce a chance element into our simulation model. Taking as our basic situation an unloading bay at which motor lorries arrive, are unloaded and then depart, we could look back at past records and set up frequency distributions of arrivals and departures over a large number of hour-long periods. Such distributions are shown in Tables 17 and 18.

Possibly the distribution of departures would be more difficult to arrive at, but, even so, a theoretically based distribution could be constructed using the mean service time and the Poisson distribution.

TABLE 17.—DISTRIBUTION OF ARRIVALS OF LORRIES PER HOUR OVER 1000 HOURLY PERIODS (*30th June–20th December* 19–7)

Number of arrivals	*Periods in which observed*	*Percentage*	*Code*
0	50	5	00–04
1	70	7	05–11
2	80	8	12–19
3	100	10	20–29
4	150	15	30–44
5	170	17	45–61
6	200	20	62–81
7	90	9	82–90
8	50	5	91–95
9	10	1	96
10	20	2	97, 98
11	10	1	99
Total	1000	100	

Suppose that we now want to simulate a pattern of arrivals, using the random numbers shown above. The table shows the percentage of hourly time periods falling in each class-interval (recall XII, **10**) and one two-digit code number has been allotted to each percentage point. By taking, systematically,

TABLE 18.—DISTRIBUTION OF UNLOADINGS COMPLETED IN 1000 HOURLY PERIODS (*at peak working*)

Number of completions	*Periods in which observed*	*Percentage*	*Code*
0	20	2	00, 01
1	30	3	02–04
2	40	4	05–08
3	50	5	09–13
4	70	7	14–20
5	80	8	21–28
6	60	6	29–34
7	250	25	35–59
8	300	30	60–89
9	70	7	90–96
10	30	3	97–99
Total	1000	100	

pairs of digits from the random number table and letting each pair indicate the number of arrivals in one period we could generate, artificially, a pattern of arrivals which was governed by the pattern of past events and yet still contained a chance element. The pattern would be governed by past patterns because there are more "percentage-codes" in the classes most frequently observed in the past. Chance, of course, governs the random number pairs selected, since it was by a chance process that the random number table was set up.

20. A two-day simulation. Selecting pairs of random numbers from the top row and then going down to the next row and working along from left to right, we can take sixteen random number pairs, each pair representing the number of arrivals in an hourly period. The sixteen selections represent arrivals over two eight-hour working days (Table 19).

So long as we use a different part of the random number table, we can simulate a pattern of unloading completions. We must take a different part of the table so that the arrivals and departures are independent. Using these methods, the following pattern of sixteen completions has been generated:

5, 7, 4, 6, 2, 10, 4, 8
3, 8, 4, 8, 2, 5, 6, 5

Combining arrivals and departures, we have the pattern shown in Table 20.

TABLE 19

	Random numbers	*Indicated number of arrivals*
Day 1	72	6
	94	8
	52	5
	78	6
	12	2
	21	3
	25	3
	20	3
Day 2	34	4
	93	8
	27	3
	89	7
	99	11
	97	10
	03	0
	95	8

TABLE 20

Day	*Hour*	*Arrivals*	*Departures*	*Queue*
1	1	6	5	1
	2	8	7	2
	3	5	4	3
	4	6	6	3
	5	2	2	3
	6	3	10	—
	7	3	4	—
	8	3	8	—
2	1	4	3	1
	2	8	8	1
	3	3	4	—
	4	7	8	—
	5	11	2	9
	6	10	5	14
	7	0	6	8
	8	8	5	11

Where the simulated unloadings have exceeded the number of lorries in the queue plus the arrivals, it has been assumed that this represented a high unloading rate which cleared up the current work *and* the backlog.

21. The advantage of simulation models. Using models such as these a pattern of occurrences can be generated which represents a very long period of actual working. The effect of proposed changes in facilities provided or in working methods can be checked out *before* decisions are made.

22. Developing simulation models. The model outlined in this section was a crude and elementary one but similar principles can be used to simulate very complex situations. We could have assumed that several types of truck were using the unloading bay, with differing distributions for each type and a corresponding variety of unloading times. It would be easy to construct simulation models for inventory situations using simulated patterns of demand for various stores items. Simulation models can also be used to check the accuracy of analytic models.

23. Computers and simulation. It was mentioned earlier that simulation is essentially a computer method. The ability to store data, to set up distributions with any desired parameters and to generate series of random (or quasi-random) numbers all make for a relatively straightforward application. In recent years so much programming experience has been gained in this field and so much "software" developed that higher level simulation languages, such as SIMULA, have been specially designed to facilitate the examination of problems by simulation techniques.

PROGRESS TEST 21

1. For a single queue, single service-point system with Poisson arrivals and exponential service times, show how the average number of people in the system would vary if an average of 12 people needed the service every hour and μ took alternative values of 24, 18 and 15 per hour. What is the probability that a person entering the system would have to queue? **(8, 9)**

2. Certain precision tools require re-setting at fairly frequent

intervals. This can be done quickly with an automatic device of which there are three types on the market.

Type 1. An obsolescent machine of simple design which can re-set a tool in 3 minutes. Only second-hand models are available; these cost £750 and have a useful life of 1 year.

Type 2. A solid machine which can re-set a tool in 5 minutes. It costs £1500 and will last for 3 years.

Type 3. A machine of advanced design which will re-set a tool in 2 minutes but costs £2000. It is not so robust as Machine 2 and will last for 2 years only. In a particular workshop, 10 workers an hour need to re-set tools. They are at work for 40 hours a week over a 50-week year. Every hour of lost time costs £3·50 per man. Which machine should be purchased? **(8, 10)**

3. (*a*)* What importance do you attach to the "traffic intensity" of a system? **(9)**

(*b*) If arrivals at a two-channel system are at an average rate of 20 an hour, but services are only completed once every 4 minutes at each of the service points (with a Poisson distribution of completions), is the capacity of the system adequate? **(9, 12)**

4. If the same system had two service points each with a mean service time of $7\frac{1}{2}$ minutes, for what percentage of the time would you expect the system to be entirely unused? **(14)**

5.* Describe how simulation might be used to show the behaviour of the system used in Question 4. What are the advantages of using simulation in connection with queueing problems? **(16–20, 21)**

CHAPTER XXII

LINEAR PROGRAMMING (1)

THE BASIC FORMULATION OF A LINEAR PROGRAMMING PROBLEM

1. The mathematical form. A function representing costs, profits or some other quantifiable entity is to be optimised. This function is represented as being dependent on a number of variables, but none of them is taken to any degree higher than he first; that is there are no squares, cubes or higher powers involved. This function is called the *objective* function and could be written:

$$Z = c_1x_1 + c_2x_2 + \ . \ . \ . + c_nx_n,$$

where c_1, c_2, etc., are the coefficients of the variables x_1, x_2 and o on to x_n. (If the notation gives you any trouble, refer back to X, **16–19**, and also glance at V, **6**, where the $+ \ldots +$ method of showing a long series of terms was used.)

In optimising the objective function, however, we are subject to a series of constraints, which might represent the amount of labour available, the capacity of a machine shop or ome similar limiting factor. These constraints can be expressed as *inequalities*. Using a general notation, we could write:

$$\begin{aligned}
\textit{Optimise:}\ \ & Z = c_1x_1 + c_2x_2 + \ . \ . \ . + c_nx_n. \\
\textit{Subject to:}\ \ & a_{11}x_1 + a_{12}x_2 + \ . \ . \ . + a_{1n}x_n \leqslant b_1 \\
& a_{21}x_1 + a_{22}x_2 + \ . \ . \ . + a_{2n}x_n \leqslant b_2 \\
& \quad \vdots \qquad\quad \vdots \qquad\qquad\qquad\quad \vdots \\
& a_{m1}x_1 + a_{m2}x_2 + \ . \ . \ . + a_{mn}x_n \leqslant b_m.
\end{aligned}$$

he dots again indicating that we may have as many constraints as the real-life problem requires. The formulation iven above is the problem in its general, mathematical form.

2. An example. It is always easier to overcome the difficulties in a mathematical problem if they are reduced to a very simple form and put in the context of a familiar situation.

Suppose that you are running a furniture workshop that is turning out rather stylish (and expensive) tables and chairs. Your output consists of a basic chair which sells at £90 and gives you a profit of £30 for each one sold and a basic table which sells at £250 and yields a profit of £40 for each one sold. Your objective function is therefore:

$$Z = 30x_1 + 40x_2,$$

where Z is your total profit for the period concerned, x_1 is the number of chairs sold and x_2 is the number of tables sold. Let the period concerned be one week. There will be a limit to the number of chairs and tables which the workshops can turn out. Suppose that production is organised in a *woodworking shop*, where the basic components are made, an *assembly shop*, where both tables and chairs are put together, a *chair finishing and leather-work shop*, where the chairs are completed, and a *table polishing and finishing* shop, where the tables are completed. The output limitations (constraints) might be as follows:

Shop	*Maximum weekly capacity*
Woodworking	250 chairs or 150 tables
Assembly	150 chairs or 200 tables
Chair finishing and leatherwork	125 chairs
Table polishing and finishing	140 tables

These output constraints could be expressed as follows, using x_1 for the number of chairs and x_2 for the number of tables actually made in the week:

Woodworking constraint:	$x_1 + \frac{5}{3}x_2 \leqslant 250$
Assembly constraint:	$x_1 + \frac{3}{4}x_2 \leqslant 150$
Chair finishing constraint:	$x_1 \leqslant 125$
Table finishing constraint:	$x_2 \leqslant 140$

Our problem is to find how many chairs and how many tables should be made in order to maximise our profit, assuming that we can sell all we make.

NOTE: The "profit" in this example may be considered as the "contribution" towards fixed overheads.

3. The problem in mathematical form. The problem outlined n the example may now be set out in a completely abstract orm. It is:

Maximise:	$Z = 30x_1 + 40x_2$
Subject to:	$x_1 + \frac{5}{3}x_2 \leqslant 250$
	$x_1 + \frac{3}{4}x_2 \leqslant 150$
	$x_1 \leqslant 125$
	$x_2 \leqslant 140$
	$x_1 \geqslant 0;\ x_2 \geqslant 0$

The last two constraints emphasise that negative outputs are ıot possible. This formulation should now be compared with he general formulation given at the beginning of the section.

A GRAPHICAL SOLUTION

4. The constraints examined. The woodworking shop could nake enough parts *either* for 250 chairs *or* for 150 tables in a veek. Any "mix" of chairs and tables between the two xtremes, resulting from making only chairs or only tables, vould be possible. Graphically the woodworking constraint ould be displayed as a line on which were all the points epresenting outputs which fully utilised the shop's capacity. This is shown in Fig. 42(*a*).

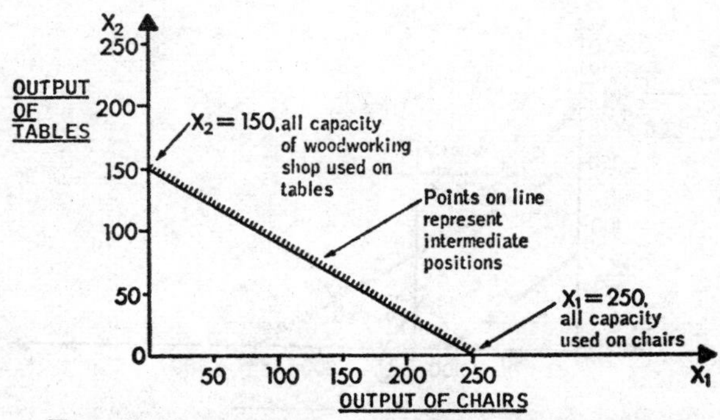

Fig. 42(*a*).—*Output constraint: woodworking shop*

If we use the hatching convention which we met in Chapter IX we can use this line to separate the graph into three parts: outputs which are just possible with the assembly shop working to capacity (on the line), outputs which are in excess of the shop's

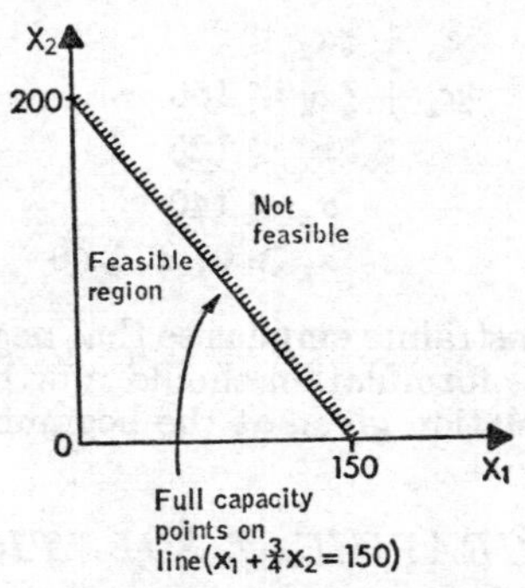

FIG. 42(*b*).—*Feasible region for assembly constraint*

capacity (above and to the right of the line) and possible or *feasible* outputs which are below and to the left of the line. This is shown in Fig. 42(*c*). The algebraic expression for the constraint can be arrived at by considering the equation for the "capacity line." In the case of the woodworking shop this line intercepts the x_2 (vertical axis) at a value of 150 and falls wit

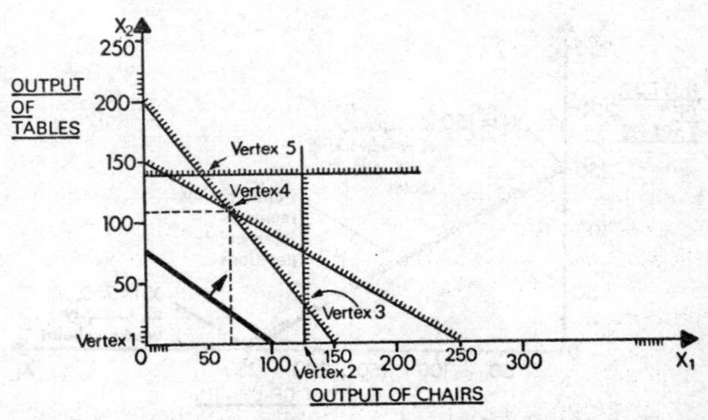

FIG. 42(*c*).—*Graphical solution of the linear programming proble*

gradient of $\frac{3}{5}$, so that, when $x_1 = 250$, $x_2 = 0$. Taking x_2 as he dependent variable (like y in an ordinary function), the quation of the line would be $x_2 = 150 - \frac{3}{5}x_1$. It is convenient o show the equation the other way round, that is as:

$$x_1 + \tfrac{5}{3}x_2 = 250.$$

Ve may now indicate the *feasible space* rather than the line equality) by writing:

$$x_1 + \tfrac{5}{3}x_2 \leqslant 250.$$

Dealing similarly with the other constraints, we can devise diagram to show all four of them and so to define the *feasible pace* that remains when all the constraints are taken into ccount (Fig. 42(*c*)).

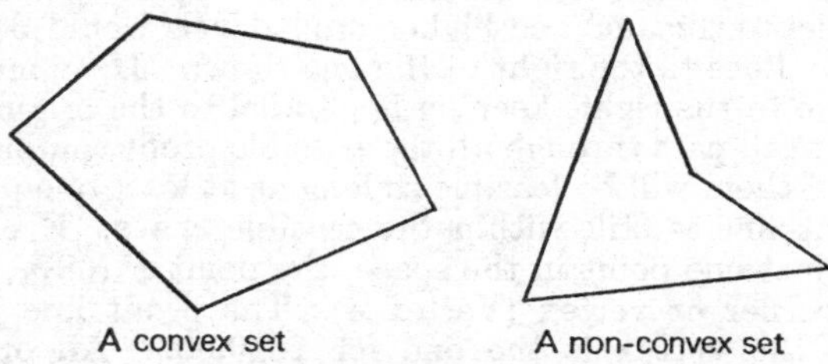

FIG. 43.—*Convex and non-convex sets*

5. The feasible space as a convex set. All the number pairs, onsisting of an x-co-ordinate and a y-co-ordinate, that repreent *possible* combinations of tables and chairs lie either on the nes that are the boundaries of the feasible space or in the pace itself. The feasible space, including the boundary lines remember that the constraints are "less than or equal to" onditions), forms a set of points. This set of points is a *onvex set* because it has no "re-entrants," no sections which are ent inwards, or, putting it another way, a straight line oining any two points inside the feasible space would not go utside the space at any point. Fig. 43 shows convex and on-convex sets.

6. The solution. Having shown the constraints graphically, ll that remains is to find which point within the feasible space epresents the production mix of tables and chairs that will give the greatest profit. To find the optimum we must add the profit function, or objective function as we called it previously. The function was:

$$Z = 30x_1 + 40x_2.$$

This is a linear function and is represented in the diagram by the heavy line. This line is one of many we could have shown, each line representing a different level of profit. The profit function shown represents all the points which would give a total profit of £3000 for the week's sales. It is easy to draw the line by putting $Z = 3000$ and x_1 (chairs) equal to zero; x_2 must then equal 75. The other end points of the profit line can be found by putting x_2 (tables) equal to zero; x_1 will then have to equal 100 and a line joining these two points will give all the intermediate points. All the other possible profit lines would be parallel to this one and higher profit levels would be represented by lines to the right of the one shown. If we move the profit line to the right, keeping it parallel to the original one, then we shall pass through all the possible profit combinations and all of them will be feasible so long as at least one point on the profit line is still within the feasible space. Eventually there is just one point in the space, the point P $(68\frac{2}{11}, 109\frac{1}{11})$ at one corner or vertex (Vertex 4). The profit line passing through the vertex is the one for £6409·09. All optimum points (solutions) will be at vertices in problems of this sort. The solution to the profit maximisation problem is to make 68 chairs and 109 tables (taken to the nearest whole number, naturally).

7. Problems in more than two dimensions. Because we were concerned with only two products, it was possible to represent this particular problem graphically. If we had been required to find the optimum mix for *three* products, say tables, chairs and sideboards, a three-dimensional model would have been required. Problems requiring more than three dimensions must be solved algebraically.

8. Integer programming. As is often the case with linear programming problems, the solution does not come out in whole numbers and therefore has to be interpreted in real, practicable terms. Usually, this presents no great difficulty but sometimes it is necessary to use a variant of linear programming which gives whole number solutions only. This is called *integer programming*.

THE SIMPLEX ALGORITHM

9. Complexity of real problems. The astute reader will have realised that, if the solution is always going to occur at a vertex, then it could have been found by solving pairs of simultaneous equations and testing out each possible solution until the one was found which gave the greatest profit. This is a possible method with a small-scale problem but real-life problems are too complicated for this method; there would be just too many simultaneous equations to handle. An improvement would be to find a method which located the required vertex as quickly as possible. There is such a method; it is called the *Simplex algorithm*.

10. Setting up the Simplex. The first step is to turn the inequalities into equalities. Since the equalities are "less than or equal to" expressions, there must be some quantity which could be added to each inequality to bring it up to the "equal to" mark. This quantity which turns the inequality into an equality is called a "slack variable." We shall add a slack variable to each constraint, giving them the symbols S_1, S_2, S_3, S_4. The problem can then be set out as follows:

Constraints:

$$x_1 + \tfrac{5}{3}x_2 + S_1 = 250 \quad \text{. . . (equation 1).}$$

$$x_1 + \tfrac{3}{4}x_2 + S_2 = 150 \quad \text{. . . (equation 2).}$$

$$x_1 + S_3 = 125 \quad \text{. . . (equation 3).}$$

$$x_2 + S_4 = 140 \quad \text{. . . (equation 4).}$$

Objective function: $30x_1 + 40x_2 = Z.$

This can represent our initial feasible solution (*see* below).

11. The algebraic solution. We now have four equations and six unknowns. There is therefore no unique solution; many values will satisfy the equations. All we need for a start is just one *possible* solution, even though it is not the optimum one. We call this our *initial feasible solution*. An easy one to start with is the "do nothing" solution; $x_1 = 0$, $x_2 = 0$. This will give $S_1 = 250$, $S_2 = 150$, $S_3 = 125$, $S_4 = 140$, these slack variables representing the *unused capacity* in each workshop. Naturally the profit will be zero, that is $Z = 0$. This situation can be represented by the layout in the previous paragraph and substitution will show that the values will make the equations true.

The coefficients of the variables in each equation represent the amount of the available capacity that is needed to make one unit of product. To find which constraint "bites" first we divide the capacity, shown by the right-hand-side constants, by the coefficients of the variables. We can choose either x_1 or x_2 as the variable to start with. If we choose x_1, the coefficients of x_1 are 1 in each case. Constraint number 3, with a right-hand-side constant of 125 is met with first. Systematised, the solution proceeds as follows:

	Action in this case
Step 1. Choose a variable	x_1 chosen
Step 2. Divide right-hand sides of each equation except objective function by coefficients of chosen variable.	Coefficients all unity. R.h.s. constants ÷ 1 give 250 150 125 140
Step 3. Choose equation with smallest r.h.s. constant after division.	Equation 3; 125/1 = 125
Step 4. Bring coefficient of chosen variable in selected equation to unity by suitable division of whole equation.	No action: coefficient already unity.
Step 5. Clear chosen variable out of other constraint equations by suitable subtractions, as with ordinary simultaneous equations.	Subtract equation 3 from equations 1 and 2.
Step 6. Clear chosen variable from objective function.	Multiply equation 3 by 15 and subtract from objective function.
Step 7. Check and interpret result.	*See* below.

CHECK:

$$\tfrac{5}{3}x_2 + S_1 - S_3 = 125 \quad \ldots \quad \text{(equation 1(}a\text{))}.$$
$$\tfrac{3}{4}x_2 + S_2 - S_3 = 25 \quad \ldots \quad \text{(equation 2(}a\text{))}.$$
$$x_1 \qquad + S_3 = 125 \quad \ldots \quad \text{(equation 3(}a\text{))}.$$
$$x_2 \qquad + S_4 = 140 \quad \ldots \quad \text{(equation 4(}a\text{))}.$$
$$40x_2 \quad -30S_3 = Z - 3750$$

Interpretation:

$$x_1 = 125, \ S_1 = 125$$
$$x_2 = 0, \ S_2 = 25$$
$$S_3 = 0, \ S_4 = 140$$
$$\text{Profit} = 125 \times £30 = £3750.$$

Note that this satisfies the equations given above and represents the position at vertex 2 in Fig. 42(c).

Choosing x_2 as our variable and repeating steps 2 and 3 establishes constraint 2 as the next one to affect us and equation 2(a) as the one to be manipulated first. Following the instructions of step 4 we must multiply 2(a) by $\frac{4}{3}$ (*i.e.* divide by $\frac{3}{4}$) and then clear x_2 from the other equations (steps 5 and 6). The result to be checked and interpreted will be:

$$S_1 - \tfrac{20}{9}S_2 + \tfrac{11}{9}S_3 = 69\tfrac{4}{9} \quad \ldots \quad \text{(equation 1(}b\text{))}.$$
$$x_2 \quad + \tfrac{4}{3}S_2 - \tfrac{4}{3}S_3 = 33\tfrac{1}{3} \quad \ldots \quad \text{(equation 2(}b\text{))}.$$
$$x_1 \qquad + \quad S_3 = 125 \quad \ldots \quad \text{(equation 3(}b\text{))}.$$
$$- \tfrac{4}{3}S_2 + \tfrac{4}{3}S_3 + S_4 = 106\tfrac{2}{3} \quad \ldots \quad \text{(equation 4(}b\text{))}.$$
$$-\tfrac{160}{3}S_2 + \tfrac{70}{3}S_3 = Z - 5083\tfrac{1}{3}.$$

Interpretation:

		£
$x_1 = 125, \ S_1 = 69\frac{4}{9}$	Profit is 125 × £30 =	3750
$x_2 = 33\frac{1}{3}, \ S_2 = 0$	*plus* $33\frac{1}{3}$ × £40 =	$1333\frac{1}{3}$
$S_3 = 0, \ S_4 = 106\frac{2}{3}$		$5083\frac{1}{3}$

This corresponds to the position of vertex 3. We can now add a further check.

Step 8. Are there any positive coefficients on the left-hand side of the objective function?

There are; the coefficient of S_3 is $+\frac{70}{3}$. We have therefore *not* reached an optimum solution and must proceed through steps 1 to 7 with S_3 as our chosen variable. Our chosen equation will be 1(*b*) as tests which give negative right-hand-side constants, as would be the case with equation 2(*b*), are ruled out. Negative right-hand-side constants represent points outside the feasible space.

Our final check gives:

$$\begin{array}{lll} \frac{9}{11}S_1 - \frac{20}{11}S_2 + S_3 = 56\frac{9}{11} & \ldots & \text{(equation 1(}c\text{)).} \\ x_2 + \frac{12}{11}S_1 - \frac{12}{11}S_2 = 109\frac{1}{11} & \ldots & \text{(equation 2(}c\text{)).} \\ x_1 \quad - \frac{9}{11}S_1 - \frac{20}{11}S_2 = 68\frac{2}{11} & \ldots & \text{(equation 3(}c\text{)).} \\ - \frac{12}{11}S_1 + \frac{12}{11}S_2 + S_4 = 30\frac{10}{11} & \ldots & \text{(equation 4(}c\text{)).} \\ \hline -\frac{210}{11}S_1 - \frac{120}{11}S_2 = Z - 6409\frac{1}{11}. & & \end{array}$$

Interpretation:

$$x_1 = 68\tfrac{2}{11};\ S_1 = 0$$
$$x_2 = 109\tfrac{1}{11};\ S_2 = 0$$
$$S_3 = 56\tfrac{9}{11};\ S_4 = 30\tfrac{10}{11}$$
$$\text{Profit} = £6409\tfrac{1}{11}.$$

This corresponds to vertex 4 in the diagram.

All these values satisfy the equations and agree with the graphical solution. Step 8 confirms that there are no negative coefficients on the left-hand side of the objective function. This method is tedious for a simple problem, but it displays the method which is used to tackle very large problems and which, programmed for a computer, can solve problems which were quite without any definite solution twenty or more years ago. A neater and more appropriate way to proceed, and one which may be expected in some examinations, is to utilise the matrix notation of X, **6–16**.

THE SIMPLEX ALGORITHM IN MATRIX FORM

12. Converting to matrix notation. In X, **12** we learned to multiply matrices and vectors. If we now take our linear programming problem, we could represent the coefficients of the variables in the four constraint inequalities as follows:

$$\mathbf{A} = \begin{bmatrix} 1 & \frac{5}{8} \\ 1 & \frac{3}{4} \\ 1 & 0 \\ 0 & 1 \end{bmatrix}.$$

The variables x_1 and x_2 could be represented in vector form:

$$\boldsymbol{x} = \begin{bmatrix} x_1 \\ x_2 \end{bmatrix}$$

Multiplication of $\boldsymbol{x}$ by **A**, using the row-into-column rule, will now give the left-hand side of the constraint inequalities:

$$\mathbf{A}\boldsymbol{x} = \begin{bmatrix} x_1 + \frac{5}{3}x_2 \\ x_2 + \frac{3}{4}x_2 \\ x_1 + 0 \\ 0 + x_2 \end{bmatrix}.$$

The product is a four-element column vector. Just as vectors may be linked by an equals sign if every element in one equals the corresponding element in the other, so they may be linked by an inequality sign if corresponding elements are all "less than" or "more than" their opposite numbers. In our case they are "less than or equal to" and so writing the right-hand-side constants in vector form as:

$$\boldsymbol{b} = \begin{bmatrix} 250 \\ 150 \\ 125 \\ 140 \end{bmatrix},$$

we may set up the whole system as:

$$\mathbf{A}\boldsymbol{x} \leqslant \boldsymbol{b}.$$

13. The initial Simplex tableau. It now remains to add in the slack variables. We can do this by using a partitioned matrix (check back with X, **19**, if necessary) and setting aside one section for the slack variables. The form of the initial tableau, in matrix notation, will be:

A	**I**	$\boldsymbol{b}$
$-\boldsymbol{c}$	**0**	**0**

where $\boldsymbol{c}$ is a row vector of the coefficients of x_1 and x_2 in the objective function. The sign of $\boldsymbol{c}$ has been changed to give a positive result for the profit and to give an appropriate system of indicators. The symbols **I** and **0** stand for the unit matrix and the zero vectors, as in earlier chapters.

Filling in the values of the elements we can show our initial Simplex tableau:

x_1	x_2	S_1	S_2	S_3	S_4	b
1	$\frac{5}{3}$	1	0	0	0	250
1	$\frac{3}{4}$	0	1	0	0	150
1	0	0	0	1	0	125
0	1	0	0	0	1	140
−30	−40	0	0	0	0	0

Values of variable will appear here (rows 1–4 of b)

Profit appears here. (bottom row of b)

Indicators (bottom row)

14. Points to note.

(*a*) The method is basically the same as the algebraic method used previously. Check each tableau with the algebraic solution.

(*b*) When a variable is in use, its coefficient will be unity. It will be "in the basis," to accept the usual jargon.

(*c*) Negative elements in ***b*** are not allowed; they mean that you are trying to go outside the feasible space.

(*d*) The various annotations in the tableau shown above are for assistance only and will be dropped in subsequent tableaux.

15. Method.

(*a*) Note the six entries marked as indicators. Are there any negative indicators? If there are, the optimum solution has not been found; pass to next instruction.

(*b*) Select a negative indicator. Call the column which contains this indicator the pivotal column. Mark this column with an asterisk.

(*c*) Test the availabilities of each resource by dividing each element of the pivotal column, in turn, into the corresponding elements of the vector ***b***. Select the row for which this division gives the minimum, but non-negative, result. Designate this row the pivotal row and mark it at the left-hand side with an arrow.

(*d*) The element at the intersection of the pivotal row and pivotal column is the pivot. Mark it in some suitable way. In the examples the pivot is shown in bold type.

(*e*) Divide the whole pivotal row by the value of the pivot. This will form a new row for the next tableau.

(*f*) Form the remaining rows of the next tableau by reducing all other elements of pivotal column to zero by subtracting appropriate multiples of the new (revised ex-pivotal) row from all the other rows.

(*g*) Continue the process for the row representing the objective function, but watch the minus signs carefully; mistakes are easy here. The extreme right-hand element of the last, objective function, row is the profit.

(*h*) Check whether any negative indicators remain. If they do, return to instruction (*b*) and repeat the process.

16. Tableaux for the furniture example.

Tableau 1 (as given).

	1	$\frac{5}{3}$	1	0	0	0	250
	1	$\frac{3}{4}$	0	1	0	0	150
→	1	0	0	0	1	0	125
	0	1	0	0	0	1	140
	−30	−40	0	0	0	0	0
	*						

Tableau 2.

	0	$\frac{5}{3}$	1	0	−1	0	125
→	0	$\frac{3}{4}$	0	1	−1	0	25
	1	0	0	0	1	0	125
	0	1	0	0	0	1	140
	0	40	0	0	30	0	3750
		— *					

Tableau 3.

→	0	0	1	$-\frac{20}{9}$	$+\frac{11}{9}$	0	$69\frac{4}{9}$
	0	1	0	$\frac{4}{3}$	$-\frac{4}{3}$	0	$33\frac{1}{3}$
	1	0	0	0	1	0	125
	0	0	0	$-\frac{4}{3}$	$+\frac{4}{3}$	1	$106\frac{2}{3}$
	0	0	0	$\frac{160}{3}$	$-\frac{70}{3}$	0	$5083\frac{1}{3}$
					*		

Tableau 4.

0	0	$\frac{9}{11}$	$-\frac{20}{11}$	1	0	$56\frac{9}{11}$	$\leftarrow S_3$
0	1	$\frac{12}{11}$	$-\frac{12}{11}$	0	0	$109\frac{1}{11}$	$\leftarrow x_2$
1	0	$-\frac{9}{11}$	$-\frac{20}{11}$	0	0	$68\frac{2}{11}$	$\leftarrow x_1$
0	0	$-\frac{12}{11}$	$+\frac{12}{11}$	0	1	$30\frac{10}{11}$	$\leftarrow S_4$
0	0	$+\frac{210}{11}$	$+\frac{120}{11}$	0	0	$6409\frac{1}{11}$	
		Dual variables					

There are no negative indicators, therefore this is an optimum solution. Note that there are *four* variables in the solution, one for each constraint.

THE DUAL PROBLEM

17. Nature of the dual problem. In the last tableau it will be noted that two values which appear in the bottom row of the columns for the slack variables, S_1 and S_2, have been marked "dual variables." These values are the solutions for a minimisation problem which corresponds to the maximisation which we have just solved.

In linear programming there is a minimisation problem corresponding to every maximisation problem. If we designate the original problem as the *primal problem*, its "mirror image" problem can be called the *dual problem*.

18. Writing out the dual problem. To find the dual problem, go back to the primal problem and read down the columns, designating four new *dual* variables, one for each constraint, as n_1, n_2, n_3 and n_4. When you reach the objective function preface the coefficient by a "more than or equals to" sign. It is probably most easy to do this using Tableau 1 of the Simplex matrix formulation. Read down the b vector in the same way, but make this the new objective function, putting it equal to w, which must be minimised. The result of turning the whole problem inside out in this way will be:

$$\left.\begin{aligned} n_1 + n_2 + n_3 &\geqslant 30 \\ \tfrac{5}{8}n_1 + \tfrac{3}{4}n_2 + n_4 &\geqslant 40 \end{aligned}\right\} \text{Constraints}$$

Objective function:

$$250n_1 + 150n_2 + 125n_3 + 140n_4 = w \text{ (minimum)}.$$

19. The solution of the dual problem. At the optimum solution the dual inequalities become strict equalities. The two variables n_3 and n_4 have zero values, and the required equalities are therefore:

$$n_1 + n_2 = 30 \quad . \; . \; . \; (1)$$

$$\tfrac{5}{8}n_1 + \tfrac{3}{4}n_2 = 40 \quad . \; . \; . \; (2),$$

the solution of these equations being easily found as $n_1 = \frac{210}{11}$, $n_2 = \frac{120}{11}$.

20. Interpreting the dual. The right-hand-side constant in equation (1) above represents the £30 profit produced by each chair made and sold. The two variables n_1 and n_2 can be regarded as the contributions made by the two scarce resources, woodworking capacity and assembly capacity. The unit of capacity in each case is the quantity of resources sufficient to carry out the operations on one chair. We could regard the values of the dual variables as the amount in £'s that we should be prepared to pay for one extra unit of capacity. That this is so can be checked by removing the woodworking constraint and seeing how much extra profit (contribution) results.

Refer back to Fig. 42(*c*) and imagine that the woodworking shop constraint has been removed. The objective function can now be moved to a higher profit level. The maximum profit that can be earned now is that which results from selling 45 chairs and 140 tables, that is £6950. The additional profit is £$540\frac{10}{11}$ and this has been earned by making and selling 31 more tables ($30\frac{10}{11}$ is the actual addition to x_2 at vertex 5) and 23 fewer chairs. A table requires $\frac{5}{3}$rds as much woodworking capacity as a chair, so the difference in capacity used is:

Tables:	$\frac{5}{3} \times 30\frac{10}{11} =$	$51\frac{17}{33}$ units
Chairs (reduction):		$23\frac{2}{11}$ units
Additional capacity used:		$28\frac{1}{3}$ units

The additional profit per capacity unit is:

$$\frac{£540\frac{10}{11}}{28\frac{1}{3}}$$

$$= \frac{£210}{11}.$$

Checking back to the optimum values of the dual variables confirms that this is the value shown for n_1. If we had the opportunity of buying more woodworking capacity, it would be worth paying up to this amount for each unit of it. Naturally, n_3 and n_4 have zero values since there is excess capacity in the two finishing shops.

PROGRESS TEST 22

1. A type of plastic article is processed in two machines, a press and a trimmer. Two variants of the article are produced. Variant A takes 5 seconds in the press and 10 seconds in the trimmer. Variant B takes 6 seconds in the press and 3 seconds in the trimmer. There are two presses and three trimmers available.

Variant A yields a contribution of 6p per article made and Variant B yields 10p per article made. At what rate should each **be produced in order to give the maximum contribution per unit of time? (1–16)**

2. Write out the dual of this problem, solve it by means of the Simplex method and interpret your answer. (17–20)

CHAPTER XXIII

LINEAR PROGRAMMING (2)

OTHER APPLICATIONS OF LINEAR PROGRAMMING

1. Versatility of linear programming. Now that the basic technique of linear programming has been outlined, it is possible to consider other ways of using it. It is an extremely versatile tool for the solution of business problems, which often require that some quantity is maximised or minimised while keeping within the constraints set by the physical or economic situation in which the firm is placed.

2. Minimisation problems. The obvious business variable to be minimised is cost. It is not difficult to find a straightforward method of handling these problems, since we have already found that the Simplex method solves a minimisation problem at the same time as it solves the maximisation one.

3. Transportation problems. Another type of problem that can easily be set out in linear programming form is that which arises when goods from a number of factories have to be sent to a number of warehouses. It is required to find the least cost allocation of routes so that the requirements of all the warehouses are met. This problem arises so frequently, in various disguises, that special routines have been developed to handle it.

4. Assignment problems. Another special case occurs when a given number of men have to be allocated, or assigned, to the same number of jobs. By quantifying their suitability in some appropriate way, the optimum assignment of men to jobs can be found by means of special linear programming techniques. This method is not considered in this book for reasons of space.

A MINIMISATION PROBLEM

5. Application of the Simplex method. The method of solving a minimisation problem is best described by means of an example. The technique used is basically the Simplex method described in XXII, 9–16.

6. The example. A firm operates two plants each of which produces animal feeding stuff in the form of a mixed output of cake, unshaped pellets and meal. The hourly output of the two plants is as follows:

	Cake	*Pellets*	*Meal*
Plant A	25 tonnes	15 tonnes	10 tonnes
Plant B	50 tonnes	5 tonnes	75 tonnes

The two plants are run intermittently as required. On a particular day the firm has orders in hand for 2000 tonnes of cake, 500 tonnes of pellets and 1350 tonnes of meal, and the plants will be run simultaneously until these quantities are available.

If it costs £10 an hour to run Plant A and £25 an hour to run Plant B, for how long should each be run in order to provide sufficient output to meet the current orders?

7. Setting up the problem. Let x_1 be the number of hours for which Plant A is to run and x_2 be the number of hours for which Plant B is to run. The product of hours times output must be at least as great as the requirements for each type of animal food. The system of constraints is therefore:

$$
\begin{aligned}
25x_1 + 50x_2 &\geqslant 2000 \\
15x_1 + 5x_2 &\geqslant 500 \\
10x_1 + 75x_2 &\geqslant 1350 \\
x_1 &\geqslant 0 \\
x_2 &\geqslant 0
\end{aligned}
$$

The objective function which is to be minimised is:

$$10x_1 + 25x_2 = w.$$

8. Putting the problem into the Simplex tableau. The Simplex algorithm, operated in the same way as before, maximises the primal problem and minimises its dual. If we want to minimise our objective function we must turn the problem round, so that the same sequence of operations produces the required result. We shall have to maximise the *dual* of the problem set out above in order to minimise the primal as we are required to do. The dual of the problem is:

$$\left.\begin{aligned} 25n_1 + 15n_2 + 10n_3 &\leqslant 10 \\ 50n_1 + 5n_2 + 75n_3 &\leqslant 25 \end{aligned}\right\}\text{Constraints}$$

$$2000n_1 + 500n_2 + 1350n_3 = b \text{ (objective function)}$$

9. The solution. The successive Simplex tableaux are presented without comment as the method of operation is exactly the same as that used for the maximisation problem. The results, the number of hours for which the plants are to be run, will appear where the values of the dual variables appeared before.

Tableau 1.

→	25	15	10	1	0	10
	50	5	75	0	1	25
	−2000	−500	−1350	0	0	0
	*			Results will appear here		

Tableau 2.

	1	$\frac{3}{5}$	$\frac{2}{5}$	$\frac{1}{25}$	0	$\frac{2}{5}$
→	0	−25	55	−2	1	5
	0	700	−550	80	0	800
			*			

Tableau 3.

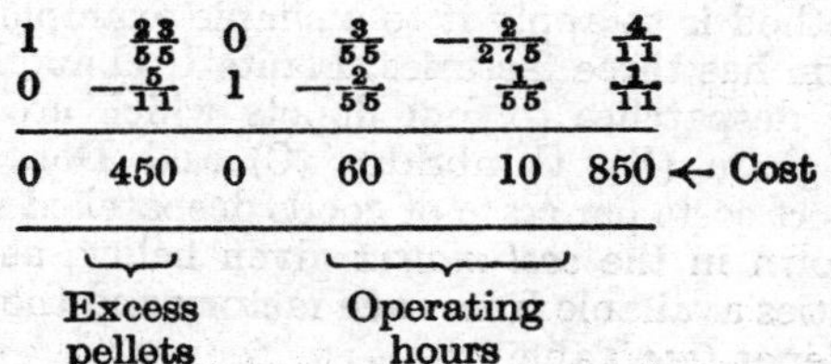

1	$\frac{23}{55}$	0	$\frac{3}{55}$	$-\frac{2}{275}$	$\frac{4}{11}$	
0	$-\frac{5}{11}$	1	$-\frac{2}{55}$	$\frac{1}{55}$	$\frac{1}{11}$	
0	450	0	60	10	850	← Cost
	Excess pellets		Operating hours			

10. Interpretation of solution. As has already been mentioned, the solution appears where the dual solution appeared in the maximisation problem. The best policy is to run Plant A for 60 hours at a cost of £600 and Plant B for 10 hours at a cost of £250, giving the total cost of £850 as shown. Although this is the cheapest possible way of producing the required quantities, it still gives an excess quantity of pellets. This, also, is shown on the bottom row of the final tableau.

THE TRANSPORTATION PROBLEM

11. The problem stated. The problem of finding the combination of routes between sources (factories, for example) and destinations (warehouses, say) which gives the minimum total transportation cost is a linear programming one provided that there is a constant cost per unit transported along each of the routes. That is to say, it must be true that it costs ten times as much to send ten units between a given source and destination as it does to send one unit. Fortunately this is quite often the case.

If the requirements of each destination are known, then a series of constraints exists, since the quantities despatched from the sources must not be more than those required by the destinations. With the sum of the costs serving as the objective function to be minimised and the availabilities from the sources and requirements of the destinations serving as constraints, the transportation problem *could* be written as an ordinary linear programming problem and solved by means of the Simplex algorithm. However, simpler methods have been devised.

12. An example. Once again, the easiest way of describing the method is to apply it to a simple example.

A firm has three factories, Plants I, II and III, which make weekly despatches to four depots which are in Aintree (A), Birmingham (B), Cambridge (C) and Doncaster (D). The transport costs per crate of goods despatched along each route are shown in the *cost matrix* given below, as are the weekly quantities available from each factory and the requirements of each depot (*see* Table 21).

TABLE 21.—COST MATRIX

Depot	*Cost per crate*				*Quantities available*
	A	*B*	*C*	*D*	
Factory I	£4	£7	£9	£2	400
II	£1	£8	£3	£9	200
III	£4	£6	£3	£5	400
Quantities required	250	250	420	80	1000

13. Method of approach. The basic approach to the problem will take the following stages:

(*a*) Set up an initial feasible solution, a routing which works, whether it is the best method or not.

(*b*) Find out what it is costing, per crate, *not* to use each of the unused routes.

(*c*) Compare this *cost of not using* each route with the additional cost incurred by sending one unit (one crate) along each of the unused routes.

(*d*) Move as great a quantity as possible along the route showing the greatest advantage.

(*e*) Check whether we now have an optimum solution.

If this series of steps has not produced an optimum solution, we go back to step (*b*), with our revised routings, and once again evaluate the routes which are not being used, following the sequence of operations right through to the final check. This is an *iterative*, that is a repeating, process which is carried on until the optimum solution is found.

14. An initial feasible solution for the example. To start the process, we require a first workable solution. To get this, we take the top left-hand cell and enter as big a figure as possible, taking into account the maximum quantity available from Plant 1 and required by Depot A. The largest figure that can be entered is 250. We must now move to an adjacent cell. We cannot move down, as requirement A has been met, and so we move to the right to Route IB. The maximum figure to be entered here is 150, thus taking up the remainder of Plant I's output. Continuing in this way, we arrive at the following initial feasible solution. Taking the number of sources as m and the number of destinations as n, there should be $(m + n - 1)$ occupied cells.

Tableau 1

Depots / Factory	[4] A	[7] B	[2] C	[4] D	Available
[0] I	[4] **250**	[7] **150**	[9] 7 (2)	[2] −2 (4)	400
[1] II	[1] −4 (5)	[8] **100**	[3] **100**	[9] 4 (5)	200
[1] III	[4] −1 (5)	[6] −2 (8)	[3] **320**	[5] **80**	400
Required	250	250	420	80	1000

Total cost £4510

15. Finding costs of not using routes. Consider Route IIA. If we send a crate along this route, we shall have to withdraw one from Route IA to keep within the requirements of Depot A. We shall also have to withdraw one crate from Route IIB to keep within the capacity of Plant II and consequently we shall have to send another crate along IB to make up the total sent to Depot B. By *not* doing any of these things, we shall forego any savings that might have resulted; these lost savings will be the cost of not using the given route.

Evaluation for Route IIA. The total costs (lost savings) for this route are:

	£
Cost of keeping one unit in Route IA	4
Cost of keeping one unit in Route IIB	8
Total costs	12
Less saving from not sending a unit along IB	7
Net cost of *not* using IIA	£5

If we do send a unit along IIA, it will cost an additional £1, the actual transportation cost, but will save £5, the net advantage being £4 for each unit sent along that route.

16. A quicker way of evaluating the routes. To evaluate each route, we shall now split the total cost into a nominal despatch cost and a nominal reception cost. These are sometimes called "shadow costs." In the initial feasible solution in Tableau 1, the actual transport costs per unit are shown in the square boxes in the upper left-hand corner of each cell. We shall assume that, for each of the routes actually used, the shadow despatch cost plus the shadow reception cost is equal to the actual unit transport cost.

To set up the shadow costs, we assume that one source (factory) has a despatch cost of zero and that this acts as a datum for the calculation of the other shadow costs. For convenience, the shadow despatch cost of zero has been allocated to Plant I. This is shown in the box on the left-hand margin. Since the shadow costs for each *used* route must add up to the actual cost, the reception cost for Depot A must be £4. This is shown in the square box in the upper margin. Expressing this symbolically, we could write $C(\text{IA})$ for the total cost associated with Route IA. This is made up of a despatch cost, $D(\text{I})$, and a reception cost, $R(\text{A})$. We may write this as:

$$C(\text{IA}) = D(\text{I}) + R(\text{A}).$$

Since we know the actual cost of using Route IA:

$$C(\text{IA}) = 4.$$

Also: $D(\text{I}) = 0$, as agreed above.

Therefore: $0 + R(\text{A}) = 4$

or: $\underline{R(\text{A}) = 4.}$

Similarly, we can show that $R(\text{B}) = 7$. Knowing this, we can continue:

$C(\text{IIB}) = D(\text{II}) + R(\text{B})$,

$R(\text{B}) = 7$, from previous calculations,

and $C(\text{IIB}) = 8$, the actual transport cost per unit,

$\therefore\ D(\text{II}) + 7 = 8$

or $\underline{D(\text{II}) = 1.}$

Having calculated a value for D(II), the shadow despatch costs for Plant II, we can calculate the reception costs for Depot C:

$$C(\text{IIC}) = 3, \text{ actual costs,}$$
$$D(\text{I}) = 1, \text{ previously calculated,}$$
$$C(\text{IIC}) = D(\text{II}) + R(\text{C})$$
$$\therefore\ 3 = 1 + R(\text{C})$$

or $\underline{R(\text{C}) = 2.}$

The remaining shadow costs can be calculated as shown on the initial tableau.

17. Using the shadow costs. The cost of *not* using the *unused* routes can now be calculated by adding together the appropriate shadow costs. Thus the cost of not using Route IIA is D(II) plus R(A). Designating this cost as N(IIA), we have:

$$N(\text{IIA}) = D(\text{II}) + R(\text{A})$$
$$= 1 + 4$$
$$= \underline{5}.$$

This agrees with the value previously calculated. The cost of not using each of the unused routes is shown in the bottom right-hand corner of each cell of the initial feasible solution.

18. Making the comparison. To find out whether an unused route *should* be used, we must subtract the cost of not using the route from the cost of using it. That is, the figures just calculated and shown in the rounded box in the bottom right-hand corner of each cell must be subtracted from the figure in the square bracket in the top left-hand corner. For cell (Route) IIA this is:

Actual transport cost — *Cost of not using* = (£1 — £5) or —£4.

This is shown in the centre of the cell and the corresponding figures are shown in the centres of the other cells. Where these are negative, it is worth while using the route. The change made will be to use the route with the "biggest" negative figure. The cell to change to is that for Route IIA.

19. Finding the quantity to move. Having selected the best cell to move to, we must now calculate the quantity to send along the new route. First of all we indicate the route by placing a plus sign in the cell (IIA). This is done in the check grid in Table 22.

TABLE 22

	A	B	C	D	*Available*
I	− 250	+ 150			400
II	+	− 100	100		200
III			320	80	400
Required	250	250	420	80	

In order to keep within the availability and requirement constraints, we must adjust other cells. To find out which ones must be changed we must adopt the following procedure:

(*a*) Put a minus sign in any other occupied cell in the same row which has other occupied cells in the same column.

(*b*) Put a plus sign in any other occupied cell in *that* cell's column, where there is an occupied cell in the same row.

(*c*) Repeat the procedure until the original column is reached.

Now inspect the marked cells and find the smallest quantity entered in a cell with a minus sign. Add this quantity to the "plus" cells and subtract it from the minus cells. Following this procedure will give Tableau 2. Note that the saving is 100 × £4 as the procedure forecast.

Tableau 2

Depots / Plants	[4] A	[7] B	[6] C	[8] D	Available
[0] I	150	250	[9] 3 (6)	[2] −6 (8)	400
[-3] II	100	[8] 4 (4)	100	[9] 4 (5)	200
[-3] III	[4] 3 (1)	[6] +2 (4)	320	80	400
Requirements	250	250	420	80	1000

Total cost £4110

20. Second iteration. The new shadow costs have also been shown in Tableau 2, and these indicate that the next move is to Route ID. Using the same procedure as before, and readers should follow this through, we find Tableau 3.

Inspection shows that comparing cost of using and cost of not using gives no negative values. There is no advantage in making further changes; this is an optimum solution.

Tableau 3

Plants \ Depots	4 A	7 B	6 C	2 D	Available
0 I	70	250	9 3 6	80	400
-3 II	180	8 4 4	20	9 10 -1	200
-3 III	4 3 1	6 2 4	400	5 6 -1	400
Requirements	250	250	420	80	1000

Total cost £3630

COMPLICATIONS

21. Degeneracy. This rather long procedure should be followed through until the method is mastered. Unfortunately there may be occasions when it breaks down. In **14** above, it was mentioned that there should be $(m + n - 1)$ occupied cells, where m is the number of rows (sources) and n is the number of columns (destinations). Occasionally, it happens that there are fewer occupied cells than this. This complication is known as *degeneracy*.

The method of handling degeneracy is to treat one of the occupied cells as if it were occupied, or, for those who like the approved jargon, "as if it had a zero allocation." Other than this, the solution proceeds as before. If this adjustment is not made, the shadow costs cannot be calculated.

22. Excess production. In real-life examples, it is obvious that the quantity available from the sources may be in excess of the requirements of the destinations. The method here is to include a dummy destination and to allocate zero transport costs to all of the routes to this dummy destination.

EXAMPLE: With other details as before, let the quantity available from Plant III be 500 crates. The initial feasible solution and shadow costs will be as follows:

Tableau 4

Plants \ Depots	A [5]	B [8]	C [3]	D [5]	Dummy [0]	Available
[-1] I	[4] 250	[7] 150				400
[0] II		[8] 100	[3] 100			200
[0] III			[3] 320	[5] 80	[0] 100	500
Required	250	250	420	80	100	1100

Note that $m = 3$, $n = 5$, and that the number of utilised routes is $(m + n - 1) = 7$. Note also that zero shadow costs must be allocated to the used dummy route. The full solution is left to Exercise 3 in Progress Test 23.

23. Computers and linear programming. The mathematics of linear programming has, in the main, been developed in the post-war years. The underlying concepts are quite subtle, although the methods as displayed in this chapter and the previous one are fairly straightforward in application. The amount of actual arithmetic involved is formidable, however, and for real-life problems, involving large numbers of products, many depots and so on, the work has become practicable only with the advent of electronic computers. Because linear programming enables many varying problems to be put into a common mathematical form, it has been possible to devise standard computer programmes for linear programming problems. It is now standard for manufacturers to supply linear programming "packages" among the software for their computer installations.

PROGRESS TEST 23

1. An animal-feed must provide at least 2000 calories and 100 protein units per day to provide required growth rates. It is possible to use three ingredients, the particulars of which are given below.

	Calories per kg	*Protein units per kg*	*Cost per kg*
Ingredient 1	1100	22	20p
Ingredient 2	440	13	10p
Ingredient 3	220	18	10p

Calculate an optimum (lowest cost) mix. (5–10)

2. Below is a cost matrix which also shows quantities available from three sources and required by four destinations. Use the transportation method to find the least cost routing. (11–20)

COST MATRIX
(*costs in £s, quantities in tonnes*)
Destinations

Sources	A	B	C	D	*Availabilities*
I	15	4	12	9	25
II	8	10	6	3	10
III	7	5	10	11	15
Requirements	14	16	8	12	50

3. Complete the example in 22.

4.* Discuss the various ways in which linear programming might be used in aid of business decisions and indicate some reasons why the practical application of these methods has depended on the introduction of computers. (1–4, 23 and previous chapter.)

PART FIVE

REGRESSION AND FORECASTING

CHAPTER XXIV

REGRESSION AND CORRELATION

THE LINE OF BEST FIT

1. Relationships. In business we are often concerned with ituations which are not so exactly structured that the elationships concerned are functional ones, but which evertheless exhibit recognisable connections between the arious quantities observed. There may be a strong conection between advertising expenditure and sales and yet he relationship is unlikely to be nearly exact enough for sales o be calculated from a given advertising expenditure.

2. A scatter diagram. In cases like this, instead of the umber pairs lying on the curve of the function concerned, hey will form a scatter of points in which a general drift is iscernible. As an illustration, consider a series of inspection osts per thousand articles produced recorded on a number of ccasions at several factories controlled by a single group and roducing comparable products. Against each level of inpection costs, the corresponding number of defectives per housand articles is recorded. A set of ten pairs of observations s obtained as in Table 23.

TABLE 23

Observation	*Inspection costs per thousand articles* (£)	*Number of defective articles per thousand*
1	0·25	50
2	0·30	35
3	0·15	60
4	0·75	15
5	0·40	46
6	0·65	20
7	0·45	28
8	0·24	45
9	0·35	42
10	0·70	22

A graphical representation of these ten pairs of observations is shown on the scatter diagram, Fig. 44.

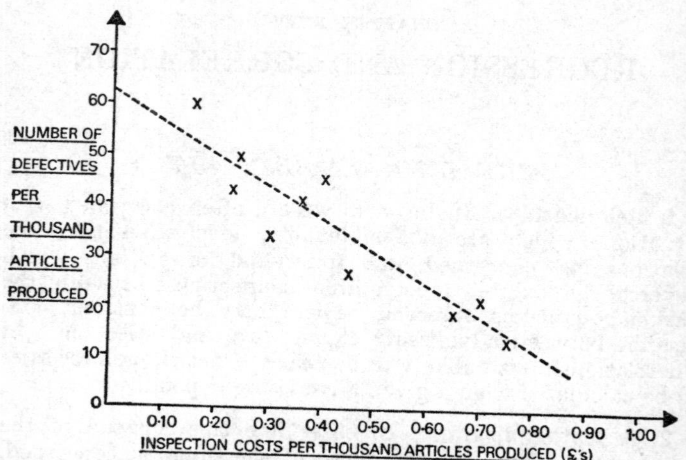

FIG. 44.—*Scatter diagram: inspection costs and defective production*

3. The line of best fit. Although there is not a functional relationship between inspection costs and the number of defectives, it does seem that there is an *almost* linear relationship between the two variables. Certainly in most cases higher inspection costs are associated with lower numbers of defective articles produced. The problem is to find the equation of the straight line which most nearly represents the relationship. To find the line, we need some criterion to judge which of the many possible lines through the scatter of points is the best one. We could say, somewhat vaguely, that the best line is that which passes closest to the points. Shifting the line closer to some points may move it farther from others. We therefore need a better criterion and the one that we shall use is that the "line of best fit" is the one which minimises the *sum of the squares* of the distances of the points from the line.

THE LEAST-SQUARES CRITERION

4. Regression lines. Consider a scatter diagram through which we are attempting to put a line, a *regression line*, the reason for this particular name being historical rather than strictly logical. The distance of any actual point from the, as yet unknown, regression line is represented by d, the distance PQ in the diagram, Fig. 45.

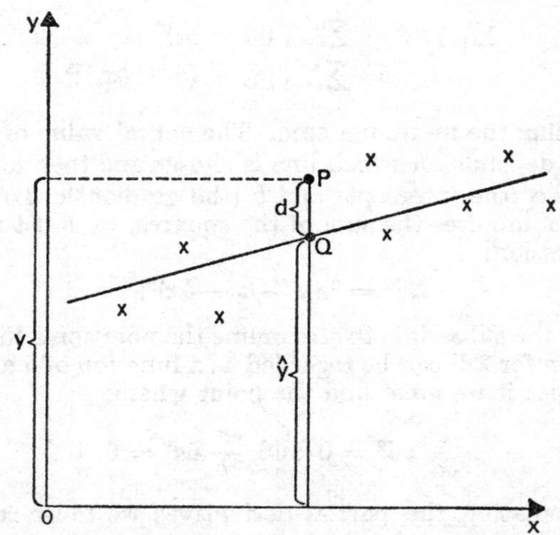

FIG. 45.—*The estimated line of best fit*

Representing a particular deviation from the estimated line as d_i, our least-squares criterion requires us to minimise $\sum_{i=1}^{n} d_i^2$. The actual y-co-ordinate of a point P_i would be y_i. Representing the corresponding y-value of a point such as Q, on the line by $\hat{y}_i$, $d_i = y_i - \hat{y}_i$, the sum of the squares of the deviations is:

$$\sum_{i=1}^{n} d_i^2 = \sum_{i=1}^{n} (y_i - \hat{y}_i)^2.$$

The circumflex marks indicate that the line of best fit is an estimated line which has not yet been found. The usual practice is to call these symbols "y-hat," "b-hat" and so on.

Since our line of best fit is a straight line it can be represente[d] by an equation of the usual linear form, that is:

$$\hat{y} = a + bx,$$

from which particular values of $\hat{y}$, such as $\hat{y}_i$, could be found b[y] carrying out the calculations:

$$\hat{y}_i = a + bx_i.$$

The least-square criterion can then be restated as:

$$\begin{aligned}\textstyle\sum_{i=1}^{n} d_i^2 &= \textstyle\sum_{i=1}^{n} (y_i - \hat{y}_i)^2 \\ &= \textstyle\sum_{i=1}^{n} [y_i - (a + bx_i)]^2.\end{aligned}$$

5. Finding the minimum sum. The actual value of the sum $\sum_{i=1}^{n} d_i^2$ depends on which line is chosen and therefore on th[e] values of a (the intercept) and b (the gradient). To find th[e] line that minimises the sum of the squares, we must minimis[e] the expression:

$$\Sigma d^2 = \Sigma(y - a - bx)^2,$$

dropping the subscripts to streamline the notation a little. Ou[r] expression for Σd^2 can be regarded as a function of a and b an[d] to minimise it we must find the point where:

$$\frac{\partial}{\partial a}\,\Sigma d^2 = 0 \text{ and } \frac{\partial}{\partial b}\,\Sigma d^2 = 0.$$

In calculating the partial derivatives we must remembe[r] three things:

(*a*) We can find the derivative of $(y - a - bx)^2$ and the[n] apply the Σ operator.

(*b*) When finding partial derivatives, first a and then b i[s] considered as a constant; x is a constant here all the time, sinc[e] it is really x_i, representing particular values of x.

(*c*) We must apply the "function of a function" rule since th[e] expression in the brackets is squared.

6. The calculations. The derivatives are found as follows:

$$\begin{aligned}\frac{\partial}{\partial a}\Sigma d^2 &= \frac{\partial}{\partial a}\,[\Sigma(y - a - bx)^2] \\ &= \underline{-2\Sigma(y - a - bx)}\end{aligned}$$

$$\frac{\partial}{\partial b}\Sigma d^2 = \frac{\partial}{\partial b}[\Sigma(y - a - bx)^2]$$
$$= \underline{-2\Sigma x(y - a - bx)}$$

NOTE: Remember that x is acting as the coefficient of the variable b here.

Putting these partial derivatives equal to zero we have:

$$-2\Sigma\ (y - a - bx) = 0$$
$$-2\Sigma x(y - a - bx) = 0$$

Dividing both sides of each equation by -2 gives:

$$\Sigma\ (y - a - bx) = 0$$
$$\Sigma x(y - a - bx) = 0$$

Applying the Σ operator to the terms inside the brackets:

$$\Sigma y - na - b\Sigma x = 0$$
$$\Sigma xy - a\Sigma x - b\Sigma x^2 = 0$$

or $\quad \Sigma y = na + b\Sigma x \ . \ . \ .$ (equation 1).

$\Sigma xy = a\Sigma x + b\Sigma x^2 \ . \ . \ .$ (equation 2).

These two equations can be solved simultaneously to give the values of a and b which will minimise the sum of the squares of the deviations from the line of best fit. Since the actual sums Σy, $b\Sigma x$ and so on can be found from the observed values, these two equations can be used to find the regression line which describes the relationship between the x and y values.

7. A development. Divide equation 1 by n:

$$\frac{\Sigma y}{n} = a + \frac{b\Sigma x}{n}.$$

Since $\frac{\Sigma y}{n} = \bar{y}$ and $\frac{\Sigma x}{n} = \bar{x}$, this could be written:

$$\bar{y} = a + b\bar{x}.$$

This is the equation for our line of best fit with $\bar{x}$ as a special value of x and $\bar{y}$ as a special value of y. The implication of this is that the line of best fit passes through the point given by the co-ordinates x, y, which is the "centroid" of the scatter of points. As the line passes through the point, the whole problem can be simplified by moving the origin of the co-ordinate system so that it passes through the point $(\bar{x}, \bar{y})$. The intercept can now be eliminated from the summation equations and remembering that the x-values, which were measured from the old origin, must now be replaced by the deviations from the mean and that the y-values, too, will be deviations from y, we have:

$$\Sigma(x - \bar{x})(y - \bar{y}) = b\Sigma(x - \bar{x})^2,$$

the equivalent form of equation 2 above. There is no real equivalent to equation 1 because $\Sigma(x - \bar{x}) = 0$, as does $\Sigma(y - \bar{y})$. We now have a way of finding b, since:

$$b = \frac{\Sigma(x - \bar{x})(y - \bar{y})}{\Sigma(x - \bar{x})^2}.$$

FINDING THE REGRESSION LINE OF y ON x

8. Method 1. Using the data given in **4–7** above, we need to know the values Σy, n, Σx, Σxy and Σx^2. The symbol n represents the number of pairs of observations and in this case it is equal to 10. The remaining values can be found by setting up a tabulation, putting inspection costs $= x$, number of defectives $= y$.

x	y	xy	x^2
0·25	50	12·5	0·0625
0·30	35	10·5	0·0900
0·15	60	9·0	0·0225
0·75	15	11·25	0·5625
0·40	46	18·4	0·1600
0·65	20	13·0	0·4225
0·45	28	12·6	0·2025
0·24	45	10·8	0·0576
0·35	42	14·7	0·1225
0·70	22	15·4	0·4900
4·24	**363**	**128·15**	**2·1926**

$\bar{x} = 0{\cdot}424;\ \bar{y} = 36{\cdot}3$

Substituting in the two "normal equations," we have:

$$\Sigma y = na + b\Sigma x,$$

which becomes $363 = 10a + 4{\cdot}24b$ . . . (equation 1(*a*)).

and $\Sigma xy = a\Sigma x + b\Sigma x^2$

or $128{\cdot}15 = 4{\cdot}24a + 2{\cdot}1926b$ . . . (equation 2(*a*)).

Solving these equations, using any suitable method, gives $b = -65{\cdot}24$ and $a = 63{\cdot}96$, thus making the equation for our line of best fit:

$$y = 63{\cdot}96 - 65{\cdot}24x.$$

This is the dotted line shown in Fig. 44.

9. Method 2. The alternative equation for b was:

$$b = \frac{\Sigma(x - \bar{x})(y - \bar{y})}{\Sigma(x - \bar{x})^2}.$$

A suitable tabulation with which to work would be as follows:

x	y	$(x - \bar{x})$	$(y - \bar{y})$	$(x - \bar{x})^2$	$(x - \bar{x})(y - \bar{y})$

In our example the relevant totals would be $\Sigma(x - \bar{x})^2 = 0{\cdot}395$ and $\Sigma(x - \bar{x})(y - \bar{y}) = -25{\cdot}76$, which gives the value of b as 65·2, as before.

10. Summary. To find the line of best fit through a scatter of points proceed as follows:

(*a*) State the normal equations:

$$\Sigma y = na + b\Sigma x$$
$$\Sigma xy = a\Sigma x + b\Sigma x^2.$$

(*b*) Set up the tabulation as in **8** above.

(*c*) Insert the values of Σx, Σy, Σxy and Σx^2 in the equations and solve for a and b.

(*d*) Insert the values of a and b so obtained in the straight-line equation:

$$y = a + bx.$$

This will give the equation of the line required, which is called "the regression line of y on x."

(e) Alternatively, use the formula for b given in 9 above.

11. Using the regression line. The regression line states the relationship between the x-values (inspection costs) and the y-values (proportion of defective articles in the final output). It is now possible to estimate the number of defectives per thousand articles produced that would be expected at any given level of inspection costs.

EXAMPLE: Suppose that it is proposed to increase the intensity of inspection in one of the works producing the article to a level equivalent to a cost of £0·60 or 60p per thousand articles produced. If other conditions of production remain unchanged, what percentage of final output would you expect to be defective?

Inspection cost per thousand: £0·6

Regression equation:

$$\begin{aligned}\text{Defectives per thousand} &= 64{\cdot}0 - 65{\cdot}2x\\ &= 64{\cdot}0 - (65{\cdot}2 \times 0{\cdot}6)\\ &= 64{\cdot}0 - 39{\cdot}12\\ &= \underline{24{\cdot}88}\end{aligned}$$

24·88 defectives per thousand is equal to approximately 2·5 per cent.

THE REGRESSION LINE OF x ON y

12. The "other" regression line. The relationship between the two quantities has not been considered as a definite functional one and the regression line is only a type of "average" line through the scatter. The regression line of y on x is the line of best fit which minimises the sum of the squares of the vertical distances of the points from the line. It would be possible to find another regression line by applying the least-squares criterion to the horizontal deviations (*see* Fig. 46).

The procedure for finding this other regression line, "the regression line of x on y," is the same as for the line of y on x except that now y takes the place of x and x the place of y.

13. The revised normal equations. Treating the y-axis as if it were the horizontal one, the normal equations become:

$$\Sigma x = na_1 + b_1\Sigma y$$

and
$$\Sigma xy = a_1\Sigma y + b_1\Sigma y^2,$$

where a_1 is the new intercept and b_1 the new gradient. It must be remembered when graphing the regression line of x on y that the intercept and gradient apply as if the axes were transposed, with x vertical and y horizontal.

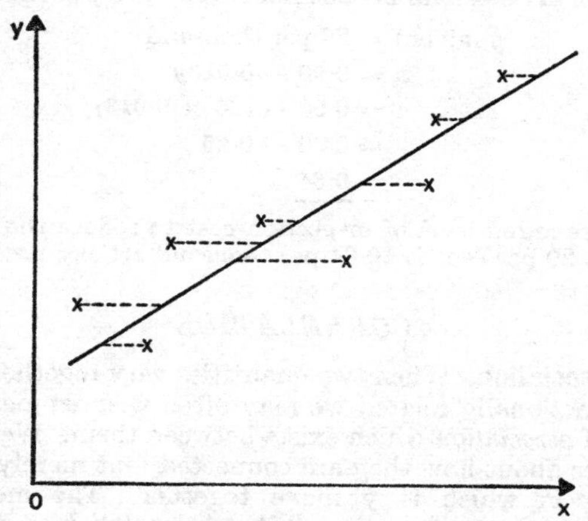

FIG. 46.—*The regression line of x on y*

14. The calculations. The calculation of the intercept and gradient proceed as before, except that we need a y^2 column in our tabulation. The Σy^2 figure is 15123, and substituting this in the normal equations, together with the other values already obtained, gives:

$$4{\cdot}24 = 10a_1 + 363b_1$$
$$128{\cdot}15 = 363a_1 + 15123b_1$$

Solution of these two simultaneous equations gives the values $a_1 = 0{\cdot}904$, $b_1 = -0{\cdot}013$. The regression equation of x on y is, therefore:

$$x = 0{\cdot}904 - 0{\cdot}013y.$$

15. The meaning of the regression equation of x on y. When ever we need to calculate x from a given value of y in circum stances such as those discussed, when the two variables are no linked by a definite functional relationship, we must find th appropriate regression equation. The regression equatio illustrates a general tendency without stating it so firmly a would a functional equation. To calculate a value of x when is given, we use the regression equation of x on y.

EXAMPLE: What inspection cost would be required to reduc the level of defectives in the final output to 2 per cent?

$$
\begin{aligned}
y \text{ (given)} &= 20 \text{ per thousand} \\
x &= 0{\cdot}90 - 0{\cdot}013y \\
&= 0{\cdot}90 - (20 \times 0{\cdot}013) \\
&= 0{\cdot}90 - 0{\cdot}26 \\
&= \underline{0{\cdot}64}
\end{aligned}
$$

The required level of inspection cost to reduce the defectiv level to 20 per cent is £0·64 per thousand articles produced.

CORRELATION

16. Association. When two quantities vary together withou being functionally related we may often wish to measure th degree of *association* which exists between them. We make n inferences about how they are connected, but merely measur the way in which they move together. The measure o association which we use is called the *correlation coefficient*.

17. Setting up the formula. If we take a scatter diagran like that in 2, we could again set up a new co-ordinate systen with its origin at $(\bar{x}, \bar{y})$. If we then consider the four quad rants of this new co-ordinate system (refer back to IV, 6 i you have forgotten what the quadrants are), we can see tha the signs of the deviations of the x-values and y-values of any one of the scatter of points are determined by the quadrant in which the particular point is found. In the first quadrant, both x-deviations and y-deviations are positive; in the second quad rant, the x-deviations are negative and the y-deviations are positive and so on. The complete picture is shown in Fig. 47

It seems reasonable to suppose that this characteristi of the deviations could be used as the basis of a measure o association, since the products of the x-deviation and the y-deviation of each point will also have a distinctive sign determined by the quadrant in which the point is located.

18. Three main cases. These are as follows:

Case 1: *Positive association.* In this case, as one variable increases, so does the other. Most of the points on the scatter diagram are found in the first and third quadrants. First-quadrant points have y-deviations and x-deviations positive and the products of their deviations are positive. Third-quadrant points have both deviations negative and consequently have *positive* products. It is not necessary for *all* the points to be in these two quadrants, but merely that most of them should. The requirement is that the sum of all the products together should be positive. Fig. 48(a) shows this case.

Case 2: *Negative association.* Here, most of the points are in the second and fourth quadrants. In these quadrants the signs of the x-deviations and y-deviations differ and so the products of the x- and y-deviations are negative. Again, it is not required

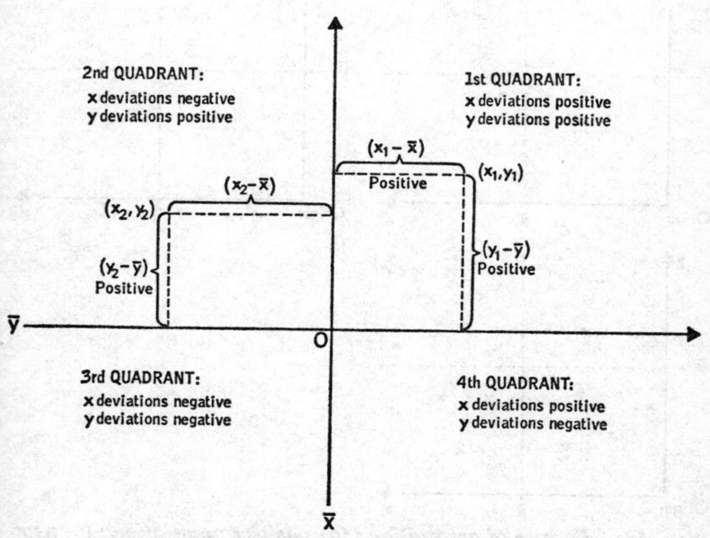

FIG. 47.—*Deviations from the means*

that every point should be in one of these two quadrants, but merely that the effect of the ones in these quadrants should outweigh that of points in the other two. This case is shown in Fig. 48(*b*).

Case 3: *No association.* In this case, points are scattered all over the co-ordinate system and the positive-product points just about balance the negative-product points. Fig. 48(*c*) shows this case.

19. The co-variance. If we wanted a very crude measure of association, we could just test whether the sum of the positive products outweighed the sum of the negative products in the case under consideration. The sum of the products of the deviations is shown symbolically as $\Sigma(x - \bar{x})(y - \bar{y})$. This measure would not be adequate by itself as it would depend on the *number* of points taken as well as on the degree of association of the variables. To adjust for this, we divide by the

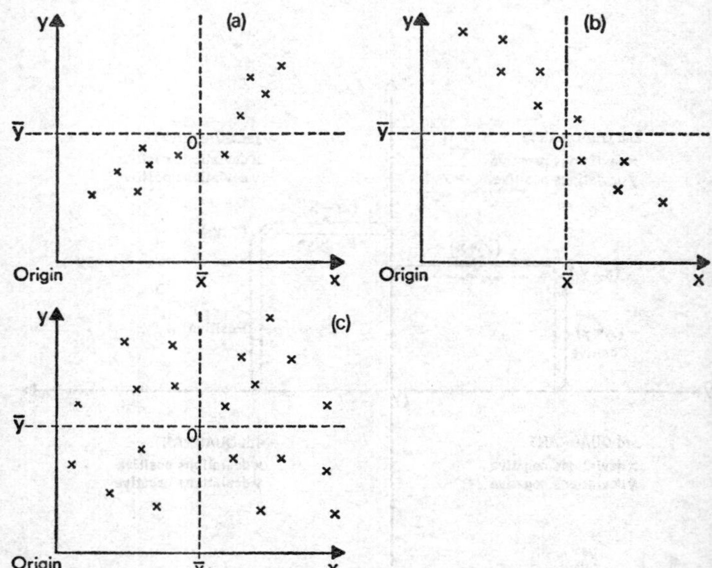

Fig. 48.—*Degrees of association:* (*a*) *positive association;* (*b*) *negative association;* (*c*) *no association.*

number of pairs of observations (n). The measure thus arrived at is called the *co-variance* of x and y and is written:

$$\textit{Co-variance} = \frac{\Sigma(x - \bar{x})(y - \bar{y})}{n}.$$

20. The product-moment correlation coefficient. The co-variance by itself is not an adequate measure of association because it is influenced by the magnitude of the original deviations. The obvious way of eliminating this little problem is to measure not in absolute units but in standard deviation units, a device which we have already employed in XII, 24–26. The formula for our measure of association then becomes:

$$r = \frac{\Sigma(x - \bar{x})(y - \bar{y})}{n\sigma x \sigma y}.$$

The symbol r is generally used for the correlation coefficient and the measure calculated by means of this formula is known as the product-moment correlation coefficient.

21. Properties of r. Perfect positive correlation will give $r = 1$ and all the points will lie along a straight line with a positive gradient. When $r = -1$, there is perfect negative correlation, with one variable declining as the other rises and all the points lying on a straight line. Values of $r = 1$ or $r = -1$ would imply that, given one variable, the other could be calculated. In cases when the relationship is less than functional, r will usually be somewhere between $+1$ and -1, that is $-1 < r < +1$.

22. An example. Taking the figures given in Table 23, we could test the degree of association between inspection costs and number of defectives per thousand. The scatter diagram Fig. 48(b) indicates that a negative correlation is to be expected. The form of tabulation required is similar to that needed for the calculation of regression coefficients (b, b_1) and is as follows:

x	y	$(x - \bar{x})$	$(y - \bar{y})$	$(x - \bar{x})^2$	$(y - \bar{y})^2$	$(x - \bar{x})(y - \bar{y})$

Entering the appropriate values and working through the tabulation will give $\Sigma(x - \bar{x})(y - \bar{y}) = -25{\cdot}51$, $\Sigma(x - \bar{x})^2 = 0{\cdot}395$ and $\Sigma(y - \bar{y})^2 = 1946{\cdot}1$. The calculation of r proceeds as follows:

$$\textit{Co-variance} = \frac{1}{n}\Sigma(x - \bar{x})(y - \bar{y})$$

$$= \frac{1}{10}(-25{\cdot}51)$$

$$= \underline{-2{\cdot}551}$$

$$\sigma x = \sqrt{\frac{\Sigma(x - \bar{x})^2}{n}}$$

$$= \sqrt{\frac{0{\cdot}395}{10}}$$

$$= \sqrt{0{\cdot}0395}$$

$$= \underline{\;0{\cdot}20\;}$$

$$\sigma y = \sqrt{\frac{\Sigma(y - \bar{y})^2}{n}}$$

$$= \sqrt{\frac{1946{\cdot}1}{10}}$$

$$= \sqrt{194{\cdot}61}$$

$$= \underline{\;13{\cdot}94.}$$

Assembling these component parts, we have:

$$r = \frac{\frac{1}{n}\Sigma(x - \bar{x})(y - \bar{y})}{\sigma x\ \sigma y}$$

$$= \frac{-2{\cdot}55}{0{\cdot}20 \times 13{\cdot}94}$$

$$= \frac{-2{\cdot}55}{2{\cdot}79}$$

$$= \underline{-0{\cdot}91.}$$

23. The meaning of *r*. A correlation coefficient with a value so near to -1 shows a very high degree of negative association. The negative sign shows that the relationship is an inverse one. Two questions remain to be answered: could this value have occurred by chance, with uncorrelated pairs of values chosen by chance, and what, exactly, does this value of r show beyond giving a measure or index of association? These questions will be answered in **24–26** below so far as the second question is concerned, and in **28–32** below so far as the first question is concerned.

REGRESSION AND THE CORRELATION COEFFICIENT

24. Explained and unexplained variation. The regression line of y on x indicated the relationship between the x-variable (inspection costs) and the y-variable (proportion of defectives). The relationship was not a functional one and the regression line only partly explained the variation in the quality of output. A useful way of analysing the variation further would be to calculate first the variation of the y-series about their mean. For reasons already discussed, it is not possible to sum the deviations from $\bar{y}$ and achieve a meaningful result. The appropriate measure of the total variation is the sum of the squares of the deviations:

$$\text{Total variation of } y \text{ values} = \Sigma(y - \bar{y})^2.$$

This total sum of squares could be split into the part that is "explained" by the regression line and the part that remains unexplained. The explained variation is the difference, for every observation, between $\hat{y}$ and $\bar{y}$, using the "y-hat" notation to denote the equivalent point on the regression line. The position for a single pair (x, y) of observations is shown in Fig. 49.

The ratio of *explained* to *total* variation, taking the sums of squares in each case, is given by:

$$\frac{\Sigma(\hat{y} - \bar{y})^2}{\Sigma(y - \bar{y})^2} = \frac{\Sigma[b(x - \bar{x})]^2}{\Sigma(y - \bar{y})^2}$$

$$= b^2 \frac{\Sigma(x - \bar{x})^2}{\Sigma(y - \bar{y})^2}.$$

In following this manipulation, recall that the regression line passes through the point $(\bar{x}, \bar{y})$ and that the difference between the y-co-ordinate of a point on the line and $\bar{y}$, the mean of y, is given by $b(x - \bar{x})$, just as it was when we switched the origin to $(\bar{x}, \bar{y})$. Recall also that the b (gradient) is a constant and can be taken outside the Σ operator, but that it was squared up by the power of the square bracket.

25. The explained variation and r^2. The various formulae associated with the correlation and regression coefficients show a wealth of interconnections. The formula for b has been calculated as:

$$b = \frac{\Sigma(x - \bar{x})(y - \bar{y})}{(x - \bar{x})^2},$$

which gives:

$$b^2 = \frac{[\Sigma(x - \bar{x})(y - \bar{y})]^2}{[\Sigma(x - \bar{x})^2]^2}.$$

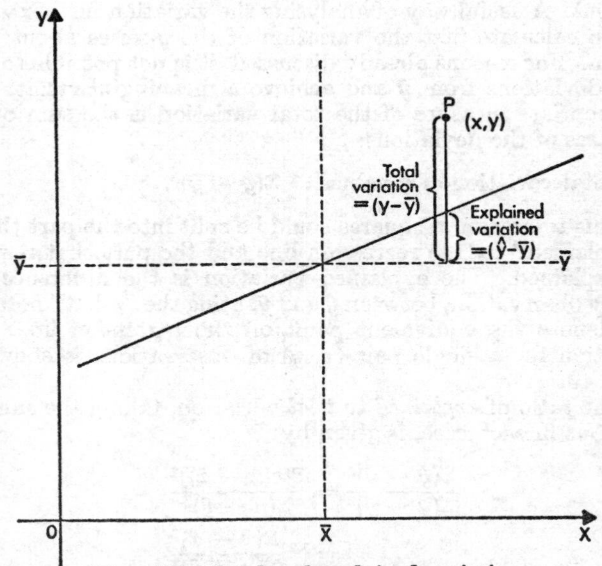

FIG. 49.—*Total and explained variation*

Following up the expression for the ratio of explained to total variation we have:

$$b^2\left[\frac{\Sigma(x-\bar{x})^2}{\Sigma(y-\bar{y})^2}\right]=\frac{[\Sigma(x-\bar{x})(y-\bar{y})]^2}{[\Sigma(x-\bar{x})^2]^2}\cdot\frac{\Sigma(x-\bar{x})^2}{\Sigma(y-\bar{y})^2}$$

$$=\frac{[\Sigma(x-\bar{x})(y-\bar{y})]^2}{\Sigma(x-\bar{x})^2\Sigma(y-\bar{y})^2}.$$

We have been using the expression:

$$r=\frac{\frac{1}{n}\Sigma(x-\bar{x})(y-\bar{y})}{\sqrt{\frac{\Sigma(x-\bar{x})^2}{n}\cdot\frac{\Sigma(y-\bar{y})^2}{n}}}$$

$$=\frac{\frac{1}{n}\Sigma(x-\bar{x})(y-\bar{y})}{\frac{1}{n}\sqrt{\Sigma(x-\bar{x})^2\,.\,\Sigma(y-\bar{y})^2}}$$

$$=\frac{\Sigma(x-\bar{x})(y-\bar{y})}{\sqrt{\Sigma(x-\bar{x})^2\,.\,\Sigma(y-\bar{y})^2}},$$

which, squared, produces:

$$r^2=\frac{[\Sigma(x-\bar{x})(y-\bar{y})]^2}{\Sigma(x-\bar{x})^2\,.\,\Sigma(y-\bar{y})^2},$$

and it therefore follows that:

$$\frac{\textit{Explained variation}}{\textit{Total variation}}=\frac{\textit{Explained sum of squares}}{\textit{Total sum of squares}}$$

$$=\frac{\Sigma(\hat{y}-\bar{y})^2}{\Sigma(y-\bar{y})^2}$$

$$=b^2\frac{\Sigma(x-\bar{x})^2}{\Sigma(y-\bar{y})^2}$$

$$=\underline{r^2}.$$

26. Application to the example. In our example $r=-0{\cdot}91$ and r^2 was thus 0·83, which in percentage form is 83 per cent. Since r^2 is equivalent to the ratio of explained to total variation, in our example the regression equation explains 83 per cent of the total observed variation in the level of defectives in the output from the factories. Going a step further, we could say that our analysis indicates that the intensity of inspection, indicated by cost per thousand articles, accounts for 83 per cent of the variation in the proportion of defectives in the output.

27. The analysis of variance. The analysis of variation which we have just carried out is a simple example of the important statistical technique known as *the analysis of variance.* This analysis is not explored further in the present text, but it offers a powerful means of resolving the total variation observed into its component parts even when the situation is very complicated.

THE SIGNIFICANCE OF r

28. Need for a test. One further point remains. Even if there was no connection between the two variables examined, could we have got the same result by chance? To test this we need some theoretical distribution of correlation coefficients calculated from samples drawn from an uncorrelated normal population. If we had such a distribution we could calculate whether our value could have occurred by chance or not.

29. Student's "t" distribution. In order to make our test we shall use a special statistic denoted by the symbol t and calculated according to the formula:

$$t = \frac{r}{\sqrt{1 - r^2}} \cdot \sqrt{n-2}.$$

When the r in this formula is computed from sets of values drawn from an uncorrelated normal population, the t statistic follows a distribution rather like the normal distribution but more suitable for use with small samples. The values of t are tabulated according to the probability of their occurrence and the number of "*degrees of freedom.*" In the formula the number of degrees of freedom is given by $\sqrt{n - 2}$.

30. Calculating t. Using our own figures, t can be calculated thus:

$$t = \frac{-0{\cdot}91}{\sqrt{1 - 0{\cdot}83}} \cdot \sqrt{10-2.}$$
$$= \frac{-0{\cdot}91}{\sqrt{0{\cdot}17}} \cdot \sqrt{8}$$
$$= \frac{-2{\cdot}57}{0{\cdot}41}$$
$$= \underline{-6{\cdot}27}.$$

31. The hypothesis. In order to make our test, we must set p a hypothesis. Our hypothesis will be that the value of r alculated *could* have occurred by chance, that is that there is o significant difference between our value and one occurring y pure chance using values drawn from an *uncorrelated* $\cdot = 0$) normal population.

We must also set up some criterion for rejecting the hypo- nesis. Our criterion will be that we shall *reject* the hypothesis nat r is not significantly different from zero if we produce a alue of t which is so large (in absolute value, that is $|t|$) that could only have occurred by chance once in a hundred times.

32. The test. From tables we find that $|t|$ for 8 degrees of eedom is tabulated at $P = 0{\cdot}01$ at a value of 3·36. This eans that values of $t = 3{\cdot}36$ and over could occur by chance nly one in a hundred times. On this test, our value of r is gnificant.

PROGRESS TEST 24

1.* What is the least-squares criterion? (3, 4)

2.(a) An examination of records supplied by ten firms estab- shed in a new town yields the following figure for capital per nployee and output per employee:

Firm No.	Capital per employee (£s thousands)	Output per employee (£s thousands)
1	4·30	1·50
2	4·00	1·30
3	0·75	0·50
4	3·25	0·80
5	1·25	0·70
6	1·40	0·60
7	2·50	1·00
8	1·50	0·80
9	2·30	1·00
10	1·75	0·80

Examine the relationship between capital and output pe employee by calculating the regression equations. **(8–11)**

(*b*) If a firm comparable to these wished to obtain an output c £1250 per employee, what level of capital per employee would th appropriate regression equation indicate? **(12–15)**

3.* What does a correlation coefficient show and how is i related to the regression coefficients calculated from two sets c figures? **(16–21, 23, 24)**

4. (*a*) Show the data of Question 2 in the form of a scatte diagram.

(*b*) Calculate the correlation coefficient for the data in Questio 2. Calculate r^2 and explain the meaning of this measure. Do yo think you would have been justified in using the regressio equations in the way required in Question 2(*b*)? **(22, 24, 25)**

CHAPTER XXV

FORECASTING

FORECASTING AND DECISION

1. Reducing uncertainty. As we saw in earlier chapters (XVIII, XIX) business decisions are necessarily concerned with future events. Often we simplify the decision by making the sweeping assumption that the future will be just like the past. We have not actually reduced uncertainty, but we have established an attitude towards the future which enables us to function. A rather more sophisticated approach would be to assume that the same *trends* that have persisted in the past will continue into the future. There are still dangers in this assumption, so a further development would be to try to identify the *processes* which have existed in the past and to extend these into future situations. The real uncertainty in the situation will still exist, however.

2. Forecasting and decision. Since forecasting helps the business man to handle decisions relating to future states of the world but does not actually dispel uncertainty, it can only be an *aid* to decision. The correct attitude to adopt is "if the forecast made is correct, *then* the best decision would be this one." Forecasting is necessarily imperfect but is essential to good decision-making.

3. Areas of application. All business decisions, then, require the best available forecasts, but since forecasting costs money (recall XIX), formal forecasts are usually confined to the major areas of business. The most important business forecasts are probably those that concern marketing, where demand forecasts and identification of the factors influencing demand are essential for good decisions. Forecasts of sales are essential, too, for the production manager and to the purchasing officer for inventory control. Other areas of decision require forecasts of future wage and price movements and it requires little imagination to see that stock market forecasts, if they were truly feasible, could be pursued with profit.

4. Methods. There are now many approaches to forecasting but in this chapter only a few of the most commonly used are discussed. The main division between the various approaches is that between methods seeking to discover and apply basic causations and those which attempt to rely only on the patterns of the data themselves. On the whole, the latter methods have tended to be more successful.

THE ANALYSIS OF TIME SERIES

5. Patterns in time series. When a series of values representing sales, numbers employed or some similar quantity, observed over a number of past time periods, is plotted on a graph, they will usually form a scatter of points similar to those previously discussed. Even though there may be a basically regular pattern of increase or decrease, this may be masked by cyclic, seasonal or random fluctuations and possibly by a mixture of all of these influences.

6. Identifying factors in time series variations. Cyclic fluctuations are those of which the pattern of increases and decreases extends over a long period, possibly over many years. Seasonal variation is the shorter-term fluctuation which probably follows the changing pattern of the natural seasons or may have some other pattern of similar duration. Random fluctuations are the unexplained chance variations which remain when the other influences have been identified and explained. For the present we shall be concerned with identifying the underlying trend about which these various fluctuations take place.

7. A time series example. Sales of T.V. electronic games are given in thousands in Table 24.

TABLE 24. SALES OF T.V. ELECTRONIC GAMES, BY QUARTERS, 19–4—8 (*thousands*)

	March (I)	*June* (II)	*September* (III)	*December* (IV)
19–4	17·9	22·4	18·9	27·3
19–5	17·5	21·5	20·2	29·3
19–6	18·0	25·5	22·0	26·4
19–7	18·1	22·5	22·0	33·0
19–8	23·1	—	—	—

A clear seasonal pattern emerges and is shown in the graphical plot (Fig. 50). Our job is to isolate the underlying trend from these figures.

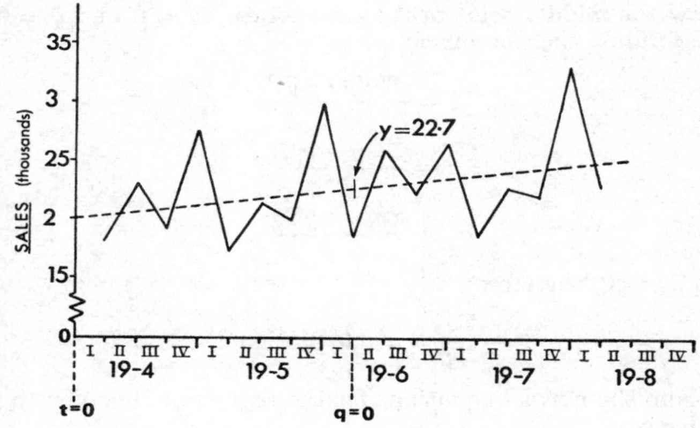

FIG. 50.—*Graphical representation of a time series*

8. The method. The task of finding the underlying trend, or secular trend as it is sometimes called, is exactly the same as that of finding a line of best fit among the points of the scatter diagram. There is no question of choice between the two possible lines of best fit, since the deviations which we wish to minimise are those of sales from trend, that is the vertical deviations. The problem can be further simplified if we recall that the quarterly intervals are evenly spaced along the time axis. If we can identify the middle point of the series, and measure from the middle quarter, the time deviations above and below it will cancel each other out. The mean of the time values will be zero.

In XIV, 9, the formula for the slope of the regression line was given as:

$$b = \frac{\Sigma(x - \bar{x})(y - \bar{y})}{\Sigma(x - \bar{x})^2}.$$

Putting q, the number of quarterly periods above or below the middle point of the time series, instead of x, the formula for the slope of the trend line becomes:

$$b = \frac{\Sigma(q - \bar{q})(y - \bar{y})}{\Sigma(q - \bar{q})^2}.$$

Since there are an equal number of quarters above and below the middle point of the time series, $\Sigma q = 0$ and $\bar{q} = 0$. The formula then becomes:

$$b = \frac{\Sigma[q(y - \bar{y})]}{q^2}$$

$$= \frac{\Sigma(qy - q\bar{y})}{q^2}$$

$$= \frac{\Sigma qy - \bar{y}\Sigma q}{\Sigma q^2}$$

but $\Sigma q = 0$, therefore:

$$b = \frac{\Sigma qy}{\Sigma q^2} \quad . \; . \; . \text{ (equation 1).}$$

From the normal equations for the regression line of y on x we have:

$$\Sigma y = na + b\Sigma x,$$

which, substituting q for x, becomes:

$$\Sigma y = na + b\Sigma q,$$

but since $\Sigma q = 0$ this is really:

$$\Sigma y = na$$

or

$$a = \frac{\Sigma y}{n}.$$

From our more elementary work (*see* XII) we know that $\frac{\Sigma y}{n} = \bar{y}$; therefore:

$$a = \bar{y} \quad . \; . \; . \text{ (equation 2).}$$

These two equations give a framework for the calculation of the trend line, but we must remember that the intercept of $\bar{y}$ is at the new origin which is at the mid-point of the time series.

9. The calculations. First, we need a tabulation similar to that for the calculation of the regression line, but the x-values are now replaced by the quarterly deviations from the mid-point in time of the series.

This tabulation is shown in Table 25.

TABLE 25

Year	*Quarter*	*Sales (y)*	q	v	qv	q^2
19–4	I	17·9	−8	− 2·1	16·8	64
	II	22·4	−7	+ 2·4	−16·8	49
	III	18·9	−6	− 1·1	6·6	36
	IV	27·3	−5	+ 7·3	−36·5	25
19–5	I	17·5	−4	− 2·5	10·0	16
	II	21·5	−3	+ 1·5	− 4·5	9
	III	20·2	−2	+ 0·2	− 0·4	4
	IV	29·3	−1	+ 9·3	− 9·3	1
19–6	I	18·0	0	− 2·0	0	0
	II	25·5	1	+ 5·5	5·5	1
	III	22·0	2	+ 2·0	4·0	4
	IV	26·4	3	+ 6·4	19·2	9
19–7	I	18·1	4	− 1·9	− 7·6	16
	II	22·5	5	+ 2·5	10·0	25
	III	22·0	6	+ 2·0	12·0	36
	IV	33·0	7	+13·0	91·0	49
19–8	I	23·1	8	+ 3·1	24·8	64
Totals		385·6	0	+45·6	124·8	408

In order to simplify the actual calculations, we shall work from an *assumed* mean sales figure. The formula given by equation 2 could be regarded as the formula for working from an "assumed mean of zero" and can be modified to:

$$b = \frac{\Sigma qv}{\Sigma q^2} \quad . \quad . \quad . \quad (3),$$

the symbol v representing deviations from any arbitrarily chosen sales value. In the example the assumed mean value is 20,000 (or $y = 20$).

Substituting in the formula gives:

$$b = \frac{\Sigma qv}{\Sigma q^2}$$
$$= \frac{124{\cdot}8}{408}$$
$$= \underline{0{\cdot}306.}$$

Since the sales figures are only given correct to the nearest hundred pounds, and the y figures are consequently only correct to the first place of decimals, the value of b is taken as 0·3 in the remaining calculations.

The intercept at the mid-point of the series is given by the mean sales value. Equation 2 gives:

$$a = \bar{y}$$
$$= \frac{\Sigma y}{n}$$
$$= \frac{385{\cdot}6}{17}$$
$$= \underline{22{\cdot}68}$$

The trend line, giving the underlying sales movement, is therefore $y = 22{\cdot}7 + 0{\cdot}3q$, since we can be no more certain than this about the real value of the mean sales figure. Should we wish to correct back to the real origin of the series, this could be written as:

$$y = 20 + 0{\cdot}3t,$$

where t is the number of quarters which have elapsed since the *beginning* of the first quarter of 19–4. This gives a value of $t = 1$ for the period 19–4/I. The trend line under both conventions is shown in Fig. 50.

10. Finding the seasonal variation. In order to find the seasonal variation for each of the four quarters, we shall divide the *actual sales figure* by the *corresponding trend figure* for each of the seventeen quarters listed. The first sales figure is 17·9 (thousands) and the first trend figure is 20·3 and the actual/trend calculation therefore gives a fraction of 0·88 or 88 per cent. The same calculation has been carried out for each pair of values and the results are shown in Table 26.

TABLE 26. PERCENTAGE SEASONAL VARIATION

	(I)	(II)	(III)	(IV)	
19–4	—	109	90	129	
19–5	81	99	91	131	
19–6	79	111	94	111	
19–7	76	93	90	134	
19–8	92	—	—	—	
Total	328	412	365	505	
Average (division by 4)	82	103	$91\frac{1}{4}$	$126\frac{1}{4}$	Bias $+2\frac{1}{2}$%
Corrected mean seasonal deviation	81	102	91	126	

Table 27 gives trend figures, uncorrected percentage seasonal variation and other derived figures for the whole series. As a measure of simplification, the percentage variation most distant in time has been omitted, thus permitting division of each of the sums by four. The variations above and below the trend line should cancel out, but there is bound to be a little residual bias in the calculations. Adding the four mean, uncorrected, seasonal variations together, we find that they add up to $402\frac{1}{2}$ per cent, whereas they should add up to 4×100 per cent $= 400$ per cent in the absence of bias. The

TABLE 27. TREND, SEASONAL VARIATION AND RESIDUAL FLUCTUATIONS

Sales	*(actual)*	*Trend*	*Actual Trend* × 100	*Corrected mean S.V.*	*Trend* × *per cent S.V.*	*Residual fluctuation*
19–4	17·9	20·3	88	81	16·4	1·5
	22·4	20·6	109	102	21·0	1·4
	18·9	20·9	90	91	19·0	−0·1
	27·3	21·2	129	126	26·7	0·6
19–5	17·5	21·5	81	81	17·4	0·1
	21·5	21·8	99	102	22·2	−0·7
	20·2	22·1	91	91	20·1	0·1
	29·3	22·4	131	126	28·2	1·1
19–6	18·0	22·7	79	81	18·4	−0·4
	25·5	23·0	111	102	23·5	2·0
	22·0	23·3	94	91	21·2	0·8
	26·4	23·6	111	126	29·7	−3·3
19–7	18·1	23·9	76	81	19·4	−1·3
	22·5	24·2	93	102	24·7	−2·2
	22·0	24·5	90	91	22·3	−0·3
	23·0	24·8	134	126	31·2	1·8
19–8	23·1	25·1	92	81	20·3	2·8

excess has been subtracted and the corrected figures rounded to give the final corrected mean seasonal variation for each quarter.

MAKING PREDICTIONS FROM THE TREND

11. Method. Our calculations have furnished us with a formula for finding the trend and a percentage mean seasonal variation for each quarter. We may combine these:

(*a*) to give past data free from residual fluctuations; and
(*b*) to extrapolate from the trend into future quarters.

12. Finding and removing residual fluctuations. If we assume that the original data are made up of the three components, trend, seasonal variation and residual fluctuation, we may represent the effects of the first two by multiplying each of the trend figures by the appropriate seasonal variation.

EXAMPLE

19–4, first quarter:

Trend: 20·3 (thousands).

Corrected mean (percentage) seasonal variation: **81 per cent.**

$$\textit{Trend} \times \textit{Corrected M.S.V.} = 20{\cdot}3 \times 0{\cdot}81 \text{ (thousands)}$$
$$= \underline{16{\cdot}4 \text{ (thousands)}}.$$

The total sales for the quarter were 17·9 (thousands) and th explained part of this figure is 16·4 (thousands). The residu variation is therefore:

$$17{\cdot}9 - 16{\cdot}4 \text{ (thousands)}$$
$$= \underline{1{\cdot}5 \text{ (thousands)}}.$$

Similar calculations have been entered in Table 27 for each quarterly figure.

13. Extrapolating from the trend. An important feature of the trend line is that it gives a ready means of estimating figures for future periods. If our equation $y = 20{\cdot}0 + 0{\cdot}3t$ really represents the underlying trend, then by taking further values of t, we can calculate future trend figures.

The trend figure for the March quarter 19–8 was found by calculating:

$$y_1 19\text{–}8/\text{I} = 20{\cdot}0 + 0{\cdot}3t,$$

where $t = 17$. We can find the trend figure for 19–8/II by putting $t = 18$ and the following quarter, $t = 19$ and so on. To make a full forecast, we should also make provision for the seasonal effect and so should multiply the trend figures by the mean seasonal variation as before.

Forecasting on this basis for the remaining quarter of 19–8 would give:

19–8	*Trend*	*Mean seasonal variation*	*Forecast Trend × M.S.V.*
Quarter II	25·4	102	25·9
III	25·7	91	23·4
IV	26·0	126	32·8

Our sales forecast for the next three quarters would have been 25,900, 23,400 and 32,800.

MULTIPLE REGRESSION

14. Simple and multiple regression. In XXIV a regression equation linking the quality of output to inspection costs was devised. Only two variables were concerned. The analysis, therefore, was a case of *simple* regression. If there had been more than one explanatory variable, so that the number of defective items depended not only on the level of inspection costs but also on other factors, we should have been dealing with *multiple* regression.

15. Least squares and multiple regression. The simple regression analysis was conducted by finding the line of best fit according to the least squares criterion (*see* XXIV, 4–7). The same approach is followed in multiple regression, but since there are two or more explanatory variables, the analysis must be conducted in three or more dimensions. Naturally this is much more difficult both to visualise and to calculate, but the principle is the same: the sum of the squares of the deviations between the values observed and those predicted must be minimised.

16. The regression equation. The general style of the multiple regression equation is

$$\hat{Y} = \beta_0 + \beta_1 X_1 + \beta_2 X_2 + \dots + \beta_k X_k$$

where there are k explanatory variables. The circumflex (hat) signs indicate, as before (*see* XXIV, 4), that the quantities concerned are the best estimates. If the observed values are shown as Y_i, then the corresponding estimated or predicted values are shown as $\hat{Y}_i$ so that the residuals for each observation are

$$d_i = Y_i - \hat{Y}_i$$

and the sum of the squares which the multiple regression procedure minimises is

$$\Sigma d_i^2 = \Sigma(Y_i - \hat{Y}_i)^2$$

17. An example of multiple regression. Suppose that a firm is one of several suppliers of a domestic appliance. Records of the company's market share are available over a number of years, together with figures showing the company's share of total advertising expenditure and the ratio of the company's price to the average price of rival products. Using the least squares technique, the following regression equation is produced

$$\Delta M_t = -0{\cdot}02 + 0{\cdot}18A_t - 0{\cdot}05\left(\frac{P_1}{P_0}\right)_t.$$

Here ΔM_t denotes the change in market share in the period t, A_t shows the share of total advertising, P_1 represents the price of the company's product and P_0 is the average price of comparable products. Possibly the prices would be most easily expressed in index form, both indices being referred to the same base period. Thus, if the company's share of advertising were zero and the prices were equal for both the company and its competitors, giving a ratio of unity, the change in market share would be

$$\begin{aligned}\Delta M_t &= -0{\cdot}02 + 0{\cdot}18(0) - 0{\cdot}05(1)\\ &= \underline{-0{\cdot}07} \text{ (or 7 per cent).}\end{aligned}$$

18. Computer packages. The calculations for simple regression were quite formidable and it will be readily appreciated that those for multiple regression are even more so. Consequently multiple regression techniques have only come into common use in the past twenty years or so, that is since computer facilities have become available. Until about ten years ago, however, using a computer for the solution of multiple regression problems was a highly technical business but now all that is required is a knowledge of the conventions for gaining access to the computer and to the required program.

19. The computer print-out. Having inserted the data into the program, a matter requiring some care since errors will invalidate the result, and having instructed the program to RUN, if that is the particular convention, there is nothing to do but to wait for the print-out. In a simple case such as that described, the print-out might begin:

```
VARIABLE        MEAN        STANDARD DEVIATION
   1            .4070          0.0471
   2            .9601          0.0500
   3            .3102          0.0101

THE DEPENDENT VARIABLE IS 3

VARIABLE     REGRN COEFF     STANDARD ERROR
   0           -0.0212          0.0051
   1            0.1801          0.0913
   2           -0.0521          0.0401

COEFF DETERMINATION      = 0.7624      R = 0.8732
```

Other information would follow and all of it would require interpretation.

20. The interpretation of the regression. Variables 1 and 2 are the independent, or explanatory, variables, the advertising share (A_t) and the price ratio (P_1/P_0). The dependent variable is the market share change and the variable marked ø is merely the constant in the regression equation. The means and standard deviations of the three variables are easily understood and it can be seen that the average market share of the firm is 31 per cent. The "Coeff Determination" is R^2, the square of the multiple correlation coefficient, R. Like the

r^2 statistic of XXIV, 25, R^2 shows the proportion of the total variation in the dependent variable which is "explained" by the regression equation. In the example, rather more than 76 per cent is so explained. The standard errors shown are those of the regression coefficients and it may be observed that for variable 2, (P_1/P_0), the standard error is large compared with the coefficient itself.

21. Multiple regression in forecasting. Forecasting market share is clearly a very necessary part of corporate decision-making and planning. In the multiple regression equation discussed above, there are two explanatory variables, each one of which is only partly under the decision-makers' control. The advertising and price ratios depend on the actions of competitors as well as on the company's policy. Prediction of the general product price and the "all firms" advertising figure would require a further forecasting exercise. This might involve other explanatory equations, using variables such as the level of consumer spending and various price indices. If a system of two or more interrelated equations is used, the approach could be said to be an *econometric* one. Alternatively, trends for the required figures might be established in ways already described without concern for the underlying explanations. The forecast figures would be inserted into the ratios and the previously established regression equation used to predict the market share.

22. Dangers in multiple regression. The methods of multiple regression analysis are sound only if quite strict conditions concerning the nature of the variables and the relationships between them are fulfilled. Discussion of these conditions would be too extended to follow here and in practice they are often ignored. Two views are possible. If an "econometric" approach to forecasting is followed, the precise values of the coefficients and the extent to which they correspond to the underlying causes are important. If the equation is used directly in prediction of future values, possibly all that matters is whether the equation "works."

EXPONENTIAL SMOOTHING

23. Exponential weights. It might seem reasonable to suppose that a forecast ought to be a weighted average of past observations, the weights declining as observations more remote in time were considered. With the subscripts denoting the period in question, the mathematical form of such a forecast would be

$$\hat{Y}_{t+1} = \lambda[Y_t + (1-\lambda)Y_{t-1} + (1-\lambda)^2 Y_{t-2} + \dots + (1-\lambda)^n Y_{t-n}]$$

The circumflex indicates a forecast and the weights go back for the past n periods. Last period, we should have forecast

$$\hat{Y} = \lambda[Y_{t-1} + (1-\lambda)Y_{t-2} + (1-\lambda)^2 Y_{t-3} + \dots + (1-\lambda)^n Y_{t-n-1}]$$

Multiplying this by $(1-\lambda)$, we arrive at

$$(1-\lambda)\hat{Y}_t = \lambda[(1-\lambda)Y_{t-1} + (1-\lambda)^2 Y_{t-2} + \dots + (1-\lambda)^{n+1} Y_{t-n-1}]$$

Subtracting from the first equation, and ignoring a very small final term, we have

$$\hat{Y}_{t+1} - (1-\lambda)\hat{Y}_t = \lambda Y_t$$

and rearranging this expression gives

$$\hat{Y}_{t+1} = \hat{Y}_t + \lambda[Y_t - \hat{Y}_t]$$

This carries the implication that a forecast based on an exponentially weighted average of past observations can be obtained very simply by taking the *previous* forecast and adding some proportion, λ, of the error $(Y_t - \hat{Y}_t)$ in the current period. The proportion λ will have a value between zero and unity.

24. An example. A series of commodity prices is available quarter by quarter for the years 19–6 to 19–8. These prices, in £s per tonne, are shown in Table 28. The exponential smoothing has been applied in each quarter and the resulting forecasts and errors are tabulated for each period.

25. The smoothing constant. The smoothing constant, λ, represents the factor which determines the exponentially declining weights in the basic model. The underlying model

TABLE 28. EXPONENTIAL SMOOTHING: DATA AND FORECASTS

Period		Price (£)	Forecast	Error
19–6	I	420	400*	20
	II	440	410	30
	III	451	425	26
	IV	440	438	2
19–7	I	445	439	6
	II	452	442	10
	III	450	447	3
	IV	432	448½	−16½
19–8	I	460	440	20
	II	450	450	0
	III	465	450	15
	IV		457½**	

* Initial forecast ** Final forecast $\lambda = 0{\cdot}5$

is not, of course, known and so the smoothing constant must be estimated as closely as possible. It is also possible that the exponential model is not an appropriate description of the process which has generated the series and in that case there will be a bias in the errors or residuals. Inspection of Table 28 shows that this is the case in the example.

26. The search for improved models. If the bias in the residuals reveals a steady linear trend, allowance can be made for it and the forecasts improved. If, however, the variations in the residuals are more complex a deeper search for the underlying pattern must be made. Methods developed over the last decade by G. Box and G. Jenkins provide a very powerful method of devising and testing models of variations in time series and the exponential smoothing case can be shown to be merely the simplest of a large class of related models.

PROGRESS TEST 25

1.* "Business men always face uncertainty when they make decisions and statistical forecasting is misleading because it assumes that the future will be like the past." Discuss critically. (1–4)

2. A retail firm's quarterly sales of washing machines are given in thousands in the following table:

	(I)	(II)	(III)	(IV)
19–5	20	45	50	30
19–6	35	50	41	25
19–7	26	55	60	35
19–8	40	70	72	40

(*a*) Calculate the trend equation for the firm's sales.

(*b*) The seasonal indices (percentage seasonal variation) for the four quarters are:

Quarter	
I	75
II	130
III	125
IV	70

Forecast the sales for the four quarters of 19–9. **(9–13)**

3. Using the "print-out" of **19**, discuss the validity of the regression equation for predicting market shares. If the company's share of advertising increased to 40 per cent and its prices were 10 per cent higher than those of its rivals, what would be the expected change in market share?

If, as marketing director of the firm, you had to choose between an increase in advertising and a cut in price in order to increase market share, what would be your decision?

4. Prices of a commodity in common household use have varied as follows during 19–8.

JAN	FEB	MAR	APR	MAY	JUNE	
0·50	0·46	0·50	0·55	0·54	0·59	
JULY	AUG	SEPT	OCT	NOV	DEC	
0·51	0·72	0·60	0·58	0·62	0·69	(in £s per kilo)

Use the method of exponential smoothing with $\lambda = 0{\cdot}4$ to predict a price for January 19–9 (the January 19–8 forecast was for £0·55). Should the method be modified to incorporate a time trend?

5.* What does the smoothing constant represent? **(23, 25)**

APPENDIX I

SUGGESTIONS FOR FURTHER READING

Those who wish to develop the subject further will need specialist works that

(*a*) give information on more advanced mathematical skills;

(*b*) investigate more thoroughly the techniques of decision-making and operational research; and

(*c*) develop the techniques of statistical analysis and forecasting introduced in this book.

Further mathematical work. There are many books which will extend the reader's knowledge of fundamental mathematical ideas and *Calculus and Analytic Geometry* by P. Franks and D. A. Sprecher (Harper & Row) is an example which may be accessible to those who have completed this book. For many readers in business life, however, a degree of application to familiar material is necessary. As a compromise, *An Introduction to Mathematics for Students of Economics* by J. Parry Lewis (Macmillan, 1969) offers a development of the calculus, differential equations, difference equations and many other topics in a clear and uncomplicated way. For those who wish to gain a deeper understanding of the *nature* of mathematics *Concepts of Modern Mathematics* by Ian Stewart (1975) published by Penguin Books would be of interest as, at a more difficult technical level, would *Basic Mathematics* by R. G. D. Allen (Macmillan, 1968). In developing specific topics at an advanced level, the *Library of Mathematics* series published by Routledge and Kegan Paul provides compact introduction to some of the most important mathematical problems.

Decision-making and operational research. There is a wealth of specialist material in these fields. In the Penguin series, *The Anatomy of Decisions* by P. G. Moore and H. Thomas (1976) extends the application of methods based on decision trees and a wider range of topics is covered in the readings in *Modern Decision Analysis* edited by G. M. Kaufman and H. Thomas (1977). M. Bacharach's *Economics and the Theory of Games* (Macmillan, 1977) presents developments of this theory which are not dealt with in the present work and *Principles of Operational Research* by H. M. Wagner (Prentice-Hall, 1975) provides a comprehensive and thorough review of major topics in this field. The ideas involved in queueing theory are developed and applied in *Queues* by D. R. Cox and W. L. Smith (Methuen) and simulation methods are reviewed in *Simulation and Business Decision* by G. T. Jones (Penguin).

Statistics and forecasting. W. M. Harper's book, *Statistics* (1977), in the M & E HANDBOOK series, provides an excellent introduction to the practical techniques of statistical analysis. The application of statistical and sampling methods in auditing is discussed in *Contemporary Auditing* by W. S. Boutell (Dickenson Publishing). An excellent and up-to-date text on forecasting is *Forecasting for Business* by D. Wood and R. Fildes (Longman, 1976), which covers a much wider range of topics than the title suggests. This book also contains an outline of the Box and Jenkins methods which are becoming so important.

APPENDIX II

MINIATURE TABLES

1. Areas under the normal curve: some critical values.

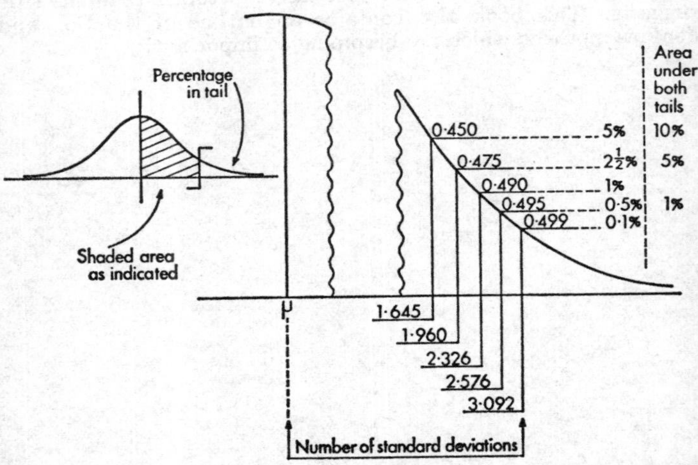

2. Some values of χ^2. χ^2 with one degree of freedom is distributed like the positive half of a normal distribution with the height of each ordinate doubled. Values of χ^2 with $\nu = 1$ are found by squaring appropriate values of the normal curve:

P	=	10%	5%	1%	0·1%
χ^2	=	2·71	3·84	6·64	10·83

For $\nu > 1$, the 5 per cent values can be calculated by taking $\chi = 1{\cdot}55(\nu + 2)$, approximately.

All the tabulated values are those that would be equalled or exceeded by chance with the given probability.

3. A selection of discount values. The values tabulated are $v_n r = (1 + r)^{-n}$.

n \ r	0·05	0·06	0·07	0·08	0·09	0·10	0·15	0·20
1	0·9524	0·9434	0·9346	0·9259	0·9174	0·9091	0·8696	0·8333
2	0·9070	0·8900	0·8734	0·8573	0·8417	0·8264	0·7561	0·6944
3	0·8638	0·8396	0·8163	0·7938	0·7722	0·7513	0·6576	0·5787
4	0·8227	0·7921	0·7629	0·7350	0·7084	0·6830	0·5718	0·4822
5	0·7835	0·7473	0·7130	0·6806	0·6499	0·6209	0·4971	0·4019
6	0·7462	0·7050	0·6663	0·6302	0·5963	0·5645	0·4323	0·3349
7	0·7107	0·6650	0·6227	0·5835	0·5470	0·5132	0·3759	0·2791
8	0·6768	0·6274	0·5820	0·5403	0·5019	0·4665	0·3269	0·2326
9	0·6446	0·5919	0·5439	0·5002	0·4604	0·4241	0·2843	0·1938
10	0·6139	0·5584	0·5083	0·4632	0·4224	0·3855	0·2472	0·1615

Percentage = 100*r*.

APPENDIX III

ALGEBRAIC PROCESSES AND ITERATIVE METHODS

1. Basic algebraic processes. Addition and subtraction have been sufficiently used in the text and are sufficiently simple to need no further discussion here.

Multiplication and division are less easy to handle and it is possible that some readers may have forgotten how to carry out these processes.

(*a*) *Multiplication.*

(*i*) Recall the distribution law for multiplication with respect to addition. If an algebraic multiplication such as $(3x) \times (4x^2 + 2)$ is to be carried out, the distribution law would give:

$(12x^3 + 6x)$ as the product. If $(4x^2 + 2)$ is to be multiplied by $(3x + y)$, then $y \times (4x^2 + 2)$ must be added to the previous result, thus:

$$\begin{aligned}(3x + y) \times (4x^2 + 2) &= (12x^3 + 6x) + (4x^2y + 2y) \\ &= \underline{12x^3 + 4x^2y + 6x + 2y.}\end{aligned}$$

(*ii*) This calculation is usually laid out as follows:

$$\begin{array}{l} 4x^2 + 2 \\ 3x \;\; + y \\ \hline 12x^3 + 6x \\ \qquad\qquad 4x^2y + 2y \\ \hline 12x^3 + 6x + 4x^2y + 2y \\ \hline \end{array}$$

Note that the commutative law applies and that it does not matter in which order the two expressions are multiplied.

(*b*) *Division.* In order to illustrate the process, a specimen calculation is shown:

$$
\begin{array}{r|l}
 & x^2 + 3x + 2 \\
\hline
x + 4 & x^3 + 7x^2 + 14x + 8 \\
 & \underline{x^3 + 4x^2} \\
 & \quad 3x^2 + 14x \\
 & \quad \underline{3x^2 + 12x} \\
 & \qquad\quad 2x + 8 \\
 & \qquad\quad \underline{2x + 8} \\
 & \qquad\quad \text{— —}
\end{array}
$$

The expression $(x^3 + 7x^2 + 14x + 8)$ divided by $(x + 4)$ gives the quotient $(x^2 + 3x + 2)$. The simple process shown above may be compared with the process of synthetic division.

(c) *Synthetic division.* If $(x + 4)$ is a factor of $(x^3 + 7x^2 + 14x + 8)$, then $x = -4$ is a root of $x^3 + 7x^2 + 14x + 8 = 0$. This root is put on the right-hand side of the layout shown below

Row 1:	1	7	14	8	−4
Row 2:		−4	−12	−8	
Quotient:	1	3	2	0	

The first row of the left-hand part consists of the coefficients only of the powers of x. The calculation proceeds as follows:

(*i*) Carry down the first digit into the quotient line.
(*ii*) Multiply this by −4 and enter the result in the second row.
(*iii*) Add the two entries in the second column to give the result +3.
(*iv*) Multiply +3 by −4 and enter the result (−12) in the second row as before.
(*v*) Continue until the last column is reached.

The result is interpreted as the coefficients of x, but with each power reduced by one. The zero gives the remainder (nil).

2. Finding the roots of an equation. The method given below is known as Newton's method. Taking an approximate value of the root as x_0, a better value, x_1, is given by:

$$x_1 = x_0 - \frac{f(x_0)}{f'(x_0)}.$$

The new approximation can be similarly improved and an iterative process set up to improve the approximation to any desired degree of accuracy.

EXAMPLE: Find the roots of $x^3 - 6x + 5 = 0$.

Put $x_0 = 2$.

$$f(x_0) = f(2) = (2)^3 - 6(2) + 5$$
$$= 8 - 12 + 5$$
$$= \underline{1}$$

$$f'(x) = 3x^2 - 6,$$
$$\therefore f'(2) = 3(2)^2 - 6$$
$$= \underline{6}$$
$$\therefore x_1 = 2 - (\tfrac{1}{6})$$
$$= \underline{1\tfrac{5}{6}}.$$

Substituting in the original equation gives:

$$f(\tfrac{11}{6}) = (\tfrac{11}{6})^3 - 6(\tfrac{11}{6}) + 5$$
$$= \underline{\frac{35}{216}}.$$

The required value is zero and that obtained is just under $\frac{1}{6}$.

Second iteration. Put $x_1 = \frac{11}{6}$, then $f(\frac{11}{6}) = 35/216$ (as shown above)

and
$$f'(\tfrac{11}{6}) = 3(\tfrac{11}{6})^2 - 6$$
$$= \underline{147/36}.$$

The new approximation is given by:

$$x^2 = x_1 - \frac{f(x_1)}{f'(x_1)}.$$

Substituting:

$$x_2 = \tfrac{11}{6} - \tfrac{35}{216} \times \tfrac{36}{147}$$
$$= \tfrac{11}{6} - \tfrac{5}{126}$$
$$= \underline{1{\cdot}8}.$$

The correct value of x will reduce the left-hand side of the equation to a zero value. Putting $x = 1{\cdot}8$ gives a value of 0·032. Further iterations will give even closer approximations. This technique is quite important as the analytical method for finding the roots of cubic (third degree) equations is cumbersome and there is *no* general method for finding the roots of equations of higher degree than the fourth.

Finding the remaining roots of the cubic. If $x = 1{\cdot}8$ is a root, $(x - 1{\cdot}8)$ is a factor of the expression. Division, using one of the methods shown, will produce a quadratic expression, from which the remaining two roots may be found in the usual way. Note that an equation of the third degree will have *three* roots, just as an equation of the second degree (a quadratic) will have two. An equation of the nth degree will have n roots.

3. Finding a square root. At various points in a number of calculations in this book it is necessary to find a square root. (Note that *root* has a different meaning in this sense from that in the previous section.) If no tables are handy, the following gives an easy method of finding a square root:

(*a*) Select an approximate, likely value of the required square root.

(*b*) Divide this approximation into the number of which the square root is required.

(*c*) Add the answer to the approximate value and divide by two to give a new and better approximation.

(*d*) Repeat until a sufficiently accurate value is found as is required.

EXAMPLE: Find the square root of 231.

(*a*) First approximation: 14.

(*b*) $\dfrac{231}{14} = 16{\cdot}5.$

(*c*) $\dfrac{14 + 16{\cdot}5}{2} = \underline{15{\cdot}25}.$

(*d*) Using 15·25 as a new approximation:

$$\frac{231}{15{\cdot}25} = 15{\cdot}15; \frac{15{\cdot}25 + 15{\cdot}15}{2} = 15{\cdot}2.$$

(*e*) $\dfrac{231}{15{\cdot}2} = 15{\cdot}2.$ This is the exact square root.

This process has the added virtue that a mistake in arithmetic in one of the stages will be compensated for at the next iteration.

APPENDIX IV

ANSWERS TO PROGRESS TESTS

Progress Test 1

2. Using the formula in the text:

$$w = \frac{2 \times 60}{m_1 + m_2 + m_3 + m_4}.$$

With $m_1 = 3$ minutes, the sum of the times is equal to 22 minutes, giving:

$$w = \frac{120}{22} \text{ tonnes}$$
$$= \underline{5{\cdot}45 \text{ tonnes.}}$$

This is a somewhat naïve approach since it assumes that there will be no congestion and that no waiting times will occur; however, it is sound for two trucks.

3. Schedules are shown for both the original times and the amended times as used in Question 2. (Note that B = start of tipping, C = start of loading.)

ORIGINAL TIMES: SCHEDULE OF TRUCK POSITIONS

Elapsed time	*Truck* 1	*Truck* 2
0	A	D
7	In transit	C
10	B*	Loading
12	D	A
19	C	In transit
22	Loading	B*
24	A	D

AMENDED TIMES: SCHEDULE OF TRUCK POSITIONS

Elapsed time	*Truck* 1	*Truck* 2
0	A	D
7	In transit	C
10	B*	A
12	D	In transit
19	C	In transit
20	Loading	B*
22	A	D

*Asterisk indicates 1 tonne discharged into hopper; 2 tonnes being discharged in each cycle which will repeat to give results consistent with the answer to Question 2.

4. The most rapid time for the completion of the cycle from

loading through to return would be 20 minutes and the least rapid would be 25 minutes. The expected (or average) time on reasonable assumptions would be $22\frac{1}{2}$ minutes. This would justify a mean blasting rate of 2·67 tonnes an hour, but the blasting rate could not be controlled to this degree of accuracy. A rate of 2·5 tonnes an hour would be prudent. With two trucks, 5 tonnes an hour could be attempted, but there would be occasional hold-ups.

Progress Test 2

1.

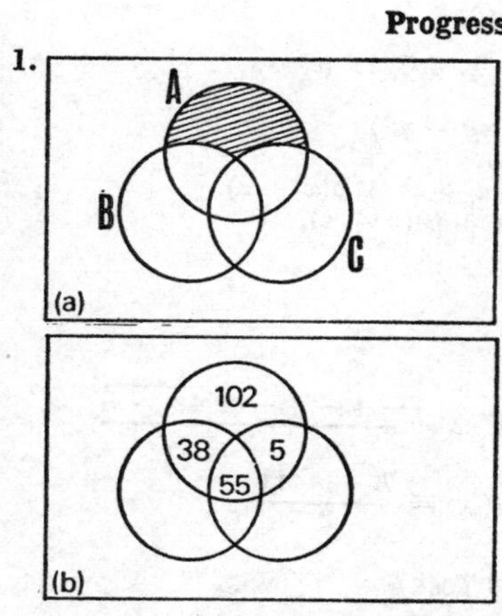

Unskilled, non-trade-union shift workers must be outside sets B and C, but within set A.

The shaded portion indicates the required set, which is the "inter-section of A with the complement of the union of B and C."

The second Venn diagram shows the numbers concerned in each of the categories mentioned. The number in the unskilled, non-trade-union category is 102.

2. (*a*), (*b*), (*c*), (*e*) and (*f*) are rational.

Progress Test 3

2.

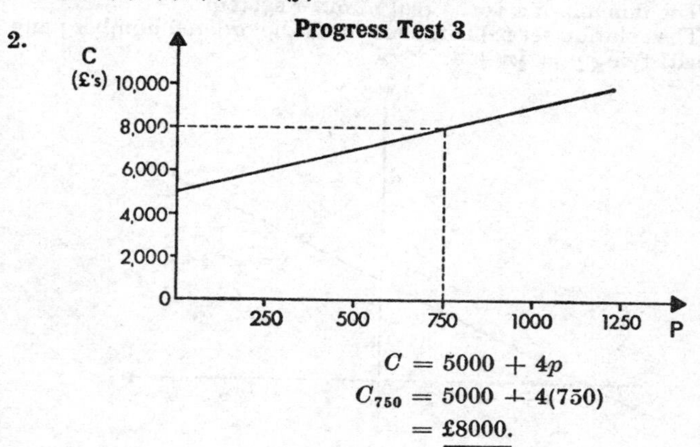

$$C = 5000 + 4p$$
$$C_{750} = 5000 + 4(750)$$
$$= \underline{\pounds 8000.}$$

3. (a) $5^3 \times 5^2 = 5^5 = 3125$.
(b) $5^2 \times 3^4 = 25 \times 81 = 2025$.
(c) $5^{-3} \times 125 = \frac{1}{5^3} \times 125 = 1$.
(d) $a^3 \times a^{\frac{1}{2}} = a^{7/2} = \sqrt{a^7}$.
(e) $\sqrt[4]{81} \times 7 = 3 \times 7 = 21$.

4. (a) 10^{-1}. (b) 10^2. (c) 10^0. (d) 10^{-2}. (e) 10^5.

5. (a) $343^{2/3} = \sqrt[3]{343^2} = 7^2 = 49$.
(b) $\sqrt{289} = 17$. (c) $\frac{1}{\sqrt{49}} = \frac{1}{7}$. (d) 1. (e) 1.

6. (a) $x^3 - y^3 = (x - y)(x^2 + xy + y^2)$.
(b) $a^2 - b^2 = (a + b)(a - b)$.
(c) $ax + az + bx + bz = a(x + z) + b(x + z)$
$= (a + b)(x + z)$.

7. (a) $3x^2 + 14x + 8 = 0$
$(3x + 2)(x + 4) = 0$
$\therefore x = -\frac{2}{3}$ or $x = -4$.
(b) $x^2 - 7x + 2 = 0$

$$x = \frac{-(-7) + \sqrt{49 - 8}}{2} \text{ or } x = \frac{-(-7) - \sqrt{49 - 8}}{2}$$

$$= \frac{7 + \sqrt{41}}{2} \qquad = \frac{7 - \sqrt{41}}{2}.$$

Progress Test 4

1. $S = \{(x_1 y) \mid | y = \frac{1}{2}x + 4, x \text{ real}\}$.
The domain of x is the real number system.
The solution set (S) is the set of all the ordered number pairs satisfying $y = \frac{1}{2}x + 4$.

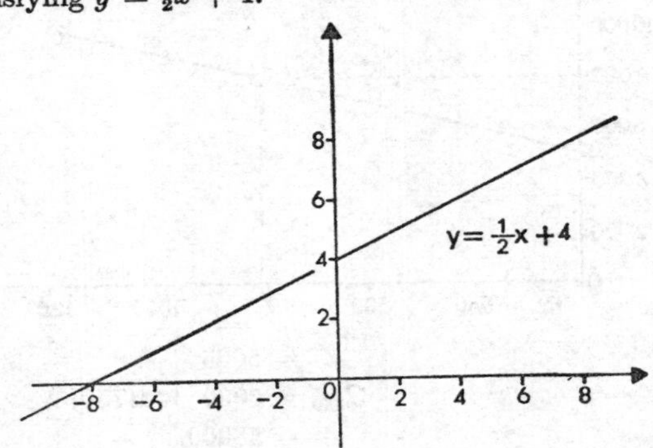

2. The domain of x is given by:

$$60 \leqslant x \leqslant 200.$$

The range of y is from $C_{60} = 480 + 7(60) = \underline{£900}$

to $C_{200} = 480 + 1400 = \underline{£1880.}$

$\therefore$ Range of y: $900 \leqslant C \leqslant 1880.$

4.

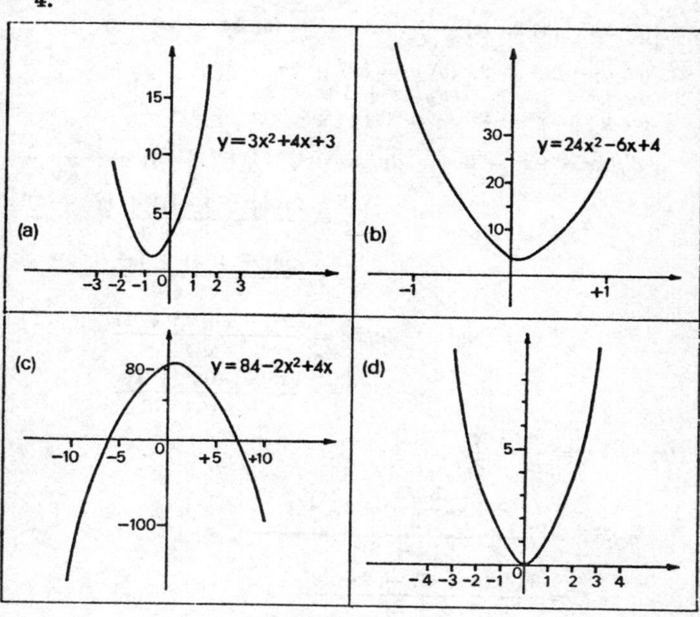

Progress Test 5

1. Sum of an $AP = \frac{n}{2}(2a + (n - 1)d)$; for first n odd numbers $a = 1, d = 2.$

Therefore $S_n = \frac{n}{2}(2 + (n - 1)2)$

$$= \frac{n}{2}(2n)$$

$$= \underline{n^2.}$$

2. (*a*) 154. (*b*) 35. (*c*) 112. (*d*) 3279.

3. (*a*) Apply 12, 13. (*b*) $\frac{3}{8}$.

4. $500(1{\cdot}02)^5 = 552$, to nearest whole number.

5. $\sum_{r=1}^{n} (2r - 1)$. (*b*) $\sum_{r=0}^{n} (2.3^r)$.

Progress Test 6

2. (*a*) $3x^2$. (*b*) 2. (*c*) $\frac{1}{2\sqrt{x}}$. (*d*) $-\frac{2}{x^3}$. (*e*) $2ax + a^2 - b$.

3. (*a*) $y = 3x^2 + 2$. (*b*) $y = 5x^2 + 2x + 3$.
$dy/dx = 6x$ $\qquad dy/dx = 10x + 2$.
(*c*) $y = 3x^3 - 2x - 1$. (*d*) $y = \sqrt{x}(x^2 + 4)^2$.

$$dy/dx = 9x^2 - 2 \qquad dy/dx = \sqrt{x}[4x(x^2 + 4)] + \frac{(x^2 + 4)^2}{2\sqrt{x}}$$

$$= \frac{2x[4x(x^2 + 4)] + (x^2 + 4)^2}{2\sqrt{x}}$$

$$= \frac{8x^2(x^2 + 4) + (x^2 + 4)^2}{2\sqrt{x}}$$

$$\therefore dy/dx = \frac{(x^2 + 4)(9x^2 + 4)}{2\sqrt{x}}$$

$$= \frac{9x^4 + 40x^2 + 16}{2\sqrt{x}}.$$

(*e*)
$$y = \frac{x \, . \sqrt{x}}{(x + 2)}$$

$$dy/dx = \frac{(x + 2) \, . \, \frac{3\sqrt{x}}{2} - x \, . \sqrt{x} \, . \, 1}{(x + 2)^2}$$

$$= \frac{3\sqrt{x}(x + 2) - 2x\sqrt{x}}{2(x + 2)^2}$$

$$\therefore dy/dx = \frac{\sqrt{x}(x + 6)}{2(x + 2)^2}.$$

4. (*a*)
$$E = 15 + \frac{x^2}{x + 7}$$

$$dE/dx = \frac{(x + 7) \, . \, 2x - x^2 \, . \, 1}{(x + 7)^2}$$

$$= \frac{x^2 + 14x}{(x + 7)^2}.$$

The rate of change when $x = 10$, that is $\dfrac{6000 - 5000}{100}$, is:

$$f'(10) = \frac{10^2 + 14(10)}{(10 + 7)^2}$$
$$= \frac{240}{289}$$
$$= \underline{0{\cdot}83.}$$

Output changes by 350, that is $x = 3{\cdot}5.$

Estimated change in E is $dE/dx \,.\, \Delta x = £0{\cdot}83 \times 3{\cdot}5$
$= \underline{£2{\cdot}90.}$

(*b*) Actual earnings when $x = 10$: £20·88

Actual earnings when $x = 13{\cdot}5$: £23·89

Change 3·01.

Derivative gives a good estimate of rate of change over a small range.

5. Cost function given by $c = 1 + 0{\cdot}5x^2$.
Revenue function is $R = 8x$.

(*a*) $\left.\begin{aligned} dC/dx &= x \\ dR/dx &= 8 \end{aligned}\right\} dC/dx = dR/dx$ when $x = 8$.

(*b*) Profit function $P = 8x - (1 + 0{\cdot}5x^2)$
$= 8x - 0{\cdot}5x^2 - 1$

$dP/dx = 8 - x$; $dP/dx = 0$, when $x = 8$.

$d^2P/dx^2 = -1$, which confirms $x = 8$ as maximum.

6.
$$\begin{aligned} y &= x^3 \\ y + \Delta y &= (x + \Delta x)^3 \\ &= x^3 + 3x^2\Delta x + 3x\Delta x^2 + \Delta x^3 \\ \therefore \Delta y &= 3x^2\Delta x + 3x\Delta x^2 + \Delta x^3 \\ \Delta y/\Delta x &= 3x^2 + 3x\Delta x + \Delta x^2 \end{aligned}$$

Letting Δx tend to zero:

$$\underset{\Delta x \to 0}{\textit{Limit}}\ \Delta y/\Delta x = 3x^2$$

that is $\underline{dy/dx = 3x^2.}$

Progress Test 7

1. (*a*)
$$\begin{aligned} y &= 3x^2 + 5x + 6 \\ dy/dx &= 6x + 5 \\ d^2y/dx^2 &= \underline{6.} \end{aligned}$$

(b)
$$y = \sqrt[3]{x} + 2$$
$$= x^{\frac{1}{3}} + 2$$
$$dy/dx = \tfrac{1}{3}x^{-\frac{2}{3}}$$
$$= \frac{1}{3\sqrt[3]{x^2}}$$
$$d^2y/dx^2 = \frac{d}{dx}(\tfrac{1}{3}x^{-\frac{2}{3}})$$
$$= -\tfrac{2}{9}x^{-5/3}$$
$$= -\frac{2}{9\sqrt[3]{x^5}}.$$

(c)
$$y = x^3 + x^{-\frac{1}{2}}$$
$$dy/dx = 3x^2 - \tfrac{1}{2}x^{-3/2}$$
$$= \underline{3x^2 - 1/2\sqrt{x^3}.}$$
$$d^2y/dx^2 = 6x + \tfrac{3}{4}x^{-5/2}.$$
$$= \underline{6x + 3/4\sqrt{x^5}.}$$

2.
$$y = x^4 - 3x^2 + 4$$
$$dy/dx = \underline{4x^3 - 6x.}$$

Putting $dy/dx = 0$, $4x^3 - 6x = 0$

or $2x(2x^2 - 3) = 0$,

therefore $\underline{x = 0}$ or $2x^2 - 3 = 0$

If $2x^2 - 3 = 0$, $\underline{x = \pm\sqrt{\tfrac{3}{2}}}.$

Stationary points at $x = 0$, $x = +\sqrt{\tfrac{3}{2}}$, $x = -\sqrt{\tfrac{3}{2}}$.

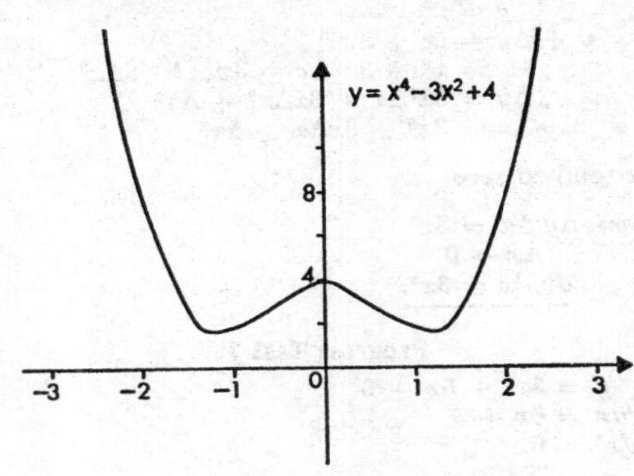

Differentiating again:

$$d^2y/dx^2 = \underline{12x^2 - 6}$$

when $x = 0, f''(0) = -6$; when $x = +\sqrt{\frac{3}{2}}, f''(\sqrt{\frac{3}{2}}) = 12$;
when $x = -\sqrt{\frac{3}{2}}, f''(-\sqrt{\frac{3}{2}}) = 12$.

Of the three stationary points $x = 0$ is a maximum and $x = \pm\sqrt{\frac{3}{2}}$ are minima.

Inflexional points when $d^2y/dx^2 = 0$. From above $d^2y/dx^2 = 0$ when $x = \pm(1/\sqrt{2})$.

4. $dC/dq = -\dfrac{3}{2(q-4)^2} + 24.$

Putting $dC/dq = 0$, $24(q - 4)^2 = \frac{3}{2}$

$$(q-4)^2 = \tfrac{1}{16}$$
$$\therefore q - 4 = \sqrt{\tfrac{1}{16}}$$
$$q = \underline{4\tfrac{1}{4}}$$

$\underline{d^2C/dq^2 < 0 \text{ when } q = 4\frac{1}{4}}$, since $d^2C/dq^2 = 3(q-4)^{-3}$.

Apparently we must employ more than 4 clerks. As q tends to 4, $(q - 4)$ tends to zero and $\frac{3}{2}\left(\dfrac{1}{q-4}\right)$ tends to infinity. At $q = 5$, the cost is rising once again. This expression is rather like some expressions that occur in queueing theory. When $q = 4$, costs tend to be very high because the number of clerks is too small and great backlogs of work occur. Either 5 clerks should be employed or some additional help drafted in (part-time workers) to get q greater than 4 although less than 5.

Progress Test 8

1. (a) $x^4/4$. (b) $\text{Log}_e x$. (c) $x^3/3 - x^{-1}$. (d) $9x^4/4 + 2x^2$. (e) e^x. (f) $\frac{1}{3}e^{3x}$; . . . all plus constants of integration.

2. (a) $\displaystyle\int_0^5 x^2 + 5dx = [x^3/3 + 5x]^5{}_0 = 125/3 + 25 = 200/3.$

(b) $\displaystyle\int_0^7 x - 4dx = [x^2/2 - 4x]^7{}_0 = 49/2 - 28 = -7/2.$

(c) $\displaystyle\int_3^5 7x^2 + 2x + 4dx = \left[\frac{7}{3}x^3 + x^2 + 4x\right]_3^5$

$$= \left[\frac{7.125}{3} + 25 + 20\right] - \left[\frac{7.27}{3} + 9 + 12\right]$$
$$= \underline{252\tfrac{2}{3}}.$$

(d) $\int_0^5 3(x^2 + 1)dx = 3\int_0^5 (x^2 + 1)dx = 3[x^3/3 + x]^5_0$

$= 3(125/3 + 5)$
$= \underline{140.}$

(e) $\int_0^1 e^x dx = [e^x]^1_0 = e^1 - e^0$

$= \underline{(e - 1).}$

Progress Test 9

1. This is a system in three dimensions. None of the variable may become negative. The system gives a convex set as show in the diagram:

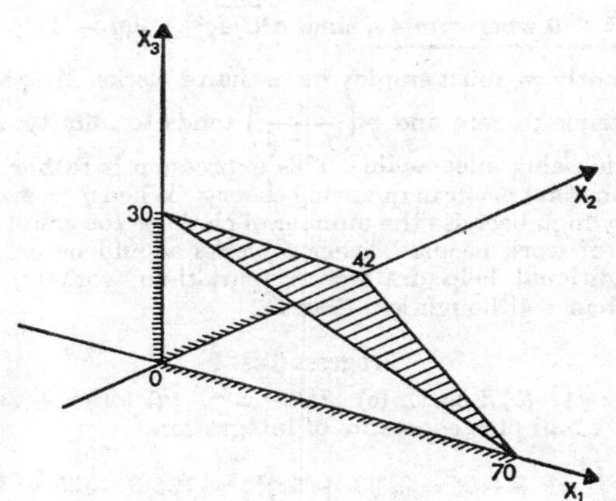

2. (a) (i) $Z = 3x^2 + 4y^3$
$dz/dx = 6x$
$dz/dy = 12y^2$

(ii) $dz/dx = 4x + y$
$dz/dy = x - 2y$

(iii) $dz/dy = dz/dx = e^{x+y}$

(iv) $dz/dx = \dfrac{3}{2\sqrt{x}}$; $dz/dy = -1/y^2$

3. (a) $\boldsymbol{u} + \boldsymbol{v}' = [4, 12, 9, 15]$
(b) $\boldsymbol{u} - \boldsymbol{v}' = [2, 6, -1, -3]$
(c) $2\boldsymbol{u} = [6, 18, 8, 12]$
(d) $\boldsymbol{uv} = [3, 9, 4, 6]\begin{bmatrix}1\\3\\5\\9\end{bmatrix} = 3 + 27 + 20 + 54$
$= \underline{104}.$

4. $\boldsymbol{qp} = [17, 4, 36, 18]\begin{bmatrix}5\\200\\4\\50\end{bmatrix}$
$= 85 + 800 + 144 + 900$
$= \underline{1929 \text{ (money units)}}.$

Progress Test 10

3. (a) $\mathbf{A} + \mathbf{B} = \begin{bmatrix}3 & 5 & 5\\2 & 5 & 16\\7 & 2 & 6\end{bmatrix}$

(b) $\mathbf{A} - \mathbf{B} = \begin{bmatrix}-1 & 3 & 1\\2 & -3 & 0\\-5 & 0 & -2\end{bmatrix}$

(c) $\mathbf{AB} = \begin{bmatrix}1 & 4 & 3\\2 & 1 & 8\\1 & 1 & 2\end{bmatrix}\begin{bmatrix}2 & 1 & 2\\0 & 4 & 8\\6 & 1 & 4\end{bmatrix}$

$= \begin{bmatrix}20 & 20 & 46\\52 & 14 & 44\\14 & 7 & 18\end{bmatrix}$

4. (a) $\boldsymbol{a} = [3, 1, 4]$

$\boldsymbol{B} = \begin{bmatrix}2 & 1 & 2\\0 & 4 & 8\\6 & 1 & 4\end{bmatrix}$

$\boldsymbol{aB} = [30, 11, 30]$

(b) $\mathbf{R} = \begin{bmatrix}1 & 1 & 4 & 3 & 2 & 8\\1 & 1 & 6 & 2 & 2 & 4\\1 & 1 & 3 & 4 & 2 & 3\end{bmatrix}$

$\boldsymbol{d}\mathbf{R} = [6, 1, 4]\begin{bmatrix}1 & 1 & 4 & 3 & 2 & 8\\1 & 1 & 6 & 2 & 2 & 4\\1 & 1 & 3 & 4 & 2 & 3\end{bmatrix}$

$= [11, 11, 42, 36, 22, 64].$

The vector d represents the number of pumps of each type required and the vector resulting from the multiplication is a vector of parts required to make up the given number of pump units.

5. $$\left[\begin{array}{ccc|ccc} 1 & 3 & 4 & 1 & 0 & 0 \\ 0 & 1 & 2 & 0 & 1 & 0 \\ 6 & 3 & 1 & 0 & 0 & 1 \end{array}\right]$$

$$\left[\begin{array}{ccc|ccc} 1 & 3 & 4 & 1 & 0 & 0 \\ 0 & 1 & 2 & 0 & 1 & 0 \\ 0 & -15 & -23 & -6 & 0 & 1 \end{array}\right]$$

$$\left[\begin{array}{ccc|ccc} 1 & 0 & -2 & 1 & -3 & 0 \\ 0 & 1 & 2 & 0 & 1 & 0 \\ 0 & 0 & 7 & -6 & 15 & 1 \end{array}\right]$$

$$\left[\begin{array}{ccc|ccc} 1 & 0 & 0 & -5/7 & 9/7 & 2/7 \\ 0 & 1 & 0 & 12/7 & -23/7 & -2/7 \\ 0 & 0 & 1 & -6/7 & 15/7 & 1/7 \end{array}\right]$$

$$\mathbf{A}^{-1} = \begin{bmatrix} -5/7 & 9/7 & 2/7 \\ 12/7 & -23/7 & -2/7 \\ -6/7 & 15/7 & 1/7 \end{bmatrix}$$

6. (*a*) $r = r\mathbf{Q} + d$, as given

$\therefore\ r - r\mathbf{Q} = d$

$r(\mathbf{I} - \mathbf{Q}) = d$, **I** being the unit symbol in matrix algebra.

Dividing both sides by $(\mathbf{I} - \mathbf{Q})$:

$$\underline{r = d(\mathbf{I} - \mathbf{Q})^{-1}.}$$

(*b*)
$$\mathbf{Q} = \begin{bmatrix} 0 & 0 & 0 & 0 & 0 \\ 8 & 0 & 0 & 0 & 0 \\ 1 & 2 & 0 & 0 & 0 \\ 3 & 0 & 1 & 0 & 0 \\ 0 & 3 & 4 & 1 & 0 \end{bmatrix},$$

$$\therefore (\mathbf{I} - \mathbf{Q}) = \begin{bmatrix} 1 & 0 & 0 & 0 & 0 \\ 0 & 1 & 0 & 0 & 0 \\ 0 & 0 & 1 & 0 & 0 \\ 0 & 0 & 0 & 1 & 0 \\ 0 & 0 & 0 & 0 & 1 \end{bmatrix} - \begin{bmatrix} 0 & 0 & 0 & 0 & 0 \\ 8 & 0 & 0 & 0 & 0 \\ 1 & 2 & 0 & 0 & 0 \\ 3 & 0 & 1 & 0 & 0 \\ 0 & 3 & 4 & 1 & 0 \end{bmatrix}$$

$$= \begin{bmatrix} 1 & 0 & 0 & 0 & 0 \\ -8 & 1 & 0 & 0 & 0 \\ -1 & -2 & 1 & 0 & 0 \\ -3 & 0 & -1 & 1 & 0 \\ 0 & -3 & -4 & -1 & 1 \end{bmatrix}.$$

To find $(\mathbf{I} - \mathbf{Q})^{-1}$, set up partitioned matrix:

Tableau 1.

$$\left[\begin{array}{rrrrr|rrrrr} 1 & 0 & 0 & 0 & 0 & 1 & 0 & 0 & 0 & 0 \\ 18 & 1 & 0 & 0 & 0 & 0 & 1 & 0 & 0 & 0 \\ -1 & -2 & 1 & 0 & 0 & 0 & 0 & 1 & 0 & 0 \\ -3 & 0 & -1 & 1 & 0 & 0 & 0 & 0 & 1 & 0 \\ 0 & -3 & -4 & 1 & 1 & 0 & 0 & 0 & 0 & 1 \end{array}\right]$$

Tableau 2.

$$\left[\begin{array}{rrrrr|rrrrr} 1 & 0 & 0 & 0 & 0 & 1 & 0 & 0 & 0 & 0 \\ 0 & 1 & 0 & 0 & 0 & 8 & 1 & 0 & 0 & 0 \\ 0 & -2 & 1 & 0 & 0 & 1 & 0 & 1 & 0 & 0 \\ 0 & 0 & -1 & 1 & 0 & 3 & 0 & 0 & 1 & 0 \\ 0 & -3 & -4 & -1 & 1 & 0 & 0 & 0 & 0 & 1 \end{array}\right]$$

Tableau 3.

$$\left[\begin{array}{rrrrr|rrrrr} 1 & 0 & 0 & 0 & 0 & 1 & 0 & 0 & 0 & 0 \\ 0 & 1 & 0 & 0 & 0 & 8 & 1 & 0 & 0 & 0 \\ 0 & 0 & 1 & 0 & 0 & 1 & 2 & 1 & 0 & 0 \\ 0 & 0 & -1 & 1 & 0 & 3 & 0 & 0 & 1 & 0 \\ 0 & 0 & -4 & -1 & 1 & 24 & 3 & 0 & 0 & 1 \end{array}\right]$$

Tableau 4.

$$\left[\begin{array}{rrrrr|rrrrr} 1 & 0 & 0 & 0 & 0 & 1 & 0 & 0 & 0 & 0 \\ 0 & 1 & 0 & 0 & 0 & 8 & 1 & 0 & 0 & 0 \\ 0 & 0 & 1 & 0 & 0 & 17 & 2 & 1 & 0 & 0 \\ 0 & 0 & 0 & 1 & 0 & 20 & 2 & 1 & 1 & 0 \\ 0 & 0 & 0 & -1 & 1 & 92 & 11 & 4 & 1 & 1 \end{array}\right]$$

Tableau 5.

$$\left[\begin{array}{rrrrr|rrrrr} 1 & 0 & 0 & 0 & 0 & 1 & 0 & 0 & 0 & 0 \\ 0 & 1 & 0 & 0 & 0 & 8 & 1 & 0 & 0 & 0 \\ 0 & 0 & 1 & 0 & 0 & 17 & 2 & 1 & 0 & 0 \\ 0 & 0 & 0 & 1 & 0 & 20 & 2 & 1 & 1 & 0 \\ 0 & 0 & 0 & 0 & 1 & 112 & 13 & 5 & 1 & 1 \end{array}\right]$$

This gives:

$$(\mathbf{I} - \mathbf{Q})^{-1} = \left[\begin{array}{rrrrr} 1 & 0 & 0 & 0 & 0 \\ 8 & 1 & 0 & 0 & 0 \\ 17 & 2 & 1 & 0 & 0 \\ 20 & 2 & 1 & 1 & 0 \\ 112 & 13 & 5 & 1 & 1 \end{array}\right]$$

$r = d(\mathrm{I} - \mathrm{Q})^{-1}$

$$d(\mathrm{I} - \mathrm{Q})^{-1} = [0, 0, 2, 4, 9]\begin{bmatrix} 1 & 0 & 0 & 0 & 0 \\ 8 & 1 & 0 & 0 & 0 \\ 17 & 2 & 1 & 0 & 0 \\ 20 & 2 & 1 & 1 & 0 \\ 112 & 13 & 5 & 1 & 1 \end{bmatrix}$$

$$= \underline{[1122, 129, 51, 13, 9]}.$$

Progress Test 11

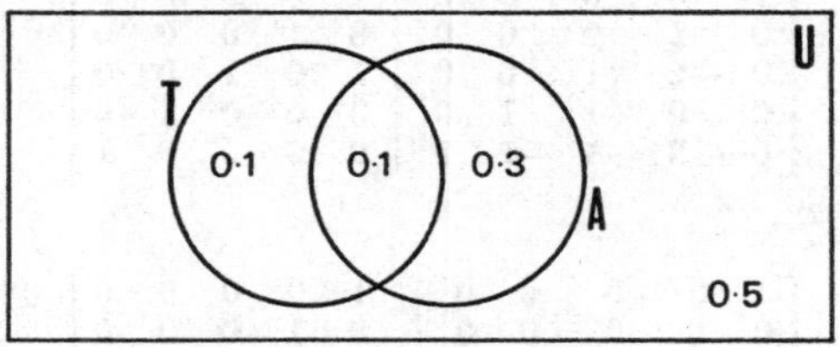

1. Probability of selling neither = 0·5.

2. (*a*) $\frac{1}{6} \times \frac{1}{6} \times \frac{1}{6} = \frac{1}{216}$.

(*b*) $\frac{1}{3}$, since out of six possible results with the second die only the 1 or the 2 will give a result of less than nine with both dice.

3. Put probability that shoes come from the major manufacturer or $Pr(a) = 0{\cdot}6$. Probability that shoes come from another manufacturer is then $Pr(\bar{a}) = 0{\cdot}4$. The probability of a pair of shoes being defective is $Pr(b)$. We require the probability that a pair of shoes was made by the major manufacturer, given that it was defective, that is $Pr(a \mid b)$.

By Bayes' theorem: $$Pr(a \mid b) = \frac{Pr(b \mid a) \,.\, Pr(a)}{Pr(b \mid a) \,.\, Pr(a) + Pr(b \mid \bar{a}) \,.\, Pr(\bar{a})}$$

$$= \frac{(0{\cdot}01)(0{\cdot}6)}{(0{\cdot}01)(0{\cdot}6) + (0{\cdot}05)(0{\cdot}4)}$$

$$= \frac{0{\cdot}006}{0{\cdot}026} = \underline{0{\cdot}23}.$$

4. (*a*) $^5C_2 = \frac{5!}{3!\ 2!} = 10.$ (*b*) $^{10}C_4 = \frac{10!}{6!\ 4!} = \underline{210}.$

(c) $^{100}C_2 = \frac{100 \,.\, 99}{2} = 4950.$

5. $$Pr = \frac{{}^{(8-3)}C_{(3-1)} \cdot {}^{3}C_{1}}{{}^{8}C_{3}}$$
$$= \frac{10 \cdot 3}{56}$$
$$= \underline{0{\cdot}54} \text{ (correct to 2 places of decimals).}$$

6. Probability of no employees with safety offence: $(0{\cdot}97)^{12}$.
Probability of one employee with safety offence: $12(0{\cdot}97)^{11}(0{\cdot}03)$.
Probability of less than two employees having a safety offence on their records = Prob (0) + Prob (1)
$$= (0{\cdot}97)^{12} + 12(0{\cdot}97)^{11}(0{\cdot}03)$$
$$\simeq 0{\cdot}95 \text{ (or 95\%)}.$$

Progress Test 12

2. $$\sigma = \sqrt{\frac{\Sigma(x - \bar{x})^2}{N}}$$
$$\Sigma x = 495$$
$$N = 20$$
$$\bar{x} = \frac{\Sigma x}{N}$$
$$= \underline{24{\cdot}75 \text{ days}}$$
$$\Sigma(x - \bar{x})^2 = 501{\cdot}75$$
$$\therefore \sigma = \sqrt{\frac{501{\cdot}75}{20}}$$
$$= \underline{5 \text{ days}} \text{ (5·01 days).}$$

3. $y = e^{-t^2}$.
Using the "function of a function" rule:

$y = e^u$
$u = -t^2$
$dy/du = e^u$; $du/dt = -2t$,
$\therefore \underline{dy/dt = -2te^{-t^2}}$.

The derivative could be written as $\dfrac{dy}{dt} = \dfrac{-2t.}{e^{t^2}}$ For negative t, the slope is positive and, for positive t, the slope is negative. There is a stationary point when $x = 0$. There is no value of t which could give negative y.

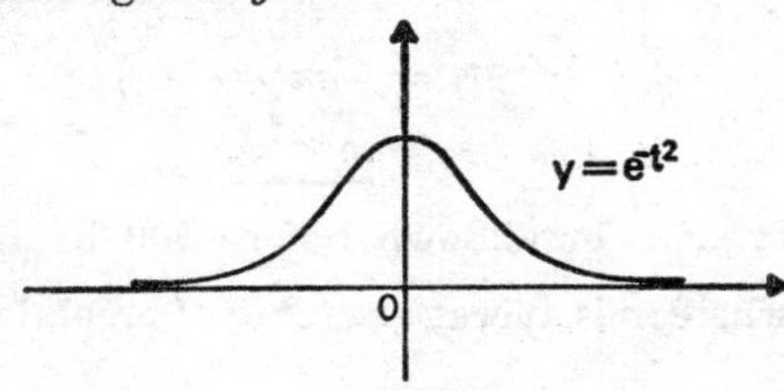

4. Probabilities of r ships arriving given by r^{th} term of Poisson distribution, *i.e.* by terms of $e^m e^{-m}$:

$$= e^{-m} + me^{-m} + \frac{m^2e^{-m}}{2!} + \ldots + \frac{m^re^{-m}}{r!} + \ldots$$

With $m = 2$, the probability of 3 or fewer ships arriving is given by first four terms:

$$\begin{aligned} Pr\text{ (3 or less)} &= e^{-2} + 2e^{-2} + \frac{2^2e^{-2}}{2!} + \frac{2^3e^{-2}}{3!} \\ &= 0{\cdot}8569 \\ Pr\text{ (more than 3)} &= 1 - Pr\text{ (3 or less)} \\ &= 1 - 0{\cdot}8569 \\ &= \underline{0{\cdot}1431.} \end{aligned}$$

The probability that more than 3 ships will arrive on any day is a little more than 14 per cent.

5. (*a*)

$$\begin{aligned} \int_0^\infty me^{-mt}\,dt &= m\int_0^\infty e^{-mt}\,dt \\ &= m\left[\frac{-1}{m}e^{-mt}\right]_0^\infty \\ &= \left[-e^{-mt}\right]_0^\infty \\ &= 0 - (-1), \end{aligned}$$

since $-e^{-\infty} = -1/e^\infty$ and $-e^0 = -1$.

and therefore $$\underline{\int_0^\infty me^{-mt}\,dt = 1.}$$

(*b*) Put $u = -mt$, then $du/dt = -m$.

Then $-e^{-mt} = -e^u$, and $\frac{d}{du}(-e^u) = -e^u$.

Using the "function of a function" rule:

$$\begin{aligned} \frac{d}{dt}(-e^{-mt}) &= -m(-e^{-mt}) \\ &= \underline{me^{-mt}.} \end{aligned}$$

6. Probability of a breakdown before 300 hours is given by $\int_0^{300} me^{-mt}\,dt$, where m is average number of breakdowns per hour

If m is average number of breakdowns, $1/m$ is time between breakdowns, therefore 240 (hours) $= 1/m$ and $m = \frac{1}{240}$.

$$\int_0^t me^{-mt}\,dt = m\left[-\frac{1}{m}e^{-mt}\right]_0^t$$
$$= \left[-e^{-mt}\right]_0^t$$
$$= -e^{-mt} - (-e^0)$$
$$= \underline{1 - e^{-mt}.}$$

With $t = 300$ and $m = \dfrac{1}{240}$,

$$\int_0^t me^{-mt}\,dt = 1 - e^{-\frac{300}{240}}$$
$$= 1 - \frac{1}{e^{5/4}}$$
$$= 1 - 0{\cdot}2865$$
$$= \underline{0{\cdot}7135.}$$

Loss due to breakdown: £5000.
Probability of breakdown: 0·7135.
Expected loss: £3567·50.

Progress Test 13

2. Standard error of mean $= \dfrac{S}{\sqrt{n}} = \dfrac{1\text{ N}}{\sqrt{64}}$
$$= \underline{0{\cdot}125\text{ N}.}$$

At 95 per cent confidence level, population mean is 31 N $\pm$ (1·96 $\times$ 0·125 N) $\simeq$ 31 N $\pm$ 0·245 N.

$$Z = \frac{\bar{x} - \mu}{s}\sqrt{n}.$$

Hypothesis is that sample could have come from output of machine with output mean (μ) of:

$$30 \text{ N if } |Z| < 1{\cdot}96$$

$$Z = \frac{31 - 30}{1} \times 8$$

$$= 8.$$

H is rejected, very decisively.

3. At 99 per cent level, confidence interval is set at $p \pm 2{\cdot}58$ standard errors.

Standard error of the sample proportion $= \sqrt{\dfrac{pq}{n}}$, and for previous sample $p = 0{\cdot}40$, $q = 0{\cdot}60$.

To keep estimate of population within $2\frac{1}{2}$ per cent limits,

$$2{\cdot}58 \times \sqrt{\frac{0{\cdot}4 \times 0{\cdot}6}{n}} = 0{\cdot}025$$

$$\sqrt{\frac{0{\cdot}24}{n}} = \frac{0{\cdot}025}{2{\cdot}58}$$

$$\frac{0{\cdot}24}{n} = 0{\cdot}000094$$

$$\therefore n \simeq 2553.$$

(*a*) A sample of about 2500 would be needed to obtain the stipulated degree of accuracy.

Unless the firm's labour force is very large, so that even 2500 represents only a fairly small fraction of the total number of employees concerned, we shall have to be aware of the fact that we are sampling from a finite population.

(*b*) Unless the tests are very easy, quick and cheap to carry out, the general manager should carefully consider whether he could not make a decision on less accurate information. For instance, an estimate of the proportion at $\pm$ 4 per cent at the 95 per cent level would require a sample of only 600.

4. (*b*) If the probability of a Type I error is to be kept to 5 per cent, we are working at the 5 per cent significance level. Our hypothesis is:

There is no significant difference between the two proportions if $Z < 1{\cdot}96$ when:

$$Z = \frac{p_1 - p_2}{\sqrt{\dfrac{p_1q_1}{n_1} + \dfrac{p_2q_2}{n_2}}}$$

$$Z = \frac{0{\cdot}26 - 0{\cdot}21}{\sqrt{\dfrac{0{\cdot}26 \times 0{\cdot}74}{400} + \dfrac{0{\cdot}21 \times 0{\cdot}79}{260}}}$$

$$= \frac{0{\cdot}05}{\sqrt{0{\cdot}00048 + 0{\cdot}00064}}$$

$$= \frac{0{\cdot}05}{\sqrt{0{\cdot}00112}}$$

$$= \frac{0{\cdot}050}{0{\cdot}034}$$

$$Z = \underline{1{\cdot}47.}$$

The null hypothesis cannot be rejected. We have *not* shown that there is a significant difference between the proportions in the two types of property.

Progress Test 14

1. $\Sigma x = 378, n = 9; \bar{x} = 42$ mm

$$\Sigma(x - \bar{x})^2 = 36, S = \sqrt{\frac{36}{8}} = 2{\cdot}12 \text{ mm.}$$

Confidence interval given by $\bar{x} \pm t_{0{\cdot}01}\left(\dfrac{S}{\sqrt{n}}\right)$,

when n = degrees of freedom + 1.

$$\bar{x} \pm t_{0{\cdot}01}\left(\frac{S}{\sqrt{n}}\right) = 42 \text{ mm} + 3{\cdot}36\left(\frac{2{\cdot}12}{3}\right) \text{ mm}$$

$$= \underline{42 \text{ mm} \pm 2{\cdot}37 \text{ mm.}}$$

2. $\bar{x} = 260$ g; $\bar{w} = 6$ g; $A_{10} = 0{\cdot}308$.

The theoretical limits would be set at:

$$\bar{x} \pm (A_{10} \times \bar{w}) = 260 \pm 1{\cdot}848 \text{ g}.$$

or, more practically, as 262 g (upper) and 258 g (lower).

This would imply that the dried fruit was weighed with great accuracy, since the *limits* are only 2 g away from the process mean. Widening the limits to, say, 255 g (lower) and 265 g (upper) would avoid resetting the machine unnecessarily but would also increase the chance of a Type II error. The extra 10 g on the process mean will avoid errors on the "wrong" side, however.

3.

Preference:	*Observed*	*Expected*
Craftsmen's Guild	69	75
General Union	81	75
Totals:	150	150

Calculation:

	$(O - E)$	$(O - E)^2$	$\frac{(O - E)^2}{E}$
Craftsmen's Guild	−6	36	36/75
General Union	+6	36	36/75
			72/75 = 0·96

$\chi^2 = 0{\cdot}96$ with one degree of freedom.

From tables, with $\nu = 1$, $P = 1$, χ^2 is given as 6·64. The null hypothesis cannot be rejected. The general manager has not been proved wrong.

Progress Test 15

1. (*b*) Formula for compound interest is $£A(1 + r)^n$; here $n = 4$, $r = 0{\cdot}04$ and $A = £450$.

At the end of 19–9 the sum invested will be $£450(1{\cdot}04)^4$

$$= 450 \times 1{\cdot}1699$$
$$= £526{\cdot}45.$$

3. £4500 is invested on 1st January 19–4 at 5 per cent per annum so that at the end of 19–4 the amount invested is £4500(1·05) = £4725. This amount now remains invested until the end of

19–5 and on 1st January 19–5 £500 is added to it. From 1st January 19–5 the formula to apply is:

$$A_t = \left(A_0 + \frac{p}{r}\right)(1 + r)^t - \frac{p}{r}.$$

In the example $A_0 = £4725$, $p = £500$, $r = 0{\cdot}05$, $t = 3$.

Therefore
$$\begin{aligned} A_t &= \left(4725 + \frac{500}{0{\cdot}05}\right)(1{\cdot}05)^3 - \frac{500}{0{\cdot}05} \\ &= (14{,}725)(1{\cdot}1576) - 10{,}000 \\ &= \underline{£7045{\cdot}66.} \end{aligned}$$

This includes the £500 added on the following day, however, and the sum on 31st December 19–7 is £6545·66.

Progress Test 16

2. (*a*)
$$\begin{aligned} P &= A\left[\frac{1 - (1 + r)^{-n}}{r}\right] \\ &= £1000(7{\cdot}2717) \\ &= \underline{£7271{\cdot}7.} \end{aligned}$$

(*b*)
$$\begin{aligned} P &= £800(6{\cdot}0021) \\ &= \underline{£4801{\cdot}68.} \end{aligned}$$

(*c*)
$$\begin{aligned} P &= £1500(3{\cdot}9927) \\ &= \underline{£5989{\cdot}05.} \end{aligned}$$

3.
$$\begin{aligned} S &= A\left[\frac{(1 + r)^n - 1}{r}\right] \\ \therefore 2500 &= A[5{\cdot}5256] \\ \therefore A &= \frac{2500}{5{\cdot}5256} \\ &= \underline{£452{\cdot}44.} \end{aligned}$$

Progress Test 17

2.

	Outflows	*Inflows*
Sums of discounted cash flows at 4 per cent	£5571·13	5615·21
Sums of discounted cash flows at 5 per cent	£5506·60	5442·28

Ratio of inflows to outflows at 4 per cent: 5615/5571 = 1·008
Ratio of inflows to outflows at 5 per cent: 5442/5506 = 0·989

Difference 0·019

Difference between 4 per cent ratio and 1 (required ratio) = 0·008.

Required discount rate is:

$$4 + \frac{0{\cdot}008}{0{\cdot}019} \times 1 = 4{\cdot}42 \text{ per cent.}$$

It is very unlikely that this rate of a little below 4½ per cent is sufficiently attractive to justify the expenditure.

3. Adding the salvage values to years 7 and 6 for machines 1 and 2 respectively, the cash flows discounted at 7 per cent are:

Machine 1: £10,718·99
Machine 2: £9573·31.

Deducting costs gives net present values of £718·99 and £573·31 respectively. Machine 1 should be chosen.

Progress Test 18

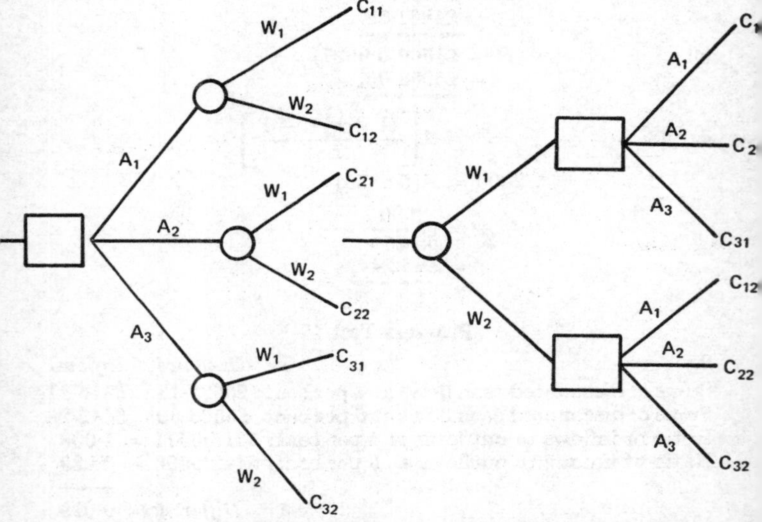

1. Decision under uncertainty Decision under certainty

PAY-OFF MATRIX

(£s thousand)

	W_1	W_2	W-	*Max*	*Min*	*Av*
A_1	5·5	7·0	4·0	7·0	4·0	5·5
A_2	6·0	6·5	4·5	6·5	4·5	5·67

Maximax: A_1; *Maximin*: A_2; *Bayes*: A_2

3. *Regret Matrix*

$$R = \begin{matrix} 0{\cdot}5 & 0 & 0{\cdot}5 \\ 0 & 0{\cdot}5 & 0 \end{matrix}$$

The regret criterion does not give clear guidance here; it does give information, however.

4. Let the weighting for the maxima be 0·3; that for the minima is then 0·7. The estimations are:

$$A_1: (0{\cdot}3 \times 7{\cdot}0) + (0{\cdot}7 \times 4{\cdot}0) = 4{\cdot}9$$
$$A_2: (0{\cdot}3 \times 6{\cdot}5) + (0{\cdot}7 \times 4{\cdot}5) = 5{\cdot}1$$

The outcome expected from A_2 (increase labour force) is slightly better.

5.

PAY-OFF MATRIX

£(000's)

Strategy	*Hurricane*	*No hurricane*
A_1: Own vessel	−4·2	10
A_2: Charter	3	2
A_3: Insure	0	4

Inequalities:

$$-4{\cdot}2x_1 + 3x_2 \geqslant g \quad . \; . \; . \; (1).$$
$$10x_1 + 2x_2 + 4x_3 \geqslant g \quad . \; . \; . \; (2).$$

Also:

$$-4{\cdot}2y_1 + 10y_2 \leqslant g \quad . \; . \; . \; (3).$$
$$3y_1 + 2y_2 \leqslant g \quad . \; . \; . \; (4).$$
$$4y_2 \leqslant g \quad . \; . \; . \; (5).$$

Writing in terms of y_1 and g identifies strategies A_1 and A_2 as those to be followed, with 2·53 (£ thousands) as the value of the game. Inserting this value with (1) and (2), with $x_3 = 0$, gives $x_1 = 0{\cdot}07$ and $x_2 = 0{\cdot}93$; that is charter 93 per cent of the time in the hurricane season but 7 per cent of the time (at randomly chosen occasions) use the company's own boats.

Progress Test 19

1. *Expectation:*

Hot-dog stall

$(0{\cdot}4 \times £1000) + (0{\cdot}6 \times £4000) = \underline{£2800.}$

Ice-cream van

$(0{\cdot}4 \times £6000) + (0{\cdot}6 \times \;\; £750) = \underline{£2850.}$

Expectation is just a little better with the ice-cream van.

2. Let I* indicate a favourable survey report and I′ an unfavourable one. W_1 indicates that minerals are present and W_2 that they are not. Then

$$Pr(I^* \mid W_1) = 0{\cdot}8;\ Pr(I' \mid W_1) = 0{\cdot}2$$
$$Pr(I^* \mid W_2) = Pr(I' \mid W_2) = 0{\cdot}5$$

$$Pr(W_1 \mid I^*) = \frac{Pr(W_1) \times Pr(I^* \mid W_1)}{Pr(W_2) \,.\, Pr(I^* \mid W_2) + Pr(W_1) \,.\, Pr(I^* \mid W_1)}$$

The prior probabilities estimated by the directors are:

$$Pr(W_1) = Pr(W_2) = 0{\cdot}5$$

Therefore,

$$Pr(W_1 \mid I^*) = \frac{0{\cdot}5 \times 0{\cdot}8}{(0{\cdot}5 \times 0{\cdot}5) + (0{\cdot}5 \times 0{\cdot}8)}$$
$$= \underline{0{\cdot}615}$$

$$Pr(I^*) = Pr(W_2) \,.\, Pr(I^* \mid W_2) + Pr(W_1) \,.\, Pr(I^* \mid W_1).$$

This is the denominator of the equation for $Pr(W_1 \mid I^*)$ and has a value of 0·65. $Pr(I')$ consequently has a value of 0·35. The tree diagram produced shows that strategy A_1 (make the excavation) will be preferred if a favourable survey report is received. The expectation from this strategy will be

$$E(A_1) = (0{\cdot}615 \times £1\text{m.}) + (0{\cdot}385 \times -£0{\cdot}5\text{m.})$$
$$= \underline{£422{,}500.}$$

If an unfavourable report is received, the concession will be sold (A_2) and £100,000 will be received regardless of the actual mineral deposits present.

The expectation with the survey information will therefore be

$$Pr(I^*) \times E(A_1) + Pr(I') \times E(A_2)$$
$$= (0{\cdot}65 \times £422{,}500) + (0{\cdot}35 \times £100{,}000)$$
$$= \underline{£309{,}625}$$

Without the survey information, strategy A_1, with a mathematical expectation of £250,000 would have been chosen. The information is therefore expected to have a value of £59,625.

3.

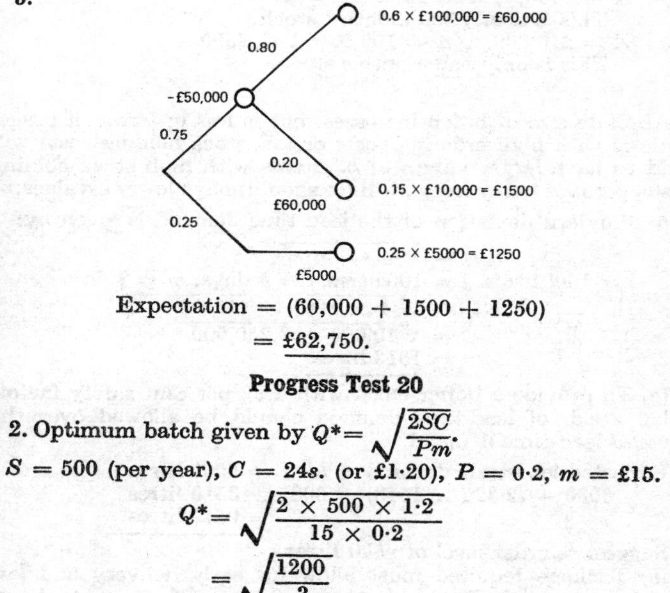

$$\text{Expectation} = (60{,}000 + 1500 + 1250)$$
$$= \underline{£62{,}750.}$$

Progress Test 20

2. Optimum batch given by $Q^* = \sqrt{\frac{2SC}{Pm}}$.

$S = 500$ (per year), $C = 24s.$ (or £1·20), $P = 0{\cdot}2$, $m = £15$.

$$Q^* = \sqrt{\frac{2 \times 500 \times 1{\cdot}2}{15 \times 0{\cdot}2}}$$
$$= \sqrt{\frac{1200}{3}}$$
$$= \underline{20 \text{ articles.}}$$

3.
$$\text{TEC} = \frac{C_s R}{Q} + \frac{C_1 T Q}{2}$$
$$\frac{d(\text{TEC})}{dQ} = -\frac{C_s R}{Q^2} + \frac{C_1 T}{2}.$$

To find minimum TEC, put:

$$\frac{d(\text{TEC})}{dQ} = 0,$$

hat is
$$\frac{C_1 T}{2} = \frac{C_s R}{Q^2}$$
$$Q^2 = \frac{2C_s R}{TC_1}$$
$$\underline{Q^* = \sqrt{\frac{2C_s R}{TC_1}}.}$$

4. Value of optimum batch $= k\sqrt{A}$.

(*a*) $A = £2500$, $\sqrt{A} = 50$, $k\sqrt{A} = £400$.
This is about two months' stock.
(*b*) $A = £100$, $\sqrt{A} = 10$, $k\sqrt{A} = £80$.
This is nearly ten months' stock.
(*c*) $A = £10{,}000$, $\sqrt{A} = 100$, $k\sqrt{A} = £800$.
This is only one month's stock.

Absolute size of batch increases, but is less in terms of usage. Articles with high ordering costs or low stock-holding costs will tend to have larger values of k. Items with high stock-holding costs, perhaps bulky items, will (or should) have lower k-values.

5. Standard deviation of the lead-time demand is given by:

$$\sigma(\bar{l}\bar{d}) = \sqrt{\bar{l}\sigma_d^2 + \bar{d}^2\sigma_l^2}.$$

$$\bar{d} = 1500 \text{ litres}, \sigma_d = 100 \text{ litres}, \bar{l} = 4 \text{ days}, \sigma_l = 1 \text{ day}.$$

$$\sigma(\bar{l}\bar{d}) = \sqrt{(4 \times 100^2) + (1500^2 \times 1)}$$
$$= \sqrt{40{,}000 + 2{,}250{,}000}$$
$$= \underline{1513 \text{ litres.}}$$

(*a*) To provide a buffer stock with a 99 per cent safety factor, 2·326 × s.d. of lead-time demand should be allowed over the *expected* lead-time demand.

Expected lead-time demand $= \bar{l}\bar{d} = 6000$ litres
$6000 + (2{\cdot}326 \times 1513) = 6000 + 3519$ litres
$= \underline{9519 \text{ litres.}}$

Suggest re-order level of 9500 litres.

(*b*) Tankage required must allow for early delivery and low lead-time demand. There must be an allowance for spare tankage. Total tankage must be:

Re-order quantity + buffer stock × safety factor
+ spare capacity × safety factor.

Using the "one-in-a-hundred" safety factor, we must allow 2·326 (say $2\frac{1}{3}$) standard deviations for the buffer to allow for a high lead-time demand and $2\frac{1}{3}$ standard deviations to allow spare tankage for low lead-time demand.

∴ Tank capacity should be:

$$25{,}000 + (2\tfrac{1}{3} \times 1513) + (2\tfrac{1}{3} \times 1513) \text{ litres}$$
$$= 25{,}000 + (4\tfrac{2}{3} \times 1513)$$
$$= \underline{32{,}060 \text{ litres.}}$$

Tankage appears to be more than adequate and could handle a somewhat higher daily demand.

Progress Test 21

1.

μ	λ	λ/μ	$\lambda/(\mu - \lambda)$
24	12	0·5	1
18	12	0·6	2
15	12	0·8	4

λ/μ gives the probability of having to queue at each service level, $\lambda/(\mu - \lambda)$ gives the expected number of people in the system.

2. *Machine* 1: This machine will last for one year during which it will be in use for 2000 hours. Depreciation per hour $= £\frac{750}{2000}$ $= £0·375$. With a resetting time of 3 minutes, $\mu = 20$/hour.

Machine 2: Depreciation per hour $= £0·25$, $\mu = 12$.
Machine 3: Depreciation per hour $= £0·50$, $\mu = 30$.

Hourly costs compared.

Machine 1: Average (expected) number of men in system:

$$\frac{\lambda}{\mu - \lambda} = \frac{10}{20 - 10} = 1.$$

Hourly cost of lost time per man	=	£3·5
∴ Cost of lost time per hour		£
for Machine 1	=	3·5
Depreciation per hour	=	0·375
Hourly cost of machine		£3·875.

Machine 2: Average number in system:

$$\frac{\lambda}{\mu - \lambda} = \frac{10}{12 - 10} = 5$$

Cost of lost time per hour = £5 × 3·5	£
	=17·5
Depreciation per hour	= 0·25
Hourly cost of machine	£17·75.

Machine 3: Average number in system:

$$\frac{\lambda}{\mu - \lambda} = \frac{10}{30 - 10} = 0·5$$

		£
Cost of lost time per hour = £0·5 × 3·5	=	1·75
Depreciation per hour	=	0·50
Total cost per hour		£2·25.

3. (*b*) For a multi-channel system $1 = \lambda/c\mu$. In this question $\lambda = 20$/hour, $\mu = 15$/hour, $c = 2$; therefore $\rho = 20/30 = 0{\cdot}66$ and the system is adequate.

4. $$P_0 = \frac{c!\,(1-\rho)}{(\rho c)^c + c!(1-\rho)\left\{\sum_{r=0}^{c-1}\frac{1}{r!}(\rho c)^r\right\}}$$

$$= \frac{2!\left(1 - \frac{12}{2 \times 8}\right)}{(2 \times 0{\cdot}75)^2 + 2!(0{\cdot}25)\left\{\sum_{r=0}^{c-1}\frac{1}{r!}(2 \times 0{\cdot}75)^r\right\}}$$

$$= \frac{2(0{\cdot}25)}{2{\cdot}25 + \frac{1}{2}\{1 + 1\frac{1}{2}\}}$$

$$= \frac{0{\cdot}5}{2{\cdot}25 + 1{\cdot}25}$$

$$= \frac{0{\cdot}50}{3{\cdot}50}$$

$= \underline{0{\cdot}14}$, which is the required probability.

Progress Test 22

1. The constraints are:

$$5x_1 + 6x_2 \leqslant 120$$
$$10x_1 + 3x_2 \leqslant 180$$
$$x_i \geqslant 0,\ (i = 1, 2),$$

and the expression to be maximised is:

$$6x_1 + 10x_2 = Z.$$

It is fairly obvious that it would be best to concentrate on Variant B, but is this confirmed by the Simplex algorithm? (It could be an intuitive but wrong solution.)

Tableau 1.

	x_1	x_2	s_1	s_2	
→	5	6	1	0	120
	10	3	0	1	180
	−6	−10	0	0	0
		*			

Tableau 2.

$\frac{5}{6}$	1	$\frac{1}{6}$	0	20
$\frac{45}{6}$	0	$-\frac{1}{2}$	1	120
$+\frac{14}{6}$	0	$\frac{10}{6}$	0	200

Interpretation:

$$x_2 = 20, \; s_1 = 120$$
$$Z = 200, \; n_1 = \tfrac{10}{6}$$

We must make 20 units of Variant B per minute. Two of the three trimmers are unnecessary and should be disposed of or put to other work.

2. The dual problem is:

$$\left.\begin{aligned} 5n_1 + 10n_2 &\geqslant 6 \\ 6n_1 + 3n_2 &\geqslant 10 \end{aligned}\right\} \text{Constraints}$$

Minimise $120n_1 + 180n_2 = w$.

The Simplex solution is exactly that for Question 1, but reading off the dual values in the lower positions. The values of the dual variables are $n_1 = \frac{5}{3}$, $n_2 = 0$, since resource 2, the trimming machines, is not scarce. These values only hold for the second constraint of the dual problem, since Variant A is not produced at all.

Progress Test 23

1. Minimise $20x_1 + 10x_2 + 10x_3 = w$, subject to:

$$\begin{aligned} 1100x_1 + 440x_2 + 220x_3 &\geqslant 2000 \\ 22x_1 + 13x_2 + 18x_3 &\geqslant 100 \\ x_i \geqslant 0 \; (i = 1, 2, 3). \end{aligned}$$

Write dual ready for setting up Simplex tableau.

$$\left.\begin{aligned} 1100n_1 + 22n_2 &\leqslant 20 \\ 440n_1 + 13n_2 &\leqslant 10 \\ 220n_1 + 18n_2 &\leqslant 10 \end{aligned}\right\} \text{Constraints}$$

Objective function:

$$2000n_1 + 100n_2 = Z$$

Tableau 1.

1100	22	1	0	0	20
440	13	0	1	0	10
220	18	0	0	1	10
−2000	−100	0	0	0	0

Following the Simplex method through successive tableau will give:

Final tableau.

1	0	0·0012	0	−0·0015	0·0094
0	0	−0·3386	1	−0·3088	0·1471
0	1	−0·0147	0	0·0735	0·4412
0	0	0·9368	0	4·4118	62·83

Taking just under a kilogram of Ingredient 1 (937 g) and a little under 4·5 kg of Ingredient 3 (4·412 g) will provide the required balance in the diet (2001 cals., 100 protein units) at a cost of 62·8p per day. The solution is barely a unique one; 2·7 kg of Ingredient 2 and 3·7 kg of Ingredient 3 will do almost as well (2002, 101·7 at a cost of 64p per day).

2. The final tableau is:

Tableau 5

Destns / Sources	A [9]	B [4]	C [12]	D [9]	Available
I [0]	[15] 6 (9)	[4] 16	[12] 7	[9] 2	25
II [−6]	[8] 5 (3)	[10] 12 (−2)	[6] 0 (6)	[3] 10	10
III [−2]	[7] 14	[5] 3 (2)	[10] 1	[11] 4 (7)	15
Requirements	14	16	8	12	50

The cost of this solution is:

	£
16 × £4	64
7 × £12	84
2 × £9	18
10 × £3	30
14 × £7	98
1 × £10	10
	£304.

3. IFS, as in 22, but with differences shown:

Tableau 6

Plants \ Depots	[5] A	[8] B	[3] C	[5] D	[0] Dummy	Available
[−1] I	[4] 250	[7] 150	[9] 7 (2)	[2] −2 (4)	[0] 1 (−1)	400
[0] II	[1] −4 (5)	[8] 100	[3] 100	[9] 4 (5)	[0] 0 (0)	200
[0] III	[4] −1 (5)	[6] −2 (8)	[3] 320	[5] 80	[0] 100	500
Required	250	250	420	80	100	1100

Total cost £4510

Final tableau giving optimum solution:

Tableau 7

Plants \ Depots	[4] A	[7] B	[4] C	[2] D	[0] Dummy	Available
[0] I	[4] 50	[7] 170	[9] 5 (4)	[2] 80	[0] 100	400
[−3] II	[1] 200	[8] 4 (4)	[3] 2 (1)	[9] 10 (−1)	[0] 3 (−3)	200
[−1] III	[4] 1 (3)	[6] 80	[3] 420	[5] 4 (1)	[0] 1 (−1)	500
Required	250	250	420	80	100	1100

Total cost £3490

There are no negative differences, therefore this is an optimum solution.

Progress Test 24

2. $\Sigma x = 23$, $\Sigma y = 9$, $\Sigma xy = 23{\cdot}74$, $\Sigma x^2 = 65{\cdot}99$, $\Sigma y^2 = 8{\cdot}96$.
Normal equations for the regression line of y on x give:

$$9 = 10a + 23b$$
$$23{\cdot}74 = 23a + 65{\cdot}99b,$$

which solve to give $a = 0{\cdot}37$ and $b = 0{\cdot}23$,
the regression equation being:

$$y = 0{\cdot}37 + 0{\cdot}23x.$$

This is the equation giving output per head as y for capital per head as x.

To calculate capital per head for a given output per head, we need the regression equation of x on y. The normal equations are

$$\Sigma x = na_1 + b_1\Sigma y$$
$$\Sigma xy = a_1\Sigma y + b_1\Sigma y^2,$$

which give $b_1 = 3{\cdot}53$ and $a_1 = -0{\cdot}88$, making the regression equation:

$$x = -0{\cdot}88 + 3{\cdot}53y.$$

With $y = 1{\cdot}25$, $x = 3{\cdot}530$.

The estimated capital per head would be £3530.

4. (*a*) For general form of scatter diagram *see* Fig. 48.

(*b*)

$$r = \frac{\Sigma(x - \bar{x})(y - \bar{y})}{N\sigma_x\,\sigma_y}$$

$$\text{Co-variance} = \frac{1}{N}\Sigma xy - \bar{x}\bar{y}$$
$$= \tfrac{1}{10}(23{\cdot}74) - (2{\cdot}3 \times 0{\cdot}9)$$
$$= \underline{0{\cdot}304.}$$

$$x = \sqrt{\frac{\Sigma x^2}{N} - (\bar{x})^2}$$
$$= \sqrt{6{\cdot}60 - (2{\cdot}3)^2}$$
$$= \underline{1{\cdot}14.}$$

$$y = \sqrt{\frac{\Sigma y^2}{N} - (\bar{y})^2}$$
$$= \sqrt{0{\cdot}896 - 0{\cdot}81}$$
$$= \underline{0{\cdot}294.}$$

Therefore:

$$r = \frac{0{\cdot}304}{1{\cdot}14 \times 0{\cdot}294}$$
$$= \underline{0{\cdot}91.}$$

$r^2 = 0{\cdot}83$. The ratio of explained to total variation is thus 83 per cent.

Progress Test 25

2. The trend equation is:

$y = 30{\cdot}20 + 1{\cdot}55d$, where d is the number of quarters that have elapsed since the end of 19–4 (*i.e.* for 19–5/I, $d = 1$).

Forecast for 19–9

	Trend	*Seasonal Index*	*Trend* × *S.I.*	*Forecast*
Quarter I.	56·55	75	42·41	42
II.	58·10	130	77·47	77
III.	59·65	125	74·56	75
IV.	61·20	70	42·84	43

3. Substituting $A = 0{\cdot}4$ and $(P_1/P_0) = 1{\cdot}1$ in the regression equation, using the values of the coefficients shown in the print-out gives an estimated reduction in market share of 0·6 per cent. In view of the high standard error of the coefficient for the price of the product relative to those of rivals, the marketing director might be unwise to depend too much on the forecast effects of a price reduction. The coefficient is not significantly different from zero.

4.

Month	*Price* £	*Forecast*	*Error*
Jan.	0·50	0·55	−0·05
Feb.	0·46	0·53	−0·07
Mar.	0·50	0·502	−0·002
Apr.	0·55	0·501	0·049
May	0·54	0·521	0·019
June	0·59	0·529	0·061
July	0·51	0·553	−0·043
Aug.	0·72	0·570	0·15
Sept.	0·60	0·63	−0·03
Oct.	0·58	0·618	−0·038
Nov.	0·62	0·603	0·017
Dec.	0·69	0·610	0·08

The January forecast would be £0·642. There does seem to be a rising trend involved but it is not a linear one.

APPENDIX V

EXAMINATION TECHNIQUE

MATHEMATICAL ability requires the development both of logic and reasoning powers and of skill in handling the various techniques. Some very capable mathematicians lean towards the one side and some to the other, but as an examinee you will have to be fairly competent in both. You must be able to set a problem out in mathematical form and then to manipulate the symbols to give the result required. This means that you must have practice. In part, mathematics is a skill like playing the piano or drawing. It has its higher aspects, but these are inhibited if the mechanical side is not handled properly. So practise, practise, practise. If your examination regulations permit the use of a pocket electronic calculator, make sure that you are familiar with the type of calculator that you will be using on the day. Competence in the use of your calculator will enable you to have more time to think out and plan your answers.

Another neglected art is that of setting out work. Examinations in mathematical subjects, like those concerned with more discursive matters, are essays in communication. Unless the examiner knows what you mean he will not give you the marks you deserve. Work must, therefore, be set out neatly and logically.

APPENDIX VI

EXAMINATION QUESTIONS

I. MATHEMATICAL METHODS AND PRINCIPLES

1. Find maximum, minimum and inflexional points of $y = 3x^4 - 4x^3 + 1$ and sketch the curve. What is the relationship between the curve you have sketched and the roots of $3x^4 - 4x^3 + 1 = 0$? (*C.L.P., B.A.*)

2. If A and B are (not necessarily mutually exclusive) events associated with the possible outcomes of a trial, if $A \cup B$ denotes that either A or B or both occur and $P(A)$ denotes the probability of event A, show that:

$$P(A \cup B) = P(A) + P(B) - P(A \cap B),$$

where $A \cap B$ denotes that both A and B occur. If $\bar{A}$ means that A does not occur, hence or otherwise, show that:

$$P(A) = 1 - P(\bar{A}).$$

Two dice are thrown: what is the probability that at least one shows a score of three or less? What is the probability of not getting a double? (*B.Sc.(Econ.), London*)

3. (*a*) Write down the first four terms of the expansion of $(1 + x)^{20}$ in ascending powers of x. Use this expansion to evaluate $1{\cdot}002^{20}$, correct to five decimal places.

(*b*) A machine depreciates each year by 10 per cent of its value at the beginning of the year. When new it costs £8000. Calculate, as accurately as your tables allow, its value at the end of 5 years. (*L.C.C.I.*)

4. (*a*) Find the value of each of the following:

$$(i) \int_2^3 3x^4\,dx \quad (ii) \int_{-1}^{+2} \frac{1}{x^2}\,dx \quad (iii) \int_1^3 (2 - x)^2\,dx.$$

(*b*) Find the area between the line $y = 2x$ and the curve $y^2 = 4x$.

(*c*) Sketch the curve represented by the equation $y = x^3 - 5x^2 + 6x$. Find the area contained between the curve, the x-axis and the lines $x = 1$, $x = 4$. (*L.C.C.I.*)

5. Show that the sum of the first n odd integers is n^2. Evaluate $\int_0^n 2x\,dx$ and relate to the above. (*C.L.P., B.A.*)

6. (*a*) State in your own words what is meant by "a derivative."
(*b*) Differentiate the following functions:

$$y = e^{x^2}$$
$$y = a^x$$
$$y = \frac{3x - 4x^3}{\sqrt{x}}$$
$$y = 3(x^2 + 4)^5.$$

(*c*) Find Z_x and Z_y for:

$$Z = e^{(x^2 + y^2)}$$
$$Z = x^2 + xy + y^2$$

(*C.L.P., B.A.*)

7. State the rule for multiplication of matrices. Write all the products of the forms **A** × **B** and **B** × **A** you can obtain from the following pairs of matrices:

(*a*) $\mathbf{A} = \begin{bmatrix} 2 & 1 & 0 \\ 3 & 4 & 5 \end{bmatrix}$ and $\mathbf{B} = \begin{bmatrix} -3 & 1 \\ 2 & -1 \\ -1 & 0 \end{bmatrix}$.

(*b*) $\mathbf{A} = [1 \quad 1 \quad 1]$ and $\mathbf{B} = \begin{bmatrix} a & b \\ b & c \\ c & a \end{bmatrix}$

(*c*) $\mathbf{A} = \begin{bmatrix} 2+3i & -i \\ -1+4i & 1-i \end{bmatrix}$ and $\mathbf{B} = \begin{bmatrix} 1-i & i \\ 1-4i & 2+3i \end{bmatrix}$

(*B.Sc., London*)

8. (*a*) The managing director is to present four engraved watches to long-serving employees, but at the crucial moment discovers that he has forgotten his glasses and cannot read the inscriptions. Being a man of crisp decisions, he resolves to give them out randomly regardless of the consequences. What is the probability that two or more of the four employees receive watches bearing their own names?

(*b*) Ten per cent of this company's very large workforce consists of men who have spent at least twelve years with the firm. If six employees are selected at random to be presented to a visiting dignitary, what is the probability that at least three of them are employees with twelve or more years' service? (*C.L.P., B.A.*)

9. (*a*)

$$\mathbf{A} = \begin{bmatrix} 3 & 4 \\ 0 & 1 \\ 4 & 1 \end{bmatrix}, x = \begin{bmatrix} x_1 \\ x_2 \end{bmatrix} \text{ and } b = \begin{bmatrix} 24 \\ 4 \\ 10 \end{bmatrix}$$

Write out in symbols the full meaning of $\mathbf{A}x \leqslant b$.

(*b*) Show this relationship graphically.

(*c*) If $\mathbf{B} = \begin{bmatrix} 1 & 3 & 0 \\ 2 & 4 & 1 \\ -1 & -2 & 3 \end{bmatrix}$ write the product **BA** and comment on the product **AB**.

Find the inverse of **B**. (*C.L.P., B.A.*)

10. The total cost of a ship per hour on a voyage is £$\left(6 + \frac{v^3}{2500}\right)$, where v knots is the average speed of the ship. Find an expression for the total cost of a voyage of 3000 nautical miles.

Hence find the value of v which makes the total cost as small as possible. (*L.C.C.I.*)

11. (*a*) If $R = R_0(1 + at + bt^2)$ and if $R = 25$ when $t = 0$, $R = 50$ when $t = 10$ and $R = 100$ when $t = 50$, calculate the values of the constants R_0, a and b.

(*b*) A man invests £P at 5 per cent compound interest at the beginning of every year. Show that, at the end of n years, he will be able to withdraw a total sum of £$21P(1{\cdot}05^n - 1)$.

Evaluate this sum, as accurately as your tables allow, when $P = 100$ and $n = 25$. (*L.C.C.I.*)

12. (*a*) If $A = P.R^n$ where $R = 1 + \frac{r}{100}$, calculate as accurately as your tables allow:

(*i*) the value of P when $A = 2000$, $r = 4{\cdot}5$ and $n = 6$;

(*ii*) the least integral value of n for which $P = 3000$, $r = 4$ and A is at least 4500.

(*b*) If $y = a.e^{bx}$ and if $y = 1{\cdot}5$ when $x = 2$, and $y = 2{\cdot}7$ when $x = 5$, calculate the value of a correct to three significant figures. (*L.C.C.I.*)

13. A motor insurance company classifies its policy holders as Class A (good risks), Class B (medium risks) and Class C (poor risks). Of their policy holders, 25 per cent are Class A, 50 per cent Class B and 25 per cent Class C. Any Class A policy holder is reckoned to have a 1 per cent chance of making a claim in any 12-month period, and the corresponding figures for Classes B and C are 5 per cent and 10 per cent. The company receives a claim. What is the probability that it is from a Class A risk? Class B? Class C?

If a policy holder goes for 10 years without an accident, what is the probability that he belongs to Class A? Class B? Class C?
(*B.Sc.(Econ.), London*)

14. An insurance salesman sells policies to five men, all of identical age and in good health. According to actuarial tables, the probability that a man of this particular age will be alive 30 years hence is $\frac{2}{3}$. Find the probability that in 30 years (*a*) all five men, (*b*) at least three men, (*c*) only two men, (*d*) at least one man will be alive. (*L.C.C.I.*)

15. The articles sold and profits of the XYZ Company Ltd. for the past five years have been:

Articles sold	27,000	30,000	34,000	40,000	48,000
Profit (£)	1250	1400	1650	1950	2300

Determine if there is a law connecting articles sold and profits, and, if so, forecast the probable profit of the company for year 6, a year of trade recession, when sales are not expected to exceed 45,000 articles. (*C.C.A.T., H.N.D.*)

16. If A, B are events in a sample space prove that:

$$Pr(A \text{ or } B) = PR(A) + Pr(B) - Pr(A \text{ and } B).$$

A man aged 35 and his wife aged 30 buy a joint endowment assurance policy, the sum assured to be paid immediately if one or other or both die within a period of 10 years or at the end of the period if both survive.

Using the information in the table below, find the probability that:

(*a*) the man dies within the period;
(*b*) the sum assured is paid before the end of the period;
(*c*) the woman survives the period but the man dies within the period.

PROBABILITY OF DEATH WITHIN 5 YEARS

Age	*Male*	*Female*
30	0·0181	0·0166
35	0·0235	0·0195
40	0·0319	0·0243

(*B.Sc.(Econ.), London*)

17. If A, B are events in a sample space S, prove that:

$$Pr(A \text{ or } B) = Pr(A) + Pr(B) - Pr(A \text{ and } B).$$

In an industrial experiment components are tested until they fail. The following table gives the conditional probabilities that a component that has survived for x hours will fail during the next 100 hours.

Period survived in hours	*Probability of failure within next* 100 *hours*
1000	0·017
1100	0·021
1200	0·028
1300	0·040

(*a*) What is the probability that a machine that has survived for 1000 hours will fail in the next 200 hours?

(*b*) If two components are tested independently and both have already survived for 1100 hours, what is the probability that one survives for a further 200 hours and the other fails? (*B.Sc.*(*Econ.*), *London*)

II. MANAGEMENT MATHEMATICS AND ALLIED TOPICS

1. One of the basic formulae used to determine the optimum size of a manufactured or purchased lot is:

$$Q = \sqrt{\frac{2RS}{i}}$$

when Q = the economical purchased or production lot in units;
R = the annual requirement in units;
S = the costs of set-up, order writing and any other costs which vary with the number of lots rather than with the number of units;
i = the annual cost of holding a single unit in stock.

Discuss the formula and state what other factors need to be taken into account in establishing control of inventories. (*I.C.A., C.M.I.*)

2. (*a*) A machine shop has two grinding machines, three milling machines and a lathe. In how many ways can a part be routed that must be ground, milled and turned on a lathe:

(*i*) if it does not matter in which order the operations are carried out;

(*ii*) if grinding, milling and turning must be carried out in that order?

(*b*) One of the two grinding machines is old and tends to break down frequently. Although the breakdowns are quite random in their occurrence, it has been calculated that the average time between breakdowns is 200 working hours. If the machine is to be worked for 50 hours a week, what is the probability that a breakdown will occur during the next fortnight?

(*c*) If the grinding and milling machines can prepare ten parts an hour ready for subsequent turning (on the lathe) and the lathe operator can turn a part in six minutes, do you consider that the lathe capacity is adequate? If not, why not? (*C.L.P., B.A.*)

3. Ships arrive in a harbour at an average rate of 5 per day. If the cost of operating the dock is £40r per day when ships can be unloaded at the rate of r per day (cost of dock labour force), and if it costs £200 per day that a ship is idle in harbour, for what value of r is the total expected cost per ship unloaded a minimum? (*B.Sc.(Econ.), London*)

4. (*a*) A firm has warehouses at each of three major ports and its principal imported commodity is sent from the ports to four inland centres for further distribution.

Transport costs per tonne are as follows:

Port	*Inland centre*			
	Gloomsville	Slagtown	Gleep	Drag
Liverpool	£4	£2	£1	£7
London	£6	£5	£8	£1
Hull	£3	£14	£5	£7

Weekly quantities available:

Liverpool	1000 tonnes
London	800 ,,
Hull	700 ,,

Requirements per week:

Gloomsville	300 tonnes
Slagtown	900 ,,
Gleep	600 ,,
Drag	700 ,,

Find the routing which would minimise transportation costs.

(*b*) What is the general name of the class of problems of which this is a particular type? Say, very briefly, what other types of problem can be solved by this general method. (*C.L.P., B.A.*)

5. Under what conditions would you apply Linear Programming techniques to solve a business problem? What are you able to deduce from the following tableaux?

Tableau "A"

x_1	x_2	s_1	s_2	s_3	s_4	b
1	0	1	0	0	0	3200
0	1	0	1	0	0	4000
1	0·5	0	0	1	0	2500
0·9	1	0	0	0	1	3600
−0·25	−0·15	0	0	0	0	0

Tableau "B"

x_1	x_2	s_1	s_2	s_3	s_4	b
0	0	1	0	−1·82	0	1927·28
0	0	0	1	1·64	0	1545·45
1	0	0	0	0·17	0	1272·72
0	1	0	0	−1·64	1·82	2454·55
0	0	0	0	0·21	0·045	686·36

(*C.L.P.*, *B.A.*)

6. Powertrucks Ltd. make two types of electrically driven trucks for use in factories, warehouses and so on. Production is grouped into four departments: metal pressings, electric traction, assembly (Truck A) and assembly (Truck B). The metal pressings shop can produce *either* enough pressings for 250 Type A trucks each month *or* enough for 300 Type B trucks. It can, of course, produce pressings for combinations of Type A and Type B within these capacities. Similarly, the electric traction department can produce enough motors for 180 Type A trucks or 360 Type B trucks. The capacity limits of the assembly shops are Type A 200 trucks and Type B 250 trucks. At the current prices of £500 for Type A and £450 for Type B, the Type A truck makes a contribution of £150 per truck towards fixed overheads and the Type B truck makes a contribution of £100.

(*a*) Show the constraints graphically and solve the problem of the most profitable product mix by means of the Simplex algorithm, making a step-by-step comparison with the graphical method. If the monthly fixed overheads are £30,000, is the operation profitable?

(*b*) Write out the dual of this problem and say what meaning you attach to the dual variables. If it were possible to produce more trucks by buying out additional electric motors, what would then be the most profitable product mix? Would the operation be profitable if additional electric motors were bought out at a price of £70 per motor, regardless of vehicle type? (*C.L.P., B.A.*)

7. Explain how discounted cash flow and the pay-back period are calculated as bases for evaluating individual capital expenditure proposals. Describe the advantages and limitations of the two methods and of the return-on-capital-employed method in this connection. (*I.C.A., C.M.I.*)

8. A man has a licence, valid for 30 days, to sell ice cream and hot dogs in a seaside town. If he fills his trolley with ice cream and it is a warm day, he can expect a profit of £10; on a cold day only £4. If he fills his trolley with hot dogs he can expect £2 on a warm day and £8 on a cold day; but he cannot put both ice cream and hot dogs into his trolley on the same day. He wants to maximise his expected profit.

(*a*) What should he do if he has no information about the weather during that month?

(*b*) He is realiably informed that on the average half the days are warm. How much is this information worth to him? (*B.Sc.(Econ.), London*)

9. (*a*) Describe what is meant by probability. By reference to a diagram or otherwise, show how the formula $P(A + B) = P(A) + P(B) - P(AN)$ is derived. ($P(A + B)$ denotes the probability of the occurrence of at least one of the events A and B. $P(AB)$ denotes the probability of the occurrence of both A and B.)

(*b*) One urn contains 58 red and 42 black balls and a second urn contains 3 red and 8 black balls. One ball is drawn at random from each urn. What is the probability that

(*i*) both balls are red; (*ii*) at least one ball is red?

(*B.Sc.(Econ.), London*)

10. A man wishes to work up to 8 hours per day making rings and brooches. It takes him 2 hours to make a ring and 3 hours to make a brooch. A ring contains 4 units of gold and a brooch contains 3 units of gold. He can only obtain 12 units of gold a day. Each article contains a diamond, and he can only obtain 4 diamonds per day. A brooch also contains 5 sapphires and he can only obtain 10 sapphires per day. He makes a net profit of £1 per article and he wishes to maximise his daily net profit.

(*a*) Formulate this problem algebraically as a linear programme.

(*b*) Indicate the feasible region, and the extreme points of this region, on a graph.

(*c*) Which, if any, of the constraints are dominated?

(*d*) Which is the optimal extreme point? How many (on average) of each article should he make each day? What is his maximum net profit per day?

(*e*) How would his net profit change if he used all the 10 available sapphires per day?

(*B.Sc.(Econ.), London*)

11. Two companies, one large and one small, both sell the same product and both wish to build a store in one of three possible towns. Of the combined population of the three towns, Town A has 30 per cent, Town B has 30 per cent and Town C has 40 per cent. A is 8 km from B and 12 km from C, and B and C are 16 km apart. Demand for the product is proportional to the population and will be wholly shared between the two companies. The large company will capture 75 per cent of the business to which it is nearer, whereas the small company will capture 60 per cent of its nearer business. If both companies decide to place their store in the same town, the large company will capture 55 per cent of the total business. In which towns should the companies locate their stores? Set up this problem as a matrix game and find the optimal strategies and the value of the game. (*B.Sc. (Econ.), London*)

12. Write down optimisation problems which are dual to each of the following problems:

(*a*) Maximise $c'x$
subject to $\mathbf{A}x \leqslant b$
$x \geqslant 0.$

(*b*) Minimise $c'x$
subject to $\mathbf{A}x \geqslant b$
$x \geqslant 0.$

(*c*) Maximise $c'x$
subject to $\mathbf{A}x = b$
$x \geqslant 0.$

In each case, **A** is an $m \times n$ matrix, b is an $m \times 1$ vector, and c an $n \times 1$ vector of strictly positive elements representing sums of money. Describe briefly a possible economic interpretation of each pair of dual problems, noting particularly the difference between cases (*a*) and (*c*). (*B.Sc.(Econ.), London*)

III. STATISTICAL METHODS

1. The figures below are the results of a series of observations made at a factory during the loading of gas cylinders on to lorries:

Time taken to load (minutes)	*Number of cylinders in load*
8	4
11	19
12	14
12	11
18	12
19	32
20	15
24	29
29	34
30	39

Express the relationship between the time taken to load and the number of cylinders in the load in the form of a regression equation. (*A.C.M.A.*)

2.

Year	*Consumers' expenditure (at current prices)*	*Value of imports (c.i.f.)*
1962	189	46
1963	201	50
1964	215	57
1965	229	57
1966	242	59
1967	255	64
1968	273	79
1969	290	83
1970	314	90
1971	348	98
1972	393	111

(measurements are all in £ hundred million)

Obtain the regression equation of Imports on Consumers' Expenditure using the method of least squares. Use the equation to predict the value of Imports for a level of Consumers' Expenditure of 250.

Compile the residual variance about the regression line and the coefficient of determination. Explain how these measures are interpreted.

For the predicted value obtained, estimate the standard error of (*a*) the mean predicted value and (*b*) the actual predicted value, explaining the difference between these. Hence give a 95 per cent confidence interval estimate of the true predicted value.

(*C.L.P., B.A.*)

3. A manufacturer is considering the introduction of an incentive bonus scheme, but fears that it may lead to an increase in the proportion of rejects produced. The following figures are the results of a sample of shifts worked over the past month:

Production of operative per shift	*Percentage of rejects*
240	1
450	2
690	1
710	3
730	4
790	4
810	5
890	6
1150	6
1370	7

(*a*) Calculate a correlation coefficient for these figures.
(*b*) How would you use it to assess the likely results of such a bonus scheme?
(*c*) What reservation would you make in using the coefficient for this purpose? (*A.C.M.A.*)

4. (*a*) Draw a scatter diagram, and calculate the product moment correlation coefficient for the pairs (X, Y) given below:

X:	1	3	4	7	10	12	13	14
Y:	9	7	3	2	5	7	10	10

(*b*) Carefully interpret your results and discuss the uses and limitations of the correlation coefficient. (*B.Sc.(Econ.), London*)

5. In two simple random samples, each of size 80, of students in London and Manchester, the mean and standard deviation of cost of journey to college were as shown below:

	Mean (pence)	*Standard deviation* (pence)
London	20	10
Manchester	14	6

(*a*) Test whether there is a significant difference in the cost of the journey to college of students in the two cities.
(*b*) Explain the meaning of your conclusion and the logical argument upon which it is based. (*B.Sc.(Econ.), London*)

6. Attendance at Infant Welfare Centres by wives of salaried workers and by wives of agricultural workers:

Wives	*Attending*	*Not attending*	*Number in sample*
Salaried workers	44·5%	55·5%	569
Agricultural workers	35·1%	64·9%	245

Assuming that these data are derived from random samples, test the hypothesis that there is no difference between the occupational groups as regards the proportion of wives attending welfare centres. Explain the interpretation of your result. (*L.C.C.I.*)

7. (*a*) A market research investigation found, from a random sample of 1000 householders, that, of two soap powders, a preference was expressed by 50 per cent of housewives for Type A and a similar preference (50 per cent) was found for Type B. At the 95 per cent level of acceptance, what is the range of error of this sample?

(*b*) The market research agency recommended that a further sample of 2000 households should be taken. This showed that 54 per cent now expressed a preference for Type A and 46 per cent for Type B. At the same level of significance (95 per cent) has it been established that there is an acceptable preference for Type A? (*C.L.P., H.N.C.*)

8. The attitudes of a random sample of 150 businessmen to Britain's entry into the Common Market are shown below by the size of the firms in which they were employed:

Attitude	*Large firms*	*Small firms*
Approve	30	30
Disapprove	10	50
Uncertain	10	20
Total	50	100

Test whether there is a significant association between size of firm and attitude to entry. Interpret your result with care.

TABLE χ^2

Degrees of freedom	*P* 0·10	0·05	0·01
1	2·7	3·8	6·6
2	4·6	6·0	9·2
3	6·3	7·8	11·3
4	7·8	9·5	13·3
5	9·2	11·1	15·1
6	10·6	12·6	16·8

(*B.Sc.*(*Econ.*), *London*)

9. Explain why time series may need seasonal adjustment. From the data given below estimate the normal seasonal movement in the births registered in the United Kingdom over 1962–4. Comment briefly on your results and discuss their use.

LIVE BIRTHS
(*thousands*)

	First Quarter	*Second Quarter*	*Third Quarter*	*Fourth Quarter*	*Total*
1962	256	252	241	229	978
1963	256	255	249	232	992
1964	254	264	257	238	1013

Source: *Monthly Digest of Statistics.* (*B.Sc.*(*Econ.*), *London*)

10. The following table shows the average amount of tobacco smoked per day over the last 10 years by two samples of hospital patients, one sample suffering from lung cancer, the other from other diseases.

DAILY AVERAGE NUMBER OF CIGARETTES SMOKED

	0	1–	5–	15–	25–	50+	*Total*
Lung-cancer patients	7	55	489	475	293	38	1357
Other patients	61	129	570	431	154	12	1357

Source: A. Bradford Hill, *Statistical Methods in Clinical and Preventive Medicine.*

Is there any evidence of association?

Defining non-smokers to be those smoking fewer than 5 cigarettes daily, test for association between non-smokers, smokers and lung cancer and other diseases.

What conclusions can you draw from these data? (*B.Sc.*(*Econ.*), *London*)

11. *Distribution of firms according to growth:*

Av. growth rate per cent per annum	Electrical	Food
Under 4	3	2
4– 7	6	4
8–11	11	11
12–15	6	8
16–19	8	4
20 and over	9	2
	43	31

(Adapted from Barna, T. *Investment and growth policies in British industrial firms.*)

Discuss the distribution of firms by growth rates shown above using appropriate statistical measures. Test whether there is a significant difference in growth rates between electrical and food industry firms. Suggest at least three ways in which growth might have been measured and discuss how the necessary data might have been obtained.

(*C.L.P.*, *B.A.*)

12. After corrosion tests, 42 of 536 metal components treated with Primer A and 91 of 759 components treated with Primer B showed signs of rusting. Test the hypothesis that Primer A is superior to Primer B as a rust inhibitor. (*A.C.M.A.*)

INDEX